The Road to the Manor

Martin Andrew

This book is a memoir. It reflects the author's present recollections of experiences over time. Some names and characteristics may have been changed, some events have been compressed, and some dialogue has been recreated.

Title: The Road To The Manor / Martin Andrew
Copyright ©2023 Martin Andrew
All rights reserved.
First Edition 2023

ISBN: 979-8-9898704-0-0
ISBN: 979-8-9898704-1-7

House of Hebyzie Publishing, Canada
www.houseofhebyzie.com
Television Performer / Biographies
Actor and Entertainer / Biographies
Memoirs

Cover Design by: Marya Heidel
Typography by: Damian Jackson
Editing by: Samira Borgosh

Cover Photo Credit: Roger Rensen

Introduction

Sitting here on a beautiful fall night in October seems a good time to reflect on my life. There are so many avenues I could venture down to enlighten you about my adventures, but I have chosen just one. There are many aspects to this one avenue, and we will explore them all in as much detail as good taste will allow. What began as a childhood dream has become a constant endeavor. From a very early age, I have held a great affinity for the arts and the world of entertainment. We all embark on a journey called life, and this is the story of mine.

Chapter One

ON JUNE 11, 1962, I BECAME THE YOUNGEST MEMBER OF THE ANDREW family. There were four of us. My mother, father, and older brother Gordon. My first vocal performance was with my father in the house where I was born. Number 9 Westgate Street, Bury St. Edmunds, Suffolk, in beautiful East Anglia, would be the setting for my rendition of the fun hit, "My Old Man's a Dustman." My father was not a dustman but an engineer at the local brewery. As I grew up, he and I would enjoy musical interludes from an otherwise distant father-son relationship. Nonetheless, my musical career was off to a flying start in the mid-'60s.

In the mid-'60s, we lived in a Brewery house on Westgate Street, but it was only a brief time before we moved to another part of the town. The new home was located on Horringer Road and would be in the family for fifty years. Having moved to a different part of town, I was consequently assigned to a new school. So, on a September morning in 1969, I crossed the bridge at the bottom of our road and became a Westgate County Primary School pupil. At this fine establishment, I would be introduced to what I remember as a very charismatic teacher.

Mr. Davis played the accordion during music lessons, led us

1

through our steps in country dancing and introduced us to the musical instrument known as the recorder. For those unfamiliar with this instrument, it could be described as the most annoying woodwind instrument if poorly played. Imagine a class of enthusiastic youngsters blowing frantically into these instruments without knowing how to play them properly. A truly earsplitting sound I can hear to this day.

I had never read music or played an instrument, but I wanted to learn. I finally grasped the fundamentals of playing the recorder. I was invited to perform with the school orchestra and sing with the choir. I showed an aptitude for music. A teacher approached my father, advising him that auditioning me at the local music and drama center would be in my best interest. He felt I could learn more than the school had to offer with its music curriculum, so the scene was set.

Early one Saturday morning, my father and I drove across town for my first audition. I remember having my recorder hanging around my neck in a case I'd made in needlework class. A dreadful sight, I'm sure, but at the time, it seemed appropriate. I had music prepared for my audition and was confident the judges would be suitably impressed with my performance. As I sat with the other children and their parents, I observed a look of terror in some of their eyes as they waited for their names to be called. However, I had no fear and felt perfectly at ease. I had practiced long and hard for this moment and was determined to do well.

My turn came, and I presented myself to the adjudicator who would decide my fate. The first words out of my mouth were I would play a piece I had prepared for him. He told me that would not be necessary and challenged me with various rhythm and pitch tests. All that time and effort I'd spent getting ready for this, not to mention the hours of intricate needlework I had endured to make my recorder case. I passed the tests and was informed I would be learning to play the violin. There were no options to play any other instruments, just a dictatorial rant from the music director. I would attend lessons on Saturday mornings and be supplied with a violin for my trouble. I was so excited. I had visions of being first violinist for the London Philharmonic, but first, I would have to learn to play the instrument.

The Road to the Manor

The lady assigned the task of teaching me to play the violin was Miss Susan Balls. As well as having a name that one could not easily forget, she was also a vibrant character who wore hot pants when giving lessons. Hot pants may have been a little racy, but after all, it was the 70s. My class consisted of three girls and myself. I felt a little awkward about this but soon became more relaxed. I can only imagine my parents' pain as I dragged the heavily rosined horsehair bow across those strings. The cat was not too impressed, often howling as I mastered my craft. I attended lessons and practiced, probably not as often as I should have, but I could play my instrument with a certain degree of competence.

After attending lessons for a while, I was told by the teacher that our class would be performing at the Breckland music festival. Breckland was a festival where young musicians got to show off their skills or lack thereof. I was unsure what this meant, but I agreed to attend with the rest of the class. Breckland would be a most terrifying yet gratifying experience for me. My father drove us to the festival, and I was extremely excited that our group would play in front of an audience.

We arrived, and the place was swarming with children and parents trying to figure out the programming for this event. Finally, we found a list indicating when I would be playing. When I would be playing?! I thought it was going to be a team effort. Then it sunk in, this was a contest, and I would be playing alone. I was terrified and sought sanctuary in the public toilets. I stood in the cubicle, which seemed to be for an eternity, racking my brains for ways to escape this perilous ordeal. There was no way out except through the cubicle door and into the auditorium. I rejoined my father, and we sat patiently, awaiting my name to be called from the list.

Finally, it was my turn. As my name was called, I felt like a gladiator walking into the arena. Judges, like Roman senators, poe faced and foreboding. The masses gathered as this sacrificial lamb was being led to the slaughter. I approached the podium with my violin, bow drawn, ready for combat. Before reaching the safety of the music stand, I was called back to the judge's bench. Some final scribbling on parchment followed by a glance indicating I could resume my march to the scaffold.

All eyes were on me as I fumbled with my manuscript. I managed to regain a certain level of composure, and as the piano accompaniment began, so did I. Honestly, I can't remember how I played the piece or even the music. However, I remember the relief of returning to my seat and sitting beside my proud father. He was not a man to show much emotion, but I could tell he was suitably impressed with my performance through his stern facade.

After all the contestants performed, the results were made public. It was announced I had received a certificate of merit. I was the only member of my class to be awarded such an accolade at this event. My teacher was pleased, and I was amazed. I had come through this experience unscathed and with my first certificate for musical achievement. What new challenges awaited me?

Since I had done so well at the festival, I was offered a position in the youth orchestra. I was thrilled when I heard the news. Even at this early age, I craved recognition. I wanted people to look at me and say, "Isn't he good!" I could have been a better violinist with more encouragement on the home front and self-discipline. I just wanted to be great and didn't appreciate I would have to work hard and be dedicated to becoming a good musician.

It felt good to be a part of this incredible group of talented individuals whose sole purpose was to come together on Saturdays to create music. There were many talented musicians in the orchestra. I admired them but soon realized I was out of my depth and struggled to keep up. I lost my place in the manuscript during a concert. I frantically tried to regain my position by glancing at the boy beside me. It was all in vain, and soon after that concert, I was relegated.

My first experience in the new class was less than thrilling. I could sense the other members were looking at me and laughing. How the mighty had fallen. I felt embarrassed and was now fast becoming a disinterested pupil. I wanted to play music from something other than the manuscript they put in front of me. I didn't like to learn how to play other people's music. I wanted to create my own compositions. If

Mozart could do it at an early age, why not me? I continued to take violin lessons in a very lackluster fashion, not really enjoying it but progressing with it, nonetheless. I needed a change; it was only a short time before one came along.

In 1973 a new school opened in town. It was just one of the old buildings with a new name, and I would be a part of this "Church of England" school. Unfortunately, the school was situated on the other side of town, so I'd have to use the bus for the first time in my career as a schoolboy. So, I walked with my big brother to catch the bus at the bottom of our road. On this fateful morning, my brother and I noticed a boy wearing a blue blazer with a crest matching ours. He was a new face on the block and didn't mix with the other kids waiting at the bus stop. I remember he carried a black briefcase similar to my brother's, with a silver chain around his wrist. Gordon and I joked that he must be a secret agent as we boarded our bus. This schoolboy would play an enormous role in structuring my character throughout my teenage years.

When we arrived at the school, I felt a sense of terror. It was old, and the buildings were scary. The same could be said for the teaching staff. The headmaster arrived in the assembly hall with the entire school in attendance. He was clad in black robes, and his head was adorned with a mortar board sporting a long tassel. He carried a cane and enjoyed the sound of his voice, especially when screaming at us from a podium as we cowered and tried not to make eye contact. It was time for class assignments, and I was assigned to Mr. Fear's class, 2F. The very name scared me, and upon seeing this enormous man, I felt my life was in real peril.

Mr. Fear stood 6' 3.5" tall. I can be precise about that fact, as he told us many times the extra half-inch was significant and should be recognized. He had flecks of red among the remainder of his balding head of grey hair. His voice, when raised, could reduce boys and girls alike to tears, and his temper was quick and severe. I liked him. Very early on, he became aware of my love for music, so he and I became friends. Mr. Fear was the school's music teacher and my form tutor. During assembly, I often used to sit beside him on the organ stool and turn pages as he played our morning hymns. He took a shine to me because he saw I was interested in his knowledge and command of music. He was a genius, and I hoped to learn from him.

For a time, I played the clarinet and the violin while attending this school. I thought it would be easy to play the clarinet, but unlike the recorder, it was a challenging instrument. The difficulty in learning and my contempt for the teacher ended the venture without any commendable results. Nevertheless, I attained the grade two standard on the violin before that endeavor also became a thing of the past.

One day at school, Mr. Fear informed me he was the choirmaster at St Mary's parish church and asked if I would be interested in joining the choir. I had never really thought of myself as a singer. I had sung in the school choir, but this was more challenging, requiring a higher level of vocal ability. I thought about it briefly and agreed to give it a try. Mr. Fear suggested I remain after class and complete some initial testing. He wanted to assess my vocal ability using a variety of musical challenges.

I told him my French teacher would be upset if I missed class, but he dismissed my concerns and proceeded to evaluate my singing capabilities. I completed the testing without difficulty before my French teacher arrived at the music room in a rage. Mr. Fear calmed the irate French teacher, and I agreed to attend future classes punctually. Mr. Fear was impressed with my abilities, and I became a chorister in St Mary's church choir. I would spend three years in the church choir, attaining the highest standard of vocal training (red ribbon) and gaining an appreciation for church music which would stay with me throughout my career. I was a model pupil. I did my homework; I was the "form" and "house" captain at school, played the violin and sang in the local church choir. A bright academic future was ahead, but things were about to change.

My brother and I had a close friendship with our newfound secret agent. Andy was about to become a part of my life, and my life was about to change. I initially met Andy as my brother's friend, but he became closer to me as time progressed. Andy was a year older than me and had what could be described as an infectious personality. He was like a drug that could have you hooked after your first experience. An instigator, a troublemaker, it's all a matter of opinion.

Andy joined the choir, and he and I shared a keen interest in music. I looked up to him because he was so wild and rebellious. Within the choir itself, Andy was a good singer. He took piano lessons and had an electric organ at his house, a popular instrument in the early '70s. The main thing, Andy was fun to be around. There was always something to do; if there weren't, he would think of a game plan, and we would execute it with intense enthusiasm. I recall many events we enjoyed at the expense of others.

Sponsored walks with the church congregation were always fun. As they walked along a forest trail, we would hide in the woods and throw fir cones at the old folks. We once offered to clean the church tower at St Mary's before the new bells were installed. It resulted in a series of comical events. On a windy day we found some old feather pillows in the tower and proceeded to empty them from the rooftop. That evening, my father remarked he had witnessed a phenomenon of feathery proportions as he gazed in amazement from his office window overlooking the church tower.

Another time my father was less than amused was when we offered to remove surplus cardboard from the brewery. We were collecting for the church, so the brewery personnel had no problem letting a couple of choristers into the port cellar to do their Christian duty. When I say port, I am not referring to the nautical left but rather the fine spirit bottled prior to its consumption.

We started with all good intentions until Andy decided it would be in our best interests to sample the port. The sorry affair ended with Andy lying face down in his vomit, moaning in desperation. After pushing a metal cart off the loading dock onto a parked car and making my escape, I sought sanctuary at St Mary's church. I lay on the cold stone floor of the church, anticipating a host of angels with wagging fingers telling me what a naughty boy I'd been when some brass-rubbing tourists discovered me. I had never been drunk before, and here I was in my pre-teen years, sauced and experiencing the misery of alcohol abuse in epic proportions. The tourists looked on in dismay at this intoxicated twelve-year-old boy. I mumbled some rubbish to them and exited on somewhat wobbly legs. It was my first drunken experience, but far from my last. Mr. Fear was tired of my antics and did not approve of my friendship with Andy. He decided it would be best if my time with the choir ended, so I was fired. I was devastated. I begged to be let back into the choir, and against his better judgment, Mr. Fear acquiesced to my pleading.

Every year the choir of St Mary's was invited to partake in a singing holiday in Cornwall to replace the regular choristers who were vacationing. The venue was Truro Cathedral, and this was, without a doubt, the highlight of the year. Two weeks away from home in such a beautiful part of the world sounded good to me. We would be singing in a beautiful cathedral and doing our fair share of travelling around Cornwall, visiting some of the best beaches in the UK. We were going to the ends of the earth as part of our holiday activities, including a visit to Lands End.

After a long coach trip, we finally arrived. Our accommodation was the chorister's boarding school facility. Unfortunately, no sooner had we settled in when the shenanigans ensued. The first night we broke into this poor man's bedroom. As he lay sleeping, we pounded him with wrapped towels and pillows. Unfortunately, the man had a heart condition. Mr. Fear had to drive him to the train station early in the morning as he refused to stay among such unruly heathens. We sang well when called upon to do so, but we were out of control the rest of the time.

One day while Mr. Fear was walking the grounds with some friends, he stopped in his tracks as suitcases left behind by the resident choristers were emptied off a top-floor balcony. Wild and joyous screams could be heard from the perpetrators of this heinous act as they gleefully dispensed with the unfortunate absentees' personal belongings. Beds were broken, rooms were ransacked, and younger boys were terrorized.

We even damaged a building by running headlong with a giant lawn roller, smashing the cricket pavilion. To top it all, when the trip ended, we stole the new hymn books from the cathedral and left our old ones behind. On a positive note, I did have a fantastic singing experience in the cathedral when I performed the solo in C.V. Stanford's Magnificat in G major. Small mercies. Upon our return to our humble parish church, things were never the same. Mr. Fear had lost all respect for me, and I couldn't blame him for doing so.

I was off the rails, and there was no turning back. I found myself torn between a love for music and my craving for alternative excitement. Finally, I wrote a note to Mr. Fear telling him I had no further aspirations as a chorister and would therefore be leaving the choir. I always wanted to be head boy and was never offered that position, although I had been told numerous times I was the choir's best singer. I realize now being a head boy meant you had to set an example as a leader with one's singing skills and strength of character. I had failed on the latter, lacking the skill set required for such a role.

It was unclear to me then, but it is so evident now. I left my note on the church organ; that was the last time I had contact with Mr. Fear. I felt regretful and ashamed of my behavior, leading to the distance I now felt. He was a true genius, and I could have learned so much more from him, but it was not to be. My time at St James school ended after only one year. There was a new middle school in town, and I was to attend its grand opening. My brother and Andy stayed at St James, and I transferred to Horringer Court Middle School. Now I was on my own.

So here I was in a new school, and my teenage years were fast approaching. Music seemed less important to me at this juncture. I enjoyed roaming the streets with my older friends and tasting the wild side of life. However, I still found time to try my hand at the piano and enjoyed creating my songs. My parents had bought a Hammond Piper organ fitted with a rhythm box, making playing fun. They often played the keyboard when we first got it, but that waned in time. My mother played piano in her youth, and my father was a competent accordionist. They were musicians of a traditional nature. I was not. So, on this keyboard, I would explore the art of songwriting.

My taste in music was not so much changing as expanding. I enjoyed the groups we watched every Thursday night on Top of the Pops, but I still had an affinity for classical music. I loved that the keyboard had a rhythm section, and when playing it, I would turn up the rock rhythm creating songs for hours at a time. It used to infuriate my father, who was an old-school musician. I recall playing a piece of music I had written to my friends. He interrupted the recital, insisting I should play something from a manuscript he placed on the music stand. Unfortunately, my sight reading was below par, so that didn't work well. If he intended to embarrass and deter me, he failed. I learned a few pieces from the manuscript, but my desires lay elsewhere. I wanted to write songs or interpret other people's music my way. I was passionate about this and would remain that way throughout my career.

The next couple of years would focus more on adolescent turmoil and domestic problems, with little attention given to music. I was living in a house that was far from a happy home. My brother had become my worst nightmare, and I feared being beaten up whenever my parents left the house. In addition, my parents were distant and preoccupied with their lives and paid little attention to mine. It was a perfect storm, and I was floundering in the eye.

I was constantly in trouble with the police and getting into bad situations. My education suffered, but I didn't care. I was hanging out with the wrong crowd, but my parents didn't notice, so why should it bother me? By the time I was sixteen and should have been considering higher education, I was ready to hit the streets. It was June 13, 1978, when I walked for the last time through the gates of King Edward 6th upper school after completing my final GCE O level exam. I discarded my briefcase into a dustbin. It had served me well through my school years, but now school was out, and it was out for good.

I left school with a modest education, still figuring out what I wanted to do. I hated my home life and, having no urgency to seek employment, joined millions of others on the dole. I spent my days wandering around the town with other lost souls, not knowing what the future held. Then, one fateful Thursday night, I watched Top of the Pops, and a band attracted my attention. Status Quo. They were a hard-rocking, boogie blues band with an image I loved: long hair, torn jeans, and a hard-driving rock-n-roll sound. A new enthusiasm swept through me. I aspired now to be in a rock n roll band.

The Road to the Manor

I had not participated in any music programs offered at school. I dropped it entirely as an exam subject by age fifteen. This new direction in my musical taste was a far cry from the youth orchestra and the church choir, but I was hooked. I had become a listener rather than a performer over the last few years, but this would only set a precedent for a while. My friend Andy moved away from Bury, but his nonconformist influence was still with me, and I decided to grow my hair and join a band.

I talked with various people about this undertaking, but nothing ever amounted to much. A lot of "wouldn't it be great to be famous" chat over a couple of cigarettes and a cup of tea with no real purpose being served. So, at age sixteen, I learned to play the bass guitar. I don't know why I chose the bass guitar. Perhaps I thought it might be easier to learn, having only four strings as opposed to a regular guitar with six. I approached my dad, who had always been a keen supporter of my classical music endeavors, unsure of his reaction to my request. I was shocked to find him receptive to my proposal, and off we went to Woolworth's, where I purchased the tools for my lifelong trade.

The amp had a single 12-inch speaker with limited eq controls, and the bass guitar was a store-brand instrument with a dark red finish: the amp and the bass guitar cost around sixty pounds. Now I was set, and my dreams could come true. All I had to do was learn to play the instrument, and fame and fortune would be at my fingertips. So, with a dressing gown chord for a strap, I began twanging away on the bass, learning a little more each day. I would play along to records of popular groups from that era. AC/DC, Quo, The Sex Pistols, The Tom Robinson Band, or anything else I could get my hands on. I had a mirror strategically placed on my bedroom wall to monitor my progress as I posed and practiced. Every night I played until my fingers were sore. I was hooked. I could play along with these famous bands and look at myself in the mirror, pretending I was part of the group. I was a dreamer, but I was doing something about it; I was learning my trade.

I spent the best part of two years working hard in that tiny bedroom at my parents' house until I felt like a reasonably competent player.

However, there was one slight problem. I was fed up with looking into the mirror pretending to be in all those famous bands. I wanted to be in a band of my own. But unfortunately, there were few opportunities for a fledgling bass player in rural Suffolk.

I was now 18 years old and faced with some serious decision-making. As well as spending time learning to play bass, I became part of a local motorcycle gang. It was nothing hardcore, just a bunch of locals from the town and surrounding villages riding together on the weekends. The "Barrow Boys" were one of a few biker gangs that frequently ended up in drunken scuffles. I liked the thrill of being part of something that would make people's heads turn when you rode into town, but it was all getting out of hand. More violent encounters with rival gangs resulted in stabbings and general brutality. I'd been in and out of dead-end jobs, and my home life was less than desirable. My musical endeavors were floundering, and I had no clue what to do to get my life back on track. Fate stepped in at this point.

A friend told me he knew somebody who lived in a little village about twelve miles from Bury. This person wanted to buy a bass guitar. Upon hearing this, I resigned myself to the fact my music career was over, and I would be a member of a bike gang for better or worse. My friend arranged a meeting, and I was introduced to a young man with long dark hair who spoke eloquently and came from a good home. I was stunned when he told me he didn't want to purchase my instrument but rather have me play it in his rock band. I sped home on my motorbike and told my dad the good news. My father was thrilled and agreed to take me to audition for the band.

We arrived at a beautiful bungalow in the village of Barningham, and my father dropped me off. The band members greeted me and helped me into the house with my equipment. It was only a short time before we were set up and ready to play. There were two guitarists, and one of them looked very familiar. I recognized him as a member of a rival bike gang. He and I said very little to each other but were courteous, nonetheless. I remember feeling nervous but also confident. I worked hard learning to play this instrument to be part of a rock band, and now I had my chance.

The Road to the Manor

It was a fantastic feeling as I locked in with the drums and finally became part of a band. No more gazing into a mirror. I was determined to play well and secure my position as bass player with my newfound friends. We knew many of the same songs, and it was so much fun to play them with real musicians instead of playing along to a piece of vinyl spinning around on a turntable. Things were going great, and we decided to take a break. During the break, they informed me they also needed a singer. I saw an opportunity and went for it. I offered my services and began to sing as well as play bass.

I was offered the job and took it. I was so happy. In an attempt to sell my bass guitar, I landed myself a job in a real live rock band. Everybody had long hair, we were young and hungry for fame, and we even had a name. I was now the official bass player and lead singer with "Beowulf." Now all we had to do was learn some songs. Before I joined, they had already written songs together, and I was encouraged to do likewise. It was a dream come true. We were like-minded people sharing a common goal. We wanted to be rock stars. We set up a rehearsal schedule, and work began immediately, formulating structured set lists.

One thing that would burden me throughout my early career was my vocal range. Some of the cover songs chosen were in a high register and difficult for me to sing. I didn't have a high screaming voice like the vocalists on the original artists' recordings. All I'd been taught as a choir boy was null and void; this was a new realm I had entered. I always liked a challenge, so there would be no complaining, just a lot of hard work. The band was lacking in the leadership department, and I felt this should be addressed sooner rather than later. Once again, I saw an opportunity and took it.

The other band members were a little timid, so putting myself forward as the band's mouthpiece was easy. I was keen to get the ball rolling on our live performance engagements even though we didn't have a show ready for public scrutiny. So, I took the helm, and everybody seemed content, allowing me to become the band leader. I assured them we would be gigging soon, and so began the search for venues to play at.

I had heard from a friend that a local act called "Turbo" were putting on a show at a village hall, and they were looking for other bands to complete the bill. I decided to meet with Turbo's band leader at a local pub. He said we could audition for a slot since he'd not heard of us, and I agreed. At our next rehearsal, I told the band what I'd done. Most of the guys were happy, but the ranks had some dissension. We took a vote, and it was agreed we would audition for the gig. At the audition, we were all a little nervous as the members of Turbo looked on. With a click of the drumsticks, we began playing our hearts out as we tried to dazzle our judges with popular hits from Thin Lizzy, Free and AC/DC. We finished our short repertoire and waited for their decision. We must have done something right because they would only let us join the bill if we agreed to headline. That was it; Beowulf, rock gods headlining our first festival. We were entitled to feel a little cocky about the whole affair, but we still had to get an entire set of songs together.

We diligently rehearsed until it was showtime. Our venue was a small village hall on the outskirts of Bury, but on this particular night, it would be a bustling place. The Barrow Boys, whom I had been hanging out with, came to the show, along with the "Walsham lot," who were friends with one of the guitarists in the band. Other bikers and locals descended upon the fair village of Ousden that night, and you could have cut the atmosphere with a knife. The hall was packed with all the rival factions in the district when it was our turn to play. As we took our places on the stage, I felt sick. I could not believe how nervous I was. I was trembling with fear as we started to play. It took a few songs before I settled in, and the trouble erupted.

Fighting broke out inside the village hall and spilt into the adjacent fields. We just kept playing as the hall emptied and more people joined the scuffles outside. I remember playing the last song of our set as the bright white lights of the venue came on. I saw a cleaning lady sweeping up broken glass and giving us a distasteful look. Finally, just her and a couple of stragglers remained in the hall with some of our close friends. At the end of the night, we got paid for our first live performance. Seven pounds each was our first wage, and we were happy to receive it. We had survived the night, and Beowulf was on the map as a local heavy metal band.

With this lineup, we would do several gigs in the local area and even venture as far as Cambridge to play with one of their leading metal bands, "Strontium." As the official band leader, I spent a lot of time organizing places for us to play. In addition, I did my best to get us as much work as possible. Finally, I met a local businessman actively involved in the local music scene. Sam Richardson was a Londoner who lived in Bury and happened to manage the town's premier rock band.

He informed me of a contest called "Battle of the Bands" and suggested it might be good for us to enter. If selected as a finalist, we would play in front of judges at the Ipswich Gaumont Theater. If we won, we would receive a recording contract. It was a prestigious venue as the Gaumont hosted all the top recording artists. I attended my first big concert at this venue when Whitesnake played in 1979. To perform on that stage would be quite an accomplishment.

We would need to submit a demo tape to enter this contest, so we prepared for our first recording session. The studio we recorded at was on a farm and had been built in one of the barns. We had a few songs written for the recording session but didn't have a clue what we were doing. We didn't care, we were recording, and that's all that mattered.

During the session, we recorded three songs. "Rock n Roll Woman," "Can You Hear Them?" and "Set Me Free." At the time, we thought they were great. The recording was enhanced with reverb, delays, and chorusing. We didn't know what they did, but it sounded neat, so we were content. We submitted our "Battle of the Bands" demo and waited with bated breath. We heard nothing. It was a bit of an anti-climax, to say the least. We thought our tape was good enough to get us into the contest, but we were wrong.

This disappointment caused a little tension in the band, and consequently, we lost one of our guitarists. Now we were three. We decided to change the band's name to "Warhorse" for a fresh start. We got our picture in the local paper and felt confident of success as a three-piece band. We were wrong. We didn't even perform as a three-piece and decided to look for another guitarist. We auditioned a few players and eventually welcomed a guitarist from another local band into our flock. However, it didn't sit well with the drummer, who thought he was a mediocre player.

In retrospect, he was right. This guy could barely tune his guitar and had a personality that could only be described as undesirable. So why did we have him in the band? Desperation! Finding players was no easy task, and trying this guy seemed like a good idea at the time. We did a gig with him at a venue in Mildenhall. Unfortunately, it would be our last show. I was devastated. How could this have all gone so wrong when it started so well? What was I going to do now? One thing I was sure of was I wouldn't give up, but I knew it would be pointless trying to form another band in Bury.

I turned to my mother for some words of wisdom. She was well aware of my situation and knew I was unhappy with life at the homestead. She suggested I talk to my aunt and uncle, so a visit was arranged. My Auntie Val and Uncle Denny had extensive and successful careers in show business. They made the trip from Uxbridge to Bury St Edmunds and regaled me with tales of their personal experiences. I remember sitting on the living room floor, listening to them in awe. I had heard enough and decided the only thing to do was to leave Bury and seek fame and fortune in the big bad city.

I had the summer to consider my options, but my mind was made up. My hometown had nothing to offer, and I didn't want to waste any more time hanging out with the wrong crowd. However, there was skepticism from people who thought I'd return, tail between my legs, having fallen flat on my face. I would prove them wrong by moving to London and meeting this new challenge on my terms. There was no room for compromise, only a desire for success.

The Road to the Manor

Gallery 1

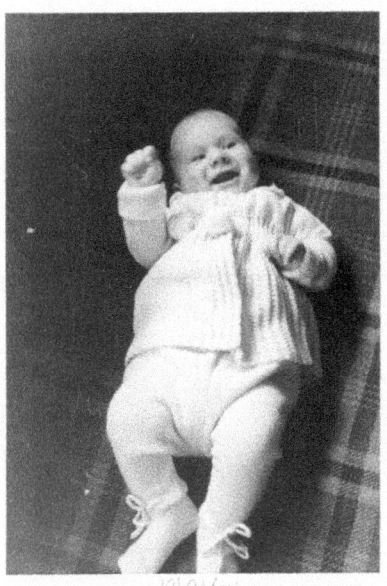

Hello world!

My Father and I at Grandmas house.

Martin Andrew

Left: The house where I was born. **Right:** Mum with her boys.

School days. **Left:** St. Mary's 1969. **Right:** St. James 1973

THE BRECKLAND
MUSIC
FESTIVAL

MERIT
CERTIFICATE AWARDED TO.

Andrew Martin

Class 4A . Violin

E. Stapleton

19th . June 1971

My first musical accolade.

Singing holiday with the choir. Mr. Fear, back row far left. Andy and I front row 3&4.

Martin Andrew

My father and I playing music.

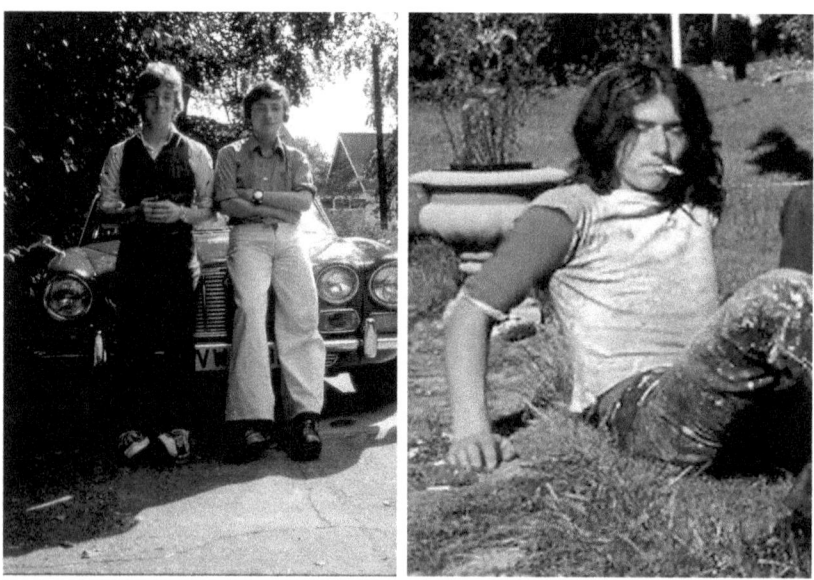

Left: Andy and I 1978. **Right:** Unwinding after work.

Left: First time in the press 1980. **Right:** Bass player & vocalist.

1981, age 19. Time to move to London.

All photographs courtesy of Martin Andrew private collection.

Chapter Two

I BOARDED THE BUS TO LONDON. I FELT RELIEF AND EXCITEMENT AS WE pulled away in the early morning hours. I wasn't going to be stuck in this little town. Instead, I was giving myself a chance to do something with my life. The journey to London took a couple of hours. I was dropped off at Victoria Station and took the underground train to Uxbridge. It was not long before I was standing at the bus station with a small brown suitcase, waiting for my uncle to pick me up. I remember seeing this wreck of a car approaching me with Denny behind the wheel.

I climbed in, and we returned to the house. I was introduced to my young cousin Jodie. She was a mere ten years old but smart as a whip and very talented. It didn't take long for me to settle in, as my aunt and uncle made me feel very welcome. However, I was determined not to be a burden, and much as I enjoyed staying with them and listening to their tales of show business, I wanted to be out on my own.

This all happened relatively quickly, and within two weeks, I had my first flat and a job. I was employed at a local industrial estate as a band saw operator. I didn't particularly care for the job, but it was an income and meant I had my own money and the luxury of independence in modest lodgings. I met a couple of local musicians at the music store in town but had yet to gain entry into the music scene. Then, one day I was looking through the wanted ads in the music papers when I came across one that tickled my fancy. A band called Heretic was looking for a bass player. I liked the band's name, so I called for an audition. I spoke with the lead singer and arranged to audition at the weekend. He sounded like he knew what he was talking about, so I prepared for my big day.

My uncle took me to the audition, and we spent forever trying to find the studio. We finally got there after banging on a pub door and being directed to the correct location by a friendly landlord. Denny gave me a great pep talk before the audition, and we both waited anxiously at the studio until my name was called. Eventually, it was my turn, and I walked in confidently. I was a little intimidated by the whole affair but soon plucked away on my bass to a couple of Heretic's original songs.

I stuck to basics and didn't try to show off. Within fifteen minutes, the audition was over. I stood outside as the band discussed their options. After a short while, they called me over and offered me the job. I was over the moon. Now it was real, and I was in a London-based rock band. That evening we got together and proceeded to have a few drinks to get to know each other.

I was also introduced to a beautiful young lady who was the singer's sister, and before long, she and I were an item. We spent a great night drinking and dreaming about the band's future. I had a friend living in Bury who was interested in being a roadie. I suggested having him join our clan would be beneficial. Everybody agreed, so I called, and Goz joined our ranks. Goz was a friend from my teenage years of turmoil in Bury. He was the one who took me to a jam session when the punk explosion was all the rage. Goz played drums and could also belt out a tune vocally. He and I worked together with Beowulf and Warhorse.

Goz wanted to be a roadie and, in his very early career, started to learn his trade working with us at the local village halls. He and I often drank tea and sat on this old bench at the bottom of Horringer Road. We would dream about touring the world, and eventually, it's what we did, but first, there was a long road ahead. Goz frequently visited me and worked with Heretic but wouldn't move to Uxbridge for a while. However, I had set the wheels in motion and, in the meantime, rehearsed with the rest of the band, learning their set of original songs.

I spent hours at Steven, the guitarist's house, trying to remember the arrangements of the songs he'd written. He was an excellent song-writer; liking the material helped with learning. Next, we started rehearsing in Iver at the drummer's house. I didn't enjoy playing with him at all. He was constantly showing off, and it wasn't easy to get things done. Although he was a good player, his days were numbered. Nevertheless, we worked hard, and slowly but surely, our show was coming together.

Around this time, my mother called and told me Andy was trying to contact me. Initially, I hadn't bothered calling him back as I'd been busy trying to get things going with my new life in London. However, I finally decided to give him a call and tell him all about the band. It was raining as I shuffled along the sidewalk to seek shelter in a somewhat vandalized telephone box. I was so excited to speak to my old friend that I could hardly get my money in the slot when the beeps went.

Unfortunately, Andy didn't answer the call. Instead, I was greeted by his brother Pete in a somewhat melancholy voice, who asked me how I was and then dropped a bombshell I could never have been prepared for. Andy was dead. He was involved in a car accident and survived, only to have a heart attack while hospitalized. At first, I thought it was a sick joke, but I soon realized this was for real. I was also told that Andy desperately tried to reach me before the accident. To this day, I wish I could have spoken to him one more time, but I was too wrapped up in my career.

Having received the details for the funeral, I walked around in a state of shock, getting soaked to the skin and shedding a few tears for my dear friend. He led a tragic life. At eighteen, he was in a wheel-chair, and by twenty-one, he was dead. It was such a waste. That night I sat talking with Val and Denny about my departed friend. The conver-sation and many glasses of whiskey eased my pain as I mentally prepared myself for the funeral I was about to attend.

The Road to the Manor

Andy's funeral attracted some of his old friends and many new ones. Goz and another friend travelled from Bury to attend the proceedings. It was great to see them, but the circumstances could have been better. The funeral ceremony was brief, and before we knew it, we were back at Andy's house, making small talk over some salmon sandwiches and a cup of tea. It was the definitive end of an era and time to move on. Growing up around Andy led me off the straight and narrow but also helped develop my self-esteem and confidence. I will always miss him.

Soon after the funeral, Heretic rehearsed at a furious pace to prepare for our live performance debut. Things were going well when disaster struck. At the end of a hard day's work sweating over a band saw, the foreman asked me to climb some racking to get a box of lighting louvres for cutting. I should have used a ladder and had somebody help me, but it was late in the day, and safety rules in the early 1980s were pretty lax. As I got to the top of the racking, I found the metal frame was loose and collapsed on top of me. I fell about twenty feet, broke my ankle, two fingers, and sustained a blood clot on my left temple.

I was in the hospital, all broken up, and had only been in London for six weeks. I remember lying on a hospital bed, thinking, why has this happened? Everything was going so well, and now this. I had to wait there for about four hours before they decided to fix my fingers and leg. Then finally, I was shipped off to a ward to recover. It was a significant setback, but I was not deterred. After a couple of weeks, I was back at rehearsals getting ready for the first concert.

It was becoming increasingly evident that we would have to change the drummer as he continued disrupting rehearsals with his childish antics. We held auditions at the local studio, and he was soon replaced. So once again, we had a full band ready for the first concert. The first show was memorable but could have been better. A bunch of friends, or not-so-friendly people, turned up to have a good laugh at our expense. We tried to look as rock n roll as possible, but we could have done better. From the opening bars of the first song, it was apparent what sort of a night we were in for. I remember thinking, play hard and keep your head down; we might get out of here alive.

I only sang one song that night, which was more than enough under the circumstances. We packed our gear and headed home when the night was over, and the heckling subsided. We even got paid a couple of quid for our trouble, so it wasn't a total disaster. However, as bad as it was, we were now, in our minds, a force to be reckoned with. We drove to all the west-end clubs in Denny's car, trying to get gigs. He would have his clipboard at the ready and about three pints of beer to motivate him. We landed some pretty good gigs in the West London area.

I will never forget one show we did, although the exact location eludes me. We started well, and the crowd was enjoying themselves. We always wanted to do the most spectacular show possible, and an easy way to get people's attention was by using pyrotechnics. The moment came, and we flipped the switch. There was an enormous bang, and the bar filled with smoke and flames.

The owner came screaming towards the front of the stage, thinking we were trying to burn down his club. He went berserk and kicked us off stage, and out onto the street. After some serious negotiating by Denny, we got paid. Unfortunately, others in our entourage were not so fortunate. The lighting guy got his gear stolen, but we all escaped without bodily injuries, readily available had we stayed around too long.

I recall the angry landlord saying, "Who do you think you are, film stars?" I believe Steve's reply was, "Not yet!" Cocky sod! We had a gathering after the gig for a drink, a good laugh, and an opportunity to lick our wounds. We even took the lighting guy with us to try and cheer him up. We worked with him often after he replenished his lighting show with some new equipment. We continued playing around London with varying degrees of success. One of my favorite venues was the Clarendon Hotel on Hammersmith Broadway. I loved this club because it was near the Hammersmith Odeon, where the big boys played.

For some reason, it made me feel good being close to the famous bands. Of course, we all hoped we would someday rub shoulders with the rock elite and share the same stages. But, if that were to happen, we would have a lot of work to do and a long way to go. London was the place to be if you wanted to get seen and signed, but I needed to get the band playing outside the city. Many other bands of that era were gigging all over the U.K., so why not us? We decided to make a bunch of promo packages (which in those days consisted of a tape, bio, and a photo) and drive up north to venues in Manchester, Leeds, Nottingham, and Sheffield, to name but a few. We would call ahead and then hand-deliver them to the club managers. I felt the personal touch would help us get a foot in the door.

We needed to record a demo tape before we could do any of this. So, we ended up going to Fast Buck Studios in London. While record-ing, we discovered that Status Quo had cut a few demos at the studio. That was a good omen, and we walked out at the end of the day with a four-song demo tape. Shortly after recording, we were approached by the owner of Bridge Studios. He said he was making a compilation record of local bands and asked if we would like to participate. Of course, we agreed, and our first vinyl release was a song called "In Time" on the "Bridge Album."

Heretic had a track on a record and a four-song demo tape. Now it was time to expand our territory, so off we went in our van searching for new venues. Unfortunately, as with all plans, they usually don't work. Our success rate was miserable. My cousin Magnus lived in Manchester. As part of our journey, we stopped to see him. I told him we were having little luck delivering our promo kits to the venues. He suggested we go to the local musician's hangout, the Phoenix Club. That is where we met Pete Dutton.

Pete was the bass player with the Manchester rock band Fireclown and dabbled a bit in booking talent. He was accommodating and assured us he could get some gigs for Heretic in the north. He became a good friend and would book most of our gigs in northern England. We were away for about a week, traveling around in the van and having a good time. Eventually, when we ran out of money and food, it was time to head home.

Not long after our return to London, we got a call from Pete with some good news. We were booked to play at U.M.I.S.T. in Manchester. It was a great venue, and we were excited about playing there. We had a great show and played well. However, it was a one-off show, and no more gigs were forthcoming. Despite our best efforts, the band was not heading in a successful direction. I also had some personal issues with one of the band members, which had been festering for some time and needed to be dealt with. I enjoyed the gigs, but we didn't have enough momentum to make any real impact as part of the N.W.O.B.H.M., which was booming in the U.K. So, the show in Manchester would be the last gig for that lineup.

When we returned to London, I chatted with the singer, and we initiated the band's break up. I always wanted to front the band and didn't enjoy being the bass player and backing singer. We announced our resignation and decided to try and get our own bands sorted out. Unfortunately, I made little headway in forming a new band. Finding players took a lot of work, and keeping a group of hungry wanna-be rock stars motivated and focused was no easy feat.

As things transpired, I reformed Heretic with myself at the helm as lead singer and bassist. It wasn't what I intended, but that's how the cookie crumbled. So Heretic was now a four-piece rock band. What we should have done at this stage is rehearse a lot and concentrate on playing in London. I wanted to be on the road. I craved the freedom of travelling around like a gipsy and moving from town to town, sleeping with as many women as possible. Without doing the work, I wanted all the party rights of a successful rock star. We completed a handful of gigs up north with the original lineup and were about to do a great deal more with the new band. Without further ado and with barely enough songs for an hour set, we got in the van and headed out on our first tour with the new lineup.

Our first port of call was Huddersfield Polytechnic. It was the first gig of a two-week tour of northern England and was important because we needed the show money for fuel to get us to Manchester. Without a certain amount of money, we would be unable to complete the tour, which would be a disaster. I had a verbal agreement from the poly-technic that all our expenses would be covered and a little extra for some fun and frivolity. Lesson # 1, get everything in writing and signed before you get out on the road.

We performed our set of songs which went well, and I was happy with the new band. After packing the equipment in the van, it was time to get paid. I expected about fifty pounds and waited eagerly to get our money. Instead, the amount I received was one pound. The bloke who paid me said they had a whip round, and that's all they'd collected. Nothing in writing, nothing to be done. I was so pissed off. But I put a brave face on and told the rest of the band what had occurred. It wasn't a good start to the tour.

We slept in the van because we were low on fuel and had to wait for the gas station to open in the morning. We weren't even sure if we had enough money to fill the tank when the station opened. The mood was somber, and the night was bitterly cold. I remember sitting in the van while everybody else fell asleep. The van had a stylish sunroof. I thought this was an asset when we bought it, but now I wasn't so sure. It started to snow, and as the snow melted on the roof, it became apparent the sunroof leaked. I just sat there in disbelief as the cold water dripped on my head. So, this was life on the road.

I shivered all night until the gas station opened in the morning. We had very little money but managed to fill up with fuel, and I bought the band a Mars bar each for breakfast. Then it was off to Manchester to play at Jilly's Rock Bar. Upon our arrival in Manchester, we had a place to stay, courtesy of Pete. He lived at home with his parents most of the time but also had a flat. It was bare necessities, but we were glad to escape the cold and discomfort of the van.

Our daily food intake consisted of a loaf of bread, a tub of butter, and a jar of marmalade. It was all we could afford. We each had six slices of toast daily to fill us up. The marmalade on toast, washed down with some hot tea, kept us going throughout the day. The gig at Jilly's went well, and the crowd seemed to like us. It was a rough bar full of bikers. We felt safe and were treated well because our friends were local heroes, Fireclown.

After the show, we could mix and mingle with the locals. I was stunned to find myself being approached by several pretty girls who were extremely friendly. It was something new to me. I'd never been popular with cute girls, but suddenly that changed. I was the lead singer/bassist with a London rock band, which was enough to impress some local ladies. It felt so good to be the center of attention. It was something I'd always wanted but never been able to achieve. I intended to enjoy every second of this new experience.

I developed a penchant for groupies at this gig. Groupies were plentiful and willing, and I took advantage of every opportunity. I indulged myself as much as I could. Sometimes I would bring girls on the road to travel with the band. I never thought having women around was a bad thing. That's why I was there! I wanted sex day and night. I couldn't resist these beautiful creatures, and the band members were relegated to second place. We tried to write new songs on our days off, but that never got off the ground. We didn't rehearse or do any serious writing together because I wanted to party. We did a bunch of dates in and around Manchester and ended up with our final night in Garstang, playing at the liberal club. Goomer was the strange man who ran the club. He was a little quirky and odd but friendly enough.

We played our hearts out and rocked the house. This was the gig where I met a girl who tugged at my heartstrings. At the time, she worked at a local egg-packing factory but aspired to do greater things. She was so hot. I remember her sitting in the front row, head banging and smiling. She wore a leather jacket with "Kawasaki Queen" written in bold green ink on the back. This same beauty would one day become a national radio D.J. and host her own show. Her name is Mary Anne Hobbs.

We had a few drinks after the show, and the other band members swarmed around her trying to chat her up. Unfortunately, I didn't get to say much to her, and when she asked for my name, the other guys made fun of me and told her it was Bozwel. It was a desperate attempt to draw her attention away from me. Nevertheless, we had such a great night, and it seemed a fitting end to the tour, or at least I thought so. When the club closed, it was time to return to London, so we bade farewell to our northern friends and headed south.

I couldn't get Mary Anne out of my head and thought about her all the way home. Driving home, I could hear the others laughing and joking about various things that happened on our small tour. It was a success because we survived, and people enjoyed the band. As I drove through the night, it occurred to me that I had a girlfriend back in London, and here I was, having feelings for Mary Anne. I had slept with a few girls during the tour, which was not good behavior by any stretch of the imagination. Would I feel guilty when I faced my girl-friend back in London? No, I had no remorse or guilt.

I enjoyed sleeping around, and as far as I was concerned, this was just the beginning. I started thinking about what to do next during the long journey home. The one place we all wanted to play was the world-famous Marquee Club. I devised a plan to get us there. Spider was a major touring act signed to R.C.A. Records and often performed at the Marquee. They played twelve-bar blues, boogie rock and were consid-ered the natural successors to Status Quo.

Being a Quo fan, I thought I'd like them, and since they played the Marquee a lot, it seemed an obvious choice to approach them. Perhaps Heretic could be their opening act if I could meet them and become friends. It seemed like a long shot, but I was determined and assumed it had to work. There was so much to think about, and still, 150 miles to go. All these crazy thoughts were in my head, but one kept returning to bring a smile to my face. Would I see my northern beauty again?

Martin Andrew

Gallery 2

Heretic.

Rehearsals early 80's.

Photographs by John Colehan.

The Road to the Manor

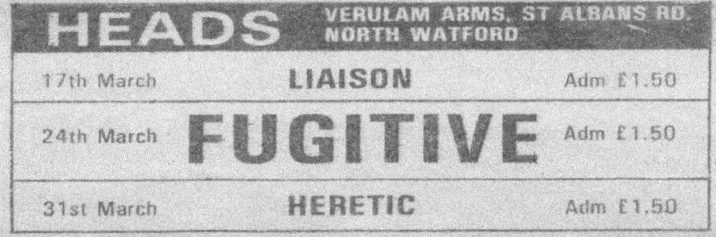

Photographs by Rock Index.

Goz.

Clarendon Hotel, Hammersmith.

Photographs by John Colehan.

Chapter Three

It was now 1982. Heretic had been out on the road in various forms for about a year, and things were picking up. It was time to try and get some high-profile gigs in London. Looking back, I'm amazed we were able to get as much work as we did. We were never outstanding, and our original songs were mediocre at best. At the time, though, I was confident we had what it took to go all the way to the top. We played a handful of gigs in London. The Clarendon Hotel on Hammersmith Broadway was a regular venue, although we never really had a good turnout there. The Marquee was the feather in the cap needed to become credible on the circuit, so that was my next conquest.

I attended a Spider show and got to meet the band. Although from up north, they lived only a few miles from the house where we stayed in Hillingdon. I was invited to their home and began nurturing a friendship I deemed helpful to our musical aspirations. However, it soon became apparent although this band was signed to a major label and seemed to be doing well, they were ostracized from the rest of the London music scene. They were branded three-chord wonders like Status Quo, the band they emulated, and ridiculed as tea-drinking party poopers. The fact of the matter was there was a lot of jealousy because Spider had achieved success, whereas many others had failed. I liked the band and enjoyed a good cup of tea, so I was happy to make their acquaintance.

Spider had the band and crew living under one roof. Their merchandising lady was a sexy blond called Debbie. Through her, I would reunite with the girl who stole my heart on our last visit up north. A Valentine's card (which I still have) was sent to Debbie, asking her to give it to the lead singer/bass player from Heretic. The envelope even had the name Bozwel on it, so the guys in the band had been more convincing than I thought. I got the card and got in touch. I wanted this girl in my life and had to end the relationship I was in, so that's what I did. I now had a new girlfriend, but my attitude to life on the road remained the same. I loved her, but I still wanted fun with the fillies.

Things were going well with the Spider relationship, and we were ready for our first show at the Marquee. It was amazing to be on that stage where so many famous people had played! We did a short set, and the crowd enjoyed us. After the encore, I remember sitting in the dressing room thinking we had come a long way in a short time. Here I was, the young lad from Bury St. Edmunds, sitting backstage at the Marquee with the crowd still cheering. So often, rock stars would come backstage after a show, and this show was no exception. We were greeted and congratulated by some of the top names in the business, including Lemmy from Motorhead. Life was good. What made it better was my new girlfriend had come to London to see me. It was a little awkward with the old and new there, but they seemed to get along and later became good friends. So now we were elevated to Marquee status, we would need a record deal.

We booked a session at a studio in London and recorded two songs, "Fever of Love" and "Watch Me Grow." The recording session went well. We did a few over-dubs, but most of the session was live off the floor. Studios were expensive, and we had minimal funds in the war chest, so the more we could get done in one take, the better. From the studio master tape, we duplicated as many copies as we could afford and did a mass mail out to the record companies. Mary Anne made us a fantastic backdrop for live shows and put together all the promotional materials and a flattering band biography. She had a flare for writing that would launch her journalism career a little later in life. Then it was the waiting game, and we waited quite a while.

In the meantime, we needed to find a new drummer and at a gig in Harwich, we met our man. We were again at full strength after a brief discussion and no audition. Our new drummer was Spick Taylor. He arranged to meet us in London and get on with the job. A new place in Hayes called Ram Rehearsal Studios had been opened by an ex-member of the band First Class: Remember Beach Baby? He was a fun bloke, and his studio attracted some interesting people. So many big names used this facility, and it felt good to be mixing with some hard hitters in the music business. Bernie Torme, Zak Starkey, Brian Connolly, Phil Lewis, and Mickie Moody, to name but a few, often frequented the rehearsal studios. Just being around these seasoned pros was a huge ego boost. It made me feel that our band was on the same level, but we were not.

We were finally taking things seriously and rehearsing quite a lot. Songs were being written, but before long, it became apparent that our new drummer had a problem. It might have been prudent to have auditioned this guy before we let him join. The problem was his ability to keep a steady tempo was terrible, but what the hell, he was a laugh. For me, that went a long way. Having a team instead of a bunch of individual egos on the stage was essential. Of course, this was not a sound policy for putting the best lineup together, but that's how I felt at the time.

Along with the new lineup, we decided to upgrade our vehicle. We bought a 5-ton furniture removal truck. It was bright red, and we fitted it with a giant bed and a couple of coach seats we acquired from Spider's old bus. We were ready to roll once again. I liaised with our agent in the north, and we went back to Manchester for another tour. This time, we were going for six weeks and sorted out all the details in writing so we would at least get paid. The tour was a lot of fun. We played all the places we had done before and added extra dates. My girlfriend came to see me when we did our show in Manchester. I remember she wore skin-tight red jeans and a black leather jacket:

Such a beautiful sight for my lusting eyes. She spent the night with me at the flat and straddled her motorbike back to her place the next day. I was getting some powerful feelings for her, but I still enjoyed playing the field.

On the last leg of the tour, I took a beautiful girl along to have fun with. Unfortunately, I was totally distracted and more interested in sleeping with her at every opportunity. This infuriated the other band members, and by the end of the tour, we were all yelling at each other. It created friction that grew for the remainder of our time together. When we dropped the girl back in Manchester, the atmosphere in the truck was terrible. There were lots of dirty looks and an uncomfortable silence. Something had to break the ice, but none of us expected what would happen next.

We were filling up with fuel when suddenly there was a huge commotion. I was sitting in the back and couldn't see through the window, but I remember hearing from the others that many police cars and dogs were converging at the gas pumps. Suddenly, this police dog came leaping into the truck, followed by a constable. We were surrounded by vehicles, with more police entering the truck. We had no insurance on the truck, and I didn't have a valid driver's license, but this seemed excessive for such minor infractions of the legal system. Before we knew what was going on, our belongings were searched.

Remember, we are four young men on the road for six weeks during summer and don't do laundry. I recall a policewoman gagging as she rummaged through a bag of socks and underwear. It was sweltering in the truck, and the stench was terrible. Another cop thought he had us banged to rights when he found some white powder in a small plastic bag stuffed down the side of a seat. We drank, but none of us did heavy drugs. Some pot was smoked occasionally, but we never bought or carried it around. I tried explaining to this young cop; he had found a bag of salt. He had to do the Hollywood dip and lick test, which I found stupid, only to pull a funny face and conclude I was telling the truth. Unfortunately, our ordeal was far from over. They arrested us and impounded the vehicle. Poor old Pete Dutton came to see us off at the gas station and ended up getting arrested. He just shook his head as we were transported to the local police station in the back of a bloodstained van. Were it not for the constable pointing out the blood on the roof and sadistically sneering, the journey may have been more pleasant. The cops enjoyed intimidating us, and I think it's safe to say we were a little nervous. I felt so bad for Pete. He only came to the petrol station because it was close to home, and now he was getting banged up with us.

When we arrived at the station, they lined us up and asked if we had scars on our arms. I thought this was a weird line of questioning, but I rolled up my sleeves as instructed. I had three small scars on my upper left arm from a brawl I had with my brother some years earlier. The fight ended when he stabbed me, and I started leaking blood all over the carpet. I digress. I was singled out from the rest of the band, taken away to a small cell, and strip-searched. At this stage, I had no idea what this was all about. Why were they interested in some old stab wounds on my arm? What the hell was going on, and more to the point, what would happen to me?

I remained sitting in a dank and dismal cell, wondering what the hell I'd done. Where were the rest of the guys? Finally, the door swung open, and in walked this burly cop who towered over me. I felt extremely vulnerable as I stood shivering, wrapped in a dirty blanket. The next utterance from the cop stunned my senses and rendered me speechless. "So, Roger...tell me about it!" Who? What on earth was he talking about? Apparently, this cop was convinced I was Roger Hodges from London, trafficking drugs in a big red removal truck. Who the hell was Roger Hodges? Back then, the problem was, you didn't have to carry identification in the U.K. This made it challenging to prove who you were.

He questioned me for about an hour, asking about my family and friends. What was the license plate on my dad's car? How many rings did my mother wear on her left hand? How the bloody hell should I know? After waiting in the cell for what seemed an eternity, I was joined by three enormous and intimidating policemen. I thought I was in for a right good kicking. Fortunately, that was not the case. They verified my story but wouldn't tell me how. So, for now, I was free to go. They stood and watched as I struggled to get my clothes on. My body was shaking, trembling with fear, anticipating a gratuitous beating. I was escorted out of the cell and relieved to find the rest of the band waiting in the corridor.

We were taken to the truck in a silent march that seemed to last forever. I expected to hear a cop call out from the station, "Arrest them!" with us being handcuffed and returned to a cell. Fortunately, this was not the case. Instead, a cop handed me the keys as I climbed into the driver's seat. I was told by the cop when we returned to London to get insurance and a valid driver's license. I suppose he turned a blind eye, having made such a big mistake with the Roger Hodges saga. Once the band climbed into the truck, we got out of there as fast as possible without breaking the speed limit. It was the icebreaker we needed.

Once again, we were friends and had a good laugh about the whole affair. We dropped Pete off and soon drove back to London on the motorway. This journey home was a little different for me. I needed a clearer idea of what was next for the band. Our drummer could have been better, and we hadn't written any new songs during the tour. This was a consequence of my womanizing and fast-evolving drinking problem. Despite our best efforts with a mass mail-out of demo tapes, we weren't offered a recording contract. Evidently, I was more interested in my new girlfriend than the band.

Upon our return to London, it was time to get a new vehicle. The truck was fine, but all credible bands had a bus. It just so happened Spider had a bus for sale. Unfortunately, it was unable to be driven and was subsequently abandoned at a coach park in Northolt. The location was not far from where we lived. I was told the bus needed an engine but other than that, it was in good condition. The sale price was three hundred pounds, but we would have to move fast to secure the deal. It was considered abandoned by the city council, and an order for its removal was issued. We promptly paid the agreed amount to Spider and devised a plan for moving the bus.

This minor problem was about a 10-ton problem. I've always advocated the saying, "Where there's a will, there's a way," so we proceeded to move this monster with as much careful planning as deemed necessary, none! I planned to use our truck to tow the bus to a new location in Hayes. The only problem was, as well as needing a new engine, the bus had no brakes. No problem. By hanging a couple of tires on the back of our truck, we could soften any impact if the bus accidentally ran into it. I had this hair-brained scheme. We could use a washing line and a length of rope to pull the bus. I honestly believed we could do it. After much discussion, I persuaded everyone this was a perfect plan and that we should execute it immediately under cover of darkness.

By then, my dear friend Goz had moved to London and lived at the band house in Hillingdon. Most of the band lived at this run-down house inherited by a somewhat eccentric gentleman, Fezz. It was a real party house, much to the annoyance of the rest of the street's inhabitants. However, Fezz worked in Scotland, so we had the run of the place and exploited the circumstances entirely. We, who are we? Allow me to digress for a moment.

I haven't said much about the band members because this is my story and memories of the events which took place. Others may have a different view and opinion, so I want to clarify these are my memories and mine alone. Again, I'm not trying to criticize anybody I worked with over the years but merely put forward a point of view and recollection of events. So that being said, let's use the first names of those involved in this debacle. The members of Heretic were Karl, Stu, Spick, and me, with Goz helping us as a roadie and driver when available. So now that's out of the way, let's get back to moving the bus!

We arrived in Northolt with our truck adapted for towing, a washing line, and a length of rope. We were aware the bus had no engine or brakes, but we hadn't factored in a missing battery and, therefore, no power for the lights. It was late at night, so lights were a necessity, but we had no alternative other than to execute our plan, as the following day, the council had the bus scheduled for removal. Goz and I crewed the bus, and the rest of the band was in the truck. Amazingly, the washing line and rope didn't break as we got the bus moving. The only major issue we had was stopping. Every time the truck slowed down, we rammed into the tires on the back and smashed the front of the bus to pieces. It must have been quite a sight as we approached a major junction, and the rope along with the washing line snapped. The truck kept going as the traffic lights turned red, but the bus rolled into the middle of the intersection, coming to an undignified stop. All I could hear was Goz yelling, "Grab the license plates and run!"

I saw the truck reversing along a dual carriageway back through the intersection, to the total dismay of all motorists on the road that night. In the middle of the crossing, we reattached the rope and washing line amid peels of nervous laughter. When I returned to the bus, I saw a police car across the street. He watched the whole affair but decided to turn a blind eye and drove on. What luck for us. The charge sheet would have read like a shopping list for a family of twelve. We managed to get the bus to the coach park in Hayes, and finally, after shunting it like a freight car for about half an hour, it was parked. The front end was destroyed. It didn't matter. We had a bus, just like the credible bands. Now all we had to do was get it running and back on the road.

I put the removal truck up for sale, and we got rid of it fairly quickly. Now we had some money to fix our new chariot. The question was, who do we contact to fix it? We didn't know any mechanics, so we turned to our friends in the Spider camp for advice. They knew a man and suggested I contact him. He was known to all as "Grizzly Filth." We called him this because he looked like the television character Grizzly Adams and habitually referred to the police as the "Filth." He was a mechanic who worked out of a small workshop in west London and came highly recommended to solve our engine problem. Having contacted him, he said he was too busy but had "just the pair" to help us, and what a pair they were.

The bloke in charge looked like George Formby, so we called him "Formby." He was an oaf of a man, but you couldn't help but like him. His heart was in the right place, but to this day, I am unsure about his brain. The next few months were spent with Formby and his partner Mitch working on the bus and the band getting jobs to fund equipment repair and getting ready for the next tour. During this time, Mary Anne stayed with me at the house in Hillingdon. We set up a rehearsal room and, at one point, invited Spider to record some demos while they were shopping for a new deal with A&M Records.

I was thrilled to have my girlfriend live with me. She was resourceful and always up for the challenge, whatever that may be. She and I both acquired jobs at a local confectionery facility. It was a factory where they packed Mars bars, Maltesers, and other teeth-rotting goodies. We hated it but did it for the money. This was a productive time. We worked during the day, and when we returned to the house, we rehearsed and wrote songs. Having Mary Anne with me was a significant stabilizing factor. She was dedicated to the band's success and had great faith in me. I wanted to work hard to please her and, in doing so, please myself.

The work on the bus took forever, probably due to our mechanic's lack of mechanical skills. Eventually, Formby and Mitch fixed the engine. It looked like a wreck with the paint peeling off, so I decided to move it into the backyard to give it a fresh coat of paint. Finally, the bus was up and running, and we had some braking capacity, but most lights didn't work. We had no insurance or tax disc, and I still needed a full driver's license to drive the beast legally. No problem. I once again persuaded everyone the best plan was to move it at night. It was only a few miles, so what could possibly go wrong? So off we went to the coach park to drive the bus back to our house.

The engine fired up, and we were ready to roll. One of Spider's roadies accompanied me on the bus, and everyone else followed in a car. We threw caution to the wind and hit the road. Within a few hundred yards of our journey, we were pulled over by the police. I tried to bluff my way out of the situation as the car following us disappeared into the distance. You may think that wasn't a very nice thing to do, but it was standard procedure for us. When the cops were involved, if you could make a run for it, you did.

I was arrested, and so was the roadie who accompanied me. We were transported to the local police station, where I ended up in the cells, locked up with a bloke who had nearly killed a taxi driver with a crowbar. After accidentally sitting on his plate of eggs and getting caught stealing his blanket, I managed to impress him enough to prevent getting beaten to a pulp. When I told him I was arrested for driving a bus, he thought I'd stolen a double-decker and was suitably impressed. Now we were friends.

Being in a jail cell isn't much fun. I had no idea what happened to the bus and wasn't sure when I'd be released. I didn't know how much trouble I was in, but I assumed it would not be favorable. Spiders Roadie was a wild Scotsman called Loki. He didn't appreciate being locked up. I could hear him yelling and damaging his cell as the hours dragged on. Eventually, we were released. When I finally ended up in court, I got a fine and a couple of endorsements on a license I didn't have. The day after the arrest, we moved the bus during daylight hours and parked it in the back garden, ready for painting. Of course, the neighbors were none too happy about this, but there was not much they could do about it.

Our work schedule was long and tedious. Mary Anne and I would get up at 5 am and be at work at 6 am. We worked eight hours and returned to the house by 3 pm. We would meet the rest of the band, who had finished their respective days' work and renovated the bus until it was dark. After a quick bite to eat, we'd rehearse for a couple of hours, then go off to bed and do it again the following day. We were getting complaints from the council about the bus being in the back garden with frequent visits from the police, citing us with noise pollution complaints. Despite all these distractions, we got some new songs in our repertoire, and the bus had a fresh coat of paint. In the evenings, I booked gigs for our next tour. The house had a pay phone. Armed with a handful of coins and a pen, I did my best to get us working again.

We were ready to get back on the road. The bus looked terrific, with a stunning Heretic logo on the back window. It was an incredible transformation. In retrospect, I should have been more concerned with the engine's condition. It felt like we'd entered the major leagues with our aesthetically pleasing mode of transport. To me, perception was everything. We named her the "Blue Goose." We had to move the bus from the back garden into the street as the local council threatened to build a brick wall, making the bus a permanent fixture. I'd upset a local councilman who asked me to move the bus several times. Unfortunately, he didn't appreciate my foul rhetoric and proved to be a vindictive bastard. The other residents in the street complained, saying it was an eyesore, and he approached me to get it moved. In my usual democratic fashion, I told him to piss off, and he, in turn, threatened to wall us in.

We started the bus and were ready to move it onto the street, only to discover the head gasket was leaking. We had no money to fix it, so we negotiated with Formby. We agreed to dig a pit in his garage in exchange for the gasket repair. Boy, we were in for a treat. We spent the whole day with jackhammers, shovels, pick axes, and our bare hands getting his pit dug. It wasn't just the band working that day. Mary Anne rolled up her sleeves and joined the rest of us in the hole for a day of hard labor. She inspired us with every swing of the pick until the task was finally finished. Formby was pleased, and consequently, our head gasket was replaced.

Our first gig was only a few days away, and we needed to get on the road. I moved the bus to the front of the house, and we loaded our equipment in the pouring rain. When we were ready to leave, I noticed an oil leak. The sump gasket was leaking, and there was no way of getting a replacement at that time of night. So, we manufactured our own gasket using a cornflakes box and some adhesive which stopped the leak. That was it; we were unstoppable! We climbed aboard and prepared for our maiden voyage on the "Blue Goose."

It felt so good driving through the local streets in our chariot. Aside from a few oil stains and a strong smell of diesel, we felt like rock stars. We were approaching a roundabout when something struck me as a little strange. Stu was turning the steering wheel, but we continued going straight. How could this be? We hit the curb and bounced around the road before grinding to a halt a mere two miles into our journey. We were stranded with no way of moving. The steering consul shattered, and dreams of a successful tour in our new bus followed suit. There was nothing we could do, so we locked the bus and walked to a house belonging to a super friendly Irish lady who was the mother of our friend Marion. We explained our situation and were invited to stay for a while. Unfortunately, we drank too much, and by the time we staggered back to the bus were brawling in the street. Tempers were fragile, so we relieved our tensions by pummeling each other until we passed out on the bus.

It took about a week to fix the bus and get back on the road. This was just the beginning of a very troubled tour. Before leaving town, we picked up a friend who volunteered as a roadie. His name was Clive, and he lived close to where we were staying. Our trip up north was to be an eventful one. The brakes on the bus were nonexistent, and the bus, at times, was being driven like a race car by an over-enthusiastic guitarist. Eventually, we came unstuck as we mounted the curb in a busy town and crashed into the awning of a butcher's shop. How people didn't get killed, I will never know. We just kept going and couldn't stop even if we wanted to. We had no brakes. All this, and we hadn't even played a note. The journey continued until we reached our destination at Mary Anne's parents' house. We received a warm welcome and a hot meal.

For some inexplicable reason, a band member developed an attitude toward my girl. He was rude and didn't like her being around the band. He didn't mind her parents' hospitality and the money she gave us to repair the bus but instead considered her bad news and bad luck. I viewed this attitude with contempt and disgust, but there was not much I could do about it, given the circumstances. I could understand if she were causing problems, but instead, she was helping our situation, not hindering it. We played our first show at Garstang liberal club, having high hopes of doing as well as our previous gig. It was a disaster. We had power issues causing long, dark delays in the show, and our performance was lackluster at best. Everybody wanted to blame each other, but the fact was we were under-rehearsed and just plain awful. We walked back to the bus in silence and climbed into our respective bunks.

The following day we were woken by the police asking questions about a butcher's shop with a missing awning and wondering where our insurance, registration, and safety inspection documents were. I delivered as much bullshit as was humanly possible and in turn was issued a five-day ticket to produce documents. We had to move the bus from the parking lot at the bequest of the local constabulary, so we parked in a country lane and began licking our wounds. Goomer allowed us to rehearse at the club since it was empty, and no other bands were booked to play there. We took him up on his offer and began writing some new material. During our stay in Garstang, we had a mechanic check out the bus to see what had to be done to pass an MOT. The news was grim. It needed a lot of work, and we had no money. We were one show into the tour, and it was over. It seemed like all the work we put into this bus was for nothing. We had been sold a lemon, and now we were stranded.

Mary Anne and I took her trumpet, jewelry, my 4/12 Marshall cabinet, and Fender bass to the pawn shop in Blackpool. This generated enough cash to get diesel money for the return journey to London. Despite our efforts, a particular band member, to my disgust, blamed all the bad luck on my girlfriend. I developed absolute contempt for him because his whole assertion was ridiculous. We limped back to London and parked at the Hayes coach park, which would be home for Mary Anne and I. Karl and Spick sometimes stayed on the bus with us, but Stu returned to his grandmother's warm house and home cooking.

During our stay in Garstang, having been allowed to rehearse at the liberal club, we learned a couple of new songs I'd co-written. Stu and Karl preferred technical music with intricate time changes, and Spick was having a tough time learning the new material. I preferred a solid beat, hard-driving guitars with a steady rhythm and melodic vocal line. We were all over the place with songwriting ideas and couldn't agree on a definitive direction. So, despite the new material and ambitions for a record deal, we just weren't ready. In addition, we were flat broke and needed a lot of money for a number of different things. Repairing the bus and paying for rehearsal space did not come cheap. Reality again reared its ugly head, and we had to pause and start looking for day jobs.

It was late 1982, and the weather in London was miserable. Mary

The Road to the Manor

Anne and I were now permanent residents of the "Blue Goose." The bus had a small gas stove so we could boil a kettle and have hot tea. We survived on a diet of "Chip Butties." A loaf of bread and a large bag of French fries from the local fish n chip shop sustained us through winter. We acquired local jobs and together walked to work on those cold winter mornings. She worked at Sainsbury's, and I had a wonderful job taping boxes in a factory. At the end of the week, the band members and Mary Anne put our hard-earned money together, and we gradually repaired the bus and purchased new equipment.

The end of the year was fast approaching, and before we knew it, the festive season was upon us. I remember waking up on the bus Christmas morning and exchanging gifts with Mary Anne. I received a watch strap, and I gifted her some leg warmers. We spent Christmas at our favorite Irish lady's home, and in the New Year, we were invited to stay at her house full-time. I used her address when mailing demo tapes. We periodically spent time there watching movies and enjoying a hot shower. She was a kind lady who made us feel part of the family. Her husband was known to us as Norm, a London transport bus inspector by day. Marion was their daughter; she'd been a friend of the band for quite some time.

One fine day we received a letter from Magnum Records. It was not a major label but a subsidiary of EMI. This was a breath of fresh air we so badly needed. They were interested in the band and wanted to meet me. I traveled to Shepperton Studios and met with the record company executives. They were very impressed with the biography we sent them and liked the songs on our demo tape. I told them about our close relationship with the band Spider at the meeting. I gave them a long-winded speech about how we would do a significant tour with Spider in the U.K. at some reputable venues. I actually believed what I was telling them at the time but would later find out it was all a pack of lies fed to me by one of Spider's band members.

After the meeting and several months passing with no news, I was terribly disheartened. Then, just when all seemed lost, a letter arrived in the mail, which put a smile on my face. The Magnum Music Group wished to enter into a recording contract with Heretic. We were thrilled with the news and signed on the dotted line after reading an agreement we didn't fully understand. They asked us to record two songs and booked us into Rock City Studios in Shepperton a few weeks later. It was a dream come true.

We garnished some local press and felt like superstars, but in reality, it was a less-than-desirable recording contract. It became abundantly clear we were not going to get the five-star treatment we thought we deserved. We were given twenty-four hours to record two new songs. The two songs from our demo tape would be used for the B-side of a 12" E.P. We had no idea how long it would take to record the songs, but twenty-four hours was definitely rushing it.

Consequently, the songs were not appropriately mixed at the end of our recording session. We were unhappy with this outcome but soon discovered the record company couldn't care less. They just wanted a quick turnaround with the E.P. on store shelves to recoup their costs.

The recording session itself was a nightmare. The bed tracks took forever because Spick kept speeding up the tempos. The guitar parts were over-written and under-rehearsed, so that took a long time to complete. When it was my turn to sing, we'd been in the studio for seventeen hours, and it was now 5 am. I was exhausted, and my voice was far from ready to sing the lead tracks on our songs of choice, "Water of Vice" and "Keep on Telling Those Lies."

In the control room were a couple of members from Spider and the sound guy they used for live shows. They didn't like how I sang the songs, and I was told to scream the lyrics out and sing in a higher register. This pissed me off; I had to rewrite the melody lines on the spot. I didn't want to scream; I wanted to sing, but I was outvoted and had to suck it up. Finally, I got through the songs, and we rushed through some vocal harmonies as our time was almost up. This was not the recording experience I hoped for, but we were out of time and kicked out of the studio before we could even mix the songs correctly.

Once the recording was mastered and ready for pressing, the record executives told me the title they wanted to use for the E.P. "Burnt at the Stake." I was not too fond of it because it made us sound like a black metal band which we were not. I made a special trip to the record company offices to plead my case, where I was formally rebuked and told to mind my own business. Nevertheless, the E.P. was released and hit the stores in early 1984.

The band thought the recording experience and the record were crap; I had to agree. I remember walking into a Virgin mega-store on Oxford Street and seeing the cover of the record for the first time. If I were a heavy metal fan, I would've been tempted to buy it at face value, but I can guarantee I would've been disappointed when it hit the turntable. We were not a heavy metal band. Yes, there were elements of that on one of the tracks, but most of the recording was poorly produced pop rock. If ever there was a reason to have a stiff drink, I had just found it. This disastrous recording experience uncorked more than a few bottles.

Since I first joined Heretic, my drinking habits had become some-what reckless. I enjoyed getting drunk a lot, and it was starting to take a toll on my health. I had no idea how hard I was about to fall. Never-theless, we were poised to do our next tour in March '84. I booked eight weeks of concert dates and named the tour "The Roar of '84." The bus was repaired, new equipment was purchased, and we were ready to hit the road. Spider promised us a lot of support dates on their upcoming tour, which was great for us as they were playing some large venues. Little did I know at the time we weren't even being considered as an opening act, but as they say, ignorance is bliss.

While I was preparing for the forthcoming tour, Mary Anne was developing a fanzine called "Crunch." Fanzines are self-published mini magazines containing articles and opinions on current music events. Most bands she interviewed for the first edition were not from the major leagues, and she was kind enough to feature Heretic alongside all the other hopefuls. After that, everything seemed to fall into place, and soon it was time to hit the road again.

The gigs were going well, and we had a lot of fun. We played some new venues and a lot of the old haunts. Goz worked full-time with Spider, but we managed to steal him away for several gigs. Another Spider roadie named Steve Hall, or "Oz" as I called him, joined us for a gig at the Clarendon Hotel in Hammersmith. Unfortunately, it was not a great night financially; I ended up paying for their services with a bag of chips smothered in curry sauce. However, they never complained and were always a great laugh. I'm still good friends with Goz and Oz to this day.

The drinks were flowing, and we were rocking across the country when disaster struck again. About four weeks into the tour, I started to feel ill with a killer headache. It just wouldn't go away. We kept touring, but I just got weaker every day. Finally, I remember trying to sing at a show in Reading and not having the energy to hold a note. The crowd mocked and laughed at me. It was so embarrassing. We had a few days off, so I suggested we return to the coach park. I couldn't get out of my bunk for a couple of days. When I finally got up to pee, I noticed something was wrong. My pee was black. I had no idea why, but I didn't doubt I was extremely ill.

Mary Anne and I moved off the bus into a squalid little flat in Southall. The bed was propped up on bricks, and the place stank of curry. I was losing my appetite and couldn't keep my food down. When the rest of the band visited, they commented that I looked yellow. Eventually, I went to the doctor and was diagnosed with hepatitis. He put me on emergency bed rest, and I was whisked away to Northwick Park Hospital and placed in isolation.

After everybody had gone that night, I lay there wondering what would happen next. The tour was over, and I would spend the next two months in hospital fighting this illness. My two-month exile in the hospital was a definitive turning point in the shambles of a career I was trying to create. I was afforded a long time in solitude to reflect upon the circumstances which had caused the situation with which I was now faced. I had a band plagued with bad luck, inner tension, and a drinking problem that could take my life.

For the duration of my stay, I would be at odds with myself on many issues. I had no physical strength. It was all I could do daily: get out of bed, walk around the room, and get back in before I collapsed. Jaundice caused terrible itching and was a constant irritation throughout the ordeal. My physical self was a mess, but my mind was working overtime. The band members only came to see me occasionally. However, it seemed apparent from their apathy toward me and the whole issue of what to do with Heretic that the winds of change were gaining momentum. On the other hand, Mary Anne stood vigil by my bedside and came to visit as often as she could.

During our frequent meetings in the isolation ward, I encouraged Mary Anne to send a copy of her fanzine to some national music papers. She was a gifted writer and deserved to be doing something more with her talents. She'd helped us with everything from writing biographies to running the lights for live shows and even digging a pit for Formby and Mitch. She told me she had submitted a copy of her fanzine to Sounds magazine, and it had been met with great interest. She was offered a job as a freelance writer and grabbed it with both hands. Her hard work and dedication had paid off. She was on her way up, and all I could sense was I was on my way down. It didn't matter. I was so happy for her; she deserved this.

I slowly recovered from my illness and looked forward to leaving the hospital. I was being examined daily to ensure I didn't have this new illness called "AIDS." I had no idea what that was, but they continued to evaluate me through physical examinations and blood work. The doctors discovered I had an enlarged gall bladder, which would have to be removed when I regained my strength. It wasn't AIDS, so that was music to my ears. I was discharged from the hospital and advised to take a convalescence period for full recovery. I was subsequently told not to live on a bus or tour with the band until further notice. Having digested the information and gathered a few belongings, I was transported back to my parent's home in good old Bury St. Edmunds.

Psychologically, this was driving me to despair. After three years of trying to fulfil my dreams, I was right back where I started. I became very depressed, and each day, I wandered aimlessly around, shrouded in melancholy and a cheap pair of pajamas. My parents did their best, and I didn't get too many "I told you so speeches," but I only stayed with them for two weeks before summoning Marion's brother to come and get me. Strapped to the back of his motorbike, I was whisked away back to London to try and pick up the pieces if I could find any of them. Mary Anne and I stayed with our favorite Irish lady and her family while following doctors' orders and convalescing.

Once I was fully recovered, a sequence of events occurred throughout the remainder of '84, which sealed the band's fate. First, Heretic was dropped from the record label for not fulfilling our touring obligations and consequent mediocre sales of our debut E.P. The fact I had nearly expired in the hospital was of no concern to them: we were history. We had no record deal or gigs and were not in the mood for rehearsing. The "Blue Goose" had to be moved to a new location, so I opted for a quiet road close to Stu's house.

Some nights the band would get together and have a few drinks on the bus to discuss future plans. After a night of frivolity and few plans of merit being discussed, we'd climb into our bunks for a good night's sleep. One morning we were rudely awakened by a car crashing into the back of the bus. We got up and staggered outside to see what happened. A vehicle was literally embedded in the back of the bus. Luckily, our equipment was not in there at the time, or it would have been destroyed. Surprisingly, nobody was hurt in the accident, which was incredible considering the force of impact. It was broad daylight, so how this idiot managed to crash into us, I will never know. Soon the police arrived, and statements were taken from all parties involved. While giving my information to the police, I noticed smoke inside the bus. I'd left my wet sweatshirt on a paraffin heater, and it caught fire. I will never forget the look on the constable's face as Spick ran into the smoke-filled bus, grabbed the heater, and threw it on the sidewalk. The paraffin poured out, and the entire area was engulfed in flames. What a scene. A car embedded in the back of a smoldering bus, with a crazed drummer screaming profanities as he tended to his scalded arms while standing on a flaming sidewalk. Such a fabulous cabaret, and all before breakfast.

The "Blue Goose" was insured for once, so we received two hundred pounds compensation, as it was deemed fiscally nonviable to effect the necessary repairs. We were delighted to get some money, as scrapping the bus was not an option. Only one course of action was open to us, and it was not pretty. It was time to employ the services of

Grizzly Filth and Formby. I had a two-hundred-pound repair budget and thought our less than reputable mechanics could salvage the "Blue Goose" for such a fee. Wrong again. We moved the bus to a car park in Southall to be closer to our unique mechanics. Unfortunately, the bus was no sooner parked when vandals destroyed it. Broken windows and graffiti now adorned our once majestic chariot. We began renovating with the help of Filth, Formby, and Mitch. Unfortunately, the poor old Goose was about to endure a disastrous makeover.

We tore sheet aluminum from a derelict van and attached jagged pieces to the bus. Rivets, glue, and duct tape were all used during this abomination. Combined with some dubious welding from Grizzly and a piss-poor paint job from the rest of us, that was a recipe for disaster. Somehow, we managed to get it road worthy and attempted to return to the road for some shows. I think we did one more tour of duty before we seized the engine and had to employ the services of Formby and friends again. You would think no other indignity could befall this poor bus, but you would be wrong.

We returned to the car park in Hayes before the engine finally seized, and we waited patiently for the dynamic duo to arrive. Formby and Mitch appeared with a truck and prepared the bus for towing. What followed was reminiscent of a scene from a Laurel and Hardy film. They removed the engine cover from the bus to access the tow bar and placed it on the ground directly behind their truck. We looked on in dismay as they reversed over the engine cover destroying it entirely.

When they were finally ready to tow us, I reminded them that our air assist brakes would only work if the engine ran. I was assured the situation was in hand, and wheels began to roll. I vividly remember being towed along Uxbridge Road at about 30 mph with no functioning brakes on the bus. The traffic was reasonably light, and it seemed we might get to our destination in one piece. Unfortunately, somebody stepped onto a zebra crossing, and Formby hit the brakes. There was no way for us to stop. Within seconds we hit the crane on the truck, and it tore through the bus roof like a wrecking ball.

It was a surreal moment as the "Blue Goose" was transformed from a hard top into a convertible. People gathered around the bus and looked on with a sense of shock. We were amazed at how many people were attracted to this demolition derby. It was the biggest audience we'd seen in months. The embarrassment was immense, and we were clearly in a state of shock. In his usual state of oblivion and sporting a ridiculous grin, Formby climbed out of the truck, assessed the damage, and uttered the immortal words, "Have you got any duct tape?"

I was speechless but managed to find a roll and handed it to him. Formby applied duct tape to the roof and having removed the crane from the bus's interior, we were once again on our way. The crowd cheered as we waved nervously, our faces shrouded with stoic expressions. Hard as it may be to believe, we fixed the roof, and Formby repaired the engine. However, the engine seized once again on its maiden voyage during a test run. That was the end of Formby, Filth, and Mitch. It was also the end of the "Blue Goose," and I reluctantly sold my beloved bus for scrap.

We'd lost our record deal, bus and had no money to show for our trouble. How the mighty had fallen. Next was the demise of Heretic itself. We went through several lineup changes, but nothing worked. The tailspin was nearing ground zero, and there was no way of pulling out of this dive of desperation. We played a few support gigs at the Marquee before Heretic imploded. Mary Anne suggested I go solo and cut ties with all that was Heretic. I didn't have to think about it too long and followed her advice. Heretic was over, and the Scoundrel era was about to begin.

Gallery 3

"Heratic," the hard rockin' London based quartet currently signed to Magnum Force Music, are not really the fearsome foursome that their name might at first suggest.

Admittedly their debut E·P titled 'Burnt at the Stake' (THBE 1004) released on the thunderbold label may also conjour up an image in the same vien, but on hearing their premier vynal vice (chuckle) you could well be surprised. The a side comprising of two very powerful tracks whereas the flip side is more lighthearted.

As for the future Heratic are looking forward to a major tour. Their debut Lp will be recorded towards the end of '84.

In the meantime, they are a treat to see, so catch them if they're in town. Their live show is made up of 99% their own material.

HERETIC
Oxford

AFTER HEARING repeated feedback about this band literally melting the Marquee a few weeks ago, I decided that for the common good they should be sought out.

Thus I found myself in Oxford, a little apprehensive about the performance I was about to witness, for the name Heretic instantly conjures up a black metal horror show with about as much subtlety as *The Texas Chainsaw Massacre*.

I couldn't have been further from the truth. Frontman Martin Andrew teased and tantalized stage and audience alike, flaunting the showmanship of a born pro as Heretic pumped out the power-crazed 'Water Of Vice' and boogie rock 'n' roller 'Fever Of Love' taken from their EP, 'Burnt At The Stake', before sliding gracefully on into the moving ballad 'How'.

Unlike the force-fed and repeatedly disappointing garbage churned from the proverbial 'rock' production line, this band know what rock 'n' roll is all about, and have without question the makings of something mega.
MARY ANNE HOBBS

Promo and press 1984.

Photographs by John Colehan.

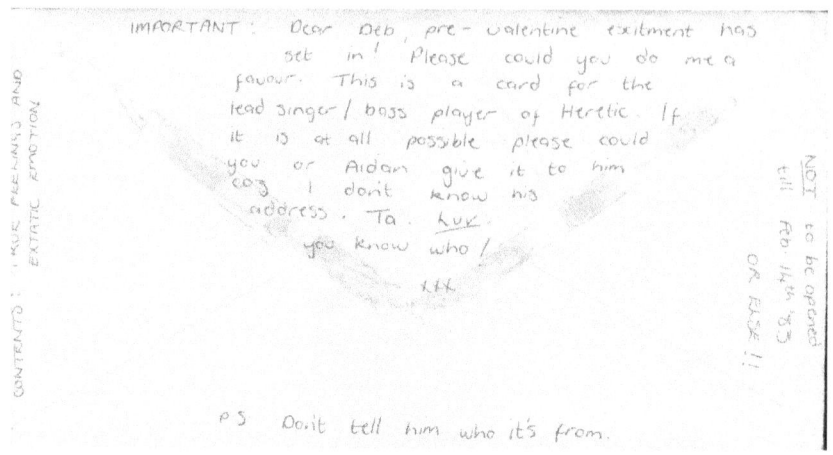

The anonymous Valentines card envelope.

Mary-Anne Hobbs and I.

Photographs from Martin Andrew private collection.

Goz and Stu in Hayes coach park with the Blue Goose.

Heretic on tour 1984.

Photographs from Martin Andrew private collection.

Left: Oz and me. **Right:** Please buy our record.

Playing at the Marquee club with a fridge on stage.

Photographs from Martin Andrew private collection.

Enter the Scoundrel. Photograph by Rock Index.

Chapter Four

WITH THE OPERATION TO REMOVE MY GALL BLADDER OUT OF THE WAY, I found myself living at a friend's house and chomping at the bit to get on with my career. Mary Anne worked diligently for her magazine, and I was healing fast and almost back to full strength. Mary Anne would be typing up interviews and attending meetings, and I felt lost. The house we were staying in had a fully stocked bar, so I spent most of my time drinking and feeling sorry for myself. Remember the accident I told you about when I fell off the rack at work? The Citizen's Advice Bureau filed a claim for me, finally settling the case. I received a settlement from my accident back in '81 and wasted no time getting a demo recorded.

I worked with a local songwriter who had some success in years gone by. He had squandered a deal with EMI records and was busying himself with a new album to try and recapture some industry interest. He was in debt up to his eyeballs and was more than willing to record me since I had some money to spend and offered to supply booze at the recording sessions. We recorded two songs. " How" is a reflective ballad from my days in Northwick Park Hospital, and "Turn Me On" (a song Mary Anne hated, and with good reason.)

She had taken me to Stringfellow's nightclub in the west end of

The Road to the Manor

London for a New Year's Eve party. While she was busy getting a scoop on the celebrities, I was off chatting up a South African beauty. She was stunning, and I spent most of the night flirting with her. I got to meet several celebrities that night. I remember brushing by Britt Eckland and being stunned by her beauty. Status Quo's Rick Parfitt arrived late at night, and I talked to him for a while. He was my rock star hero. Watching him on television inspired me to embark on a musical career. I was in heaven.

A veritable who's who of the music business to mix and mingle with, but I still found myself more interested in flirting with this South African hottie rather than shaking hands with the music elite. I made sure I got her number before leaving the club. I saw her for a while and enjoyed the adrenaline rush of having an illicit affair. While Mary Anne did all she could to help my career, I was busy getting laid and lying to her. This is how I repaid her. I feel bad just thinking about it now, but I didn't care at the time. I was having fun, and that was all that mattered. The song "Turn Me On" was initially called "Hold On," I had written it for my better half. I changed the lyrics, and now it was about the girl I cheated with. How low could I go? I was only getting started.

Mary Anne suggested reviewing my rock persona and improving my appearance. I'd always steered clear of dying my hair or doing anything which would make me look remotely effeminate. With some gentle persuasion, I could leave those fears behind and create a new image. Blond streaks were added to my hair, and I was a changed man for the worse. My devoted girlfriend gave me a new look and all the confidence in the world, which would be our relationship's very undoing. She created an egotistical monster.

By February '85, I was making every excuse possible to get out of the house and meet my drinking mates at the St. Moritz club in Wardour Street. It was the club where everybody partied. Any night, you might see Iron Maiden, Motorhead, Girlschool, Rock Goddess, Tank, and many others. I was back drinking and sleeping with as many girls as would say yes, which back then was a lot. My new blond locks were a hit with the ladies, and I exploited that to the full.

As a couple, Mary Anne and I were drifting apart. She was prepared to put up with me, but I wanted my freedom. It was cramping my style, knowing that girls in the industry wouldn't come near me for fear they might get a bad review from my girlfriend. This would be one of the dumbest decisions I'd ever make. It was terrible when I told her I wanted to split up. I knew what I was doing was wrong and for all the wrong reasons. Yes, she was upset but, through tearful eyes, remained so dignified.

I was honestly not worthy of this woman. For Valentine's Day, I took her to the island of Ibiza for a farewell holiday. We had a great time, but we were over. When we returned, we went our separate ways. She moved uptown, and I became one of the many lost souls experiencing homelessness. I'd outstayed my welcome at the house where we were staying and spent all my money from the settlement.

I was in a real mess. All I had left was my van, which was worse for wear after crashing it into a tree one fine morning when I was hung over. I had little to my name but managed to salvage the Heretic backdrop she made, and it was now my blanket as I slept in the van. Despite everything, Mary Anne submitted my demo tape to Electra Records. A band called Rogue Male was signed to Electra after one of the A&R reps saw an article on the band, she had written for Sounds music magazine. Heretic had been the opening band for the Rogues when they played at the Ad Lib club in Kensington. The article she wrote paved the way for their deal.

She submitted my demo and several other bands, and they picked up on it. Around the same time, a show on channel 4 called ECT featured live performances from all the middle league bands. I'd convinced them that having me on the show would be a great idea. So here I am with a major label interested and a possible television slot for a band that doesn't exist. My ex had created the name "Scoundrel" for my solo persona. No prizes for why she chose that name. The record company said they wanted to see the band, and so did the folks at Channel 4. Getting the gig was easy.

I arranged a showcase at the Marquee opening for Bernie Torme. It was time to prepare for the chance of a lifetime. The scene was set. All

I needed now was a band. I called on some players I'd worked with to see if they would do it, and they agreed. More time and planning should have occurred for what was at stake here. Unfortunately, impatience and delusions of grandeur blinded me. None of the players would get signed because this was a solo deal. They were aware of it, and it's fair to say they would not lose any sleep preparing for a gig with no glorious outcome for them.

We spent more time making outrageous costumes and planning ridiculous stage antics than rehearsing. I only had about five songs and needed ten for the show. Rather than spend time writing some good new material, I padded the set with vintage Heretic and some cover songs just thrown in for good measure. What was I thinking!? I wasn't, but it was game on. We did one rehearsal, and that was it. Show time. Past performances at the Marquee had gone well, with a great crowd reaction and a sense of achievement. This would be different from those nights.

From start to finish, it was a disaster. From the first note of the first song, the drums were all over the place. The sax player was drunk, and our elaborate costumes fell apart as we played, causing us to hit some nasty notes as our fingers were compromised on our respective fretboards. The crowd was not impressed with our appalling performance. It was a small turnout, and those there enjoyed the cheap beer more than the band.

I'd arranged for the record company A&R people and the production folks from ECT to be on the guest list. I could only hope they didn't show up, but I was out of luck. The following day I spoke to the record label, who brushed me off and told me to come back in a couple of years when I had a good band, and the ECT people wouldn't even take my call. I was left with an enormous egg on my face and had ruined some great opportunities by trying to cut corners. So that was my last gig in the U.K. trying to promote any songs I'd written. There was only one thing to do. Hit the bottle and hit it hard.

Throughout 1985 I spent most of my time blagging my way into nightclubs in the west end and drinking at various hot spots: Dingwalls, The Embassy Club, Hippodrome, and St. Moritz Club. Apart from the occasional gig on American air force bases around the U.K., I was no longer playing much. There was no more original music for this kid. I was content to play top forty cover songs for inebriated American service members. When socializing, I would still put on my best togs, get my hair looking good, and party as much as possible. I met a lot of fun people. So many other lost souls hid behind a glass of cheap booze and a cigarette. My behavior left much to be desired as I became very loud and boisterous when under the influence.

One night at the Embassy Club, I was attending a party hosted by the Ramones. To the celebrities ' dismay, I went berserk and caused a dreadful scene. I was so pissed off for some reason that I cannot recall and proceeded to fight with a drug dealer who took offence at my asking him for a kilo of cocaine and a kiss. A big brawl ensued in the lobby, and I was thrown out on the sidewalk. Not to be deterred, I climbed behind the wheel of my car and drove along the sidewalk toward the shocked bouncers and crowd that had gathered.

There were no fatalities or injuries, but it amazes me how I never got busted for drinking and driving or even made it home that night. I was just another washed-up musician with anger issues and a drinking problem. People soon began to distance themselves from me, and I don't blame them. Goz stayed a faithful friend and was doing well as a roadie travelling the world. Around this time, he was working for Iron Maiden and Waysted. He landed himself a beautiful girlfriend from New York, and she was in London with her sister. They stayed at a nice hotel in London's west end and enjoyed nights out at rock clubs.

Goz invited me to tag along and hang out with his girlfriend's sister. I reluctantly agreed but was glad I accepted his offer. She was gorgeous. I just loved her American accent and attitude. Since I was couch surfing and Goz stayed with the sisters at the hotel, he arranged for me to stay there. And so, the love affair began. I was despondent when it was time for the girls to return to America. I had just fallen for this girl, and now she was leaving. In retrospect, this was all about lust and not much about love, but at the time, it seemed authentic.

Goz returned to his life on the road, and I had to find a place to live. I ended up staying with George and Jan. They were father and stepmother to Stu, one of the guitarists from Heretic. I'd drifted apart from Stu when the band split up, but we would still hit the town occasionally. His parents had always supported the band, whether fixing buses or just listening to me rant and rave. Over the years, we spent many nights sitting in a cloud of smoke, drinking tea, and debating whatever came to mind. However, it was not a happy household. A lot of domestic violence combined with mental health issues is never a good recipe for a happy home. They gave me room and board for free, allowing me to get a job and save up to go to America. Yet another hair-brained scheme!

I landed a job at a local builders' merchant and met Steve Barton. He was my boss, and we hit it off right away. I told him about my situation and intention to go to America to be with my new girlfriend. He helped me to achieve my dream. We worked a fiddle, and soon I had money to go to the States. I don't want to go into great detail about what we did, but it was far from being above board. Enough said! I got a passport, and after weeks of corresponding with my American beauty by mail, it was finally time to fly to New York and see her in person.

I had a great time in New York and loved the American way of life. Things seemed more relaxed, and opportunity seemed more readily available for those with dreams. I stayed on Long Island and was given royal treatment for the duration of my stay. I was hooked and decided to leave the U.K. and move to America. Life would be good; I would become a rock star and live happily ever after with my new girlfriend. At the conclusion of my brief visit, I was driven back to the airport, said my teary farewells, and promised to return soon. What could possibly go wrong?

I was motivated to get some money together when I returned to the U.K. I even sold the immigration plan to my father, who agreed to match any amount I could save. Now there was some incentive. I was worried about the situation working with Steve. The company was investigating an unexplained inventory depletion, so I quit my job and searched for another. I managed to get employed working in the warehouse of a local record manufacturer. At Damont Records, I often had to sweep floors and tidy up the boxes that had fallen off racks. Sometimes the boxes would split open and spill record sleeves all over the floor. One such day when I was sweeping up, I came across a sight that stopped me dead in my tracks.

The scattered box remnants containing "Heretic…Burnt at the Stake" lay on the floor before me. I felt awful. First, I had recorded the record thinking I would be a rock star, and now here I was, picking up the old sleeves and throwing them away like a loser. It was a hard pill to swallow, but I was on a mission, so a stiff upper lip was the order of the day. I worked as many hours as I could each day and then raced home to see if a letter had arrived from my American beauty. I loved receiving those scented envelopes until, one day; the aroma turned stale.

As I sat down to read, I noticed the letter's tone was different. As I read on, I soon figured out why. My girlfriend told me she was pregnant and wanted an abortion. She said she needed money, and I was to send her as much as possible because the procedure in America was expensive. What could I do? I felt I had to help her, and without any question, I sent all the money I had saved. I waited to hear back from her, but there were no more letters.

Goz flew over to New York as he was still dating her sister and had some grave news for me when he arrived back in the U.K. He told me she had a new boyfriend and was out and about enjoying herself, and there had been no mention of an abortion. I was devastated. I didn't know if it was all a lie or whether she had just found somebody new and was over me. Either way, I was done with all this falling-in-love crap. That night I burnt all her letters and hit the west end. It was time to get laid.

I quit my job because there was no real need to save money, and besides that, I was not too fond of the place. I was back on the dole and spending more and more of my time in the nightclubs. My meagre government allowance was enough to put fuel in the car and get me a drink, and that was all I wanted. I was getting laid and drunk, and it all felt good. It was like being a rock star without worrying about achieving success. The clubs were full of the real stars, and you could blend in if your hair was long, and you could tell a good story. It suited me just fine.

One of the bands that were regular patrons of the nightclub scene comprised three hard-rocking beauties who hailed from Wandsworth. Rock Goddess was doing well on the A&M record label and had successfully toured with Iron Maiden and Def Leppard. The bass player, in particular, caught my attention. I'd seen her on television and had been introduced to her once by Goz at a Marquee show where he worked as her roadie. She was the hottest girl in rock at that time, stunning to look at and very approachable.

I used to hang out with her at the clubs and always enjoyed our intimate discussions. One night I finally plucked up the courage to ask her out on a date to the cinema. She said yes, and I couldn't believe my ears. I told everybody that would listen I was going on a date with Dee from Rock Goddess. I was so excited. We arranged a time and decided to see the movie, Teen Wolf. We got a few drinks inside us, and the night progressed from the cinema back to Dee's apartment in Wandsworth.

It was a massive house on the high street, and each girl in the band had an apartment, with the manager living in the basement. On the top floor was the rehearsal studio, where the girls put in a lot of work each day. I spent my first night with her, and that was it; we were an item. It was not long before I discovered the situation with the band was not all it seemed from the outside. She wasn't happy as they'd lost their recording contract with A&M and were struggling to get placed with another label. Their only income was from playing live shows at the Marquee Club. These shows were a regular occurrence, so much so they could have been mistaken as the resident house band.

We decided to move in together and get away from Wandsworth. There was little privacy at the Rock Goddess house, and it always felt like Dee was on call. An ex-girlfriend of mine and her boyfriend were contemplating moving at the same time, so we decided to rent a house together. We moved into a run-down house in Hayes, and life continued with our respective careers taking front and center. Rock Goddess was negotiating a contract with the hugely successful management team Smallwood/Taylor. They wanted to take the band to L.A. and revamp them entirely. It was all going well, and the prospect of relocating to Los Angeles was very appealing. But it was not to be. Literally, overnight, the deal was off. Goddess released a third album, "Young & Free," which garnished limited success. So, the tide had turned, and the band was all but washed up.

We were treading water with little going on with my career or hers. I recorded a couple of new songs and shopped them around without success; Dee was still commuting to Wandsworth to rehearse for gigs they didn't have. Something had to change to shake things up and get us moving again. We fell behind with the rent at the house and ended up moving in with my old friend Steve Barton. He was married and had a young family, screaming kids! That was the last thing I needed, but I was grateful to him for putting a roof over our heads.

Days drifted into weeks, and life was rather mundane until I was hit with some news that almost gave me a heart attack; Dee was pregnant. So here we were, living with a friend and his wife, trying to make ends meet. We were on the dole, and our careers were circling the drain. How on earth were we going to cope with a baby? I could barely be responsible for myself, let alone a newborn child. Dee told me she wanted this child and assured me we could cope, and I could continue with my music aspirations. It certainly wasn't instant, but I came around to the idea and looked forward to having a child. The circumstances could have been better, but I'm sure many people would tell you that. These were the cards dealt to us, and we just had to get on with it.

I met some excellent musicians during my nights at the clubs and found some who were looking for new opportunities. A lot of bands had signed record deals achieving limited success for a variety of reasons. Everybody was trying to save face with all kinds of stories about how they were recording new material or thinking of moving stateside. The record companies had spent a lot of money on bands that had yet to break into the big leagues. Consequently, the acts got dropped from the labels and hung around in the clubs, hoping to run into an agent or manager who could jump-start their careers.

The Road to the Manor

The proprietor of our old rehearsal space suggested I contact his agent. He played in a band and made a living performing to the Americans at air-force bases in the U.K. It wasn't news to me as I had dabbled in playing at these venues with limited success. I knew they weren't interested in original songs but wanted bands who could play some old favorites and hits of the day. My peers frowned upon this, but I was starting a family and needed the money. I wasn't thrilled about doing it again, but I revisited the situation to evaluate its merits.

I contacted the agent and was told he had plenty of work for me if I wanted it. I called Stu to see if he'd be interested in trying it. He was curious, so we auditioned for a drummer and acquired one in reasonably short order, but we still needed another guitarist. I didn't want to work with Karl again, so who would I contact to fill the vacant position? As fate would have it, I hired the guitarist who gave me my start back in Bury St. Edmunds. He'd moved to London, and I ran into him at a show and chatted about the old days. He was working with a band but agreed to join our venture.

Now we had a full lineup but needed a name. I suggested we call the band Scoundrel, and surprisingly, everyone agreed. What was supposed to have been my solo career was now shaping up to be a cabaret band. We decided to play at the American military bases to make money and perhaps collaborate on writing some original material in our downtime. This might work! First things first, though. We had to learn enough popular songs to perform for ninety minutes. After a brief period of rehearsing, it was only a short time before we drove to our first show, wondering what to expect. Watching the audience enjoy our performance was a big relief when we began playing. It was relatively easy to please the audience because all the songs were hits, and you couldn't put a foot wrong so long as you played well. The agent gave us plenty of work; maybe I could make some decent money this time.

Throughout Dee's pregnancy, I continued playing at the American bases, and we survived with the combined income of gig money and dole checks. It was getting crowded at Steve's house, so we opted to use the welfare system to try and get on our feet and have a place of our own. We ended up living in Slough in what was called "Emergency

Housing." It was awful. We had to be out of the house by 8 am (supposedly looking for work) and back in the place for lights out at 11 pm.

Dee had a daughter from a previous marriage who was now living with us. We were all cramped into one room, sharing a bathroom with the other occupants of the house. After a short stay in this living hell, we were moved to Southall. This place was even worse. It was a tiny room in a complex where you had to share a kitchen and bathroom. Our food was frequently stolen, and the loud booming of reggae music kept us awake all night. There were prostitutes, drug dealers, and violent people all around us.

Dee was three months into the pregnancy, and our living situation was diabolical. It was so cramped, and we had just enough money to survive. As we approached Christmas in 1986, I had little to no festive spirit required for the season. I sank into a deep depression and gave up on ever getting out of this place. We were on a council waiting list for a flat but had yet to determine when we would be able to move. Goz was travelling the world, and all my other friends had decent places to live. Here I was, expecting a child with nothing to show for my endeavors.

One morning, Dee presented me with a copy of the Sun newspaper. She grinned as she gave it to me. I could not believe my eyes. There was my ex-girlfriend, Mary Anne, on the front page. She'd been at a nightclub with a mutual friend who landed himself a part on the television show Eastenders. A sneaky photographer snapped a picture of her and the soap opera star and ran a fictitious love triangle story. Simon, the soap star, was dating Mary's sister. For the next few days, this real-life soap opera played out on the front page of the national press.

I was living in squalor, awaiting the birth of my first child, and my ex was splashed all over the front page of the national press. Was I jealous? Yes, I was, but I was also proud. She was going places and would continue climbing to heights she could never have imagined. Dee continued a relentless quest to get us out of Southall and into a flat. Where we relocated didn't matter; we had to escape our present situation. I was worthless at this time, wallowing in self-pity, making the occasional trip to the west end to get drunk with my friends. Dee spent long days at the DHSS haggling with the local authorities trying desperately to get us moved.

Christmas came and went with little celebration or ceremony; 1987 was soon upon us. Finally, we got some good news. We had been approved for a flat and could move in immediately. The only problem was it was on the other side of London in Woolwich. Neither of us knew the area, but we didn't care. If it had a roof and four walls, we were moving in. As they say, "Be careful what you wish for." When we checked out our new home, we were a little unnerved. It could have been in a better area, and the flat needed a great deal of work. It had no carpet, light bulbs and bare walls. There were no appliances, and our welcome basket was some old chicken bones lying helplessly in front of the gas fire. Nevertheless, it was a take-it-or-leave-it offer, so we took it.

We had the bare necessities we'd been given by friends and family. Our neighbors were an amiable couple and had a baby girl. We were made to feel welcome, but I needed to find a way to fit into this new lifestyle. I didn't enjoy all the small talk about children or shopping. I had very little in common with anybody in our new community. Already there were telltale signs our relationship might be in jeopardy.

The agent booking our U.K. dates had a cancellation to fill for a month's work in Spain. His original band had pulled out, and he wanted Scoundrel to take their place. The only problem was we had to pretend to be them. What did I care? I was going to Spain for a month in June of '87 to have some fun in the sun. I contacted the band, and everyone was excited about playing in Spain. None of us cared about pretending to be the other band, so we became "Jacuzzi." We managed to get enough money to put a down payment on a small P.A. system and rehearsed diligently.

The contract stipulated three forty-five-minute sets were to be performed six nights a week. We had two sets ready to go, so it was easy to learn the extra material. I would be doing most of the singing, but my guitarist friend from Bury was able to offer some relief in that department. We had this great idea; we would be able to write a ton of originals while we were in Spain and then come back to England with a new original band. That was the idea, and it was a good one, but realizing it would be something entirely different.

I'm sure many people can't understand how I could leave the country when my first child was due to be born. I didn't realize that Dee might require my assistance at that time. I was more interested in getting away to foreign shores and having a good time. Our journey would begin in Ramsgate, boarding the ferry to Dunkirk. From there, we would drive for two days through France and Spain. At first, the journey was exciting, but that soon changed. There were no GPS systems or smartphones to aid our navigation. All we had was a map book and a few words of French at our disposal. We stopped briefly in Paris for a cafe au lait, but other than that, we continued driving day and night. There was no interest in sightseeing; we just wanted to get to our destination and start playing.

Our destination was Rota near Cadiz. After two days in the van, we arrived at a beach in Rota. We parked, and I remember thinking, "What a dump." The beach was filthy, and a pungent stench hung over the dunes. This was not what we were hoping for. We went into the town and met some locals, some of whom spoke English. They told us we parked on "Garbage Beach," a local dumping ground. The good beaches were on the other side of the harbor. We were relieved and enjoyed the company of locals with some cheap beer and cigarettes.

After spending the night with a couple of ladies in the American Navy who were more than willing to make us feel at home, it was time to load in and get set up at the venue. Rota was a high-security naval base, so we were issued passes at the guard house and escorted to the club. The Windjammer Club was a three-hundred-seat venue, joined by a restaurant and casino. The equipment we brought was unsuitable for a club this size, but since they didn't relish a high level of volume, it would suffice. The night manager of the club was a great guy and ensured we had everything needed for our nightly performances. We were allowed one meal a day at the club and as many soft drinks as we could handle.

After setting the gear up, keys were issued to an apartment in the town, and we were escorted off the base. The apartment was no palace, but all we needed and only a stone's throw from the beach. We did our first show at the club, which was a huge success. People loved that we were an English band, and the drinks flowed all night. After the show, we went out on the town to visit various rowdy night spots. This town was geared up to entertain the American troops, and the partying continued until sunrise. It was my kind of town. I was here for a month and determined to enjoy every second. Daytime was spent lazing on the beach with a cold beer in one hand and a beautiful senorita in the other.

One of the first days at the beach, I remember running into the sea and laughing hysterically. I screamed at the top of my voice, "I'm getting paid for this!" and I was. At that moment, in a haze of beer and lust, I was on top of the world. Nothing could spoil my day, and nothing did. As soon as I opened my mouth, I was surrounded by willing beach beauties, and as soon as my glass was empty, somebody filled it. I was in heaven, or at least I thought so. Everything I should have been concerned about back home didn't even enter my mind. I was oblivious to everything not in front of me or underneath me.

We started with good intentions of writing songs, but it was not long before I detached myself from the rest of the band and was involved with a woman at the club. She was a bartender, and we hit it off immediately. She and I would go to the beach for the day and, after the show, spend the night at her house. Her husband was in the Special Forces and away for long periods. He was due to return before the end of June, but she was all mine for now.

One day we were at her house, rolling around the floor watching porn films. All of a sudden, there was a knock at the door. The way the house was laid out, I couldn't leave the room without being seen. The door was just a transparent screen, so I had to hide my naked body behind the couch. Some friends of her husband had grown suspicious of her extracurricular activities and tried to get an invite into the house. I was terrified they would force their way in, but she managed to get rid of them. From then on, viewing porn and other sexual activity was restricted to the bedroom. The last thing I needed was a jealous navy seal seeking retribution, but the thought of that didn't stop me from seeing her, and the affair went on. Tensions continued to grow within the band as I became more and more ostracized.

One day we went to the club to adjust the lights. Stu was up a ladder complaining about how dark his side of the stage was. The stage walls were covered in mirrors, and he wanted to shine a white spotlight onto them. I argued this would reflect in the audience and blind people. The discussion soon became a yelling match and physical, with me attacking him with a screwdriver. It was just a lot of shouting, and nobody got hurt, but the damage was done.

I decided to quit the band, so I arranged a meeting to propose we split up. The way the split worked was straightforward. I would keep all the money from the tour, and they would get the van and P.A. equipment. We agreed, so the band dissolved, and the dream of writing new songs and returning to the U.K. triumphantly was over. We had to continue performing at the club until the end of June to fulfil our contractual obligations. Many shows were packed with unruly sailors. We had an excellent time on stage, which eased the tension somewhat, but the band was over. A somber mood hung over me, and I started thinking about my firstborn, due any day.

On the 25th of June 1987, just before I was about to get on stage, the night manager asked me what it felt like to be a father. I told him I would let him know when I became one. I was then told he received a message from the U.K. My child was born, and I was officially a father to a bouncing baby girl. I can't begin to describe the incredible sensation I felt at that moment. I had a daughter who would later be named Tanya Lee Andrew. The following day, I talked to my girlfriend and heard how beautiful our little girl was. With only a few days left to perform in Spain, I was anxious to get home.

When I returned to England, I would have to smarten up, so there was no time to waste. I had several one-night stands and made the most of the time I had left to party in Spain. Our final gig was a sold-out, rowdy affair. Hundreds of drunken sailors were in attendance, and mayhem ensued. Nevertheless, it was a great way to end the month in Spain. We had a good time on stage that night, delivering a killer performance. Equipment got soaked in champagne, and so did we inside and out. It was a triumphant departure from the stage that night despite the tensions within the now-disbanded band. Once the night was over and the new day arrived, it was time to pack our bags and be on our way. None of us were looking forward to the trip, but I was excited to get home to see Tanya. What did she look like? Would she like me? How do you hold a baby? Nappies!

We drove in virtual silence, having become two separate and hostile entities. They were in a band together, and I was on my own. I had no concerns about what to do next as I knew a lot of players from hanging out in the clubs and retained a good working relationship with my agent. I plotted and schemed my next move as the silent journey continued. It was so hot in the van as I feasted on a diet of bologna sandwiches and warm soda. By the time we got to Dunkirk and set sail, I was glad to be able to walk around on the deck of the ferry. I could see the English coastline and felt nothing could slow us down now. The van was running smoothly, and it was only a couple of hours to get back to Woolwich. All we had to do was clear customs, and I would be home.

When we arrived in Ramsgate, the customs officer was a real bitch. She looked down her nose at us, and we were treated as inferiors. The condescending tone continued as she asked if we had any illicit drugs in the van. I should have kept my cool and just said no. Instead, I unloaded a string of sarcastic remarks about how we were smuggling everything from heroin to hash inside the equipment. Note to self: never try to be funny with a customs officer if she's a bitch. A team of officers ripped the gear apart, and hours later, we were still putting it back together before we could resume the final leg of our journey.

The mood in the van for the remainder of the trip was now at an all-time low, with everybody pissed off at me. If I had kept my mouth shut, we would have cleared customs much quicker. Instead, I caused a massive delay by being a smart arse. I remained in the doghouse for the rest of the journey home. We returned to London, and I was dropped off outside my flat. We parted company for what would be the last time. No pleasantries were exchanged, but it didn't matter to me. I was home and greeted by my beautiful daughter Tanya Lee Andrew.

She was tiny and looked so fragile. Her pure white skin was in such contrast to my tanned flesh. I sat in a chair and held her in my arms in wonderment and amazement. Could I really be part of this beautiful creation? Would I be able to change my ways and become a regular family man? Of course, the obvious thing to do was to settle down and lay some solid foundations for us as a family. I could never have imagined what fate had in store for me at this point in my life. For now, though, I was content to sit in my chair and cradle my beloved Tanya.

Gallery 4

Debut gig

LOCAL band **Life** make their debut on Monday at Silks, supporting top London rock band **Scoundrel.**

Led by Thatcham guitarist Dave Benson, the quartet are all experienced local men. Keyboard player Pete Courtney comes from Tadley, drummer Andy Collins from Kintbury, and bass player Jed Walters is from Inkpen. Dave's last well-known local band was Prairie Dog. It's the first time this line-up has played live together, and they're hoping their brand of American melodic rock will go down well with rock fans.

On the night they'll be supporting Scoundrel, a new band formed in May 1986, and already set for a busy time touring this year.

The night before they're due at Silks, they'll be returning to the scene of their debut — London's famous Marquee Club, where they've already built up a fine reputation.

After Silks, they set off on a UK tour, to take in places like Portsmouth, Cardiff, Edinburgh and Glasgow. In August they head for Spain for a four-week tour, with recording studios waiting for them when they get home.

Local rock fans better catch them while they can!

Local band Life will be supporting Scoundrel (above) at Silks next week.

Left: First cassette release. **Right:** Press for the new band.

Photograph by Rock Index.

Have you read the paper?

Martin Andrew

Invite You To Meet

at The Red Fort
77 Dean Street
London W1

after their
Hammersmith Odeon Gig
On Friday October 5th
11.30pm — 2.30am

Drinks and Buffet

This invitation admits one only

R.S.V.P.V.
Bernadette Coyle
Phonogram Press Office
01-491 4600

Party Time!

Photograph from Martin Andrew private collection.

80

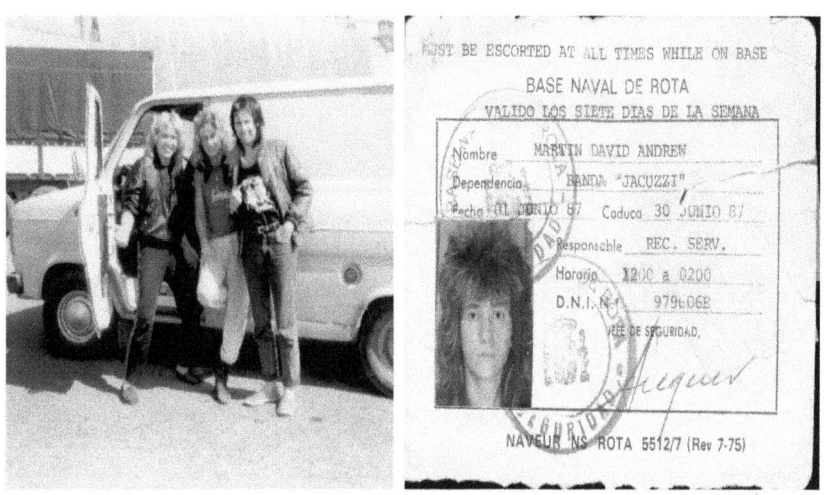

Left: En route to Spain. **Right:** ID please!

A night out with Dee from Rock Goddess.

Photographs from Martin Andrew private collection.

Baby T and me.

Photograph from Martin Andrew private collection.

Chapter Five

I SETTLED IN AS BEST AS POSSIBLE TO THIS NEW LIFESTYLE OF responsibilities and did everything a new father does. I made a mess of putting on the one nappy I changed and had no control over Tanya when she cried. I was like a fish out of water. I loved my daughter but needed to figure out this new way of life. I wasn't into visiting next door and talking about the kids over endless cups of tea. I soon returned to the west end night clubs where I socialized with my drinking mates and began planning my return to foreign shores.

There were a lot of wayward souls hanging out at the clubs, and this is where I would find my new band. Getting musicians to work with you was difficult if you had no gigs, but I had something to offer this time. Fun in the sun and money for nothing, apart from learning some cover songs and performing them six nights a week.

Spider was no longer a working band. They decided to call it a day after losing a couple of record deals and a lead guitarist. Stu was hired as a replacement lead guitarist, but his time with the band was brief as his playing style was totally wrong for them. However, I remained friends with one of the band members. Far from his tea-totaling days in Spider, Colin was now a beer-swilling out-of-work musician. Spider was a twelve-bar blues boogie band, and Colin was well-versed in the art of pumping out a solid rhythm which was the backbone of that particular genre of music. I approached him about playing some US bases in the UK with some dates overseas in the works, and he jumped at it.

Cliff Evans and Gary Taylor were both in the band "Tank." The band was still together, but they were not actively doing much. Cliff and Gary were looking for work, so a new group was formed with the four of us. We did a few rehearsals and could have used a few more. It didn't matter; we were up and running and started playing very quickly. I'd bought a van with the money from my payout on the last Spanish trip and also acquired a small vocal PA system which was adequate for what we were doing. Towards the end of the year, I managed to put together a three-month tour in Europe. It began in Spain for a month, then Sicily, and finished in Germany.

We had a few more gigs in England before we left, and Colin was not fitting in. Gary, Cliff, and I became close and worked well on stage, but Colin didn't seem right. I admired his skills so much as the guitarist from Spider, but he was not suited to playing the styles of music from the other bands we were portraying. So, one night after a show, I had to fire him. Here I was, sitting across a table from someone who toured the world and played sold-out shows promoting albums on RCA and A&M records. I was telling him he was out because he wasn't good enough.

I felt awful doing this, but it had to be done. Colin and I went our separate ways, and it would be several years before we talked again. Removing Colin from the equation had put me in a pickle. I needed another guitarist, but who could join at such short notice? Cliff, Gary, and I were having a pint at the Intrepid Fox on Wardour Street one night, trying to figure out who we could get to join the band. A burly gentleman approached us and said a guitarist was sitting in the snug. This lonesome guitarist was looking for a gig.

I couldn't believe my eyes when I was introduced to Nasty Suicide. How the mighty had fallen. This guitarist from Hanoi Rocks was now rumored to be a washed up has been with a drug problem. He sat down and blankly stared over the brim of a glass. He wore the outfit he used to wear when performing on stage, which was a little overdressed for the pub in question. He said he could do the tour if I could get him a guitar and amp. He was a mess, and I wanted nothing to do with him. I sarcastically told him the gig paid twenty pounds for the three-month tour, thinking he would get the message and leave. Instead, he thought about it and accepted my offer. The three of us finished our drinks, and we were the ones that got up and left.

We hit a serious roadblock. Nobody else could leave at short notice, so I had to swallow my pride, pick up the phone and talk to one of my old guitarists from Heretic. Karl and I hadn't spoken since Heretic's demise. Neither of us was too keen on the other, but I had no choice. He came over to my flat in Woolwich. After a night of drinking cheap beer and a few tales of old, he was in the band, and we were ready to go on tour. We managed one drunken rehearsal and left for Spain in late November 1987. We should have rehearsed more, but none of us took the tour that seriously. It was about having a good drink and banging as many willing ladies as possible. The channel crossing was rough, but we soon headed south through France after landing on foreign soil. The weather was terrible, and we got lost in Paris. I almost got us killed reversing along a motorway intersection after I missed our turn-off, but we survived.

In Spain, we parked at a service station where some hostile Spanish truck drivers met us with utter disdain. They didn't like the look of us, and although we didn't understand a word they were saying, we knew it was not good. We left the services and drove down a mountain road when the van started to shudder. The vibration got worse and worse, and it was all I could do to keep the van on the road. When we were finally able to pull over, I found the front wheel nuts had been loosened. Three guesses as to "Who dunnit?" Having tightened the wheel nuts, we continued en route arriving in Rota without further incident.

We got there in the early evening, and this time, I knew exactly where to go. When I was there in June, I made several lady friends and was pleased to find they remembered me. The rest of the band was impressed when we walked into a bar, and all these beautiful girls swarmed me. They had their fair share within seconds, and this seemed like a fun ride. Having gone through the same ritual of getting our passes and an escort on to the base, we were set up and ready to play. This time the club had a new PA system we could use, which we integrated with our own. The first night was a success, and we were ready to rock and party like there was no tomorrow. Unfortunately, before the first week ended, we were involved in controversy.

We were out one night in one of our drunken stupors when Gary, Cliff, and I realized Karl was missing. Karl was a loner, so we didn't think too much about it and partied until the wee hours of the morning before staggering back to our apartment. We slept most of the next day and woke up with our usual hangovers. Soon it was time to be transported to base, and there was still no sign of Karl. We ended up in the dressing room, confronted by the club's managing director, asking where Karl was. He was a mousy little man with a big attitude. He was livid, so we played it up that maybe Karl had fallen victim to the local gypsies who were known for mugging people. When the yelling was over, and the angry manager left the room, we all looked at each other in disbelief. We had barely gotten started at the club, and here we were, getting a severe reprimand and the possibility of having to play as a three-piece.

Moments later, we spotted a somewhat disheveled Karl at the main entrance to the club. He was staggering around with a stupid grin and foaming at the mouth. We dragged him into the changing room and told him that if asked why he was late, he should say he was mugged and drugged. Clearly, he was high on something, but if the club manager thought he'd been taking drugs of his own accord, we would be history. So that was our story, and no sooner had we got it straight than the angry manager walked in the room demanding an explanation. We couldn't believe our ears and eyes when Karl laughed in the manager's face and muttered something about his watch stopping.

The next day we were summoned to the base commander's office.

He said he called our agent in London and wanted to fire us but, after calming down, decided not to. We were to keep a low profile for the rest of our stay, and any further incidents would mean instant dismissal. The three of us were so pissed off at the stupidity of our fellow musician. We decided he was bad news and not one of the gang from that day on. Having been told to keep a low profile, we went out on the town that night and got hammered. What a smart thing to do after being threatened with instant dismissal.

It was just our luck as Cliff staggered across the street and fell over a police car while projectile vomiting all over the trunk; the club manager was stopped at the traffic lights and saw the whole debacle. Next, I was seen being carried unconscious out of the same club by a bunch of rowdy marines. I think he was so taken aback by our blatant disregard for the lecture we had been given; he just looked the other way and hoped for the best. He needed a band in the club and knew the audience liked us. If he reported this incident, he, too, would be in trouble for us having a lack of respect for his authority. He drove away, and we slept it off.

I hooked up with the lady at the bar I'd been seeing on my first visit to Spain, but her husband was in town this time. We were cautious, but to be honest, I was not ready to get beaten to a pulp just to get laid, so I moved on. Gary, Cliff, and I embarked on a drinking spree that damn near killed us. We remained drunk both day and night. I was unaware of how much damage I was doing to my system, but it was a lot of fun at the time. We became terrific friends and had a blast. The month passed quickly, with us chasing a lot of pretty girls and some dodgy boilers. Christmas was a bit weird; we got a little homesick, but the New Year soon arrived, and we were on our way to Sicily.

A girl who had been partying with us wanted to go to Naples, which was on the way; she had gas coupons to pay for her ride. So now there were five of us crammed into the van, and we would be on the road for four days. You would think this would be easy to remember, but having recently spoken to Gary about this, he remains oblivious that a girl travelled with us for those four days. All this despite the fact that he was curled up with her on the van floor for most of the trip. They say heavy drinking kills brain cells; I guess they were right!

We drove the eastern coastline of Spain without incident for most of the journey. At one stage, we heard gunfire a little too close for comfort but continued our travels without anyone getting shot. Driving through the south of France was absolutely breathtaking. We stopped off in Monte Carlo and admired the view for a while but had a schedule to keep, so it was back on the road before long. When we finally got to Italy, we decided to make another pit stop in Pisa. We climbed the famous leaning tower, and although I'm glad I did, I was so scared at the top. There were no guard rails to speak of, and I'm afraid of heights.

Not long after we visited Pisa, it was time to part company with our lady friend. Her gas coupons made the journey much less expensive; we were grateful for that. When we arrived in Naples, it was early morning. The area where we dropped our female passenger off was very sleazy. She got out of the van and disappeared into the fog. That was the last we ever saw of her. We got lost in the back streets of Naples, a little unnerving. We locked the doors and kept moving with one eye on the road and the other on the map. At this stage in the journey, we were feeling very fatigued and still had a fair trek to reach our destination. Eventually, we arrived at the Reggio Calabria ferry on the southern tip of Italy. From there, it was a short trip before arriving in Sicily.

We immediately got off on the wrong foot at the American base in Sigonella. I'd been given camouflage trousers from a marine in Spain and, for comfort, wore them for the trip. The night manager at the club (a big, fat, miserable man who we affectionately referred to as the sharp-dressed pig) told me to get out and come back with civilian trousers. I argued with him just for the sake of it, finally acquiescing to his demands. This gig was a nightmare. We expected to play three sets a night, and they made us play five. We thought we would play in one club, and they made us play in two. That meant we had to do a teardown and set up twice a week. The staff was horrible, and the management was worse. It was going to be a rough ride, so there was only one thing for it, drink more alcohol!

Our time in Sicily was the most drunken debauchery I have ever been involved in. We were constantly getting written up, and I was in the office more times than I care to mention. I recall we got in serious trouble on one of our nights off. The club had a redneck DJ spinning country songs with an audience of hillbillies in attendance. We decided to join them for a convivial evening of libations and frivolity. The DJ was making derogatory remarks about us all night. We had gained a lot of friends in our time at the club and an equal number of enemies. Provoked by all the remarks, I made my way onto the dance floor with a chair and proceeded to mock the hillbillies.

My interpretation of their dance moves did not go over too well, and verbal abuse flew in both directions. The antagonistic atmosphere continued all night until it was time to leave. When we exited the club, our tires were flat, and a bunch of rednecks had gathered around the van. I lost my mind, grabbed a tire lever from the van, and started swinging it at the crowd while yelling obscenities. First, I was approached by the duty officer, and she told me to calm down. I told her to fuck off. Then another girl came over with a pump and began inflating the tires on the van, much to our amazement. It was absolute chaos, and it was not going to end well. Then, out of nowhere, a calming voice told me to relax and stand back. Suddenly, we had some older special forces troops on the battlefield. These older soldiers who were rock fans took it upon themselves to stick up for us, and the fight was on.

While the brawl ensued, the girl with the pump was successful in her quest to inflate the tires, so we jumped in the van with her and left the battleground for quieter pastures. I realized she was a girl I'd chatted up in the bar and invited back to the apartment. I was driving like a lunatic and almost hit a car, which later turned out to be the duty officer I'd told to "go away" so nicely. The night was just getting started. We stopped off at the girl's house so she could pick up an overnight bag, and then it was back to our apartment for some fun.

She agreed to party with us all, so after my solo shag-fest, I shared her with the rest of the band. She handed out various sex toys, and we indulged in carnal pleasures of the flesh. That was all except Karl, who hid under his bedclothes while the rest of us enjoyed a drunken gang-bang. Things were about to get out of hand, and I would again be the cause. The girl who'd taken care of us so obligingly arrived with me, so I figured she would sleep with me for the night when we were done. My ego would not allow for any other scenario.

She took a liking to Cliff and ended up in his bed. I was yelling and screaming at both of them. As they took cover under the sheets, I started throwing beer bottles against the wall. The bottles smashed above his headboard and showered the bed with broken glass. I should point out that although we had a four-bedroom apartment, we opted to sleep in the same room for such occasions. The room was now covered in broken glass, and here I was, naked with a hard-on, smashing anything and everything I could get my hands on. As I punched the glass globes on a chandelier causing even more broken glass to cascade onto the ground, Cliff skillfully launched a dildo at my head, which knocked me flat on my back. I had cuts all over me. Gary, although barely able to stand, helped me back onto my feet.

During all the chaos, Gary and I noticed that a new day was upon us, and along with it, a procession was making its way along the street. We walked out onto the balcony with a beer in hand and me with my body covered in blood. By now, I had calmed down and accepted that Cliff would have a lovely young female body to keep him warm for the night. My focus now was on the spectacle before me as Gary and I gazed through bloodshot eyes at the parade. Unaware of its purpose, we cheered and waved at this montage of Sicilians. What a sight it must have been for them. Two long-haired men standing naked on a balcony, one covered in blood, both drinking beer in the morning sun. Unfortunately, we would later find out we witnessed a mob funeral parading in the street, and our behavior was somewhat inappropriate.

Many other incidents followed this night, including me insulting the chief of police while chewing on a pizza crust. We were at Mama Elios Pizza parlor having a bite to eat after a show when there was silence among the locals. At the main entrance, a distinguished and fierce-looking man in uniform was flanked by a couple of armed police officers. This stoic figure surveyed the establishment's patrons, and an atmosphere of terror was quite apparent. As usual, I was drunk and unaware of who this man was and decided to make a humorous quip. I yelled out, "Holy shit, It's Mussolini!" You could have heard a pin drop. But, luckily for me, he found my remark somewhat amusing. After a few moments, he grinned at me and left the establishment. Did I dodge a bullet? I think so.

We left the base one night so drunk I couldn't get us home, so I parked the van at the side of the road, and we passed out. In the morning, we were woken by a loud pounding on the side of the van. It was the Carabinieri. This was a no-nonsense police force with dubious ties to organized crime. I felt sure they were not waking us to offer coffee and a pastry. While opening the door, I was grabbed and pulled from the vehicle with machine guns pointed at me. The rest of the band was treated similarly, and we were lined up against the side of the van. They ransacked the van's contents while yelling in Italian at us. I was smacked on the back of the head whenever I tried to talk to them. Eventually, I just shut up as I was getting more of a headache than the regular hangover I was used to. After a good rummage through our belongings, they left us facing the side of the van and drove away. We waited a few moments to count our blessings and returned to our apartment post haste.

We became aware our excessive drinking was taking its toll on our health and decided to do something about it. There were a bunch of fields close to the apartment, so we decided to go jogging and see if that improved our stamina. We made it once around the field before somebody suggested we should have a beer. Undeterred, we decided to go for a hike in the countryside and walked across the field into a more hilly and wooded area.

Soon into our journey, we noticed three men following us. That in itself would have been fine, but these men were brandishing shotguns and yelling at us. We decided to see if we could outmaneuver them and get back to the relative safety of our apartment. We lost sight of them for a while, only to round a corner and come face to face with the men who had pursued us. I was terrified. I thought we would get shot and buried in a shallow grave. But, lucky for us, they just wanted to say hello. Through broken English, we ascertained they were rock fans and heard we were the band from England and just wanted to meet us.

We got ourselves into all kinds of crazy situations during our stay in Sigonella, but for the most part, we had a great time. As time passed, we grew weary, and tempers began to fray. One night at Mama Elios, I was feeling particularly homesick. Cliff invited a girl he met at the show to join us. She was cute but annoying. Usually, that wouldn't have bothered me. So long as she spread her legs and made Cliff happy, it didn't matter what she had to say, but this night was different. I remarked how I missed home and looked forward to seeing my girl-friend. She scoffed at my remark and said something derogatory towards Dee.

That was the spark that ignited the powder keg. I lost my temper and called her all the whores under the sun. My remarks pissed Cliff off, and now we were causing a scene in the pizza joint and subsequently asked to leave. The argument became more heated when we got outside; even Karl chimed in. Soon it was a full-scale brawl, with Gary trying to pull me off the others as fists were flying. The police arrived, and somehow, Gary managed to calm the situation and get us out of there.

In the morning, we all awakened with our usual hangovers. My knuckles were bloody, and my face was swollen. Cliff had a black eye, and Karl was in a real mess. Apparently, I threw him over a wall, and he fell about twenty feet down a ravine, getting cut to ribbons by some branches on the way. My behavior was out of control. Things were about to come to a head when we performed at an outdoor festival.

It all started great. The festival was for about five thousand troops returning from six months at sea and many locals. Bands and enter-tainers flew in from England, and we would all perform in a massive circus tent. We performed two sets per day, which were much less than required in the club, so we were pleased about that. The circus came to town, and along with it came a lovely girl who walked on a large ball and swung from a trapeze. Loredana would be my next conquest.

The Road to the Manor

She couldn't speak a word of English, so we managed to communicate with a dictionary and a lot of sign language. Her family owned the circus and actively participated in some of the main attractions. This was like no circus I had seen. It was a real low-budget affair. The equipment was rusty and falling apart, and the funfair that accompanied the big top was quite deadly. Her mother was known as the electric lady. They literally plugged her into the mains and made sparks fly off her head. She looked significantly worse for wear with sagging facial features.

We played our first day at the festival. The crowd liked our antics, but the female agent who'd flown in with the rest of the acts was not impressed. She became even more hostile towards me, mainly after she told me to get the band on stage despite a bomb scare. In my usual abrasive fashion, I told her where to go and even threw in a finger gesture for good measure. After the first show, I spent the night in the girl's trailer, keeping as quiet as possible after she indicated her dad was next door and had a gun, along with a bad temper.

The following day when Gary, Cliff and I returned to the tent, we found Karl lying on the stage next to an empty bottle of vodka. He was in such a mess he couldn't speak. We had to be on stage at noon, which was only an hour away. We dumped him in a cold shower and did our best to sober him up, but our efforts were in vain. He was obviously out of it, and the show officials were there to see it. We knew we were in trouble, although nothing was said at that time. We didn't have to play again until midnight, the night's final act. We spent the day getting loaded and arrived on stage that night with Cliff and I in full military fatigues.

We did everything we had been told not to do. We were a band of drunks who didn't care what any of the promoters thought, raising hell regardless of their rules and regulations. That night was to be one of the wildest stage performances I have ever been a part of. The audience invaded the stage. The night went from bad to worse, with me uttering the immortal phrase, "Italy is the toilet of the world, and you people are the shit in it." I wasn't being malicious, just drunk, and stupid. Fights broke out in the crowd, and the security guards couldn't contain the situation. We just kept playing; my rhetoric throughout the show fueled the fire. The event was captured on film. When it was all over, we packed our gear and returned to the apartment quite pleased with ourselves.

The next day we were due to play back at the club, so we set off on our short drive from the apartment with hangovers from hell. When we arrived at the guard house, we were met by an armed escort who told us to turn around and get off United States of America's property. I was then escorted as band leader to see the head of entertainment. He was the most obnoxious individual who resembled "Jabba the Hut" from Star Wars. He told me we were fired. The complaints were endless, from scenes of sexual deprivation on stage to ridiculing the natives of the country. The promoter from England had us in mind for a tour in Russia right up until she met me. She said she had never met such a liability on two legs as Martin Andrew. There was nothing more to be said. We were told to get out of Sicily, and if we returned to the base, we would be arrested.

With those kind words, we drove to Palermo to catch a ferry. Having boarded, we sailed to Pisa. The crew of this vessel was multi-tasking as we saw the same guys loading baggage and mopping the decks serving our food. Hopefully, they'd washed their hands between duties. The trip lasted a good twenty hours and was an interesting experience. Exiting the vessel and leaving the harbor, I had one last bit of fun with the dock workers. I drove through a massive puddle and soaked a bunch of workers as they were having a coffee break and munching on some pastrami. It wasn't the kindest gesture and almost backfired when we had to stop at a checkpoint before leaving the docks. I remember watching these soaked and furious Italians in hot pursuit as we anxiously awaited the gates opening.

When we reached the Italian border, I was so glad to see the back of the place. We had enough money to get us to Bitburg in Germany, our next gig, and the final part of the tour. Incidentally, to this day, Gary has no recollection of ever going to Germany despite my attempts to jolt his memory. The power of the pint!! For this last part of our European excursion, we only had to play for two nights, and that was about all we had left in us. We were so burnt out it was starting to show. In my case, this was hardly surprising since I wasn't even supposed to be drinking due to my liver damage in 1984.

When we arrived at our hotel in Bitburg, we were pleasantly surprised. It was a beautiful setting with a trout farm at the rear of the building. Our rooms were plush, and the staff at the hotel made us very welcome. Both nights at the club were reasonably slow as the troops were on maneuvers. Those in the club enjoyed us, and we were pretty tame on stage compared to earlier shows on the tour. We drank a little with some locals, then returned to the hotel, where this dear old lady greeted us. She spoke in broken English and asked if we were hungry. We were musicians; of course, we were hungry. We took her up on the offer of making us a late-night snack. We were seated at a table and presented with sandwich platters and other goodies, insisting we have a glass of beer and leave everything for her to clear up in the morning. We'd been given the royal treatment and loved every last bite of it. When we were done, we went to bed, and it wasn't until the next day we were presented with some shocking news.

The landlord was fuming. The woman who served us was a resident at the hotel and somewhat mentally challenged. The food she served us was for a wedding party, and guess who had to pay for it all? This was just typical. We settled up, played our final show, and drove through the night to Dunkirk to catch the early ferry to Ramsgate. Despite our efforts to catch the morning ferry, the weather was appalling, and our journey took longer than expected. We watched the early ferry disappearing into the horizon as we arrived at the Dunkirk terminal. Having waited all day, when we finally boarded, a warning was issued about severe gale force conditions.

The crossing was the worst I've ever experienced. Waves crashed over the decks as we bobbed like a lost cork around the English Channel. With our beer in hand, we laughed about the events of the last three months to mask our fear of the ship sinking. We docked in Ramsgate and cleared customs without incident. From past experience, I learned to keep my mouth shut and speak when told to. I drove everybody home and was soon alone, returning to my fledgling family in

Woolwich. It was now mid-February 1988. This tour had taken its toll. I put too much alcohol through my system and knew It was time to slow down. What would be my next move with this shaky career of mine? Tanya was eight months old; I'd been away for half her life. Could I be a father to this child, or was I destined for failure? Lots to think about, but first, I had to load the gear into the flat, say hello to my family and get some well-deserved sleep.

Gallery 5

Karl, Gary, Me, Cliff.

Left: US naval base Rota Spain. **Right:** Euro invasion.

Photographs from Martin Andrew private collection.

New year's day in Spain 1988.

En route to Sicily January 1988.

Photographs from Martin Andrew private collection.

Time to work at the club.

Time to party with the Marines.

Photographs from Martin Andrew private collection.

Martin Andrew

Left: Loredana. **Right:** Knickers & Drumsticks.

Left: The leaning tower of Pisa. **Right:** Cliff and I house hunting.

Photographs from Martin Andrew private collection

The Road to the Manor

Gary wants a drunken chat!!

Late night rendezvous in Loredana's caravan...Shhhhh!!!

Photographs from Martin Andrew private collection.

Martin Andrew

1º January 1988

From: Mess Coordinator
To   : Band leader, Martin Andrew

Subj: WARNING

Ref : (a) Memo from head security guard of 17 Jan 1988
      (b) Entertainment contract, sample of

1. Reference (a) informed me of several infractions you or your
band members made on Friday, 17 Jan 88. If the Band's attitude
does not improve and if your Band does not show more cooperation
with club personnel you will not be allowed to perform any
longer at NAS Sigonella! Ref (b) (attached) will refresh your
memory on how you and your members should act while on NAS
Sigonella.   Further, you are to respect the local nationals who
are hired by the Crater Club and you shall not defame them or
use obscenities towards them.   They are paid to do a job and
should be respected at all times.

2. As you well know, your performances are as follows:

   Crater Club:

   Mon, Tue, Thu: 1945-2330 (45 min. on, 15 min. off)
   Fri.   : 2045-0100 (45 min. on, 15 min. off)

   Lava Lounge:

   Wed. and Sat.: 1900-2300 (30 min. on, 30 min. off)

      You are expected to depart the club as soon as possible
after your performance ends!!!

3. Final Notice.

P.S. Keep the volume at
     a reasonable level!

                                          T. DEXTER

copy to: D. Tringali
         S. Petrucci

Our final warning before we were banished!

Chapter Six

I'd been looking forward to getting home, and now that I was here, all I wanted to do was get back on the road. I've always seen the grass as greener on the other side, but it's usually the same when I get there. What stays constant is oneself. If you're still searching for self-awareness, where you go doesn't matter. You're going to be in big trouble. I felt so awkward living at the flat with my young family. I loved Tanya but didn't feel like a father. How could I be? I was so irresponsible.

Being a dad was something I had fallen into and was definitely not prepared for. I struggled to do what was right, but I had serious issues with where we lived and the people around us. It's not that they were terrible people, I just found it challenging to fit in, and Dee was right at home with it all. When we started our relationship, we were both musicians. Now she was a housewife and a mother, and I didn't know how to feel about that. Everything seemed to have changed, and I was falling into the trap of my own making. I didn't want to be on the dole living in Woolwich and just getting by, so something had to change.

I met up with Gary and Cliff at a pub called the Ship on Wardour Street. We were all out of sorts and wanted to get back on the road. The problem was being unable to return to venues we'd just played at, as our behavior left such a bad taste in the promoter's mouth. I was not about to get on my knees and start begging people I had little to no respect for, so we decided to do more shows at the U.S. bases in the U.K. This was not a healthy choice. We kept drinking and even brewed our own beer to take to shows.

I remember one day when we were loading the van outside Cliff's house, a surreal situation developed. Two doors down from Cliff lived the singer from T'Pau. We were cramming our gear into my old Ford transit van along with the beer we had brewed. We even printed our own labels for the bottles and called the poison "Ye Old English Grundles." As we struggled to get all our gear into the van, a colossal limo pulled up to pick up T'Pau. We chatted briefly with them and were told they were travelling to Wembley Stadium for the Nelson Mandela concert. We were off to Greenham Common air base to play to the Americans and try to sell some home-brew to make extra cash. Although we joked about it, we knew our careers were in the toilet, and it was only a matter of time before somebody flushed it. There will be no gig at Wembley in our future but rather more of the same in our downward spiral of debauched antics cloaked in the guise of a rock 'n roll band.

A few weeks later, we played a two-night gig at the Lakenheath U.S. air force base, where I met the northern rock band "Mad Hatter." They were a band who followed our European tour and had just returned to the U.K. Their tour was also not without incident. They had an old bus that broke down in Switzerland and was stuck there for about three weeks while one of them hitched home to England to get parts to repair it. I thought we had bad luck, but these guys really took the biscuit. They were from Stoke on Trent, and we had a good time with them that weekend. They would play a significant role in future events, which I could not have imagined at this time.

We only did a handful of gigs after Lakenheath before Gary moved to America. His wife was American, so he was relocating to Virginia Beach. Once again, it was time to find a new drummer for the band. Cliff and I knew a fellow drinking buddy called Steve. He had been on the scene for quite a while and played with the Rock band Fastway.

Steve was the perfect fit for us, and we continued on our path to rack and ruin until one day, my body said enough. The excessive drinking was about to catch up with me again. I was about to take a substantial metaphorical fall.

I had been to the town to do some shopping and was on my way home when I felt short of breath. I had to sit down a couple of times and take a breather. I managed to get back to the flat and decided to lie down. Unfortunately, I developed a crashing headache and continued having trouble breathing. Suddenly, it felt like somebody had jumped full force onto my stomach. I started hyperventilating, and my left arm and leg became contorted, and I couldn't move. It was like something out of a bad horror film. The ambulance was called, and I was taken to the hospital.

Upon my arrival, they took me straight into the emergency room. As a bit of comic relief, I remember this older man watching me as I sped past him on a stretcher. Then, looking in amazement, he yelled, "Hey, I was next!" Despite my condition, it struck me as funny. I was in a mess, and my liver was extremely sore. A group of doctors gathered around me. The next thing I remember was an injection and being told I would vomit. Now this lousy horror film just turned into The Exorcist. I hurled pea soup into a bucket until I was empty. My next recollection was waking up in a ward. Now paranoia has set in.

I was convinced the nurses were trying to poison me for some reason, so I called home, expressed my fears, and said I was planning my escape. No sooner had I hung up the phone than a call was made from my house, letting the doctors know my deranged state of mind, and I was immediately sedated. I remained hospitalized for about a week while they tried to flush my liver of various toxins. History had repeated itself. I'd overindulged and landed myself in the hospital. I wish I could say I had learned my lesson at this stage of my memoirs, but that is not the case.

The saddest part of all this was not my pain and suffering but the pain and suffering I inflicted on my family. I can still, to this day, see little Tanya's face staring at me from the bottom of the bed, wondering why her dad was sleeping in the hospital and not at home. Her confused expression still haunts me to this day. When I got out of the hospital, I was told by my doctor never to drink again. It was a sobering speech that I'd heard before and ignored. Maybe this time, the advice given would be worth following. I made a decision, and that was it. I was on the wagon.

After several weeks of convalescing and regaining some of my strength, I sought opportunities to revive my career. The next option that came along was in the form of a used car salesman. I had met him at Ram Studios and was introduced to him after a rehearsal. As a used car salesman, he told me he had become involved with some executives at a car dealership. He said he was integral to marketing a new car that the company would launch shortly. He wanted to do an advertising campaign incorporating me singing an old Sweet song with the original lead singer Brian Connolly. The idea he pitched to me was an old meets new concept with the two singers. Brian Connolly is the old legendary singer from The Sweet and me being the new one. I was aware that our second-hand car dealer and Mr. Connolly knew each other. Still, to this day, I wonder if he ever approached Connolly for this project.

I met Brian several times at the rehearsal studio and was thrilled at the idea of recording a song with him. He was a teen idol of mine in the early 1970s, so for me, this was huge. It sounded great. All I had to do was sing the song, and I would be part of a national advertising campaign for the company. In addition, I was told I would get a brand-new sports car which made it sound even more appealing. How could I say no? I was sucked into the vortex of my dreams and began recording a demo tape for the song.

I honestly thought at the time that this would be the deal to solve all of my problems. How wrong I was. Weeks passed, and I kept calling and being told we were getting closer, and the deal was almost done. After about three months, he said the final meeting was scheduled, and we would get the green light for the project to proceed. The meeting day came and went, and I didn't hear a thing from him. The following day I called him and asked how the meeting went. He told me he couldn't attend the meeting because he had to go shopping. I went ballistic. How could he miss this final meeting? The deal was off the table, and after a heated exchange on the phone, we never spoke again. One of two things happened during this debacle. The deal was lost because he went shopping and missed the meeting, or the man was full of shit from day one. As I look back on this, the second explanation warrants much more merit than the first.

So here I was again in my little flat, wondering what to do next. Enter Mad Hatter. The band I played with at Lakenheath called me out of the blue and offered me a gig. Their bass player/singer had quit, and they wanted me to take his place. I didn't immediately jump at this opportunity because they were a band based in Stoke-on-Trent, which was way up north. But, after mulling over my options, I realized I had only one. So, I got in the car and headed to Stoke-on-Trent for my first rehearsal with the northern lads.

When I arrived, my hotel was a tour bus parked outside the guitarist's house. We had our first rehearsal at a welding workshop which was cold and aromatic, but it was free. I felt uneasy with this band. I had been used to calling the shots and working with people who were my friends. I was miles from home with strangers trying to learn a new set of songs, including some of their originals. They were hospitable and friendly, but it felt wrong. The rehearsal was fine, and we pressed on with getting a set of songs together. I don't remember how long I was there on that first trip, but I was glad to return to London.

Before long, the band was ready to play and play we did. We were booking through a couple of agents and working on the same circuit as I had done before. Since we were not overloaded with gigs, they would rent the bus out to bands during our downtime to make extra cash. It was a time of survival, and we did whatever was necessary to fund the band. Things were plodding along, but fate was about to step in, wearing fishnet stockings and high heels.

On a Sunday afternoon, I was sitting in the flat when a phone call changed my life. That may sound a bit dramatic, but it's true. It wasn't the call's content but the decision I made after the conversation that would turn my whole world upside down. The band called to tell me that another outfit wanted to rent the bus and asked if I could help as a second driver. Naturally, I didn't want to go. I hated driving that bus but was broke and needed the money, so I agreed to do it.

The guitarist from Mad Hatter, who I will call "Micky the Pimp," had a small flat in West London. For some reason, I'd stayed at his place the night before we were due to set off on the tour. In the morning, the band arrived with their manager. The manager was a lackey at EMI who fancied himself as a hotshot. I don't remember his name, but I recall naming him the egg man. The egg man brought a friend with him in the form of a young teen hottie from Canada. She was nineteen, and he was well into middle age. At first, I thought she was his daughter, but he announced to everybody apart from her that she was his girlfriend.

The band had been recording late, drinking into the wee hours of the morning, and were hung over. I decided to introduce myself to this young Canadian beauty, and she told me her name was Karen. From the moment we boarded the bus, I knew what my conquest would be. I didn't like the egg man, so it would be fun to try and steal his girlfriend. Karen was the merchandising salesperson for the duration of the tour, so it would be easy to talk to her at the gigs while the egg man was busy. We arrived at the first venue, and showtime was soon upon us. Once the band was on stage and the egg man was flapping his lips trying to impress people, I took it upon myself to get to know Karen. She was dressed in a stunning outfit conducive to 1980s fashion. She wore Fish net stockings, high heels, and a short black dress that looked like it had been applied with latex spray paint. She was hot!

I found out that night she was staying with her grandmother in Hornchurch. Her parents sent her to the U.K. for six months after she graduated from school. This was her big adventure before returning to Canada to get on with her life. She also told me she was not the egg man's girlfriend and was quite horrified that he had made such an assertion. Game on. I liked her and decided I had to have her. During the tour, she spent less time with the egg man and more time with me. What this guy was thinking, I don't know. She had attended a recording session with the band, and now the egg man figured if he invited her on tour, she would be his girlfriend. It wouldn't happen, and as time went on, he figured that out.

Things got a little heated on the tour when I was accused of ripping the band off by charging extra for fuel. I don't think I did, but between that and his threatening to have Karen kicked off the bus and left at the side of the road, let's say we were not having a perfect time. I ensured the egg man knew I was sleeping with his "Girlfriend." We were at it like rabbits. One night we were on the bus outside a gig when some bikers tried to break into the bus. We didn't care. We were stark bollock naked and having way too much fun to worry about them.

When the tour was over, and we were back in London at Micky the Pimps' flat, I remember standing in the kitchen with Karen when the egg man's friend asked her to leave with them. She told him no thanks; that was the last I saw of them. I had won the conquest. Here I was with a beautiful nineteen-year-old, and I was twenty-six. The only problem was I had a girlfriend and a daughter. I told Karen this up front, she didn't mind. Why would she? She was just over here for a good time, and I am sure she never expected us to last for very long. I don't suppose I did either, but we both were wrong. This chance meeting was going to change everything.

I dropped her off at her grandmother's house and returned to Woolwich. It became a route I would travel extensively over the next little while. When I got home, I lied through my teeth and said the tour had been tedious and uneventful. I was firmly entrenched in an affair and felt good about it. This was what I needed to feel good. I knew my love for Dee had waned by now, and there was no turning back. It was easy for me to deceive her and continue seeing my new girlfriend. I was always out with Cliff and the lads, so I had a perfect excuse. I don't know what about Karen got me hooked so fast. I was like a kid in a sweet shop with a sugar craving needing to be filled and fill it I did.

I set up a love nest at Micky the Pimp's flat. I had given him the nickname because he accommodated letting us stay at his place. He only charged me a few horny details of our sexual exploits for using his bed. My routine was set. I would meet Karen in Hornchurch and, when she had finished working in the pub, drive back to the flat in the west end, where we would shag the night away. In the morning, I would drop her off and then return home to the flat in Woolwich with nobody any the wiser to my antics. Dee was used to me staying out as travelling around London in the middle of the night could be a little dangerous, so staying at a friend's was seen as a sensible move.

During my visits to Hornchurch, I became a friend of the family at Karen's grandmother's house. Many nights, I would sit and drink copious amounts of tea with her while Karen worked a shift at the pub. Her family had no idea about my situation, and I became entrenched in a labyrinth of lies and deceit. Her grandmother and I discussed various topics, including her experiences during the Blitz in World War two, which was very interesting. We also talked a lot about Canada, and I heard a great deal about Karen's family. From day one, I was drawn to the Canadian stories. It sounded like a different world out there in North America.

I think the main thing I envied about Karen's life was the apparent closeness of her family and the seemingly "Brady Bunch" household atmosphere. Growing up, I had not experienced that kind of relationship with my parents and brother. I lived in a cold and loveless home, and this seemed like such a perfect family. I wanted to be a part of it, but my situation was ridiculous. I had a family, and now I wanted to be a part of another in a different country.

Karen and I saw each other often, and I always called her on days we couldn't get together. It was like being a teenager again. Not too ridiculous when you factor in that I was dating one. Even though I was besotted with my Canadian beauty, I was still intent on fooling around, and my insatiable lust for sex would rear its ugly head occasionally. No pun intended! One incident I remember well was the day I slept with three women in three locations within five hours.

I went to my agent's office to pick up a cheque for a gig we had done the previous weekend. At the office, there was a secretary who I always fancied. Unlike my agent, she was always in a good mood and made the visit special on this particular day. I arrived late afternoon. We indulged in our usual flirtatious chit-chat as I left the office to cash my cheque. She mentioned she would be finishing work soon, so I asked her to meet me for a drink. She accepted my offer with a naughty smile, and I left the office.

At around 5 pm, she arrived at the pub. She said she had the keys to the office, so why not get a couple of beers to go and sit in a more relaxed atmosphere with some music? I didn't have to be asked twice. We ended up in my agent's office, drinking beer with some tunes playing in the background. One thing led to another, and soon, we were banging away like rabbits on my agent's desk. When we were done, she mopped up and locked up, agreeing to do it again sometime soon, but for now, I was running late and had to get home.

I boarded the tube in a semi-drunken state and headed for Woolwich. Upon my arrival, I was still in the mood and wasted no time getting it on with girlfriend #1. Not content with this, I made my way to Hornchurch and managed to get my leg over with girlfriend #2 before 10 pm. This is how out of control I was. My music had taken a back seat to my lusting after women; it seemed I was bound to remain in this state for quite some time. I saw the sultry secretary a couple of times at her house, but when I found out she had a bodybuilder boyfriend with a bad temper, I decided it would be best to stay away.

I played occasionally with Mad Hatter during this period, but the gigs were few and far between. I didn't feel comfortable playing with this group, but it was a way to say I was still a performer and out there rocking. Karen often accompanied me to gigs; she and I were called John and Yoko. It was becoming evident to the band this was more than just a fling I was having with this young and attractive Canadian. My double life was in full swing, and they were concerned about where this was leading. I was also worried about how long I could keep this charade going.

One day I was sitting at home when, for some reason, I just blurted the whole thing out. I came clean and admitted to Dee I was having an affair and felt we should split up. Sometimes the right thing is the worst thing you can do. She was devastated; I hurt her beyond all expectations. She was distraught, rightly feeling betrayed at this revelation; I felt so bad. I thought she might have lost her love for me, but I was wrong. I hated seeing her so upset, but what could I do? After a few days of formulating a plan, I conceived an idea. I decided to tell her an even bigger lie. I begged her forgiveness, said I was ending the affair, and everything between us was perfect and would remain that way. She was happy; I was up to my neck in it once again. Now what was I going to do?

I concocted a scheme whereby I would leave the country and live in Canada with Karen. Absurd, I hear you say? It was ridiculous, a totally irresponsible and selfish thought had taken hold of me, and I couldn't shake it off. I had no faith in the band doing anything more than we already did. The original music we were playing was out of date and going nowhere. We were heading toward the end of the '80s, with big hair and complex vocal harmonies soon becoming a thing of the past. However, if I played my cards right, I could use my position in this band to my advantage. I devised the following plan.

Karen lived in London, Ontario, which was close to Toronto. Toronto was a short flight from New York in the good old U.S. of A. I would need to convince the band that our days in England were numbered. Sending me ahead to Canada when Karen returned home was the best way of getting a foothold in North America. I would go to Canada with a demo of the band, find us an agent, and when a tour was set up, they would fly over. They could sell the band equipment in England, and we could buy new things in Canada. Although this sounds ridiculous now, at the time, quite a few bands had relocated to the West Coast of the USA and tried their luck in the Los Angeles market. Somehow, I convinced them this was a good idea, and they agreed, even paying for my airline ticket. Now all I had to do was think of a way to explain this to Dee.

With our newfound romance in the air, it was easy. I told Dee the plan; she supported me because she was used to my colorful schemes and always wanted to see me happy. So, it was done. There was only one major problem, Tanya. In all my scheming, I hadn't thought about the ramifications of leaving my beautiful daughter behind. She was barely eighteen months old, and I knew my decision would change everything. Nobody persuaded me to leave her behind. It was 100% my decision. I created the illusion that once things were set up in

Canada or the USA, we would be reunited as a family, so Dee had little concern about our long-term future. I knew that was not my intention, and if I left, I would cause a lot of suffering in both of their lives. There are many reasons why I decided to go, but only one matters.

I knew if I stayed, I would wreck my own life and theirs by my selfish overindulgence. However, by going to Canada, I could achieve a better way of life for myself and, in turn, create more significant opportunities for my daughter in the coming years. My relationship with Dee was over in my head and heart, but my daughter and I had just begun. Most people will probably condemn my actions. However, at the time, I was able to sell this idea to myself as the right thing to do. It may have been executed in an unorthodox fashion, but the result would justify the means. Wishful thinking? My mind was made up, and there was no turning back.

It was time to record a demo for Canada, so we went to Glasgow, Scotland, to perform this task. Karen came with us, and we spent the best part of a week at a rundown house owned by a friend of the other band members. He was a crazy Scotsman who inherited a home in an awful part of Glasgow. However, the studio was adequate for the task at hand, and we laid down some tracks for the demo. It turned out alright, and we were soon returning to London. Unfortunately, the drive back was not without incident. Flight 103 was blown out of the sky that night, not far from the road we were travelling on by a terrorist bomb. Although we were not directly affected by this act of fanatical lunacy, it was a little disconcerting just knowing we were in the neighborhood at the time of so many deaths.

Mad Hatter had a handful of gigs remaining before the end of 1988. I drove to Stoke on Trent at Christmas for the shows, and that was it. We were done, and it was time for me to travel to Canada. I spent New Year's Eve with my daughter cherishing every single moment. While Dee was next door babysitting, I was battling my emotions and the demons in my head, trying to make sense of the situation I'd got myself into. I was so distracted from reality that I missed the clock striking at midnight. I just sat with Tanya trying to justify the actions I would be taking and hoping when older, she would understand why I did it and forgive me.

So here it was. 1989. I was about to leave for Canada to seek my fortune, but that would have been too easy. Yet another lie was about to rear its ugly head. As I spent my final hours playing with my daughter before leaving her for the last time, she just stared at me. It was as if she knew I was going for good. I wanted so much to explain to her, but how could I? I will never forget her face on that day as I said farewell. I had a train to catch; I kissed my fledgling family goodbye and walked down the hill to the train station. My head was full of doubt; I couldn't believe I was actually going through with this.

I sat at the station waiting for the train to arrive that cold January morning. As the train slowly approached, I was filled with anxiety and indecision. I knew I could walk back up the hill and confess my sins. Maybe all would be forgiven. It was not to be. I boarded the train, which was supposed to be the official start of my journey to Canada. So, that other lie is about to rear its ugly head. Contrary to the itinerary I had given Dee, I would secretly be going to Spain for a vacation with my new girlfriend.

Karen saved some money from working at the pub in Hornchurch and decided it would be a good idea to go to Spain for a final party before returning to Canada. How could I say no since I was broke and she was paying? When I arrived at her grandmother's house, she was finishing a shift at the pub. They were throwing her a farewell party. I sat and chatted with her grandmother; eventually, she showed up some-what worse for wear. She wasn't very good at holding her liquor and usually became sick. This night was no exception.

In the morning, we left the house in Hornchurch, bidding farewell to Karen's grandmother and a couple of her uncles. Soon, we were boarding our aircraft to Majorca at Gatwick Airport. We spent about ten days in Majorca and enjoyed the fact we were no longer hiding our relationship. We could walk hand in hand on the beaches and have romantic dinners in the evening. It was a breath of fresh air, and I was filling my lungs.

When our vacation ended, we had to return to the U.K. for a few days before flying to Canada. I told everybody I was in Canada, and now here I was, back in England, hanging out in London. Micky the Pimp was in on the plan, so we stayed at his place until it was time to leave the country. Once again, we made our way to the airport, only this time; the destination was Hamilton, Ontario, Canada. We were delayed for a while because the plane had a mechanical problem with one of the engines. I was a little nervous about flying, so this was not music to my ears. The plane we boarded was a crate, and I'm surprised it even got off the ground.

We ended up sitting apart; the flight gave me time to reflect on the past and ponder the future. I was determined to make this work but nervous about failure at the same time. After many hours in the air, a stomach full of reheated food and warm coffee, we arrived at Hamilton airport. I managed to get through security and immigration with relative ease. This trip was before 9/11, so immigration officers were less intimidating. I was not faced with too many awkward questions about why I was visiting Canada. Next, it was time to meet her parents and experience my first Canadian winter. The parental reception was warm, but the weather was the most bitterly cold temperature I had ever encountered. Struggling with my luggage to the awaiting car, I thought I would freeze to death. Snow was piled high in the parking lot, and it felt like I was walking on an ice rink. Welcome to Canada.

Martin Andrew

Gallery 6

Housing estate in Woolwich.

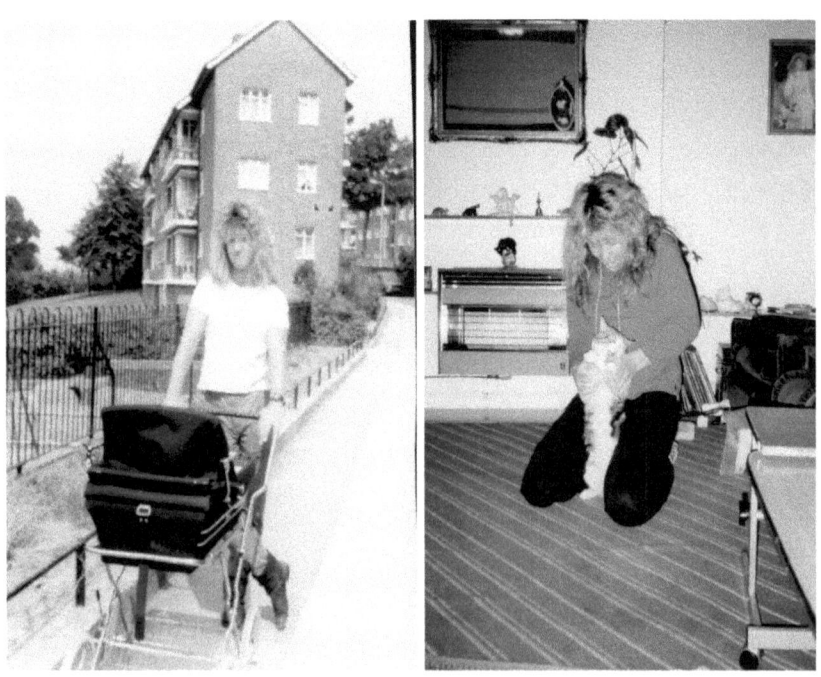

Left: Taking Tanya for a walk. **Right:** Sgt. Wilson the cat.

Goz and I after a night on the town.

Living a lie but loving my beautiful baby girl.

Martin Andrew

Mad Hatter.

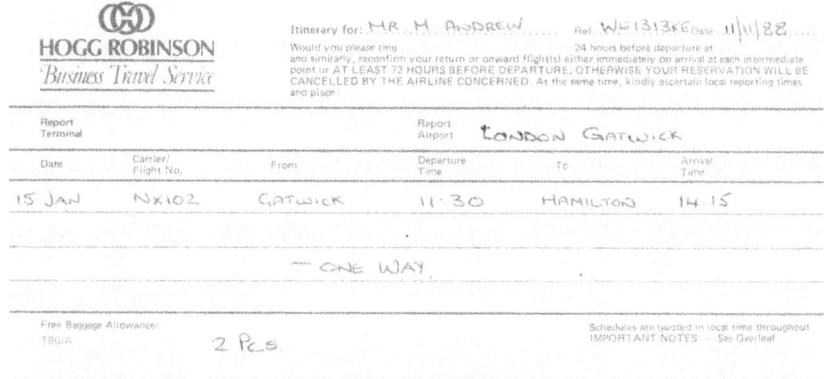

Leaving on a jet plane.

Photographs from Martin Andrew private collection

Chapter Seven

THE DRIVE TO KAREN'S PARENTS' HOUSE ONLY TOOK A COUPLE OF hours. Before I knew it, I was sitting comfortably in an armchair, nursing a hot cup of tea. Karen's parents were great, and her younger brother was a happy soul. I was officially a member of the London, Ontario, Brady Bunch. The house itself seemed enormous. I was used to homes in England, so this four-bedroom beast seemed palatial. After some brief pleasantries and copious amounts of tea, I was ushered to my room across the hall from Karen's.

As I bedded down for my first night, I felt I was in a void. It was like I had found this wonderful family and girlfriend, but in doing so, I regressed to being a teenager living at home. This would become more and more of a problem as time passed, but for now, I was just happy to have made it to North America. I drifted off thinking about the challenges ahead without any real idea what they were.

I sensed problems in my relationship with Karen very early on. She had a lot of good friends and some baggage I didn't care for. I could see her drinking and pot smoking as a situation causing problems, as I was abstaining from alcohol and not interested in smoking pot. She was different when intoxicated, as we all are, and we often argued. I still hadn't shaken my evil ways for chasing ladies, so we would probably be in for a rough ride.

Exploring London, Ontario, was so much fun. I would walk to the town center and spend hours just looking around. The big question was how to start my music career in this new land. I had brought some ¼" master reels from my recording sessions in England and decided to get some cassette copies made. I went to a local studio to get the transfer completed. I got talking to one of the sound engineers about the local scene. I told him a bit about myself and my aspirations, and he gave me a couple of numbers of local musicians to call. Having made several calls, I was invited to join a local band for a jam session. Karen's dad bought me a bass guitar at a music store called "Music Mart." Here, I met a very talented gentleman named Dan Brodbeck. He worked at the store, a family-run business. We would become excellent friends later in life, but it was off to the jam session for now.

The session went well, and I was invited to join the band. I hoped they had a structured set of songs with gigs waiting, but I would be wrong in that assumption. We practiced for weeks in a tiny house which was fine in and of itself, but to this day, I don't know what direction we were going. A bunch of originals, some covers, and no gigs would be a good summation. There was no money to be made, and I desperately wanted to earn Canadian dollars. I tried to avoid getting a regular day job, but this outfit seemed unlikely to make money anytime soon. I wasn't even supposed to work without a government-sanctioned work permit; technically, I was just on vacation. I really hadn't thought this through, but I was knee-deep in my crazy Canadian relocation scheme. I had to do something, and so it was that I got my first job in Canada.

The guitarist's brother had a flooring installation company, and I was offered a cash-in-hand position ripping up floors. It was back-breaking work; I hated every minute of it. The job didn't last too long, and neither did the band. I decided to record a new demo and approached Dan Brodbeck to play guitar and produce it. He had a great studio in his house and agreed to record my songs. Karen offered to pay for the recording.

The Road to the Manor

She inherited some money and was prepared to cover the studio expenses. I wanted to help out with the cost of recording but was unemployed and broke. Karen helped again and put me in touch with a local landscaping company. I started pushing a lawnmower by day and writing songs by night. Soon I had a little money put away and four compositions ready to record. It was time to return to the studio and lay down some tracks.

Joining the landscaping company introduced me to a whole new circle of friends. I started to get into the loop of local musicians. There was one particular group of folks who I referred to as "Dicky and the Anne Street Gang." Dicky was the lead singer of a prominent local band called "The Persuasion" and had quite an entourage of followers. He was also my foreman on the landscaping crew.

We used to party quite a lot at his house on Anne Street even though, at the time, I was on the wagon. The drummer from the Persuasion had a girlfriend who was originally from northern England; she and I became friends with a common U.K. bond. This relationship would cause some grief down the road, but at this stage, she was just a lot of fun and one of the gang. Dicky's band got involved with my recording project, which kicked off in November 1989.

I had so much fun in the studio. Dan was such a talented individual. It was one of the most fun recording sessions I have been involved in. By Christmas, the 4-track E.P. was completed. I liked it and had high expectations for what could be done with these new songs. The first thing was to get the word out that a new kid was on the block. CKSL was a local rock radio station with a show called "The Battle of the Bands." I submitted my new recording to a D.J. named Dave Burgess. He, in turn, invited me on to his radio show.

The way the contest worked was as follows. A local band would get their song played along with a new release from a well-known artist. Listeners were then invited to call in and vote for their favorite song. The local band would get their friends to call the radio station to vote for their song. At the end of the show, they would inevitably win and move on to the next round. This would go on for five days, and the local band would finish the week being retired undefeated. It was an easy way to get some airtime and give yourself a false sense of achievement. I followed suit; the title track of my E.P., "Night After Night," was retired undefeated, having beaten acts such as Kiss and Cher. I was delighted even though I knew it meant nothing. I interviewed at the radio station and felt like a rock star for at least three minutes. 1989 ended on a high note with my new E.P. ready for the record companies to scrutinize and hopefully fawn over.

My personal life was a mess. My now ex-girlfriend in England was under the impression that we were still a couple. Why wouldn't she? As far as she was concerned, I was in Canada trying to forge a new life for us. Come to think of it, Mad Hatter was under the same impression. I had deceived them all, but how long could I keep this facade? I honestly thought Dee would have dumped me after a couple of months, but I was wrong. I had spoken to one of the band members in Mad Hatter; he was wise to my scheming. He realized my intentions had been less than honorable and shared his thoughts with me in a profanity-laced tirade during a telephone conversation.

To add more fuel to the fire, I started a relationship with Sharan, the drummer's girlfriend from The Persuasion. So how did that all start, I hear you ask? I stayed at her apartment one night because I had no ride back to Karen's. It all seemed above board as we were good friends; I tried to be good, but who was I kidding? I ended up in bed with her, and we were at it all night. She was a beautiful creature of East Indian descent; sex with her was incredibly sensual. As usual, I had no guilt; all I could think about was how to keep this going.

Sharan was a very sexy girl; I'd tasted her forbidden fruit and wanted more. During our first night's naked encounter, we talked about our sexual fantasies. I'd experienced threesomes and hearing her talking about her desires turned me on. I had a girlfriend who was Sharan's friend, so how would I handle this situation? I had a crazy idea, but I thought it might just work. All I had to do was get her and Karen to have sex with me in a menage a trois; that is precisely what happened. I couldn't believe my luck. I set it up, and it worked. So now I had two girls to sleep with and a girlfriend in England looking after my daughter. How much more ridiculous could this get? A lot! More about that later.

Sharan was the manager of a local record store and had dealings with the record company reps who decided what would be for sale in the store. She offered to sell my E.P. at the store through a consignment deal. Since Sharan was the manager, she assured me the E.P. would get a prime location in the store to afford me the best opportunity for increased sales potential. She could also bring my new recording to the attention of record company reps who frequented the store. There was no doubt in my mind that Sharan was a serious asset in business as well as being exceptional in the bedroom.

It seemed the logical way to keep her close at hand would be to have her handle my affairs; again, no pun intended, so she became my manager. She got me into the local newspaper for an interview and review of my E.P. and helped promote my new music. Living with Karen's parents was great for a while, but I soon grew tired of it. They were terrific people, but I felt smothered and needed some space. I was not a teenager and felt that, at times, I was being treated like one. I was used to being my own boss for so many years I just couldn't adjust to this family life. Ironic when you think about it. One of the main attractions I had about moving to Canada was to be part of a loving home, and here I was, thumbing my nose at it.

Tensions were growing in the house between Karen and her mother, and soon it was time to move out. We got an apartment close to Sharan's place on Talbot Street. We had an extra bedroom, and Sharan wanted to be rid of her roommate. We all ended up at the "Love Shack," as it was affectionately known. It was a lot of fun, to begin with, and I spent most of my time bed-hopping or indulging in amazing threesomes. I was one lucky guy and enjoyed every minute of it.

I had some new photos taken, and it was time to put together a complete promo package for the record companies. This was all well before the days of sending out an EPK via email. A lot of time and effort went into the packaging. We made parcels that looked like sticks of dynamite and stuffed them full of pictures, biographies, and the essential item, the cassette tape. We were confident we would get a positive response from the record companies, so the packages were sent out.

It was a great feeling sending the promo out, but not such a good feeling getting the responses back. I recorded a polished, harmonious rock E.P., and we had entered the grunge era. Big hair and big production were all but over; I had missed the boat. I'd finally managed to get my songs recorded how I liked them, but nobody was interested. It was a new decade. The 1990s had arrived, and I needed to be updated. What a blow to the system. I thought this would be my moment, but once again, I encountered the bitter taste of defeat.

My days pushing a lawn mower dreaming of my songs being picked up by a major label were just that, dreams. So here I was, still pushing the lawnmower and shoveling shit but with no real purpose. Sadly, I must confess that I'd broken down and started drinking alcohol again. It was always my go-to solution when times were tough. I thought my liver would probably cope since I had been dry for so long. Time will tell. I felt down but not entirely out and decided to try a different approach. What if I were to put a band together and do a showcase? I could film the show and present a promo video to the record companies. If they saw the visual aspect of my performance, they might reconsider their position concerning my music.

I was racking my brain to figure out how to salvage this situation. Karen invested a great deal of money into this project, and I was determined for her to see some return. The highly polished nature of the production on the E.P. had perhaps factored into the equation of why they thought my songs sounded dated. I decided to remix the E.P. I contacted my friend, the guitarist with the heavy metal band Lee Aaron. John agreed to help me and remixed the E.P. to make it sound more edgy. I preferred the original mix, but I was keen to get him involved in the desperate hope of his involvement opening some doors for me. So that was the recording taken care of, and now it was time for the live show and a subsequent video.

I was working on putting a band together when a friend of a friend of a stranger hooked me up with this real winner. He was an art student or something of that nature and aspired to become the next Spielberg.

He wanted to film my video for free, so he was employed with no questions asked. As the old saying goes, you get what you pay for. He was intent on shooting a video with a storyline instead of just filming a live show. I was not opposed to that and wrote a script for the title track of the E.P., "Night After Night," and we began filming.

I got a bunch of Karen's friends to perform in this epic musical saga; we had a lot of fun during filming. Unfortunately, not so much fun was had when I saw the footage, which was absolute crap. This guy had no idea what he was doing; the filming had been a complete waste of time. I was so pissed off with this idiot that I never returned his equipment. If memory serves correctly, I believe I sold it and kept the money.

All was not lost. I went ahead with the showcase, and it was a very successful night. Dan Brodbeck and his band "The Guns" were doing a scheduled performance at a club called Kipling's. They agreed to be my backing band for a quick showcase during their regular show. The band was comprised of top-notch players, which gave me great confidence on the night. It was my first live performance since I left the U.K. I was performing my new songs under my name as a solo artist. I felt on top of the world.

Dave Burgess from CKSL introduced me, and with a hail of pyrotechnics, I blasted my way through four songs. The crowd consisted of most of my friends, so they were easy to please, but I was grateful for their energy and support. I was flanked by Karen and Sharan, who were filming the show on stage with me. They were dressed in highly provocative attire, which attributed to the crowd's excitement. It must have been quite a scene to behold, but an underlying problem had to be addressed.

Leading up to this show, I had been drinking more to quell my disappointment after the unsuccessful mail-out campaign. I managed to stay off the booze for quite a while but had slipped back into my bad habits. After only four songs, I was exhausted and noticed the area around my liver was swollen. The showcase itself did me no good at all. If it were an ego boost, I was after, it would have been a massive success. I was hoping that some music business guru would be at the show, see me, and take an interest in my original work and perhaps my merits as an entertainer. Unfortunately, nobody from the world of entertainment was looking, just a bunch of my friends having a good time.

So, let's look at the big picture and see what I have achieved up to this point. I had been in Canada for about fourteen months and managed to record four new original songs. All the Major labels had rejected my recordings, and my showcase and live video shoot had come to nothing. Karen and Sharan looked great on the night, but the video footage was not of a standard that could be used for promotional purposes. I suppose one saving grace was that I was having a great time in the bedroom.

This was not the list of accomplishments I had hoped for during my fourteen-month stay in the colonies. My failing health was again becoming an issue due to my lack of self-discipline concerning alcohol consumption. I was an illegal alien, and things would have been very awkward if I had endured severe liver problems. I had no health insurance, so visiting the hospital would be out of the question. I was experiencing extreme discomfort, and the telltale signs of overindulgence again reared their ugly head. I decided the only sensible course of action was to take a trip back to England to get myself checked out.

Before I knew it, my suitcase was packed, and I was on my way to the airport with my two ladies. Things had become strained between the three of us. Sharan was fed up playing second fiddle to Karen's relationship with me. Who could blame her? I sensed she was ready to move on, but I had become so attached to her that it was hard to let go. I said my farewells, not knowing how long I would stay in England.

As the aircraft took off, I had to shake my head and ask myself what I was doing. What would I say to Dee when I saw her? As far as she was concerned, we were still an item, and here I was, embroiled in a love triangle with two other women. I wondered if my little Tanya would even remember me. It was going to be awkward. My old bandmates were not on my list of people to see. I had lied to them to get my plane ticket to Canada, giving them false hope about relocating to North America. They knew what I had done, and if I did run into them,

I was sure it would be a meeting full of hostility. On top of all this, I just felt rotten. Had I damaged my liver even more? What would be the prognosis this time for my health and my future? There was no turning back at this point, so I just closed my eyes and waited for the jolt of the wheels hitting the runway to bring me back to reality.

Soon enough, I was back on my home turf and struggling with my luggage to get from the airport to the flat in Woolwich. I felt like I'd never been away as I travelled across the city. Soon I was at my old front door and being welcomed home. Tanya was at school, so we dropped off my bags and went to pick her up. I was so nervous. I didn't know what to say or how she would react when she saw me. As the school bell rang for the end of another grueling day for the under-fives, I waited impatiently, scanning all the tiny people looking for my daughter. When she cautiously approached, I had a lump in my throat. She looked so beautiful in her little lavender coat. I don't think she knew who I was, but she smiled all the same, which made me feel good.

I was back in familiar surroundings. After a couple of cups of tea and some travel chatter, things were back to normal. I slipped right back into where I left off. It was time to come clean about what happened in Canada during my fourteen-month exile. I explained to Dee what had occurred concerning the two women who were now in my life. She didn't seem too bothered. It was almost as if she had expected it from me. I felt great relief and figured that if she could deal with that, anything else I divulged would be met with the same sentiment.

All was well until we went to bed; things went a little pear-shaped. For the first time in my life, I had this overwhelming sensation of guilt. What was happening to me? Here I was in bed with a beautiful naked lady, and for some reason, I didn't want to have sex. It didn't feel right, and she was not amused when I tried to explain my emotional conundrum. I don't blame her. I didn't feel guilty having my threesome in Canada, but now that I was home with her, I had a problem. She was right; I was being a bastard. The issue never got resolved, and I slept on the couch for the rest of my stay in the U.K.

While in Woolwich, I visited the hospital to see what was happening with my liver. There was a problem and a simple solution. Stop drinking! So once again, I went on the wagon and committed to an exercise regime to get back in shape. The lady next door had an exercise bike she rarely used, so I borrowed it and spent half an hour each day pedaling frantically to the overtures of Motley Crue. After two months of this intense exercise, I was in great physical shape, but my mental state was not so good. I knew there was no way I could ever return to living in this flat. I also knew that would mean completely isolating myself from Tanya.

Neither Dee nor I knew how to approach this situation, so we avoided the subject, and life went on in as typical a fashion as possible. We visited with some old friends and tried to maintain a certain level of dignity in public. I am sure we were both aware of the impending end of our relationship, but neither of us wanted to confront it. Tanya was still very young, and there would have been no way of explaining the situation to her. I knew I had to leave her behind. I hoped I could keep her in my life until I achieved my own selfish goals. Perhaps then I could be a good father. Maybe I would be able to offer her so much more than if I had stayed in an unhappy home with her mother. Hope was all I had: that and my insatiable desire for success.

When my two months were up, my suitcase was packed again, and our neighbor gave me a ride to the airport. As I was chauffeured to the airport, I thought of my little girl. I just hoped this would all play out and make sense one day. I was soon back in the air crossing the Atlantic. Now my thoughts turned to the love triangle I'd created and how that would play out. Was I falling into moral turpitude? Probably. Did I care? Not really! I kept telling myself this was fun. This was what rock 'n' roll was all about. Screw the music and bring on the wild sex! My cavalier attitude knew no bounds, and I was ready to pick up where I left off. My stay in the U.K. had taught me nothing. All that time to self-analyze and perhaps better myself had yielded zero results, so the train wreck continued.

The Road to the Manor

Gallery 7

January 1989 Welcome to Canada ...Brrrrrrrr.

A day out at Niagara Falls.

My first job in Canada & Lazy days at the Loveshack.

Recording the Night after Night EP with Dan.

The London Free Press

SECTION C   C3

Transplanted 'Brit' makes local impact

Martin Andrew left the other London for greener pastures in the Forest City.

I told you so.

It was bound to happen.

Today, we debunk two great London myths.

First, that London can not attract quality musicians to participate in its scene.

Second, that nobody from this wasteland of indifference, supposedly devoid of any marketable talent, can make the break into the major leagues.

Enter Martin Andrew, British ex-patriot, now London, Ontario, resident. Last summer, Andrew made the move from London, England, to Ontario. Before coming to Canada, he fronted various British outfits, touring England and continental Europe extensively.

After years of road work, he realized his band was on a one-way street, with nowhere to go but down, even though they had released an album on a major independent British label. He took stock of his ambitions and decided he needed something more stable — a long-range career in rock 'n roll.

Enter fate. While some London, Ontario, kids were vacationing in England, they befriended Andrew. They soon broached the topic of our music scene. I'm sure they must have exaggerated a tad, because Andrew seriously began to think about setting up shop here.

Canada, and especially the Forest City, began to look musically and financially attractive.

OFF BEAT
Steve Stunning

Once here, Andrew met members of The Persuasion and The Guns. The groundwork was laid. Andrew would record his new material at the highly successful dB Studio. Dan Brodbeck (The Guns) was hired as producer, engineer, and guitar player.

Last month, the final product was made available to industry people and the general public. The cassette package, titled Night After Night, was put in record stores to recoup costs, as well as test public reaction. So far, both have been positive; a second 500 copies have been ordered for sale, while the title song, Night After Night just went five nights in a row on CKSL's battle of bands and was retired undefeated. This positive reception to the song means it should get some kind of regular rotation on CKSL's play list.

The sound has been compared to everything from Queen to Journey. It has excellent vocals with nothing earth-shattering lyrically, but well-crafted love songs.

So, obviously, London is beginning to attract attention and musicians to its small but growing scene. It will not be long before a few record company executives start sniffing around our clubs, looking to sign some of our excellent but somewhat media-shy musicians.

Let the invasion begin!

ROCK NOTE: The Brunswick presents its second instalment of Alternative Wednesday next week with the heavy sounds of Stab-A-Katt. Sweet songs for you and yours to share Valentine's Day.

First press in Canada.

TV interview to promote the Night after Night EP.

A couple of contest winners on my promotional blitz.

FM 96 On Track Winners
THE GUNS
Live Video Shoot with
special guest
Martin Andrew
Sun., March 18

Greg Simpson's Monday
Nite Jam with hosts **The
Piranha Brothers**
March 19 & 26

Every Tuesday in March
The African rhythms of
Native Spirit
March 20 & 27

Top 40
**Andi Hardy & The
Wildcats**
Wed., March 21

London's Hottest Salsa
Band
HERENCIA LATINA
featuring jazzman Oliver
Whitehead on guitar
Wed., March 28

Entertainment Line
668-3218

Pop Rock
with an edge
**National
Velvet**
Sun., March 25th

KIPLINGS
981 Wellington Rd. S. 668-2695

My first show in Canada.

Flying back to the UK with a liver in need of repair.

Photographs from Martin Andrew private collection.

Chapter Eight

I WAS ONCE AGAIN BACK ON CANADIAN SOIL, AND IT WAS TIME TO TAKE
stock of my situation. While away, Goz had been smuggled across the
border and was now a resident at the "Love Shack." He had been living
in Florida while working with the rock band Poison, but circumstances
had changed, and he wanted to head north. I put him in touch with
Karen and Sharan. In my absence, they hatched a scheme to get him
into Canada. They literally drove across the border and bundled him
into the car's back seat. He was then covered with a blanket, and they
returned across the border with nothing to declare. It was ridiculous
and could have landed all parties in jail, but it worked, and Goz and I
were reunited.

I hadn't seen him for a long time and hadn't lived with him since
our time together in Hillingdon. It was a grand reunion; we danced a
jig outside a local restaurant before catching up with all the gossip. He
lived with us, and I got him a job working with me at the landscaping
company. We worked by day and partied on the weekends. My situation with Karen and Sharan changed during my exile in England.
Sharan got herself a boyfriend, but things were a little strained between
her and Karen. I didn't care about their personal issues so long as they

didn't interfere with our bedroom fun, but that was soon coming to an end.

I did another showcase to try and promote my music; it was fun to have Goz as my roadie once again. It was a night of frivolity and loud rock music, but nothing transpired. It seemed like I would be landscaping for the rest of my days. Days turned into months, and life became stagnant. Goz was getting very disgruntled with life in Canada. After an incident when he threw a plate at the wall while preparing himself some food in the kitchen, it became apparent on all sides that he would be leaving. One fine day, we dropped him off at the Greyhound station, and that was it. He was gone again; I wouldn't hear from him for several years.

I was bored with everything. Nothing seemed to be working out until one day, I got a phone call that would change my situation entirely. A young man asked me if I would like to come and sing for his band. To this day, I am still confused about how he got my number. He said he got my contact information through the musicians union. I wasn't a member, but I wasn't complaining about his inquiry. He talked the talk on the phone, so Karen and I drove to his house. I was surprised to find out he lived with his parents. Upon arrival, I was introduced to his family. The parents were devoted to their two sons, who were both in the band. One played bass, and the other played guitar. They already had a drummer and needed a singer to complete the lineup.

The trio were young and very inexperienced but had lots of enthusiasm. I sang a couple of songs with them, and they were suitably impressed, so why not give it a try? There was nothing remarkable about this band, but if it got me gigging again, so be it. I agreed to sing for them, and that was it. I was now part of a band called "Guilty as Sin." I was told they had an agent in Toronto named Mark Ireland who was ready to book the band when they had finalized their lineup. Mark was contacted with the good news and began putting a schedule together.

Our first show was booked; I was told we would be performing at a club in Welland, Ontario. I was relieved knowing the rest of my life would not be spent pushing a lawnmower. Perhaps there was a chance to return to the road after such a long hiatus. I was so ready for this. Having rehearsed and learned almost enough material for a whole night, it was time for our first show.

I was stunned when prior to our leaving, I was offered pocket money from their parents. They gave each band member some cash and loaded the van with so much food we could have fed a small village. Early on, It became apparent that there was a problematic age gap between the other band members and me, not just in years but in personality and general life outlook. I was by now a reasonably seasoned road musician. Embarking on this new venture with such inexperienced band members could become an issue. Time will tell.

We travelled in a van with our back-line equipment and met the production crew when we reached the venue. Unfortunately, soon after our arrival, it became pretty apparent we had employed the services of a complete idiot named John Fox. I wonder if that was his real name or just one, he had chosen for himself to assert a more manly prowess. Either way, the man was an egotistical moron of epic proportions. However, he brought along his assistant Ed, a gentle soul, and I had a lot of fun hanging out with him. So, the scene was set, and we played our first week. Aside from the antagonistic John Fox, who persisted in singing along using a spare microphone behind the mixing board and a lack of songs, we did alright.

As always, I had a roving eye and homed in on a pretty girl who caught my attention. She introduced me to the fine art of drinking Tim Horton's coffee while basking in the calming waters of a bubble bath. I must say it was quite a novel experience. I was up to my old tricks and could not resist the charms of a beguiling woman. Being back in business as lead singer with Guilty as Sin was a great feeling. More gigs were being booked, and It would soon be time to head out on the road full-time. Mark was a great agent; it only took a couple of weeks before we had enough gigs to get us rolling.

Mark suggested we use the same production crew for our forthcoming tour. I couldn't stand the thought of touring with Fox but had little say in the matter as our agent endorsed him. Ed would be joining us on tour, so I focused on the positive of having him along and gave little credence to the Fox factor. We worked across Ontario, taking in such beautiful places as Kirkland Lake and Thunder Bay before heading west to Saskatoon. The gigs were not A-list rooms, but they were suitable for getting the band tight and paying a reasonable wage. Early on in the tour, I handled the band's finances and dealt with the club owners. I had the knowledge and experience of how to run a touring band, and my self-appointed position was never challenged.

The band was received well, and we had a great time. When you spend time on the road with a band, you get to know the people and break off into splinter groups. I just tolerated Fox for the simple fact we had to have somebody running sound. Ed was a great person constantly getting yelled at by Fox, so I befriended him and made Fox aware that Ed's future held a greater certainty with the band than his. The other band members were adequately competent for the small-town venues, but upon our arrival in Saskatoon, we ran into some problems.

We performed at a prestigious club called Rylys which had been host to some polished and accomplished bands. Our set list comprised a lot of mediocre material, but it was all the musicians were capable of playing. Despite having several gigs under our belt, the band had not improved, and the reception we got from the audience was tepid at best. The owner called our agent, telling him he liked me but didn't like the band. Mark called to tell me what was happening, and I decided to cancel the rest of the tour.

The band was oblivious to their shortcomings and would have wanted to continue, but I had enough, and having spoken to Mark didn't want to waste any more time with this lineup. Clearly, a good band could play at decent venues, and I no longer wanted to be on the B circuit. I had to figure out how to end the tour without hurting people's feelings.

I hatched a plan with Ed to tell everyone Mark had warned me immigration was waiting at the next town with a deportation order. I would have to make my escape to England. Any fool could have seen through this load of rubbish, but they bought it, so the tour came to a grinding halt. I boarded a bus back to Toronto. The band and Ed took the van and went home. Prior to my leaving, Ed and I talked at length. We learned a lot about each other and galvanized a lasting friendship. When I arrived in London, I got off the bus, and returned to the love shack to plan my next move. I literally hid for a couple of weeks at the apartment, having no contact with the band and pretending I had gone to England.

When I made my apparent return to Canada with all my alleged affairs in order, it was time to reconnect with the other band members. I knew I wanted to change the players in the band, but I also learned how difficult it would be to find new ones, better ones. I decided that a gradual process of elimination and replacement would be most conducive to achieving my goals. With this in mind, I arranged a meeting with the others to determine my first move.

It turned out that when the rest of the band left the club in Saskatoon, the drummer had stolen a snare drum. The club manager was furious and called our agent, demanding the return of the drum. Unfortunately, he also called the cops to report the theft, which meant our drummer was in deep trouble. So that was it; he was the first to go. A perfect candidate to throw under the bus, paving the way for a new drummer.

Ed had a friend named Rick who lived in Toronto and was a drummer. I took Ed at his word that Rick was a competent player, and he joined the band without an audition. I had always liked having two guitarists in Heretic and wanted the same format in this band. I suggested we got a second guitarist and was met with no resistance, so the search was on.

I scoured the classified ads in the music papers and happened upon an advertisement that caught my eye. A guitarist who matched the criteria I was looking for was available, but he lived in a different province. He was from Winnipeg, Manitoba but assured me he would be prepared to attend an audition in London, Ontario. He was a good player, and I offered him the position of lead guitarist. His level of playing far exceeded the other guitarist, so our sound would hopefully improve. A gradual personnel change was achieved; it was time to get the show on the road. We followed the same route from the previous tour, working all the B circuit rooms and freezing to death on travel days. Winter in Canada is no joke; the road conditions can be brutal.

About mid-way through our tour, we did a show in a small town called Estevan in Saskatchewan. We played at a dingy little bar managed by a coke-snorting lunatic. Our lodging situation was less than desirable, and the company was even worse. I have to say this was one of the most disgusting places I have ever stayed. The hotel rooms were filled with older men who could not reach the bathroom as fast as they should. It stunk of piss and shit day and night. The owner was a deranged lunatic who took pleasure in abusing his elderly guests. I saw him punch an older man and nearly kill him just because he got in his way. I was a long way from the Marquee Club, that was for sure.

We fulfilled our contract, and the small crowd that attended our shows seemed to enjoy themselves. We tried out some new material, and I was keen to get a couple of my original songs in the show. The band was excited about playing some original material and was prepared to learn some of my songs. Even though we were playing in such a dump, it had been quite a successful week. I was curious about who else was out on the road playing at venues like this when I ran into the following week's main attraction.

The lunatic owner introduced me to a man I did not recognize but was a Canadian legend. I thought the owner was full of it and asked the guy if he worked behind the bar. He smiled at me and went about his business. I later found out I was talking to Kenny Shields from Street-heart. In my defense, I wasn't familiar with many Canadian bands. I didn't expect someone of that caliber to play in such a dodgy venue. However, Ed informed me it was common for some classic Canadian acts to play in bars. I felt terrible, but what was done was done. It was time to move on.

We backtracked to Thunder Bay for our next gig at a glorious bar called The Horseshoe. Thunder Bay was the town where we had the most fun. We had to stay in a band house which was a dump but great for partying. The venue's owner was a Chinese lady. She was always in a good mood and made us feel at ease. We were booked at the Horseshoe for two weeks. During this time, I met two people who would significantly impact my life for different reasons.

The first was a local agent, Mike, who worked with some credible acts and took an interest in booking me. Unfortunately, he was critical of the band and suggested replacing all of them. This was getting to be a familiar criticism that I would take heed of later on. The second was a beautiful lady called Tannis. Life on the road is a lot of fun, but there is a great deal of downtime. I didn't have too much in common with the rest of the band members, so I used to take my leave and venture to a club just a few blocks away from where we were playing. The club was called "Bunnies," a strip joint. I loved these places. You could go alone, sit in a corner nursing a beer, and nobody bothered you. As a bonus, an array of pretty ladies wearing next-to-nothing performing striptease shows on the main stage every twenty minutes.

The girls in this club were obliged to do table dances between their main stage shows. For those non-aficionados of the strip club industry, these are dances performed on a little box right in front of your chair rather than on your table. I got chatting with a girl and, in my usual arrogant and confident tone, asked her to hang out with me. She declined with a wry smile and suggested I talk to her friend. Her friend was Tannis. She was a beautiful blonde with a killer body and a wonderfully sarcastic nature. We hit it off, and I invited her to the club to see the band play.

I didn't think she would show up, so in jest; I promised her a table dance in the band house if she did. As luck would have it, she did show up with three friends and demanded her pound of flesh. After the show, I did my duty and climbed onto a table clad in a pink g string. I ended up naked with the four of them, earning a few dollars in tips and a large pizza for my trouble. I didn't get lucky, but we had a good time. I was very attracted to Tannis and enjoyed her company. I spent my days at the strip club and nights at the bar performing with the band. Unfortunately, the band felt stagnant, and I could only see a slight improvement despite my best efforts to mold this unit into a professional act. Mike attended a few of our shows and expressed the same sentiment.

One of the brothers was becoming increasingly more challenging to work with because of his lack of guitar skills and poor stage presence. Having chastised him several times, he took it upon himself to get back at me by trying to contact an immigration official. I wonder where he got that idea? It ended with a minor scuffle and was an excellent excuse for me to get rid of him. The funny thing was I didn't stop there and got rid of all of them.

I was the band leader, so it was easy to keep the agent for myself and dump the rest. I enjoyed the final night in Thunder Bay and breathed a sigh of relief when the gig was over. The rest of the band decided to leave after the show, and Ed opted to go with them to get a ride back to Toronto. Tannis was at the final show, and I ended up alone with her at the band house. We spent a convivial night just talking and enjoying each other's company. Somehow, I persuaded her to stay the night, and we slept together. She was horrified that she had let her guard down but admitted to enjoying our time together.

After Tannis departed, I had a final chat with Mike in the morning. We agreed to stay in touch with a view to him working in collaboration with Mark in Toronto. We decided this would only occur once I had a new and improved band ready to play. I don't remember how I got back home for the life of me, but when I did, I found myself obsessing over Tannis. Before she left the band house, we agreed to see each other when she visited one of her dancer friends in Toronto. I thought this would also be a good opportunity for me to scour the city for musicians to form a new band.

I advertised in a Toronto music paper, and the search was on for yet another new outfit. Ed offered to have me stay with him in Toronto to look for new players. He lived in an area close to all the action and nightlife, so it made sense for me to hang out at his place. This was great! I had a legitimate reason for being away from home and would also get to see Tannis. As always, I had no guilt about what I was doing. I don't know why; it just seemed a regular thing to do, right or wrong.

I always believed that what people didn't know couldn't hurt them. Despite this philosophy and ideology, I was, without a doubt, hurting any chances Karen and I might have of establishing a future together.

Unfortunately, I wasn't fazed and continued with this pattern of infidelity which had been a constant in all my relationships. So off I went to stay with Ed for a while. It would be an understatement to say the place where he lived was not a palace. I stayed in the basement and had to share my day-old doughnuts with the ants infesting the area around the old mattress I was sleeping on. It was the best way to keep them from crawling all over me while I slept. We were broke and desperate, but the search was on to get new players for the band. I periodically visited with Tannis, which was always a welcome relief from the squalid conditions of my lodgings. She always had money and was very generous with it. She made me feel good.

After several weeks of auditions and multiple disappointments, we finally had our new lineup. A drummer, bass player, and guitarist joined our ranks under the banner of the "Martin Andrew Band." We got ourselves rehearsed and, once again, were ready to head out on the road. This new endeavor had the potential of being strike three. If it all went pear-shaped this time, I felt the agents would have had enough, and I would be sent packing. So, this time, it had to work. Ed was now the band's full-time roadie, and I had employed the services of a new sound and lighting production company. We had about six weeks booked in northern Ontario. The agent (Mike)from Thunder Bay, who had become a friend on the last excursion, was helping us with some dates and sharing the booking burden with the other agent (Mark) in Toronto.

The characters in this lineup were as colorful as ever. The bass player was a compulsive liar and a basic troublemaker who enjoyed nothing more than to indulge in gossip and creating rumors. The guitarist was a young, naive lad who missed his girlfriend until he encountered his first groupie; then, he acted like a rabbit in the mating season. The drummer was a strange chap who missed his mum and dad despite being a fully grown man. He also became a voyeur who enjoyed watching other people's sexual exploits.

It was a strange brew, but this would be the first incarnation of the Martin Andrew Band. It was time for a tour. We had some of the same venues on our itinerary but added others with the help of Mike. Despite their quirks, the band members were all competent players and worked well as a unit. Our show developed quite nicely, and unlike other excursions, we got the band tight and expanded our repertoire. However, I still felt like an outsider and unable to relate to the other band members on a personal level. I was fine when we were all on stage, but after the shows, I often looked elsewhere for an alternate form of stimulation.

I made a big mistake during this tour by seeing a girl for an extended period. She was fun to hang out with and very innovative in the bedroom. On one such night in the bedroom, I noticed the drummer leering through a window at us. He was getting off watching us. She didn't seem to mind having an audience, so all parties were fulfilled. I liked having her around but gave her my address like a fool. This would cause many problems when I finally arrived home, but we had a few more weeks before I had to face that music.

During this tour, I celebrated my 29th birthday in a small town called Atikokan. We were there for the week, and It was time to party. It was our final gig of the tour, and I was determined to go out with a bang. During the show, we drank ourselves into a stupor, much to the delight of the patrons in attendance. It was a drinking town, and these people liked to party. After our show, I ran around the hotel roof naked with a crowd of onlookers cheering. The drummer decided to visit the local gas station to get more drinks. He presented himself to the attendant wearing nothing more than a toga and a smile. It was a wild night, but nobody got hurt, and the club manager enjoyed all the antics. I remember calling Karen from the club before we left on our journey home. She sounded a little strange. I couldn't figure out what was wrong, but something bothered her. I knew from the tone of her voice there was a problem, but I had no idea what. Unfortunately, there was nothing I could do about it, but it played on my mind all the way home.

We met a couple of strippers at the club. One of them asked if she could accompany us on our journey. We had no problem with that, so our journey began with our special guest sprawled out in the back of the van. She was a wonderful distraction for the long journey that ensued; we shared a few intimate moments along the way. We didn't have sex, just a lot of fun fondling until I became aware of an uncomfortable burning sensation in my twig and berries. Like an idiot, I had not used condoms while indulging in my sensual pleasures. I was concerned I was taking home more than a few naughty memories.

Soon we were back at the Love Shack. Nothing could have prepared me for how I was about to be greeted. Three of us arrived at my front door after dropping the other band members at their respective homes. There was the stripper, the young guitarist and me. As we waited for the door to open, we laughed and joked about the tour and the arduous journey we had just been through. In the back of my mind, I was thinking about my phone call to Karen. Why did she sound so strange on the phone? I was about to find out.

The door opened, and there stood Karen smoking a freshly lit cigarette. As we walked into the apartment, I noticed a bunch of boxes piled up by the front door. It soon became apparent that these boxes had been filled with my belongings and were stacked next to the door for a speedy exit. My fellow travelling companions got the message that a confrontation was about to occur and decided to leave. No sooner had the door closed than a letter was thrown at me. It had been mailed by the girl I saw in Thunder Bay and arrived on Karen's birthday. What made matters worse was the envelope had a detailed description of sexual acts this girl had performed with me and others she was looking forward to doing the next time I was in town. It had been sent deliberately to annoy Karen and done its job.

I wasn't about to deny anything, so I offered to leave and stay with the guitarist. After hours of discussion and a couple of packs of cigarettes, I was allowed to remain but with a very shaky future. No longer could I be trusted? I was in a very precarious position. I was still an illegal alien and could be deported if things got nasty. Things never really got back to normal between us. There was always that air of suspicion, and rightly so. I was a rogue who couldn't keep his pants on, and Karen knew it. To add fuel to the fire, the bass player decided to take it upon himself to tell Karen all the activities I'd been up to while painting a portrait of himself as an angelic choirboy. After that, I was done with him, and now I would face the same old problem of finding players.

If that was not enough, I soon found out I had a dose of the clap. The guitarist thought he might have caught something, so we went to the clinic. He was fine, but I was not so lucky. I got a prescription and a lecture and was sent on my way. This was definitely a low point. It was strike three, and I needed to figure out how to fix things. My life was a mess of widespread infidelity and zero trust in my relationship with Karen. Both agents would probably drop me if I couldn't get another band together quickly; I had to act fast. The band members weren't critical as the band was being pitched under my name, and all the promo sent out had my face on it. So long as I had a functional band, the agents wouldn't care, but I didn't have one, and that had to be addressed immediately. There was much work to be done.

The drummer quit because he didn't like being away from his parents, and I did not intend to work with the bass player again. I did, however, have one member of the band who was still willing to work with me. The young guitarist, who matured rapidly during our time on the road, was still on board and prepared to give it a go. I liked him and even gave him a nickname. From here on, he will be called Crusty. You can make your minds up about why he got that name, as I genuinely can't remember.

Crusty had a friend who was a drummer. He was young and keen to play, we offered him the job, and he accepted. Now all we needed was a bass player. We advertised, and before too long, we were able to find a willing candidate. He was more into the new grunge sound coming out of Seattle but agreed to play the old classic rock songs in our repertoire. He was an interesting character and told us he would like to be known as "Worm." The Red-Hot Chili Peppers had Flea for a bass player, so we were content to have Worm as ours.

I had a full band and began rehearsals at the drummer's house. We worked long and hard to get everybody up to speed and adjusted our set list to incorporate some newer material. It was a good lineup, and I was excited about taking it out on the road. We rehearsed a couple of my songs from the four track EP I recorded, and they were added to our repertoire. I felt so good about having some original music in the show. It was a far cry from the early days of Heretic when our whole show comprised of songs we had written, but it was a start.

While we were readying for the next road trip, Karen and her parents went on vacation to Florida. Tannis had been in touch and told me she was booked into a Sudbury, Ontario, club for two weeks. I decided I needed a break, took a little vacation, and went on a road trip. It was a long haul, probably close to a hundred miles, but well worth it. I met Tannis at the club and watched her stage shows. I was as spellbound by her performance as I had been when I first saw her in Thunder Bay. After her last show, she told me she had a surprise.

She had rented a particular room for us. It had a hot tub, a waterfall, and a full bar. She paid for everything, and we pleasured each other the whole night. She was so wild and crazy. I liked hanging out with her, not just because she paid for everything and treated me like a King. I had genuine feelings for this dynamic lady. We shared some excellent times together. Spending time with Tannis was a great way of escaping the rigors of putting a band together. It seemed like all I did was play for a few weeks, then split up and start again. I could never find the right people, or maybe I wasn't the right person for the job. I had more questions than answers and felt very unsure about the future.

My visit with Tannis had relieved my stress in more ways than one, but now it was back to the job at hand. I had to get the band ready for the next tour, and we still had a lot of work learning songs. We continued rehearsing at a frantic pace. Eventually, we had enough material to get out and play. The one thing we didn't have was a means of transport. Karen did something unbelievable. She bought me a car and got me a credit card on her account. All I had to do was pay the car off with the money I earned on the road. Since it was transport for the band, a fee could be deducted from each gig to help pay for it. I had mistreated her, and still, she showed incredible kindness in supporting my dreams. I didn't deserve her, but I was grateful for her actions.

The transport arrangements for this tour differed slightly from what I had been used to on previous outings. The band would travel in the Ford Granada that Karen bought for us. The equipment would be transported in a U-Haul trailer towed by the car. We had some difficulty loading the trailer in such a fashion as to stop the car's front end from lifting off the ground. We were seriously overloaded, but we were ready to go. This time, we would be joined by a miserable sound engineer with the personality of a dead kipper.

I hadn't worked with him before, but some other guys had. He was known for his miserable demeanor but was affordable and available. He drove the truck with the PA system and lights and usually travelled alone. It would have eased the load in the car if somebody had opted to travel with him, but nobody wanted to. I had a bunch of gigs booked through the agent in Toronto and some more from our contact in Thunder Bay. I didn't know it then, but this would be the last time I would live in London, Ontario, or for that matter, with Karen. I had done irreparable damage with my road indiscretions. We were falling apart and out of love, although we were not prepared to face it at this stage.

Aside from the car overheating a few times, we made it to Kirkland Lake without incident. We were booked for two weeks, settled into our gig, and got a little better each day. The gig had its usual ups and downs, and we all indulged in what the ladies of the town had to offer. It's a funny thing on the road. The first night you are in town, you try to find a girl who has their own place and some food in the fridge. One thing you can always guarantee is if you get offered dinner, it's nine times out of ten going to be spaghetti. It's also a bonus if you can get your laundry done while getting laid every night. I was usually the lucky one who landed the girl with a house, and as a rule, the whole band would be invited to hang out. One of the perks of being a lead singer and having a "cute accent" was I could get to the front of the queue when it came to groupies.

You must be careful to ensure the girls you end up in bed with are of age. You can't just take for granted they're not a minor because they're in the bar drinking and having a good time. I bring this up now because of what I will tell you next. A couple of days before we were due to leave town, we got a visit from the police. The drummer was accused of having an underage girl in his hotel room. The cops were now involved, talking about rape charges. Let me clarify that I in no way condone sex with underage girls, but in his defense, this girl was in the bar and could quite easily pass for eighteen. However, the damage was done, and we decided it was best for him to get out of town, just not in the same direction as the rest of us.

Worm knew a drummer and suggested he could quickly fill the position, so we did a dramatic changeover. Our new drummer arrived in Kirkland Lake the night we were leaving and sat in the audience learning the show. We loaded his kit into the U-Haul when the show was over and sent the old drummer packing. I have no idea what happened to him or the outcome of that incident. Our latest member arrived with his wife. He was a married man named Dave. They watched us play on that final night in Kirkland Lake. In the morning, he kissed her goodbye, and we were on our way to a godforsaken place called Manitouwadge.

There were two ways of getting to this remote town, and neither was appealing. We were low on funds, so I opted for the shorter route, which was not a paved highway. I have an overloaded car towing a trailer full of our equipment, and a gravel road is the optimum route. What the hell was I thinking? Our lives and the tools of our trade are in my care, and here I am behind the wheel of this car, travelling down a road that a tank would have a hard time driving on. Here is a quick note for anybody who decides to travel to northern Ontario, stick to the main roads! The further we travelled along this gravel road, the worse it became.

My frugal instincts in choosing a route had taken us onto a logging trail. Unfortunately, it meant that large trucks transporting tree trunks used this trail, and consequently, there were potholes and debris everywhere. However, I took my hat off to the Ford Motor Company because, against all odds, the Granada just kept going. As we dodged massive logging trucks and swerved to avoid craters in the road, we eventually emerged from the cloud of dust that enveloped us to enter the fair town of Manitouwadge.

We arrived late and had to get the gear on stage as quickly as possible. It was hysterical. Everything was covered in dust, including us. No sooner had we got the equipment on stage than we had to start playing. Remember that our new drummer had only ever watched the band and had yet to rehearse before this performance. It was a mess, but we got away with it. At the end of the night, we breathed a sigh of relief and settled into the trailer provided for us.

Two girls we had been partying with in Kirkland Lake arrived at the club a couple of nights into our gig. It seemed a long way to drive just to get laid, but I had no complaints, and it helped the week pass. By the end of the week, the band sounded good, and having said our farewells to the town and the girls, we were heading west. The next port of call would be an interesting one. We were going to be playing in a shopping mall. That was novel enough, but the ensuing drama was fit for an afternoon soap opera. Having found the venue and loaded in, we promptly set up everything and did our sound check. When I arrived in a new town, I went for a walk to look at the local surroundings after sound check.

I happened upon the local store and decided to pop in for a browse. While cruising the aisles, I encountered this beautiful girl clad in a skimpy T-shirt and very short shorts. She was crouching down and stood up as I approached, and we almost banged heads. She was stunning in appearance and had a friendly personality, which is a rare combination. We chatted for a while, and I invited her to the gig. She seemed interested, and I kept my fingers crossed she would show up.

That night during the show, she appeared at the bar and was very friendly. I checked her fingers for rings. She had no wedding ring, so it was game on. If a woman were married, I didn't care, but in a small town, you could get yourself in deep trouble by sleeping with one. We chatted after the show and went to her friend's house. We sat up till the wee hours listening to music and having a great time. I didn't score, but it was a fun night, and I was there for the week, so I still had time.

It was the last night we were there that everything went wild. She invited me to her house after the show. The place was set up for a night of passion when I arrived. I left my car at the hotel and told the band I would see them in the morning to continue our journey west. My night at her house began with her dancing for me in a lace outfit with lingerie underneath. It was so erotic. It seemed like such a magical night until the phone started ringing. Somebody on the end of the line was not happy.

Unbeknownst to me, the person on the phone was a lunatic known in the town as "Bates:" As in Norman Bates from Psycho. He was this girl's ex-boyfriend and had been to the hotel banging on doors and brandishing a knife looking for me. He challenged the band for information about my whereabouts, stating he wanted to kill me. All this was being articulated rather forcefully through a haze of alcohol and smoke breath. Meanwhile, back at the ranch, I am just getting pissed off that the phone call is interrupting my fantastic night of dancing which I hoped would lead to gratuitous sex and carnal pleasures of the flesh.

After the call ended, she stripped down to her lingerie and continued the eroticism. It was evident in every way how ready she was for the body ravaging to begin. I was ready to explode when there was a bang on the door. It was a thunderous bang! It was Bates. I still didn't fully comprehend the situation until she quickly explained and suggested I grab my clothes and seek sanctuary in the basement. As I picked up my underwear, I could hear the pounding on the door accentuated by a stream of profanity and threats towards my life. I had no sooner entered the basement, and the front door burst open. Bates was in!

"I'm going to kill him!"…"Put the knife down!"…The exchange of words was terrifying. It was a small house, so I had to be very quiet. I could hear my heart beating loud and clear. I looked for an escape route, but there was none. The basement windows were boarded up. I needed a place to hide. I noticed a pile of laundry next to the washer and drier, and there was a gap between the machines. As the arguing and threats continued overhead, I squeezed between the two machines and pulled a couple of sheets over me. Only then, while I was sitting there cowering, I realized the gravity of the situation. Despite my fears and naked state, I retained a full erection throughout the ordeal.

All I could think of was the headlines. "Man stabbed to death between washer and dryer wearing a bed sheet and sporting a fine erection!" Eventually, the commotion upstairs subsided. Did he kill her? Had they made up and they were going to kill me? Then, just like in the movies, the door to the basement opened, and I could hear footsteps slowly coming down the stairs. I was terrified, not knowing who it was or whether or not it was both of them. I was so relieved to hear the words, "He's gone!"

I tried to regain some composure as I struggled to free myself from the mighty grip of the washer and dryer. When we got back upstairs, we lay on her bed, and she told me the sorry story of Bates. This character was a local nut with whom she had a drink one night, and he had been stalking her ever since. Fortunately, the drama was over, and we pleasured each other for the rest of the night.

Early in the morning, I looked out the window only to find that Bates had parked his truck just down the street and had probably remained there all night to ensure she was alone. Since Bates was still there, I couldn't leave through the front. Leaving the house through the back door led to an open field. If I had just walked casually away, I would have been spotted by Bates. Even if I ran for it, he would probably see me and mow me down with his truck. The only way to escape would be to crawl the length of the field until I was out of sight and return to the hotel.

I kissed her goodbye and proceeded commando style to cross the field. The mission was a success, and I ran back to the hotel as fast as possible. I quickly grabbed my bags and met the rest of the band, who told me all about Bates and his antics at the hotel. I would save my story for the journey ahead. We got in the car, fired up the truck, and left town in a cloud of dust. Who knew so much could happen playing rock n roll at a mall in a week? As I told the band my story, we continued our journey west. Next stop, Saskatoon.

Gallery 8

On the road again.

Martin Andrew

Tour Promo 1990.

A wall mural created by some exotic dancing friends.

Say hello to Ed aka Slothy Bigguns.

Martin Andrew

A light snack before the gig.

It's showtime!

Photographs from Martin Andrew private collection.

Chapter Nine

I WANT TO TAKE A QUICK TIME OUT HERE TO DISCUSS THE SIGNIFICANCE of the next leg of our journey. We were driving into uncharted territory. Up until now, we had only travelled throughout Ontario and Manitoba with this lineup. I played at a club in Saskatoon with Guilty as Sin, but this was the new Martin Andrew band. We were about to enter a new province and likely encounter new adventures with fresh challenges. So, what was I leaving behind? I had a great relationship with both agents the band had worked with. Despite all the lineup changes, Mark in Toronto had been solid and kept booking the band. Mike in Thunder Bay had given me some harsh truths about the quality of the bands I had presented him with. He also told me to focus on writing songs. I only had a handful of originals, and he told me I needed much more to be taken seriously as a writer.

My love life was a complete mess. I was having sex with many obliging groupies but still had a girlfriend willing to give me a second chance after discovering my infidelity. I had feelings for Tannis but would likely not see her again as I was moving in a different direction in a very literal sense. Life on the road tests the integrity of a person and the strength of any relationship they may be involved in. I had to reside myself to the fact that monogamy was not in my future. It had never been a problem before, and it probably wouldn't be now, but that's not to say I wasn't utterly impregnable to Cupid's arrow. As we drove across the prairies, I had lots to think about, but first, it would be time to forge a relationship with our new agent.

The agency in question was an outfit run by a recently split couple. He had moved on, and she was still running the business out of her home in Saskatoon. Upon our arrival in town, I was told we would stay at the lady's house. I was not too bothered by this as it had been explained that the house was large and quite beautiful. However, our miserable sound man was not so happy. He kept demanding to be housed in a hotel but soon changed his tune when we arrived.

The place was like a palace. It had an indoor swimming pool with a bridge to get you to the other side of the water without getting your feet wet. Every bathroom had a jacuzzi tub with an ample supply of bubbles. For those with a sporting inclination, there was a pool table in the basement with a well-stocked bar. We were set. When I first saw our host, I was taken aback by her beauty. She was what today they would call a MILF. Around 40 years of age, blond and beautiful with all the toys a wealthy lady should have. She was very accommodating and made us feel welcome at the mansion.

She booked us into a relatively new club; we had a blast playing there. The club owner was fantastic, as were the rest of the staff. The audience was small but very friendly and enjoyed our shows. Saskatoon was to be the new base for the band for a while as we became firmly entrenched and enjoyed all the amenities at our new residence. During our stay at the house, we had a free run of the place and took advantage of all the available facilities. I enjoyed many an hour soaking in the spa and sweating in the sauna.

One night after a show, we were all in the hot tub just hanging out and chatting when the lady of the house arrived. She was clad in a skimpy bikini and lowered herself into the hot steamy water. We sat with her in the spa feeling a little awkward. Here we were with our agent, who was half naked, trying not to have her notice us checking her out. One by one, the guys in the band left the spa until it was just the two of us. I sensed she was not just in the water to relax; these thoughts were confirmed when I sat on the side of the spa, and she moved towards me.

She gracefully removed my swimwear and began an oral mission that would have blown my socks off if I'd been wearing any. I was invited to her private chambers upstairs, where the real fun and games began. She looked me in the eye and told me she had no sexual boundaries, and I could do whatever I wanted to her. I couldn't believe my ears. She was terrific; I was hooked from that night on. The gigs didn't matter anymore. I indulged to the full of whatever fantasy I could think of. Life was good. She didn't even mind if I was shagging other women so long as I was practicing safe sex. Other women were at the club, and yes, I did have fun with them, but she was my drug.

After about two weeks in Saskatoon, she booked us into a club in Edmonton, Alberta. The drive from Saskatoon to Alberta would be one we would make a few times over the coming months. Since I'd entered these sexual relations with our new agent, I had an excellent reason to return to "Toon Town." She was wealthy and had a great home with all the toys you could ever wish for. It was a good deal. For now, though, it was time to venture into the fair province of Alberta for the first time to see what trouble we could get into.

The venue was situated at the west end of the city. Having arrived in our two-vehicle convoy, we parked and began the load in. This bar was a good size but had a very dingy atmosphere. We knew nothing about Edmonton and were unaware of the good and bad areas. This area of town was a bit dodgy. However, the bar staff was fun, and the crowd for the week was adequate. We got shifted out of the hotel and sent to another mid-week which was an inconvenience but other than that, it was a smooth run.

The last night we were there, I met a long-legged beauty who caught my eye. She was a stunning and vivacious brunette. I was singing "Hot Legs," and the song could have been written for her. She had a friend, and after the show, the drummer and I took them to a hotel across town. I rented a room with Karen's visa card and hoped for the best. The girl the drummer was with soon became tiresome and wanted to leave. He followed suit, so my long-legged beauty and I were left alone with the hotel room at our disposal. It wasn't long before pay-per-view porn was on television, and we were shagging like crazy. She was terrific; I couldn't believe I scored with such a beautiful woman.

When we satisfied our cravings, we cuddled up and spooned until checkout. No numbers were exchanged, and we took separate rides home. I didn't think I would ever see her again. It had been an incredible night; I was again falling for another beauty. As fate would have it, I'd see her again, but not for a few years. For now, though, it was back to the business at hand of playing rock n roll.

The gigs had been a success. The audience received my original songs well, which pleased me to no end. The band members were getting along, and life was good. However, one issue had to be dealt with before we left Edmonton. I had a decision to make. The sound man had been a pain in the arse from day one and, in my mind, was not that good. There had been an incident earlier in the week when my monitors were feeding back so much and humming so loud you could see the speaker cones vibrating. When I gestured for him to do something about it, he ambled to the front of the stage, strolled back to the soundboard, and solved nothing.

I had become so disgruntled with him that I threw my wireless microphone across the stage and smashed it. I was fed up and decided it was time for him to go, so I fired him. He, in turn, made an angry protest telling me I couldn't do what I was doing. I told him to piss off. He and his equipment were soon on their way back to Ontario. So now we need new production. I ended up hiring the cheapest outfit in town to run our sound. We were not making much money, so I decided to use a budget sound system to save cash and stay afloat. So now we had a new production company and sound man.

Our new sound tech was a huge and daunting figure but very mild-mannered most of the time. It was best to keep out of his way when he got angry, but his appearance and sometimes aggressive nature made me feel safer when playing in some of the rougher clubs. Edmonton had been a success, and now it was time to make our debut performance at the Athabasca Hotel in Jasper, Alberta. The gear was loaded onto a school bus, the band members got into my car, and we headed west. Jasper was a beautiful mountain town with deer and many young winter sporting enthusiasts wandering the streets. The Athabasca Hotel was plush and a great place to stay for the week. Once we had settled in, it was time to be greeted by our contact at the venue.

Our contact had the same last name as our new agent. Could they be related? It turned out this contact was, in fact, her ex-husband. When I first saw him, I couldn't relate to them being a couple. This guy resembled an older version of Ronald McDonald. He looked me straight in the eye and asked me about my stay in Saskatoon. I told him with a wry smile I had enjoyed my time there immensely. I endured a few hours of idle banter with him before breathing a sigh of relief and having a few chuckles under my breath. He would be a character that periodically crept back into our lives on the road, but we were done with him for now.

The gig was fun but not a huge success. It was a young crowd, and we played many older classic rock songs. It was often suggested that we play newer material and broaden our repertoire. I was not inter- ested in doing that because I could only see merit in writing original songs and didn't want to spend time learning other people's material. That's probably not a good policy for a cover band. Cover songs were how we made money; we were supposed to play what people wanted to hear. My main goal was to write more original tunes and to follow up the "Night After Night" EP with an album. Regrettably, I did not appreciate most of the new music I encountered. I didn't like it. The rest of the band was not interested in my songs as they felt the production value was dated. They were probably right, but I was not prepared to give an inch at the time. My stubborn attitude seeded some discontent that would ferment over the passing weeks and months to come.

Another problem for me was getting sucked into the party lifestyle again; my priority when I arrived in each new town was getting laid. My excessive drinking was starting to rear its ugly head again. More often than not, I was downing beers and taking shots of whatever liquor was put in front of me. The warning bells rang, but I was not in the mood to listen. I was travelling across the great nation of Canada and having a blast.

We did a lot of sightseeing in Jasper. It felt more like a vacation than work. We would see people from all over the world who invested a small fortune to stay where we were staying, and here we were, having a similar experience and getting paid to be there. That is one of the great things about being in a touring band. The fact is you go to a lot of places that you usually couldn't afford to travel to. Jasper was a prime example of this.

When we were done in Jasper, it was back to the mansion for another round of gigs in Saskatoon. We played back at the club we had just performed at, and then we had a gig at a total dump. When we arrived at the venue, I was told we had to use the house system and tech. I needed clarification on this because what was our soundman supposed to do? He still had to get paid. It was time for negotiating; I was told to introduce myself to the house technician. I couldn't believe my eyes when I saw who it was. Fox! Was there no escaping this idiot? He was his usual smug self but became quite humble when faced with our giant soundman. I negotiated to have our man run sound, and with Fox benched, we were set for the week.

We stayed in lodgings at the venue as it was a long way back and forth to the mansion. After the shows, a trio of gothic Asian girls entertained us most nights with outrageous games of truth or dare, ending in the usual display of naked bodies. The gigs were not much fun as the venue was sadly inadequate and didn't attract much of an audience. We had more fun post-show than during our nightly performances. Several venues in Saskatoon accommodated a variety of bands of different statures. We were at the bottom of the pile. I was happy to hear that Lee Aaron was coming to town to play at one of the more prestigious concert halls. I enjoyed visiting them and catching up with my old friend John.

Watching Lee Aaron play at one of the larger venues in town was a bittersweet experience. It put into perspective where I was with my career. Here was a band with significant success playing all original songs, and what was I doing? I was wasting more and more time trudging around the B circuit with a cover band playing moldy oldies. I felt like I was in a giant rut, but it was one of my making. I'd lapsed into this world of pretense. I was playing shows, people were cheering, and if I consumed enough alcohol, I'd believe it was legitimate adulation. It wasn't.

I was touring with a glorified jukebox. The cheers were for songs I merely reproduced from artists who had legitimate success. This constant feeling of self-loathing made me drink more to escape reality. I seemed incapable of love and instead tried to substitute real feelings by sleeping with any woman who had a heartbeat. Easy to admit now but challenging to be fully aware of at the time, and so the figure of eight continued.

During this particular stay in Saskatoon, I was getting uncomfortable with the whole situation at the mansion. I liked the lady of the house, and the sex was incredible, but the situation didn't sit well with me. She offered me her world, and I couldn't accept it. It just didn't feel real, and I didn't feel like I had earned it. It would have been nice to live in the house and drive the fancy sports car, but it would never really be mine. I had to taper off this evolving affair.

The next gig she booked for us was in a small town called Whitecourt, Alberta. Before we left, she and I had an intense business conversation. She informed me that the Feldman organization would try to steal me away from her. Feldman was the biggest agency in Western Canada at the time. Being on their roster of bands would mean some A-list rooms for us. As it had been time to move on from Mike and Mark, perhaps it was now time to move on from this situation. If I received a call from the Feldman agency, I was not about to say no. This transition might help distance myself from the relationship I'd been developing with her. Time will tell.

Whitecourt is a tiny town in Alberta. The club we were booked at was small. As always, we churned out our three sets a night and got a great response. However, I felt unfulfilled by this and sought appreciation elsewhere. Around the second or third night, two girls approached me at the end of the show. They were cute, very friendly and invited me out for a night of drinking at a late-night venue. For some reason, I felt a little uneasy about going. The girls were a little loaded; I didn't want to drive with them, so I offered to take my car. I couldn't open my car doors because the locks were frozen, so they insisted I go with them. They were cute and available, but something in my head just said no. I kissed them goodnight, and that was that.

I was in the restaurant having breakfast the following day when two uniformed police officers approached me. They started questioning me about the two girls. I told them my story and then inquired why I was being interviewed. Both girls were dead. A tractor-trailer decapitated them. Their car spun out of control shortly after leaving the club and had been cut in half by the tractor-trailer. I didn't know how to feel. Lucky, I suppose. Perhaps I had a guardian angel or something. Usually, I would have gone with those girls without hesitation. Had I done that this time I would surely be dead.

The rest of the week in Whitecourt was a pretty somber affair. However, we met a couple of nice girls who would be joining us for some fun at our next gig. I got a call from our agent in Saskatoon telling me we were off to the "Windsor" in Red Deer, Alberta. I heard a lot of tales about this particular venue, but none of them were good. Nothing could have prepared me for the hell I would venture into.

It was the middle of winter. Travelling on roads covered in snow and ice was very treacherous. Nonetheless, we pressed on and headed south toward Red Deer. This town was a dump. I just had a bad feeling about it from the moment we arrived. When we pulled into the parking lot of the Windsor Hotel, I was horrified. It looked like a derelict building. However, a Billboard proudly displayed my name. "Martin Andrew from London, England." It would've been a little more flattering had it been advertising a show at a more credible venue, but I was pleased to see it just the same.

The man at the front desk weighed about 400 lbs. and was a disgusting slob. He completed our guest registrations and directed us to our accommodations. We were ushered into a dark, damp, dingy room with four beds. The heating system had failed due to a faulty boiler. It was so cold the water in the toilet was frozen. We were exhausted from the journey and just wanted to sleep. We kept our clothes on and got under the smelly blankets on our respective beds, hoping for a few hours of sleep. I lay there with my eyes closed, praying for the heat to be restored.

The second floor of this building was falling apart. A section had been closed off because it was deemed unsafe. It was, however, a perfect haven for some runaway girls who decided to make it their home. These girls survived by hanging out with the bands and offering sexual favors for some food and alcohol. We were in a dystopian world with seemingly no escape or means of enjoyment. The only saving grace at this venue was strippers performing during the day, which would help pass the time.

I remember getting ready to perform for the first night. I always wore tight black trousers but decided to wear pink for a change. What a mistake. The Windsor was a biker bar, and when we hit the stage, I thought I would be lynched. I don't know who was scarier. The tattooed women clawing at my trousers or the snarling men insulting my sexuality. Poor old Ed spent most of his time trying to stop people from stealing merchandise. It was an absolute nightmare, and we had to endure five more nights of this. I breathed a sigh of relief when the night's final chord was played.

For the duration of our stay, things didn't improve, but we managed to survive. Towards the end of the week, I was told the Feldman agency had left a message asking me to call them at my earliest convenience. What I was warned about in Saskatoon was about to come true. The big bad agency from the West wanted to talk business. I was thrilled to hear this news and called them to listen to what they had to say. I was told if we worked exclusively with them, they would book us six weeks of work right away, just for starters.

Knowing we were in a crappy venue and hating life, the ploy was that they offered us some outstanding gigs, knowing we would take them. It was a method they used to acquire bands who were working for other agencies. We must have been doing something right because they only had bands on their roster, they deemed suitable for A-list venues. Without further discussion, I agreed to be handled exclusively by them, and they booked us at the Generator in Prince George, BC. It was one of the best gigs on the circuit. When I relayed this information to the rest of the band, the mood was very positive.

I called our lady agent in Saskatoon and told her about my conversation with the Feldman office. She expected this to happen and wished me well, knowing her run was over with the band and myself. It was for the best, and we both knew it. We completed our contractual obligations at the Windsor and looked forward to bigger and better things. A new agent with better opportunities created an enthusiastic mood among the band members. I counted my blessings that the week ended with no bloodshed or loss of limb and asked the management for payment.

Apparently, the venue went bankrupt during the week, so the manager refused to pay me. He surrounded himself with some unsavory characters and told me to piss off. You couldn't haggle or intimidate these people by mentioning contractual obligations. They were thugs; I had to suck it up and leave. It was a devastating blow to my wallet as I had to pay the band members. I took out a cash advance on the visa card to cover their wages, but Ed and I received no payment for our ordeal at the Windsor. The worst venue I'd ever performed at, and I got ripped off. It had been a bad week, but we were on to better things as we joined forces with Sam Feldman and associates.

The Road to the Manor

Gallery 9

I'm so excited!

It's a dirty job but someone's got to do it!

Me & Dave.

Crusty & Slothy.

Waiting for the bus.

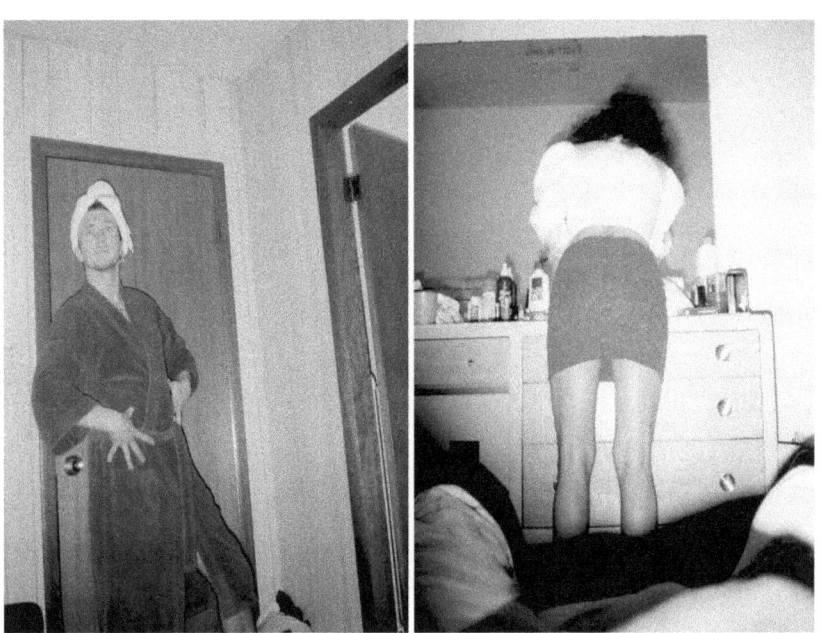

Left: Getting ready for a hot date. **Right:** My hot date.

Photographs from Martin Andrew private collection.

Chapter Ten

THE SHOW AT THE GENERATOR WAS A GREAT START TO OUR BC TOUR. We had a fantastic time, with large crowds and a great response to the music we played. During our stay, we added a couple of newer songs to our set list, contributing to a fresher and re-energized approach to the stage show. Many of you reading this book may think my main focus has been the antics surrounding the music, with very little focus on the shows. You would be right because that's the way it was.

When performing with a band, it is routine. Of course, there are small things that go wrong on stage which you remember and tend to focus on too much, but as a rule, the performance itself is repetitive. It always struck me as funny that we, as musicians, claimed to be beating the system by living our lives on the edge as rock n roll gypsies. We were doing the same as everybody else except without job security. So, you do the same show repeatedly, say the same pithy comments in between songs hoping for a response and work like a dog for a pittance of pay.

We claim to be our own bosses, but instead, suck up to an agent who doesn't give a shit about you or your music so long as he is getting his 15%. The escape comes when you let your hair down and have a good time; that's what I was doing during these years on the road. I never managed to pen a hit record or achieve the success I'd hoped for when I started, so it was game on for a good time. If more time had been spent on developing writing skills and rehearsing, things might have been written differently in this book.

Unfortunately, I was not too fond of the plasticity of the people in the business and could not conform to the mutual backslapping and backstabbing in the same breath as the bulk of my peers seemed able to do. Instead, I succumbed to the vortex I was swimming in. There could only be one end in sight. However, for now, that end was some distance away from my otherwise unpredictable future. For now, it was a travelling circus. We just stepped up a league into the realms of Feldman and associates.

We continued travelling and enjoying the new gigs. We were rocking all over the place week after week, but it was starting to take its toll. We spent Christmas of 1991 in the northwest territories playing at a club called "The Gallery" in Yellowknife. It was a hellish place where there was not much daylight in the winter, and it was freezing. We had been flown up there and enjoyed the bar on the plane immensely. I was back in full swing with my drinking by this point. The routine of touring and being around the same people was very wearing, so my alcohol consumption eased the pain.

The bass player (Worm) was getting into the whole Seattle scene (which was emerging rapidly) and didn't enjoy what we were doing anymore. Crusty was following suit, and tensions were definitely on the rise at this point. I spent most of my time writing new song ideas. I had a sequencer and a keyboard we used during our shows to fill out the sound. During the daytime, I would use both to record new song ideas. I worked alone on these ideas as there was very little interest from the band in my musical tastes. I was cataloguing songs for another day and maybe another band. Either way, it was gratifying, and I enjoyed doing it.

There was controversy at the club, starting with the sound check on the first night. Half the audience hated us due to their redneck distaste for any man with long hair and a physique unbecoming of a fat slob. The other half enjoyed our performances, and we had a good time most of the time, with some nights being better than others. A few days before Christmas, I noticed a cut on my finger had become infected. The infection spread. A red streak rose on my left arm toward my armpit. I went to a clinic. I was told I had blood poisoning, and my hand might have to be amputated. Merry Christmas! Fortunately, a course of strong antibiotics cleared the infection, and I slowly recovered. As well as this, I was hit with a dose of the flu and spent Christmas day at the band house alone. It was a miserable time.

I had lots of time to think about the band's future and approached them about adding more original music to our show. They didn't care much about my songs, but a collaboration might lead to some good material. Unfortunately, they were not impressed with my suggestion, and it would be my final attempt to do any structured writing with that particular lineup. Christmas passed, and I made a full recovery. We continued with our shows until the contract was fulfilled. Then it was time to leave the frozen wasteland of Yellowknife and return to an equally bitter climate in Edmonton. Having returned to Edmonton, we did many more dates until we finally ended up in Medicine Hat, Alberta. For whatever reason, I arrived separately from the rest of the band and went straight to the restaurant for breakfast. Over a plate of ham and eggs, it was here that the bass player announced he was quitting the band and returning to Toronto. I was not bothered in the least. It was time for a change. Crusty also decided to leave and he would return to Ontario.

I talked to the drummer, who wanted to stay in western Canada and create a new lineup. We played our final week together, and that was it. During the week, I hooked up with a dusky and very beautiful stripper, which was the only thing that kept me going, as the gigs themselves were pretty tedious. We were on autopilot, not paying attention to each other or the crowd. It was a sad way to end things, but that's how the cookie crumbles sometimes.

Dave and I loaded our gear into my car and drove directly to Edmonton. My dusky friend joined us as she had a gig at a strip club in the city. We shared a few laughs on our journey. When we arrived in Edmonton, she and I parted ways. Dave and I realized we had no more gigs and, consequently, nowhere to live. Fortunately, I knew a girl who lived in Edmonton and called her to see if she would let us stay at her place. Her name was Mickie. She agreed to let us stay at her apartment, which would become our base of operations for the next little while.

It was the end of an era. We had no clue what lay ahead of us. I wondered how things would work out. I had a colossal visa bill and no band to generate income. Our agent told me to stay in touch but was unconcerned with my situation. There would be another struggling band playing at the Windsor for him to prey upon, so our dilemma was of little consequence to him.

Mickie lived in the west end; I had known her since we played a show in Whitecourt. She had come out to a few of our gigs. Having spent considerable time with me, it's fair to say that an intimate relationship existed between us. There were girls you met on the road that were just one-night stands and others that developed into friendships of differing degrees. Mickie was a girl I liked to be around. She was smart, not too clingy, and always ready to help where the band was concerned.

Here we were in Edmonton with no band and not knowing what to do. We were flat broke and couldn't even afford fuel for the car. However, our hostess was good to us, let us stay with her for free and ensured we had food in our stomachs. A band she was friends with was playing at the CI West, so we went to the show to see if we could get any leads on some players. We chatted with the band's manager, who told us we needed to contact Don McKenzie. Apparently, he was the man in the know. He ran a rehearsal facility in a building by the Edmonton Greyhound station.

The next day, having scrounged some gas money, we headed to the rehearsal space to see if we could find the man in question. We waited all day to try and catch him, but he never showed up. It was so bloody cold and very disheartening not to meet the man. Finally, however, we met a fellow musician in one of the rehearsal studios. He gave us a rundown on the Edmonton scene and told us about Don. It turned out that he was dating one of Don's daughters. I remember as I was listening to him talk, I could feel the lining of my stomach being consumed by my digestive juices. I was so hungry. He was kind enough to give me $5 for food and coffee. It may not seem like much, but it was everything on that day.

We waited about three days to see the elusive Don, but he never arrived. One night we slept on the floor of one of the rooms in the rehearsal space as we had insufficient gas in the car to get back to Mickie's. It was freezing cold, and we didn't even have a blanket. This was a low point for sure. I remember lying there shivering in the cold, trying to stay positive but feeling extremely pessimistic about the situation. We made it through the night. In the morning, I was awakened by the door of the studio opening.

As I struggled to focus, I could see a man in the doorway staring at us with a look of surprise and concern. It was Don McKenzie. He spoke softly and asked me to come to his office when I was ready. I didn't know what to think. Was he going to charge us for staying the night? Was he going to call the cops? What did he want? As it turned out, he and I hit it off right away. We chatted for a couple of hours as I smoked many of his cigarettes.

He was a genuinely kind man who had been in the business for a long time. He was the founder of the Studio City music agency, which, in its day, was the biggest and best in Western Canada until Feldman moved in. Don's empire had been crushed by Feldman and a bunch of rogue agents who had worked for him, then moving on to open their respective agencies. It was strange, but in a way, we were both in the same boat. I was trying to get my band back together and, on the road, he was trying to get his agency started again. It was the genesis of the next phase of my career in Canada.

I told Dave about my conversation with Don. We both felt somewhat inspired. There was definitely a light at the end of the tunnel. Dave mentioned that one of his old guitarists from another band might be interested in joining us. I knew who he was talking about as I'd met him when we played a gig in northern Ontario. The offer was made, and now we were three. Buffy, as he came to be known, was a typical rock guitarist of that era. Skinny and always eating chocolate bars. He was a good player and fun to be around, so now all we needed was a bass player, and we would have a full band again.

Mickie knew a guy who played bass and suggested we ask him to join our ranks. Brad was already in a band, but it was at least worth a go to see if we could steal him away. He was a good-looking fellow and very personable. Brad expressed an interest and agreed to come to a rehearsal for an informal audition. We talked to Don, who allowed us to use a rehearsal space for free. We fired up the amps, cranked out a few songs and were happy with the sound we created. It worked; a bit loose but good enough to get out on the road. We needed money, and gigging was the only way to generate an income.

Don advised me to call the Feldman agency, see what they had to offer, and then get back to him if there were any problems. I called, and they reluctantly booked us into the York Hotel in Calgary. At best, it was a low-end B circuit gig, with the clientele being a colorful mixture of junkies and hookers. Feldman wanted to assess the band by sending one of their scouts to check us out. That was fine by me. I just wanted to get back on the road. The gig had a house PA system, so hiring production was unnecessary. The team would only be complete with my old friend in attendance, so I contacted Ed. He had been hanging out with a hooker in Edmonton, having a wonderful time, but agreed to join us. So, we set off for Calgary to showcase the new band.

The York was no palace. It was in the heart of downtown Calgary and the local haunt for every low-life in a five-mile radius. When I checked into my hotel room, I was somewhat disturbed to find a couple of bullet holes in the wall. However, this was our big chance to show-case the new band for Feldman's scout and get back to business. The lady who came to see us was a total bitch; I got off on the wrong foot as soon as she arrived. I later discovered she worked for Don at Studio City before luring many bands and clients away and starting her own agency. To put it politely, she was an opinionated woman who enjoyed unleashing her forked tongue at every opportunity. Unless you licked her boots, among other things, you would not be viewed favorably by her. We played well but got a bad report and, despite our best efforts, were not rehired by the Feldman agency.

Martin Andrew

I called Don, who told me not to worry and to return to Edmonton after the week. His new agency "Talent Corp" was now up and running, and he said he would book us. So began the Don McKenzie era. This man would become a very close friend of mine for many years. I had come to Canada to pursue my career as an original artist, and this was still my goal. I had been very clear about this during my first meeting with Don. He agreed this should be my primary objective. When I'd been staying in Ontario and working with John Albani (Lee Aaron guitarist) on the "Night After Night" EP, he warned me about the pitfalls of playing in a cover band. He said getting sidetracked and labelled as a cover artist was easy, and he was right.

As this new era with Don began, it had become more a survival time than anything else because I had to keep the band working to generate an income. Alas, working six days a week and travelling on the seventh only allows a little time for getting the original material together. Granted, I had new songs I'd penned along the way, but what good were they doing me just lying dormant and gathering metaphorical dust? The other thing I was up against was the band itself.

Most of the bands on the circuit were content to play cover songs and party as much as possible; I, too, had found a certain appeal in this. Aside from adding the occasional song, there was no real work involved, and you could live the life of a rock star without ever really being one. We were called the "Martin Andrew Band," so there was no incentive for anybody in the group to pursue original music if it was to be released or performed under that banner. My view of originals differed from the other members, and they were already influenced by the whole grunge scene, which I despised. I had always preferred the lighter side of rock instead of the frantic guitar playing of the '80s. Now this mundane whining of the '90s had become even less appealing. These were issues that were not going to be resolved quickly.

Having mentioned to Don that I was a songwriter, and he supported this, it was decided that he and I would collude in expanding my catalogue of songs. He had been an influential character in his Studio City days and appreciated my songwriting style. We decided while Don was working at securing the band some live engagements, I would record a

176

new demo tape. The building where his office and rehearsal spaces were housed also hosted a small recording studio. Don heard my "Night After Night" EP, liked it, and wanted to listen to some new material. As an artist, whenever anybody takes the slightest interest in your work, it is flattering, but when they like it and tell you they like it, you want to dance naked in the streets. Unfortunately, Don had secured some dates for us before we could schedule a recording session, so I had to get back on the road. I would have to wait a little longer to return to the recording studio, but knowing I would be recording again soon made me very happy.

So, we went touring around Alberta and BC, playing as many venues as possible. Don was able to keep us busy, which kept everybody happy and put some money in our pockets. This would be par for the course for the following year. Recounting every gig would be dull, but a few key moments are worth exploring. We played at the Bulkley Hotel during our visit to Smithers in BC. It was a dilapidated building with a crowd to match. The gig was not that memorable, but the following incident was quite colorful. During our week-long stay in Smithers, I decided to get my hair done. At the local salon, I met a beautiful girl. We chatted as she colored my hair; I asked her to come and see the band play. After that night's show, I returned to her house, and we slept together.

The week all of a sudden took on a different vibe. I liked hanging out with Donna. It was great to escape from the daily routine of waking up in a hotel and twiddling my thumbs. Instead, I was invited to stay at her place and enjoyed her warm personality along with some home-cooked meals. The week passed. Aside from a few bar brawls, there were no actual incidents of any consequence. She and I said our farewells at the end of the week, and I returned to the hotel to get paid. The idiot who ran the bar did not have enough money to pay me and said he was $1000.00 short. I told him since we were playing in Kitimat, only four hours away, I would return to pick up what he owed me in a few days. He agreed. We shook hands, and I and the rest of the band went to Kitimat for our next engagement.

Kitimat was another small town in northern BC, but the local fillies were fun, and the club was quite grand for such a remote place. Two days into the gig, I returned to Smithers to pick up the $1000.00 from the degenerate bar manager. I could make it there in four hours, so I left after the gig and was knocking on my love interest's window by six in the morning. Donna was pleased to see me; I got into her warm bed for a few hours before she had to go to work at the local mall. I hung out at her house most of the day and relaxed comfortably. Later in the afternoon, I went to the hotel and picked up the $1000.00 in cash. Rather a lot to carry around, but it was a small town, and I thought everything would be fine.

As I drove around the town, I noticed a lot of police cars. It seemed that everywhere I went, there was a cop, and they always gave me a funny look. At the time, I didn't lend too much credence to it, but all the same, it did seem strange. It was close to 5 pm when I decided to go to the mall and meet my local beauty. I still had a few minutes to kill, so I had a quick coffee while waiting. I entered the restaurant and was followed by this fellow who also ordered coffee. As I took my seat, I noticed him chatting with the staff, and then all of a sudden, people started to vacate the premises. I figured they were getting ready to close up, but it seemed odd. The man then sat behind me and began reading a newspaper.

So here we were, just the two of us, having a nice, quiet cup of coffee while he read the local newspaper. When my coffee was done, I left the restaurant but still had a few more minutes to kill. On the way out of the restaurant, I spotted a jewelry store and was looking at the display in the window when a man stood beside me. It was the same man who followed me into the restaurant and sat behind me, reading his newspaper. What happened next took me by total surprise. He announced he was RCMP and that I should put my hands out in front of me. I thought he was a lunatic and told him to piss off. He was no lunatic. He had a gun and a badge and reiterated his request. I complied. He then walked me to the mall's main entrance and into the parking lot, where a crowd had gathered.

All these people were staring at me with nervous expressions on their faces. I had no idea what was going on. Suddenly, two police cars with their sirens blaring came speeding across the parking lot and skidded to a halt just feet from me. The cops leapt like gazelles from their squad cars with guns drawn and pointing in my direction. I still had no clue what was going on. I was dragged to one of the cars and slammed over the trunk. As they read my rights, the cuffs were put on me just like in the movies. I was then bundled into the back of one of the cars.

In a stunned state, I saw Donna emerge from the crowd. She was talking to one of the cops, and they kept looking at me. I should point out that during one of our conversations, Donna told me her brother was an RCMP officer. Our nights together led to her telling me about her family, and I also confided in her that I was an illegal alien. Now my mind was racing. I stared at her through the rear window of the police car, but she wouldn't make eye contact with me. Had she told the cops that I was illegal, and this was the first stage of my deportation? I didn't know what she was talking to the cop about, but I was terrified.

Soon the car was in motion, and we were off to the police station. I kept asking what I was being arrested for. I was told it was for armed robbery. This whole situation was ridiculous. I wanted to laugh, but the fact of the matter was I was in cuffs and being taken to jail. It was no laughing matter. I was taken to an interview room, and the cuffs were removed. I remember sitting in this small room and having all these cops staring at me. I could hear them saying things like, "That's him!" "We got him!" and "You're going down for a long time!" What a nightmare this was turning into.

I asked if I could make a phone call. The cops said I could make one call and brought a phone to me in the interview room. I was supposed to call a lawyer but called Karen's parents instead. They thought I was joking but soon realized I was serious and in a lot of trouble. I explained to them that the whole thing was ridiculous. They agreed to help me in any way they could if things didn't get resolved quickly. The other thing that was going through my mind was that I had a gig to do that night, and my not showing up could get the band fired. I explained this to the cops, but they just ignored me.

After a few hours, I was taken out of the room and presented to a detective who was quite a decent man. He began to apologize to me and explained what had happened. The moron at the hotel told them that a person fitting my description had stolen $1000.00. The cop explained that the description given fitted me exactly and the car I was driving was the apparent getaway vehicle. However, this alleged robbery occurred at 11 pm the previous night, and they dispatched a police officer to Kitimat to verify my story that I was on stage. My alibi was confirmed by the staff at the hotel, and I was subsequently in the clear.

Nothing was ever said about my legal status in Canada; I was so relieved. However, one issue still had to be resolved, and I brought this to the detective's attention. By the time I drove back to Kitimat, I would be late for the first show, so I asked for a note explaining I had been detained for questioning by the RCMP. This note would hopefully excuse my tardy arrival and save us from any financial retribution due to my incarceration. He obliged, and I was soon on my way. It had been a harrowing ordeal; I was glad it was over. Before leaving town, I had to pick up a bag of my clothes from Donna before heading out on the highway.

I explained the whole debacle to her when I arrived at her place. She was relieved but told me she was unsure if I was guilty or innocent. The bag I left at her house also caused her concern. She wondered whether or not I'd hidden a gun in it. I showed her the bag's contents. She was relieved to see some old socks and a couple of shirts. I bade her farewell and made my way back to the gig. I put the pedal to the metal, making good time on my journey and finished the night with the rest of the band. Word got around about my ordeal. When we played the Clash hit "I Fought the Law," we got a great response. Many of the gigs we did during the Don McKenzie years were chaotic. We had numerous vehicle breakdowns, equipment stolen off-stage, bar fights and drunken parties.

I had been using my car for the band to travel in and it had taken a beating. It was time to find a new mode of transportation. Don suggested we look at an old tour bus parked at his acreage. He used it during his touring years and said it might be helpful to us. It was a 1959 flat-nose Bluebird with a 12-speed split-shift gearbox. The engine was sound, but the bus had been sitting for several years. Hence, it needed a paint job and a mechanical evaluation. We had it checked out by a local mechanic. Aside from having a dodgy braking system and some electrical issues, it was deemed roadworthy. Don handed over the keys, and once again, I was the proud owner of a tour bus. It seemed only fitting to me to name it "The Blue Goose 2" in honor of the old Heretic bus.

Don had spared no expense on refurbishing the bus's interior. It was pretty plush, considering its age. It had a sleeping area with four bunks, a toilet, sink, stove, fridge, and seating for eight with tables that could fold down and be used as double beds. I added a stereo and television with a video so we could travel in style. There was enough room in the back of the bus for our equipment and a small PA system. We still used my car for some gigs, but the bus soon became our primary mode of transport.

One particularly memorable venue we travelled to on the bus was the Rock Pit in Red Deer, Alberta. During the early '90s, many clubs were experiencing financial difficulty, and bands often suffered at the hands of greedy club owners. They would sign contracts knowing full well that the bank was taking over their club, and therefore, they had no intention of paying the band. They would only let you know this the last night when you were packing your gear. By then, it was too late to do anything about it. Remember the Windsor? Such an incident occurred at the Rock Pit.

We were packing down after our final show when the owner announced there was no money to pay us. I suggested to the rest of the band that we take goods from the bar to the value of funds owed. We all agreed and set the wheels in motion. At this gig, we had two sexy girls sympathetic to our situation. I instructed them to keep the bartender occupied while we started taking things out of the bar. They did a great job distracting him. We grabbed everything we could get our hands on. We loaded the lights, CD players, mixing consoles, you name it, onto the bus.

A slight problem arose when one of the female owners noticed Ed and Otto dismantling her lighting rig. Otto was a relatively new member of our crew. He ran sound for us and also doubled as the bus driver. Anyway, back to the frantic, nasty lady. She gazed around the room, noticing that many other things were missing and started yelling, calling me a thief. By this time, I was pretty drunk and tore into her calling her all the fat bitches from here to kingdom come. That was it; she was calling the police.

All the gear was on the bus in plain view, so if the police came, we would be in deep trouble if they decided to search our vehicle. As if by magic, a friend of ours arrived for a surprise visit. He barely pulled into the parking lot when I quickly explained our predicament. We frantically loaded his car with the gear, and he did an about-turn and made off with the goods. One last thing we had to deal with was a big screen projection television that we removed from the club with the intent of loading it on the bus. We had it out in the parking lot, and there was no way of hiding it. Three of us picked it up and dumped it over a loading dock, where it smashed into a thousand pieces. What a satisfying sound and sight that was. We stood and relished the moment, but then it was time to venture back into the club to greet the police.

The same woman was there talking to the police and calling me a thief. I yelled obscenities back at her, and the poor cop was caught in the crossfire. He asked if he and his colleague could search the bus. I agreed and watched as they scoured every inch of it; of course, they found nothing. The items in question were heading at high-speed south toward Calgary. He apologized to me and eventually told the woman, who had continued yelling throughout the search, to shut up. Undeterred, she continued ranting but to no avail. She couldn't figure out where all her beloved equipment was. I just smiled and laughed in her face. Before we left the bar, the girls managed to grab a couple of bottles of vodka. As we hit the highway, it was party time.

Otto was trying to keep the bus in a straight line as I poured vodka down his throat. It was one big party zone until we saw a cop car behind us with the siren wailing and lights flashing. We quickly put the booze in the fridge and tried to compose ourselves as we pulled over and greeted the officers in pursuit. These were the same cops from the gig. They wanted one final look to see if we had stolen anything, but just as before, they found nothing. They didn't notice that we were drunk and let us go without further incident. What a week it had been. We never got the gear our friend smuggled away from the crime scene. We later discovered he was a junkie; so far as I know, the equipment paid for his habit. It didn't matter; I was just glad that we fought back against a crooked club owner and, in our minds, had won.

This lineup of the band came to an end in 1992. It was me that quit the band after a gig in Calgary. It had become evident that the other guys weren't happy with the things I wanted to do. We didn't share the same musical tastes, and any friendship we once had was now all but gone. This band had run its course; it was time to move on. Once again, I was in familiar territory with nowhere to live and no band. After our final show, I dropped everybody off along with their equipment at their respective homes. I finished my journey by parking the bus on the street outside Don's office. Here I was, living on a bus again, only this time I was alone. I had no money, band, or idea of what to do next.

Gallery 10

The Martin Andrew Band. Brad, Dave (up top), Ed (aka Buffy) & Me.

Don McKenzie at Talent Corp headquarters.

Mickie working the phones!

The Blue Goose 2.

Luxury travel on board the bus lol!

The Road to the Manor

The Bulkley hotel in Smithers before my arrest.

Royal Canadian Gendarmerie royale
Mounted Police du Canada

ĊST DAMIEN .

847 - 3233 .

Canada

MARTIN. ANDREW.
WAS AT Smithers RCMP. Rt
FoR QUESTIONING .

A note from the RCMP for my agent.

One of many breakdowns.

Otto busted for speeding.

Hanging out at the Saxony Hotel in Edmonton.

Yogi Blossom & Slothy Bigguns........nuff said!

Otto & Ed.

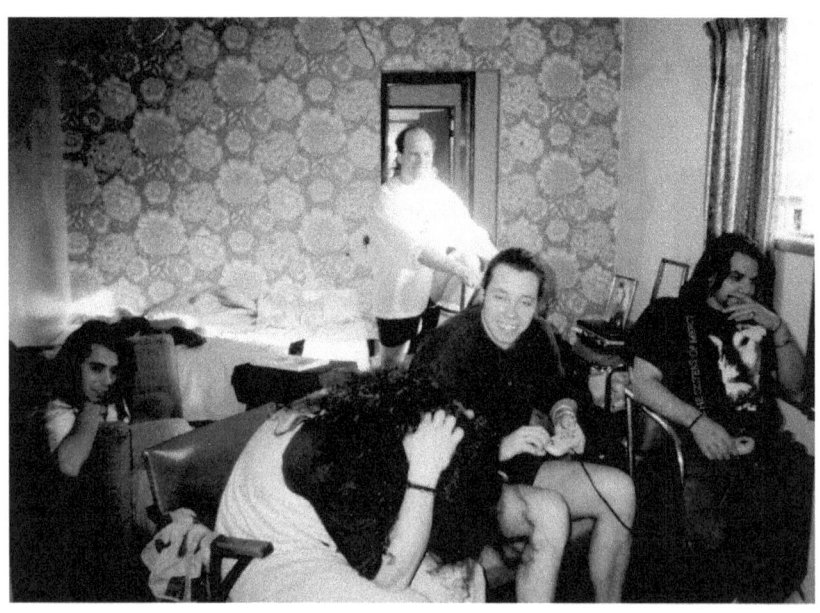

The Lads killing time before a show.

All photographs from Martin Andrew private collection.

Chapter Eleven

I HAD A LOT OF TIME ON MY HANDS TO CONTEMPLATE MY achievements since arriving in Canada. I came to this country for a fresh start and had high hopes of doing well as an original artist. It had been my dream to better myself and, in doing so, create a brighter future for my daughter. A place where she could have an opportunity to do well in life rather than being stifled by the poverty and hardship of life in working-class London. So, what had I achieved four years into this venture of mine? I recorded some demos and wrote new songs, but that was about it. It could be argued that I made a bit of a name for myself by touring extensively throughout the country. Perhaps, however, this newfound notoriety was for all the wrong reasons.

During this wild touring extravaganza, it had come to my attention that a disgruntled agent was trying to get me deported. It was no big secret that I was an undocumented worker. It made me an easy target for the bloated, blood-sucking agent to take aim at. Karen and I decided to get married to eliminate this problem. If there had not been the legal pressure to do this, I am sure we would have waited, but as it was, we decided to proceed with the marriage. I married Karen to stay in the country. It's fair to say that any love we shared had dwindled.

The day I set out on the road; our relationship was doomed. She saw other guys, and I had my fair share of women. We never really stood a chance at a proper relationship, but we were about to become husband and wife on paper. It was a whirlwind affair with a short ceremony followed by a brief stay in a hotel in Toronto. I flew out the next day to resume touring in the West, and Karen continued her life in the East. My life and future were destined to be forged in Western Canada. The London, Ontario days seemed far behind me. It was time to look to the future in Edmonton, Alberta.

I had a great friend in Don and got to know the rest of his family quite well. His eldest daughter Heather had sung on my demos. She and I became close friends. She was a beautiful woman and very talented. I enjoyed being around her as she always put a smile on my face and had great energy complimenting her beguiling personality. I had spent too much time fooling around on the road and not paying attention to business. Don had done his best for me but was burnt out too. He would never admit it, but I am sure he could see the writing on the wall that his days in the music business were coming to an end. He had no money and struggled to stay afloat. We were two of a kind.

One night, he and I went to a bowling alley across from his office. It had been a hot day, and we were both parched. I had a few dollars left on my visa card. We shared a pitcher of cheap ale. We convinced ourselves it was worth another go getting the band together, so I started looking for new players. I would get a few guys together and play a few gigs, and then someone would quit, and it was back to square one. At one point, I even drove to Calgary to pick up this Scottish drummer. During a telephone call, he told me he'd played with a famous band in the UK called "Glasgow." I'd heard of this band, which was a credible outfit, so I just gave him the job and assumed all would be well. How wrong I was. He was awful, and after a couple of hours of painful rehearsal, he was sent packing back to Calgary. After a long and tedious search, I finally found the right players for the job.

This following lineup was the best I'd had to date. After one night's rehearsal, we were the new Martin Andrew band. I had an exceptional guitarist named Cory who possessed the ability to play a variety of genres and was incredibly expressive. The drummer (Scott) was rock solid, and Scotty, the bass player, was as mad as a March hare but also a fantastic player. He and I became instant lifelong friends. When Scotty answered my ad, I agreed to pick him up for his audition. Unfortunately, he broke the door handle when we loaded his gear into my car. I joked that he would have to be in the band now because he had a vested interest in fixing my vehicle. This was the lineup I would be most proud of.

Don got to work on the telephone, and before long, we had a tour booked which would take us across the country to Ontario. He got in touch with Mike, my old agent in Thunder Bay, and got a bunch of dates for us in some of my old stomping grounds. I contacted Karen to let her know that I would be coming out east. She had been dancing for a few years and was able to get booked at a hotel in one of the small towns where we would be playing.

I had not seen her in a while. I thought this would be an excellent opportunity to rekindle the flame, flickering in such a vulnerable fashion for so long. I felt energized and confident this tour was going to be great. We had a couple of warm-up gigs before heading east. The final show was at the CI West in Edmonton. The week at the CI passed by without any significant events. We were able to try out some new songs and get our lighting show sorted out. Then on Saturday night, an event took place that would change my life forever. Before I go any further, I should make you aware of something.

During my exploits on the road, I had hundreds of one-night stands, which were fun but mostly meaningless. A handful of women breached my defenses and emotionally engaged with me. I have mentioned a few in earlier chapters, but there are others I should recognize before continuing my story. The lady I met at the CI West who joined me for a night of pay-per-view porn and passion was Lisa. I connected with her on several occasions, each time enjoying passionate interludes. We were never lovers, but I was especially attracted to her and enjoyed her presence. She had other love inter-ests, which caused a serious issue one night in Calgary. I had to be hustled out of a club and hidden in a hotel room when a jealous boyfriend came looking for me. He was armed and dangerous.

Following that incident, I distanced myself from her, but my desire never diminished.

I met Jennifer at the Generator in Prince George, BC and whisked her away to Edmonton. We were close for a while, and she travelled with the band. My roving eye caused us to drift apart, but we always remained cordial, and I genuinely cared for her. Jennifer's roommate was a beautiful young girl. Katherine and I embarked on a relationship that was doomed from the outset. I was twelve years her senior and married. I fell in love with her, but she was smart enough to realize my flawed advances would lead nowhere. She was young and a free spirit. I was much older and entrenched in a marriage that I gave no indication of ending. My promiscuous behavior was apparent. If I were cheating on my wife with her, what assurance did she have I wouldn't treat her the same way? The answer is none. Despite my understanding, her rejection was a deep cut that took time to heal.

The point I'm trying to make is the need for someone to share my life with was constant throughout my cavalier sexual exploits. I enjoyed the wild sex but craved true love. It was a genuine case of wanting my cake and eating it too! I had a reputation as a womanizer, an attribute for bedding groupies but hardly an endorsement for any woman to enter into a serious relationship with me. Besides that, I was married. The marriage was over in my head, but a ring remained on my finger. It would take an extraordinary lady and set of circumstances to break the vicious circle I'd created. Such a lady and circumstance were about to be revealed. So back to Saturday night.

We'd completed our three sets and were about to end the night when a rowdy group entered the bar. They were boisterous and seemed to be in the party spirit. Our final song was "Rock n Roll All Night" by Kiss. The song enticed two ladies onto the dance floor. I made eye contact with one of them as she danced provocatively in front of me. I was stunned by her beauty and how she moved. I was so intent on watching her that I forgot my words, becoming a bumbling fool on stage. She smiled and began to sing the lyrics to the song, putting me back on track. The song ended, and she returned to the pool tables at the rear of the building. I had to meet her.

The Road to the Manor

When we finished playing, I positioned myself at the bar so she would have to pass by me when exiting the building. As she approached, my heart was pounding. I'd never felt this surge of passion for a woman in my whole life. It was wild. I hadn't even spoken to her, and I was besotted. Finally, she was right in front of me, and I was able to talk to her. Her name was Paula. She had such a happy demeanor. Her eyes were mesmerizing. She invited me to a party, but I declined the offer stating that I only went to parties with the other guys. In saying this, I hoped to get her to stay with me at the bar for a few drinks. Instead, she said farewell, and I found myself chasing her into the parking lot, asking for directions to the party. I wanted to spend some time with her, and we agreed to meet at the party without my entourage.

I felt a little awkward at this gathering as I didn't know a soul. To make matters worse, soon after I arrived, Paula announced she had to take her friend home but would be back shortly. So here I am, sitting alone at a party with nobody to talk to, wearing eye makeup, teased hair and feeling very out of place. Everybody there was pleasant enough to me, but I felt I didn't belong. I started thinking I'd been dumped and was about to leave when Paula returned.

We talked for hours and enjoyed getting to know each other. We spent the night together at a friend's house, and I soon realized I was hooked. It was love at first sight for me, and I hoped for her too. In the morning, we said our farewells, and then it was time for me to get back on the tour bus and travel across the country to Ontario. This situation was so surreal. I was going to Ontario to see my wife in an attempt to kick-start our marriage, but I had just fallen in love overnight with another woman. Why had this happened? I had no idea, but I was given lots of time to think about it as we travelled across the country to our first gig.

When we arrived in Thunder Bay, it seemed like I had travelled back in time. I played here before with my first Canadian touring band; returning was maybe not such a good idea. I didn't feel like the returning conqueror but more like I'd been relegated to a lower division. Nonetheless, we were here and would play around the area for six weeks. During the second week of the tour, I met up with Karen. It was great to see her, although I felt a little awkward considering my feelings for Paula.

In Atikokan, Karen was dancing at one club, and the band and I performed at the other. The gig was somewhat dull, but during our stay, we had both ends of the spectrum, from gross to sexy, regarding the town's women. One day we looked out the window to see an elderly woman scraping fecal matter from her underwear and legs with her bare hands. She was doing this in broad daylight under a fire escape. The sights one sees in the wilds of northern Ontario. On the other end of the spectrum was a beautiful blond girl I liked the look of, so I invited her to join Karen and me for a ménage à trois. It was fun recreational sex but did nothing to rekindle our love life.

Karen stayed with me for about three weeks. During this time, there was a rumor that she slept with Otto, the sound man. The story came from Otto himself. He never said anything to me about it, but he was bragging to everyone else that he nailed my wife. Karen dismissed the gossip and warned me that he was trouble and that I should get rid of him. To this day, I am not sure what happened, but it is fair to say that Otto was no longer a friend.

After Karen left, I felt a sense of despair. It seemed to me we had achieved nothing regarding our marriage. We had been apart too long and quickly became a lost cause. I was torn apart emotionally because I felt so good about meeting Paula and so bad about the way Karen and I were fast dissolving. As well as all this, there was a chink in the armor of this new touring act with the situation surrounding Otto.

The tour continued but slowly fell apart as we had gigs cancelled. It became a struggle to stay afloat financially. Finally, we ended up in Sioux Lookout. Upon our arrival, we were informed that the hotel rooms we had been promised were not available. Staying on the bus was acceptable between gigs but unsuitable for a working week. We needed a place to shower and prepare for the shows. Since our accommodation for the week no longer existed, I had to find alternative lodgings and find them I did.

A local festival was taking place in the town with live entertainment on an outdoor stage. I had an idea. I asked if we could get up and do a song or two to promote our forthcoming show in the town. The people in charge agreed to let us play, and we hit the stage. During our extended version of "Roadhouse Blues," I changed the song lyrics to plead for a place to stay. The people in charge met this with scornful looks, but the crowd got a kick out of it.

When we departed the stage, I was approached by a pretty young lady who asked me if I was serious. I told her we were very serious. She agreed to let us stay at her cabin. She was a doctor and had a beautiful cottage on a private lake. We lucked out. We stayed at the place for the entire week. The gig became very unimportant as we all enjoyed the serenity of the outdoors. I spent a lot of time with the doctor and enjoyed many an afternoon floating around the lake as our naked bodies soaked up the sun.

She was always a bit nervous about having all these strange rocker types in her home. While we were trying to sleep one night, her nerves were almost shattered. Scotty had a habit of getting a little insane when he consumed too much alcohol. We called this condition "psycho mode" and usually gave him a wide berth when it took effect. This particular night he had gone into psycho mode. He was acting somewhat strange by skulking around the cabin chanting incantations while he was stark naked. Cory had a habit of screaming while asleep. Periodically, we would hear these blood-curdling screams as Scotty paraded his naked form for all to see. These antics would have been a little disconcerting for anyone, let alone a poor defenseless doctor alone in the woods with a rock band. I assured her she was safe, and we made it through the night.

As the week progressed, I had many discussions with the doctor about my ambitions of being a successful songwriter. She showed a keen interest in my aspirations and offered to help me financially. I knew she had the money but couldn't believe she wanted to help me. Nevertheless, she was serious and saw some merit in me as a person and songwriter. She was prepared to write me a check for $20,000 with nothing more than a handshake. It would have been easy money, but I couldn't bring myself to do it. I told her if I were to accept the money, a contract would have to exist between us whereby she could recoup her investment if I were lucky enough to get a recording contract. This financing would have paid for an excellent recording, and I could have easily walked away with her money, but I was intent on doing the right thing by having a contractual agreement. I made Don aware of the situation. He put a contract together, which I, in turn, sent to her.

When we parted company at the end of the week, she returned to the USA. She told me her lawyer would look at the agreement and get back to me when a decision had been made. Her lawyer must have taken one look at that contract and told her to forget it, as she withdrew the offer shortly after returning home. I can't say that I blame her. After all, what was she thinking? She had just met me, slept with me, and decided to hand over $20,000 for a recording project with very little chance of getting a return on her investment. Of course, I was upset that I couldn't record, but my moral compass had pointed me in the right direction for once.

Our tour was over, and it was time to head west. Having arrived back in Edmonton, we only did a few more dates before Cory announced he'd been offered another gig. A band called Specula Black was doing rather well at the time and needed a lead guitarist. He asked me what I thought of the opportunity, and I told him he should go for it. They had a great chance of getting signed, and I was genuinely pleased for him. So, it was the best lineup of the Martin Andrew Band that ended after only a few months.

Once again, we needed a new guitarist; I offered the job to a colleague who had a reputation for being an awkward person to work with. I never had a problem with him. Leon had been the manager at a local hotel where we played quite a lot and was no stranger to me. I hired him despite the rumors of his bad attitude as they bore no merit and because he was an outstanding player. Our drummer agreed to let us rehearse at his house. We had a couple of weeks to get ready for the next gig. During this time, I decided to get to know Paula better.

I called and invited her to join me for a movie night. We went to see the Harrison Ford thriller "The Fugitive" and returned to her home after the show. She had just moved into a small apartment in St Albert,

Alberta, and lived alone with her two children, Mark, and Randi Lee. Paula was going through a divorce, and I was headed that way, so we had much in common. This woman made me feel so good. I loved being around her. It was a special love that I had not experienced before. It was early days, but I knew this was my soul mate and the woman of my dreams.

Some days when I was supposed to be rehearsing, I would make excuses just to lay in bed with her. Such behavior was not regular for me as I always tried to put the band first over any woman, but not this time. I fell increasingly in love with her, but I was about to take a fall I was not expecting. Paula was seeing another guy before she met me, and he dumped her the night I met her. He would rear his ugly head and cause me a lot of heartache in the coming weeks.

One day after rehearsals, when I went to Paula's place, she announced that we were done. Done, I asked? We had barely begun, so how were we done? She said I could be her friend, but that was it because she was getting back together with this other guy. There was no room for discussion. Her mind was made up. I let my guard down and opened my heart to this woman, only to be blindsided by this callous dismissal. I was genuinely heartbroken. I bared my soul to her and had been rejected. I spent one last night with me lying on the floor beside her while she slept in bed.

In the morning, I gazed one last time at her beautiful face and said farewell. I felt so sad as I walked to the car. I was grateful the band had a gig so I could get my mind off this desperate situation. We were away from Edmonton for a couple of weeks, but I couldn't get Paula off my mind. I wrote her a letter, wondering if she would read it. Maybe I had just been a fling to her as so many women had been to me. Whatever the case, I sent the letter and called her upon returning to Edmonton. I remember pacing up and down next to a pay phone at the West Edmonton Mall, not knowing what to say if I did call. Would I be rejected again?

As I fumbled with the quarter in my sweaty hand, I finally decided to make the call. To my surprise and relief, she sounded pleased to hear from me and invited me for a cup of tea. The big question now was, do

I go? What had caused this change of heart with Paula? I didn't want to feel that sharp sting of heartache again if she were to change her mind. I decided to meet her. I needed to know what had gone wrong.

She greeted me with a radiant smile. We hugged in the doorway for what seemed an eternity. There was no denying the feelings we had for each other. After exchanging the obligatory pleasantries, I asked her the question that had bothered me these past few weeks. Why? She told me soon after I'd left and she was reunited with the other guy, she realized she made a big mistake. She thought there was no way a guy like me could be interested in a single mother of two small children.

She felt inadequate, leading to her decision to exclude me from her life. Her colleagues and teachers at the beauty school she attended told her I was a perfect match and she had made a big mistake. Lucky for me, she heeded their advice. I was reunited with her, and it felt so good. From that day forward, we became inseparable, and our love continued to grow and still does to this day. I had found my soul mate, and nobody could ask for more in life than that.

Having Paula by my side made me feel complete, but the only problem was I was still married. It was time for me to talk to Karen, so I called her to discuss the situation. We'd known for a long time that our marriage was over, but neither wanted to initiate the necessary conversation. I finally did, and we both let out a sigh of relief. Karen had found another love interest, and I was intent on being with Paula. We decided to get a divorce and went to Karen's parent's house in Calgary to sort out the paperwork. It must be the happiest divorce in history. The four of us and Karen's parents sorted everything out quickly. We wished each other well and parted company on good terms.

The Christmas of 1993 was fast approaching. It was time to venture back to the Northwest Territories for a month in Yellowknife. I had been there before and did not relish returning, but it was a good paycheck, so I confirmed the gig. The band was ready, but we had one slight problem getting to our northern destination. We had no money for fuel. None of us in the band had any money, so Paula ended up lending us $800.00 for the trip, which more than covered fuel costs. We made our final preparations and headed out on our journey.

The last time I performed in Yellowknife, we had flown from Edmonton, but this time, we would be using a different mode of transport. I don't know what I was thinking, expecting a 1959 Bluebird bus to make the journey without any problems, but that was my choice. Travelling to Yellowknife at that time of year was a dangerous journey with a sensible vehicle, so opting to make the journey in an old bus was not a product of the most prudent thinking. The temperatures we would endure could be well below -30 C, and we didn't have adequate heating on the bus for such a frigid climate. Our best efforts to insulate the damn thing had not succeeded; it got frigid quickly.

The halfway point was High Level. We stopped there for the night. We were able to find a gas station with a power outlet where we could steal some electricity. This would allow us to have some heat from an old electric fireplace Don had given us. We bedded down for the night. The bunk area at the back of the bus was quite toasty. As I dozed off, I was relieved we had made it this far without incident and looked forward to a good night's sleep.

I was rudely awoken by screams of "Fire!" As my eyes opened, I could see thick smoke engulfing my bunk; I could hardly breathe. The back wall of the bus had flames licking at it, and panic soon ensued. We scrambled to get out as fast as possible. We were choking on the thick smoke as we desperately tried to navigate to the front of the bus. I could barely see who was in front of me as my eyes were stinging from the irritation caused by the smoke.

We found ourselves engulfed in this inferno due to a drummer who had cold feet. Moving his feet closer to the electric fireplace caused his sleeping bag to catch fire. This, in turn, ignited his mattress and set fire to the back of the bus. We hauled the burning mattress off the bus, dumped it at the side of the road and watched it smoldering in a pile of snow. What a sight we must have been to passers-by. Five guys standing at the roadside in their underwear while a burning mattress does its best to melt a snowbank with an old bus puffing black smoke from every orifice.

We hadn't had time to put any clothes on before we escaped from the burning bus, so we stood by the side of the road half-naked until the smoke dispersed from the Blue Goose 2. Cooked goose, more like it! Was this an omen? Was this trip doomed? Only time will tell. Eventually, we escaped the terrible cold and resumed our slumber. In the morning, we surveyed the damage, which was minor, aside from a few scorch marks here and there. A long road was still ahead, so we headed north, leaving behind the smoldering mattress in the snowbank.

The further north we travelled, the colder it got. Before long, the freezing temperatures became unbearable. We ran the propane stove to get some heat, but all that did was create moisture in the bus, and the windshield kept icing up. So now, we had me scraping ice off the windscreen and Scotty spreading washer fluid everywhere to have a fighting chance of seeing the road. It was unbelievable; I'm amazed we got to Yellowknife in one piece. However, despite these appalling conditions, we arrived and settled into our accommodations.

After loading our frozen equipment into the club, we had a brief sound check and were up and running for opening night. Nothing much had changed since the first time I had been there. The crowd was just as belligerent as ever, and it was easy to feel unappreciated, but this was a good paycheck for me, so I didn't care. Early in the first week, some lady whined about a song she wanted to hear and wouldn't shut up. Eventually, I gave her a verbal assault peppered with rather colorful metaphors. She became distraught. As a rule, that wouldn't matter, but this lady just happened to be a friend of the owner.

The owner was a complete bastard who owned a bunch of property in Yellowknife and was Mr. Big in this stagnant little pond. He called and informed me we were fined $400 for not having a suitable set list and that we had better learn some new songs or be fired. I argued with him until I was told in no uncertain terms that I could like it or lump it. Apparently, he could do as he pleased because we did lose $400 and were forced to learn some new songs, including the one the loudmouth bitch had requested. This autocratic behavior from the owner would be par for the course in Yellowknife during this visit. The only thing that made sense was to drink and stay drunk. So that is what I did.

The Road to the Manor

I hung out at the local strip joint and made friends with the two girls working there. They came over to the house towards the end of the run. We got high and had a fun party. The rest of the band followed suit, entertaining ladies, and drinking as much alcohol as possible. We survived the month, and soon, the ordeal was over. Despite the unfair deductions from the club owner, I finally had some money in my pocket, and the rest of the band was happy with their respective remuneration.

We had insulted and pissed off as many people as had heckled us, so it was as we loaded the gear on the bus a drive-by beer bottling pelted us. When we returned to the house to collect our personal belongings, I noticed some mechanical problems. The engine spluttered like crazy and would die whenever the lights were turned on. This was not good, considering it was pitch black, and we had a long journey ahead of us in icy conditions.

The bus had proved to be lacking in the insulation department. We had suffered as a consequence of this on our inbound journey. The house we were staying in had an unfinished basement, so I instructed the rest of the band to rip out the insulation and use it on the walls of the bus. While they were busy doing this, I tried to rewire the fuel pump. It was so cold I could barely move. At one point, I filled a kerosene heater with gas and tried to ignite it. Despite repeated efforts, it wouldn't ignite. Lucky for me as the explosion would have destroyed the bus and killed me. After a few hours, I solved the fuel pump problem but couldn't get the lights to work. There was nothing more to be done. I had to ask myself whether we wait until daylight to travel or hit the road and take our chances. It was about 3 am when I decided to get going and hope for the best.

The club's owner had mistreated us; now it was payback time. We dumped a month's worth of garbage out in the backyard and some of it in the house. The basement was left in a state of disrepair, with most of the insulation having been removed. What we didn't take, we just ripped out of the walls and left it in a pile on the floor. Having destroyed the band house, it was time to get out of town, so we embarked on our journey back to Edmonton.

It was now December 23, 1993, and I will never forget this journey. The first five hours of travel were spent with me driving and Scotty hanging out the door, ensuring I didn't veer off the road and into a ditch. We only used the lights when a truck was coming the other way. I flashed the lights so we wouldn't get hit by the oncoming traffic. Having the lights on caused the engine to splutter a bit, but when the truck had passed, and we were back in stealth mode, it would run smoothly again. It was absolute hell and so cold because now we had the front door open. We managed to distance ourselves from the gig, and the bus kept going, which was good news. Otto was still our soundman, and he took over driving when we pulled in for gas. As a rule, the driver would always check the oil when filling the tank. Because of the extreme cold, he didn't bother or just forgot to check the oil. Either way, the consequences of this inaction would be disastrous.

As we approached High Level, an awful banging sound came from the engine, and we lost power. The noise got louder, and as we coasted to a halt, it became apparent we had a severe problem. We were about fifteen miles from High Level, and the engine was wrecked. As I removed the dipstick from the red-hot engine block, a milky fluid could be seen seeping out. It clearly indicated the engine block was cracked, and we were in deep trouble. We were stranded in the middle of nowhere. It was dark, and the temperature was around -35 C. We were in a dangerous situation in more ways than one. We broke down on the main highway that all the trucks used and had no hazard warning lights. The passing trucks came so close to hitting us. The situation was terrifying.

Scotty and I decided to go for help. We started walking along the highway in the bitter cold with the sound of howling wolves and other creatures of the night ringing in our ears. Finally, a small truck pulled over and offered us a ride. The truck's occupants were two drunken bull riders who said they would like to help us fix the bus. As they regaled tales of various bull riding exploits, we held on for dear life as their truck executed a U-turn and swerved around the icy roads until we were back at the bus. They added thick oil to our wounded engine and tried to get it started. It fired up briefly before a loud bang, and it seized solid. That was it; the engine was dead.

We thanked our rodeo friends for their concerted effort, and before long, they were driving off into the night. It was pitch black and freezing cold as we hunkered down for the night. It was so cold I wanted to die. My bones ached, and every organ in my body felt chilled. I couldn't sleep, and I don't think any of the others got much rest that night. I didn't know if we were going to survive this ordeal.

In the morning, as the sun rose, it warmed the bus a little. I breathed a sigh of relief; we survived the night. I remember looking around and cracking a smile as I witnessed a surreal sight. We had been regular customers at the tanning salon in Yellowknife and were subsequently an excellent shade of brown. It occurred to me how ridiculous we would have looked had we frozen to death in the night and been discovered by some passerby. I could envision the headlines. "This morning in the wilderness of northern Alberta, a busload of long-haired corpses with golden brown tans were found." After this brief moment of levity, I had to figure out how to get home.

It was now Christmas Eve. We had a long way to go, but there was no way the bus was moving. We gathered our essential belongings and hitched a ride into High Level. We were able to get a ride and subsequently dropped off at a Ford dealership. I met with the manager and arranged for them to tow the bus to their facility. Having sorted that out, I rented a truck at the local U- Haul. The drummer and Otto announced they had to get home for Christmas and could no longer be a part of this debacle, so they decided to take a Greyhound bus to their respective destinations. Talk about leaving the sinking ship. When the tow truck and our deceased vehicle arrived at the Ford dealership, Scotty, Leon, and I transferred the gear onto the truck and set off on our journey back to Edmonton.

All the money I'd saved from the gig was now gone. I had always put the band on a wage to ensure they got paid; therefore, I was responsible for dealing with the disaster that had befallen us. Aside from Leon throwing a fit on the way home and beating up his winter coat, we travelled without further incident. Paula met us at the CI West, where we parked the truck for the night. After that, it was just a short car ride to a lovely warm house. At around 10 pm, Paula and I arrived at her parents' house to have a large scotch and celebrate what was left of Christmas Eve. I was relieved to return to Edmonton and extremely happy to see Paula.

Christmas came and went. We were left with one final gig to round out the year. Since we had no bus, we drove to Drumheller in a vehicle supplied by our drummer. Paula and her friend Tracy came with us to the show, and we would all celebrate the New Year's festivities together. The gigs leading up to New Year's Eve went very smoothly, but things changed when we began celebrating early on the 31st. We were pounding back as many drinks as possible on the day of the festive show. I told Paula about my liver problems. She was very concerned about my drinking habits. I assured her I would take it easy but instead was swigging vodka in the DJ booth at the club.

We could barely stand when it was time for us to perform. Having struggled through two sets out of four, we retired early after the count-down. The owner was none too pleased when I announced we were done for the night. As I was making excuses to him for our drunken behavior, I heard a familiar voice shouting out loud, "Sgt Major, Sir!!" I knew who it was, but nothing could have prepared me for the sight of Scotty standing butt naked in the middle of the dance floor, saluting me. My apology to the owner fell on deaf ears; he went berserk. He was not alone, as the rednecks in the bar wanted to kill us all.

Scotty was instructed to go and put some clothes on before returning to the bar. In his defense, Scotty did return wearing clothes. The only problem was he borrowed one of Paula's dresses. Once again, he paraded around the dance floor to the sheer dismay of all present, and so it was we ended up getting thrown out of our own gig. When we got upstairs to our rooms, Scotty had to be subdued as he became aggressive and started smashing the place up. The drummer started spouting off at me in a drunken stupor. He and I ended up in a brawl; it was chaos.

When we finally ran out of steam, and all bottles present were empty, we decided to gate crash a local party. It was a wrong move and didn't end well. As Leon squared off with some of the locals, I collapsed in a snowbank and had to be carried back to the hotel by Tracy and Paula. Battered and bruised, we decided to call it a night. Finally, there was a calm over the fair town of Drumheller. By the time the morning rolled around, our hangovers had set in. Opaque memories of the night's antics caused us alarm and a certain amount of regret. We played in Drumheller a lot. This would be the last time, as we were never invited back. 1992 had come to an end in a haze of drunken debauchery. We left a bad taste in the mouths of the populous of Drumheller. Nevertheless, the New Year was upon us, so we licked our wounds and departed without fuss or fanfare.

Gallery 11

Celebrating at my wedding.

Back on the road with the new line up; Scotty & Me, Papa Louie, Scott & Cory.

Welcome to the Danger Zone.

Auditioning for Basic Instinct... lol!!!

From mild..........

To wild!!!

Paula posing on the pool table in Drumheller.

All photographs from Martin Andrew private collection.

Chapter Twelve

So here it was,1993. A brand-new year, and I was starting it with a severe hangover. Paula and Tracy returned to St Albert, and we were off to Calgary for our first show of the year. Unfortunately, it became apparent early in the week that I had overindulged in my drinking exploits and needed to see a doctor. When examined, I was told I had alcohol poisoning, and the toxins in my liver were high. Having described my history of drink-related ailments to the doctor, he advised me to stop for good. I paid heed to his advice as I'd done in the past, but I had no idea how long it would last this time.

So now I was back on the wagon and wondering what '93 would have in store for me. It occurred to me that every time I decided to reflect on my achievements, I faced the harsh reality I had yet to achieve any of the goals I'd set upon my arrival in Canada. I was sucked into this shallow lifestyle of drinking, playing cover songs, and getting nowhere. It had become a vicious circle of having to keep working to be able to afford to work. One good thing that happened to me was meeting Paula. I was so happy to have her in my life, but that, in turn, made this life on the road seem so much more pointless. How much longer could I keep this up?

As the year went on, the band went through many lineup changes.

The Road to the Manor

Scotty ended up quitting to go to film school in Vancouver. He had seen the writing on the wall, and by this time, I also was taking a good look at it. I tried to keep the beast alive, but gigs were getting harder and harder to come by as so many clubs were closing their doors. The straw that broke the camel's back was when my dear friend Don had a heart attack. Thankfully, he survived, but this led to a lifestyle change for him as he quit the music business and joined the investment world. As the weeks passed and the band's demise became more and more apparent, I felt like an old boxer fighting way past his prime. I played bass guitar and changed the band members more than my strings.

My final gig with the Martin Andrew Band was in Lloyd Minister as a three-piece outfit. It was the only way to make money with such a low-paying engagement. Unfortunately, three days into the gig, it became evident the bar was struggling to survive. They were running out of beer, and the sewers backed up one night. Our audience consisted of a handful of drunks and a pool of raw sewage working its way to the stage. To add insult to injury, I was called into the office in the morning and informed we were fired. The poor attendance had been blamed on us, and the raw sewage got a get-out-of-jail-free card. That was it; I was done trying to keep the act going. I couldn't do this anymore.

Paula was with me on this final week. When the bus was loaded, the band members said farewell, and we returned to St Albert. I dropped the bus off at Don's acreage, its home for many years after Don finished his touring days. I parked it in the bush behind his house. As I locked it and left it in the undergrowth, I thought I would never use it again. Paula and I drove in her car to the little apartment in St Albert, where we had started to make a nest. What the hell was I going to do now?

I had to assess my situation and think hard about how to move forward. I was no spring chicken anymore. If I were going to achieve anything in the fast-changing world of the music industry, I would have to get on with it quickly. I had the best secret weapon a man could have; a woman who loved and supported me fully with any decision I made. For now, I just wanted to relax and enjoy the comforts of home.

I'd spent so much time on the road it was great to sit in the apartment and do regular things like dusting and cooking. I know it may sound ridiculous, but it was a pleasant change for me at that time.

I enjoyed having Paula's children around, and the whole feel of family life lent a certain appeal. However, I wasn't ready to throw in the towel just yet, so I needed to formulate a plan of attack. Once again, my good friend Don would come to the rescue, and I would end up doing a job I'd usually never have considered. Don was working for a company called Investors Group. I'd frequently visited him at his new office in downtown Edmonton. He and I always used to meet to chat and figure out a plan of attack to take the music business by storm. On this particular day, he'd come up with a solution to my financial needs by referring me to a client of his.

This client of his talked about a vacancy for a DJ at a local strip club. Don told him about me, and he was interested in meeting. I went to see about this new career in the sex industry and subsequently got introduced to the club manager, who insisted I audition for the vacant position. I'd been to so many strip clubs over the years that I knew the vernacular the DJ's used and got the job on the spot.

One of the D J's I'd be working with had been a singer in a band. He, too, ended up as a strip club DJ. He was a nice guy but seemed a little jaded and somewhat worse for wear from drugs and alcohol. As I looked at him, warning bells went off in my head. I didn't want to be a washed-up singer talking about the good old days and drowning my sorrows as I ogled sexy young girls. On a positive note, this was a steady job, and it paid quite well when you added tips from the girls. It was not a job that required much thought, which allowed me to focus on writing some original songs and getting that whole side of my career kick-started again.

I settled into the routine of working at Rusty's and was even given a nickname for my trouble. To the other staff members, I was known as "Tetley." They were friendly, and I enjoyed working with my new colleagues. I worked four weekly shifts, 10 am to 6 pm, giving me plenty of free time to focus on my passion; I began to write some new material. I bought a four-track recorder and set up a small studio at

Paula's apartment. She had this enormous closet in her apartment, which we converted into my first recording studio. I borrowed some equipment from Don and added that to some of my own. With this small amount of recording equipment, I could create some half-decent sounds and enjoyed working in the closet.

The music I was writing was diverse and needed more direction. I have always enjoyed all music styles, which became evident as the material I produced explored different avenues. I wanted to get some female voices on my songs, and once again, Don came up with the goods. He introduced me to two girls involved in local musical theatre who were great singers. It was a different situation for them, but they religiously came to the closet every Wednesday, and we worked on songs together. Both of these ladies would go on to become television and radio personalities in western Canada, but for now, they were firmly entrenched in the closet with me.

As I got more material together, I would see Don at his acreage and let him hear the songs. He always supported my work and was primarily interested in the ballads I wrote, but we always hit the same brick wall. Who do you send the songs to? Writing them is easy; getting the material to the right people who can help you get a deal is the problem. What I couldn't see then was everything I'd written sounded nothing like the music on the radio. I didn't listen to the tune of the day. Grunge was not my thing, and the songs I'd written could not be pigeonholed into any particular category.

When I played the songs to other people, they didn't know what to make of them other than to say it sounded different. Different can be good, but it can also be a problem if you are trying to get signed to a label that wants something more mainstream. It didn't matter because, as far as the A&R departments of any record company were concerned, this material would not see the light of day.

Years ago, Don may have been able to do something when his Studio City empire ruled Western Canada, but now he needed contacts and an accurate idea of what to do with the songs. That made two of us. The songs piled up and went nowhere. It was so frustrating. I was convinced I had something to offer but nobody to show it to. The old days of just sending out a demo tape were at an end. Nowadays, all material has to be solicited by a lawyer or a music management company to have any chance of being heard. So, it would be a waste of time if you didn't have a reputable manager or music lawyer looking out for you. I didn't have either. That, coupled with the fact I was living in northern Alberta, where there was no real music industry, put a significant damper on any chance of success.

Despite this, I kept writing and remained a DJ at the strip club. I tried several things, including a failed attempt at being Edmonton's number-one jingle company. A friend of mine had created some jingles in his day, and we decided to team up and form our own jingle company. "Jukebox Jingles" was supposed to revolutionize the jingle industry. Instead, it cost us a bunch of money, time, and effort, then fizzled out before it even got going.

One day I got a call from some folks in Kimberly, BC. I made some good friends when we played there with the band. Lo and behold, they called me with an offer that tickled my fancy. They'd opened a new restaurant and wanted me to write and record a birthday song for them. The song would be played every time a patron celebrated a birthday, and I would get a paycheck for creating the tune. I wrote a little ditty for them and agreed to perform at the new facility.

They had a tiny budget that matched the size of the restaurant itself. They didn't have room for a drum kit and asked me if I could play the piano alone. I offered a compromise by proposing a performance at their restaurant as a duo. I would bring a guitarist, and we would use programmed drums to make it sound like a full band. They were very excited, and a suitable date was arranged for this new musical venture.

I had to get some songs ready and find a guitarist who was willing to go with me to perform at the restaurant. Using a drum machine for a live performance was something I'd never done. I'd used a sequencer with the band and drum sounds on my keyboard when writing songs, but this was new. Midi files were not readily available then, so writing all the parts for the setlist I was preparing took a fair amount of time and effort. If I was going to do this, I wanted it to sound good, so I added other instruments along with the drums.

The Road to the Manor

Once that was done, I found a local guitarist prepared to accompany me for this one-off duo gig. We rehearsed in the closet and were soon ready to hit the road. It was great to see the old gang in Kimberley. The gig was a lot of fun, and we had a blast. We were drunk by the night's end, and the crowd loved it. I was back in the game playing rock n roll, but now there were only two people on stage. We only did one gig, but I knew I was on to something that could make money. Life would be good if I could perform as a duo, work at the strip club, and keep writing my originals. The big question was, who would want to do this gig with me, and could I curb my drinking habits and stay healthy? All good questions and ones that could be answered solely by moving ahead with the rock duo, which I named "Take Two."

I got in touch with one of the numerous guitarists I worked with in the Martin Andrew Band and, before long, had a rock duo ready for the road. Cory's time with Specula Black had not delivered the recording contract he sought, so he was once again a gun for hire. He was a brilliant player and also had a keen business sense. The deal I offered him was a 60/40 split. I would handle business and supply all the equipment, and he would play guitar. It was an arrangement that suited both of us. We decided to move forward with the project and get some work.

I negotiated with a local agency that handled a lot of minor acts and would be suitable for booking "Take Two." So, it was we began our career as a rock duo act. We only played on the weekends, which was perfect. I worked at Rusty's Sunday through Wednesday and could perform with Cory Friday and Saturday at out-of-town shows as needed. We took the duo very seriously for about five minutes until we realized whether we were well-dressed or rehearsed didn't matter.

The clubs we played in were ones we would never have even considered when we had a full band. They were dumps, and the clientele consisted of drunken men and loud-mouthed women who would scream and yell at us throughout our night's performance. However, the money was adequate for our efforts, and we settled into this new routine of being weekend warriors on the duo circuit. It worked well for about a year, but Cory eventually wanted to branch out independently. He had a girlfriend who could sing and decided to go his own way and form a duo with her. I advertised for another player and was soon joined by a guitarist who came to my house for an audition.

Paula and I moved from St Albert to Edmonton and now lived in a small townhouse northwest of the city. I turned the basement into a small studio where I could continue writing songs and rehearse the duo. My new partner (Paul) had been doing some duo work of his own. He was an earthy character but brought quite a lot to the table. He had a PA system and computer with a seemingly endless amount of song tracks. We decided to blend our two shows and provide a broader spectrum of music for the patrons of the venues we performed at. We kept the name "Take Two" and prepared for our first tour.

During these preparations, a minor disaster struck. Rusty's, without warning, closed its doors, and I found myself out of a job. I worked there for the best part of two years and was accustomed to getting my paychecks and having cash in my wallet from the daily tips. Paula was working as a waitress, and her wages would barely be enough for us to get by. As much as I was looking forward to this new project, it made life a little stressful since I no longer had any financial security.

Paul and I booked some shows and were soon ready for our first engagement. I was always excited about leaving on tour, but on this occasion, I was hesitant. It had nothing to do with the shows but instead with Paula's health. She had some dental problems and became quite ill due to an infection in her gums. Much as I hated to leave her, I had to go and make some money, but it didn't sit well with me. I ensured she was comfortable and had everything she needed before I hit the road.

It was now January of 1997. We were in the middle of another Canadian winter with the usual snow and ice everywhere. The roads were treacherous as we drove north to our first gig. It was all we could do to keep the van on the road. We were presented with a rather odd work schedule when we arrived at the venue. They asked us to perform on Friday and Saturday and then again on Monday and Tuesday. I agreed to the split schedule, but there was no way I could stay in this dump of a hotel on Sunday.

When the gig was over on Saturday night, I drove home in a snowstorm only to find our house had met with disaster. As I opened the front door, I was nearly knocked over by a disgusting stench from the living room. I saw Paula lying on the couch, and it was clear her condition had not improved. The house was freezing. She explained the roof had cracked under the pressure of the snow, and water was leaking into the upstairs bedrooms.

It was more than a leak. The house was soaked from top to bottom, with water pouring out of the lighting and electrical sockets. There was no heating, and the place stank like a stagnant pond. My poor Paula looked terribly ill. She couldn't eat because the dental issues had infected her mouth so badly. She'd lost a great deal of weight and was down to around 95 lbs. which is very light for a grown woman of 5'8". It was still early morning, so I cuddled up with her on the couch, and we tried to stay warm. Randi and Mark were huddled up with some blankets. As I lay there looking at my family suffering in this mess, I decided to resolve the situation.

Around 10 am, I told everybody we had to take drastic action. I had spoken to the company we were renting from, and they offered little to no assistance in the short term. They told me they had a couple of vacant townhouses close to us, but upon inspection, I decided to look elsewhere. There was only one thing for it, we would have to move, but the big question was where? It was the middle of winter on a Sunday. We had to move within twenty-four hours if I were to make it back to the gig. I had no idea how this would be achieved but had no intention of staying in this house a moment longer.

Having grabbed a local newspaper, I scoured the pages for rental homes and found one reasonably close by and in our price range. I drove to the location and met the landlord, who was busy cleaning and preparing the place for new tenants. I explained our predicament, and he agreed to let us move in immediately. The house looked alright, but it wasn't easy to assess the neighborhood as the entire area was blanketed in snow. So, with a lack of options, we took the risk of moving and started gathering our belongings.

I had a Minivan, so we moved our belongings from the old house to the new one by transporting several small loads. It was bitterly cold and a grueling ordeal. At one point, our upright piano rolled unexpectedly. It almost fell on me as I slipped on the ice and lay flat on my back. However, by the end of the day, we had three bedrooms set up at the new place. Achieving this afforded us a place to sleep, and the rest of our belongings could be sorted out when I returned from the gig. By nightfall, we were exhausted but able to enjoy a nice cup of tea in a warm, clean house. Unfortunately, I had to drive back to finish the gig the following day. Having fulfilled our contract, I returned home. By the end of the week, we were fully moved into our new house.

Paula's health was still a significant issue, and she didn't seem to be recovering. I was so worried about her and wanted to be home to look after her, but this was not to be. We got a booking in Trail, BC and would be there for two weeks. We decided to take two vans on this trip. It was the middle of winter, and we would be in big trouble if we broke down. By having two vehicles, we had a backup just in case one had mechanical problems.

It was a treacherous drive, and we encountered some dreadful road conditions on our outward journey. When we arrived in Trail, I was unsure the trip to this town had been worth risking our lives. What a sad and melancholy place this was. It was grey and miserable; I felt like leaving as soon as I arrived. The thought of spending two hours, let alone two weeks, in this place was enough to drive a sober man to drink.

We settled into the old hotel and tried to make ourselves as comfortable as possible. Paul had been to this gig before and knew a couple of the locals. He seemed to enjoy the place, but it was not a good fit for me. All I could think about was my poor girlfriend I'd left behind. Would she get better? I called her frequently to see how she was. She would always try to sound perky and never complained, but I could tell she was not well by the timber of her voice. It was driving me crazy because I could do nothing to help her. I couldn't even give her a hug.

Once again, I hit the bottle hard to ease the pain of being away and dealing with this hell hole we were playing in. The bar was nicknamed the "Hug n Slug," an appropriate name for a venue hosting some of the drunkest degenerates I'd seen in a long time. Their primary mission was to get drunk as quickly as possible and start a fight before closing time. Now the drinking part I could relate to. I had vodka in my room and would get hammered before getting on stage. Regarding the nightly performances, I can only say my heart wasn't in it.

I didn't like half the songs we were playing, and most of the time, I just mimed the bass parts letting the sequencer do all the work. Things finally came to a head one night when I was so bored and drunk that I decided performing with my trousers around my ankles was a good idea. So here I am, standing in front of this hostile crowd with my best underwear exposed to the masses and as drunk as a lord. The owner was not impressed and shut us down.

That spark ignited the powder keg, and I went absolutely berserk. I should point out that prior to this night's performance, I'd spoken to Paula about her visit to the doctor. The news was not good. The doctor thought she might have Crohn's disease and was sending her to the hospital for further testing. I was so upset hearing this news and a complete mess when I hit the stage that night. Not only was I drunk, but my emotions were running wild.

Having been kicked off the stage, I argued with the club owner, told him what I thought of him and then decided if I wasn't allowed to perform, I was leaving. I staggered back to the stage and started packing my gear away. Paul was pissed off with my behavior and began yelling at me, so I punched him in the face, along with a flurry of verbal abuse. I was so drunk it seemed to take forever to get my gear packed into the van. I drove to the gas station in a drunken haze, only to find I'd left my wallet in the hotel room. When I returned to my hotel room, a girl was inside and refused to open the door. I kicked the door in and grabbed my wallet from the bedside table. She looked on in stunned silence. I had no idea what she was doing there, but after a brief exchange of colorful metaphors and having smashed a couple of beer glasses, I was returning to the gas station.

What I didn't know at the time was all my antics had been observed from the roof of the hotel by an assortment of regular customers and my bewildered duo partner. I was belligerent as I staggered around the street, telling anybody who would listen that Trail was a dump, and I was leaving. When the van was finally refueled, I was on my way and drove off into the snow-capped mountains, barely able to see from my bloodshot eyes. I drove for hours until I could drive no more. I called Paula and tried to explain my actions to her. As always, she was totally on my side and asked that I rest before completing the journey home. She was concerned for my well-being, and rightly so. I slept in the van for a few hours and awoke with a massive, pounding hangover at dawn.

At first, I had no idea what had happened, and then it all started coming back to me. What had I done? I'd just walked out on a gig and left my duo partner to fend for himself. Strangely enough, I didn't feel too bad about it. My main concern was Paula. I had to ensure she got the treatment needed to become healthy again. I hadn't enjoyed doing the gigs with Paul; honestly, I don't think he liked doing them with me. We were very different people, and if I was going to play, there had to be some fulfilment, personally and musically. Standing on a stage miming bass parts to songs wasn't cutting it for me. I probably shouldn't have quit how I did, but as they say, "Shit happens!" There was no turning back and a long drive ahead of me. I eventually reached the outskirts of Edmonton in pretty rough shape, but it didn't matter because soon I would be home and reunited with my darling Paula.

Upon my return, I crawled into bed in an attempt to escape from the turmoil I'd caused by my foolish actions. I was in a terrible state of mental instability, with my mind and body soaked from a flood of alcohol abuse. It was not long before we received a call from the club owner in Trail. He was not happy, but Paula dealt with the situation, telling him I had a nervous breakdown and was heavily sedated. I never heard from Paul again, and that was the end of our relationship. Paula ended up in the hospital for a while but was soon on her way to making a full recovery. She didn't have Crohn's disease; she regained some weight and felt much better before long.

I decided to stop playing live shows and concentrate on recording new songs. It was time to replace the equipment I'd used for live performances with new digital recorders. Once my gear was sold, I bought a Fostex DMT 8vl digital recorder and built a small studio in the basement. If nothing else was working out for me, I was at least getting proficient at building basement studios. Maybe I should have made that my new enterprise, but I digress. I decided the studio could be a small commercial enterprise for me. With that in mind, I put an ad in the paper for clients who wanted to record a demo. I waited with bated breath for the phone to ring and felt comfortable being off the road for a while. With the duo exploits behind me and Paula's health back to normal, we were in good stead as another chapter of our lives was about to unfold.

Gallery 12

Duo days with Cory.

A quick pint on a trip to the UK early 90's.

Paula enjoying some fish n chips English style.

Paula with some friends from Rusty's in the studio.

Trying my hand at filming in Kimberley B.C.

Career in the toilet.

All photographs from Martin Andrew private collection.

Chapter Thirteen

ALTHOUGH THE STUDIO I BUILT WAS ADEQUATE FOR DEMO RECORDINGS, it was unsuitable for recording material up to a releasable standard. I enjoyed working with other musicians in the studio but needed a high-quality recording of my new songs. Once again, I approached Don with my dilemma. He pointed me toward a friend who operated a local studio. Don had known him for a long time and vouched for his skills as a studio engineer and producer.

I decided to record four songs. Since I had no idea how modern music should sound, I let the producer take things in whatever direction he saw fit. I always steered towards a raw, edgy rock n roll, but this could be an opportunity to explore a new sound with a different approach. The four songs ended up with a polished blues/pop sound, and I wasn't sure if I liked it. However, everybody involved with the recording reacted positively to the result, so I just went with the flow.

The age-old problem of what to do with it upon its completion was about to stare me in the face. I had no contacts in the recording industry, and neither did Don. After a great deal of debate and waffle, nothing happened, and not one demo was sent out to anyone. I recorded four new songs that would sit and collect dust with the rest of my demos. The only difference with this new batch was the expense of recording them, but at least they sounded good. I employed the services of several excellent local musicians. The quality of the recording reflected their talents. The songs were solid and would have been received well, but this business is all about who you know; I needed more credible contacts.

After a few weeks of trying to figure out what to do next, Don came up with a suggestion. He wanted to send the demo to a colleague running a successful studio in Vancouver. I had mixed feelings about this character and wasn't 100% comfortable with him getting involved, but there was nothing to lose at this stage. So, we sent a copy of the tape to the studio and waited for a reply. It was only a short time before we got a response. The demo review was mixed but somewhat encouraging.

Having listened to the tape, the summation was that it held some merit in the songwriting department but didn't sound modern enough for today's market. I had no recourse other than to agree. The sound could have been more stylish, despite our best efforts in the studio to overcome that, so what did he propose to do about it? He suggested I start from scratch and come to Vancouver to record a new demo at his studio. I'd just spent a great deal of money recording a demo, and now he wanted me to do another one. How could I possibly afford to do that? I reached out to everyone I knew, trying to solicit funds to record some more songs, but there were no takers until I approached an unlikely source.

I was still in touch with Karen. Our relationship remained convivial despite our divorce. Paula and I had been to visit with her and her parents. As part of a general inquiry about my career, I mentioned I needed funds for yet another recording project. They were only too glad to help and became the sole investors in this new venture. I couldn't believe my good fortune and assured them I would pay them back every penny with interest when I had my first hit single. I was sincere in my assurance, but in retrospect, I lived in an alternate reality. It was a reality where I thought I could reach the top of the music charts. First, I would have to convince the rest of the world of this feasibility, and maybe then I could make good on my assurances.

Martin Andrew

I had my funding, so it was time to prepare a trip to the studio in Vancouver. By now, my dear friend Scotty was firmly entrenched in the movie business in Vancouver and offered me shelter for the duration of my recording session. Before committing to this new venture, I decided to check out the facility and arranged a ride to Vancouver with a truck driver friend. Then, if it all seemed legitimate, I would make the necessary arrangements to do the recording and return at a later date.

The trip to Vancouver was long and tedious, but I was glad to see Scotty again upon my arrival. He was living in a bad part of the city, but it didn't matter as he and I always managed to have fun, whatever the circumstances or location. We chatted a little about the studio I was going to take a look at. Scotty recommended I tread with caution. He had less than agreeable dealings with them and hadn't been paid for some session work. Despite some reservations, I arranged a meeting with the people at the studio, and we discussed the forthcoming project.

The studio was situated in Port Coquitlam, just outside Vancouver, in a residential area. It had good equipment, and the female engineer/producer seemed competent and approachable. During a lengthy discussion, we also broached the topic of an opportunity to perform in Asia. There was an apparent relationship with the Feldman agency, which sought capable bands to play on that continent. The idea intrigued me somewhat, but my focus was primarily on recording. When the discussion ended, I felt comfortable booking time at the studio and moving ahead with the recording, even though Scotty's warning still resonated in my head.

I spent one more night with Scotty then it was time to return home. Upon my return to Edmonton, I had to get some songs ready for the studio, and an alteration had to be made to my appearance. Another part of the discussion about modernizing my music pertained to my self-image. I was told to be taken seriously; I would need to cut my hair and get with the times. I had worn my hair long for so many years it would be tough taking the shears to it, but I decided if I was going to try and get back on my feet as a legitimate recording artist, then maybe it was time for an image change.

The Road to the Manor

With my new look and a head full of dreams, I was now ready to proceed with my journey and the project at hand. In May of 1997, Paula helped me load up our minivan, and I set off on my trip to Vancouver. I hoped this would be it. If everybody did what they said they would, I could play with a band in Asia and get a record deal with the songs I'd written and recorded. I had lots to think about and plenty of time to do the thinking as I made my way to my destination. My original plan to stay with Scotty was impossible as he was busy filming, and I didn't want to commute daily from Vancouver to Port Coquitlam. The weather was relatively mild, so I decided to sleep in the back of the minivan as my budget didn't afford me the luxury of a hotel room.

I parked by a secluded area of the highway and bedded down for the night. I didn't get much sleep that night as my mind was racing, still trying to figure out some arrangement ideas for the new songs. It was soon morning; I made my way to the studio with a quick stop at a burger joint to get breakfast and a wash in the restroom. When I got to the studio, I was met by the employees and fully expected to get started right away. However, I was blindsided by the owner and engineer, who presented me with what I considered a very slimy ploy.

They wanted to scrap my songs and for me to record some of their originals. They felt their material had a more modern sound and, therefore, more chance of success. What a load of bullshit this was! It was apparent from that moment all they wanted to do was secure the rights to any songs I or anybody else recorded at their facility. I played along and listened to their wonderful songs, but as anticipated, there was nothing earth-shattering. I insisted on recording my material, and they backed down. It wasn't the start I'd hoped for on my first day at the studio. All I could hear was Scotty's words of warning reverberating in my head.

Nothing went according to plan from that day on. Trying to get things done was a struggle. I ended up paying a lot of money for session players to come in and record the bed tracks. At one point, I even had to pay the power bill so we could continue working after the electricity was cut off. I thought I'd be working with a more efficient unit rather than a bunch of opportunists who saw my money and myself as easy targets. Some people in this industry will exploit your enthusiasm and love for your craft by telling you what you want to hear, knowing they can't deliver the desired results. Unfortunately, I had fallen prey to such manipulating characters, but there was no one to blame but myself. I had decided to record here despite the warnings from Scotty, and now, I was in too deep to pull the plug on this fiasco.

I didn't care for the way my songs were being produced. Various parts needed to be fixed, but the lady at the mixing console kept wanting to move on. Ultimately, I had enough and let loose a barrage of insults concerning her recording and production skills. That brought the recording session to an abrupt end as she left the studio in a flood of tears, and I walked outside to get some air. After some mediation and damage control, we continued recording the next day.

On a parallel course with the recording was a search for band members to form a group to go to Asia. I was very interested in this, but searching for competent musicians took a lot of work. Several people were interviewed before one guy who grabbed my attention appeared for an audition. He looked good, sang well, and was a very competent guitarist. He spent some time in Asia and regaled us with tales of his exploits as we listened intently. Shortly after our initial meeting, he agreed to join the new act and also offered to sing backing vocals on a couple of my songs.

The search continued for other musicians, and before long, we found a competent drummer and the "Hippie." The Hippie was a bass player from the east coast who had recently moved to Vancouver looking for work. He was a tad slovenly but could play the bass guitar and be made to look respectable with sufficient showers and hair prod-ucts. This was the first incarnation of the new band. It was hardly suit-able for playing at dance clubs in Asia but was indeed a working unit for some of the rock clubs in Canada.

We were keen to start playing, so our production team set about booking dates in some of the old haunts I'd played in many times before. While the small tour was being booked, I was putting the final touches on the three songs I recorded at the studio. Despite all the problems and lack of competence surrounding this project, it sounded alright. The finished product was sent out to Don's friend for a listen. Upon his approval, he would hopefully work his magic with the record companies. While his opinion was pending, we set out on the road for a five-week tour.

I was glad to be out of the studio, as living in the back of my van had not been fun. However bad the accommodations were on tour, it had to be better than that. So here I was, back on the road and looking forward to playing in a band again. The duo days had paid some bills but had not done much else for my bruised ego. I hoped this band would work out, but early on in our small tour, it became evident that the "Hippie" would have to be replaced. He didn't fit in, and after the first week of shows, I told him so. He didn't seem bothered by my remarks, and we continued the tour, venturing as far north as Yellowknife. It was a place I vowed never to return to, but here I was, once again annoying the people of the northwest territories.

I found it hard to take gigs like this seriously as the club patrons were usually so drunk, they didn't pay much attention to the entertainment. We almost got fired because the crowd attendance was so low. I had become increasingly drunk on stage just to get through the seemingly endless nights. It was summertime. Twenty-four hours of daylight played havoc with one's circadian rhythm. We would finish the night, and the sun was still up in the sky when we left the club at 2 am. It was hard to get any decent sleep. We often resorted to drinking more than we should.

Before we knew it, five weeks of entertaining the toothless and inebriated concluded. The tour ended, and we were back in Vancouver, searching for musicians. The Hippie returned to his homeland. It was time for the rest of us to find suitable players for a more polished dance band. To play in Asia, we would need a whole new set list of current commercial hits, and some added sex appeal in the form of a female singer. I set up a date for auditions, and the response was overwhelming. The promise of the tour in Asia was very appealing to all those who auditioned, but the fact of the matter was we were bluffing. There was no guarantee of any work in Asia, just the chance that we would be considered if the band performed well at a showcase for the Feldman agency.

A girl and a guy from Bellingham, Washington, appeared for an audition and seemed the perfect fit. She was a beautiful, talented singer, and he was a good-looking, clean-cut bass player, which was just what we were looking for. There was no clash of personalities; they were enthusiastic about joining us, so we offered them the job, and they accepted. Time was of the essence, so we set about getting our new show together. During this time, I needed a break. I decided to drive home and drop off the van.

I had to escape the madness, and what better way to do that than to get home and see Paula. She'd been out to visit me during my exile in Vancouver, which was great, but I was glad to spend some time with her away from the others. We had a picnic in the house; I loved every moment of sitting sipping wine and eating her invention, the "bagel pizza." I missed being with her but knew I had to return, so with my batteries recharged, I flew back to Vancouver.

After a couple of weeks of sorting through songs, we ended up with a fragmented set list which we showcased for the Feldman agency. They liked the initial showcase but had some reservations. It was apparent to them this was a new act. They decided the band needed to work for a while to see how it developed. Luckily, there was an opening for a dance band at a club in Terrace, BC. The band performing there had run into some medical problems and was not able to continue. It was a six-week engagement and seemed ideal for us to get the act tight. The only problem was we needed a complete set of songs, as our contract required us to play four forty-minute sets six nights a week. It was time to get rehearsing.

We rehearsed at a veritable dump in an industrial part of Vancouver. Our production team was picking up the tab, so I had no complaints. I stayed with Scotty off and on but decided to sleep in the rehearsal space and make that my home base for the remainder of the time spent in Vancouver. The only drawback with sleeping in the rehearsal space was it was also home to a regular rave. I bedded down one night and was enjoying a good night's sleep when all hell broke loose.

I awoke to about a hundred people bursting in through the door. The door was locked, but whoever was running the rave had a key. To my amazement, they all ignored me and proceeded to set up the equipment. Before long, the party was in full swing. I couldn't escape the madness as I no longer had a means of transport at my disposal. Loud pounding music and ecstasy were the order of the night. The rave went on for a few hours, then they simply packed up and went home. It was a bizarre night.

The club in Terrace asked for our set list and a promo picture of the band. The photograph we sent represented who we were, but the setlist did not accurately reflect the material we would be performing. The list we sent them contained songs we were learning for potential shows in Asia. We barely had enough material to play for an hour, let alone the four shows we were contracted to perform per night. It was too late to do anything about it now, as we had run out of time. Maybe we could learn some more songs on our journey?

We loaded the van on a scorching hot day in the middle of summer and set off on our long trip north toward Terrace, BC. The van was seriously overloaded. We had a lot of mountainous terrain to navigate. This was not a good combination. A few hours into the journey, there was an enormous bang, and fluid began spraying under the van. The transmission failed, and we were immobilized. It was a bloody disaster! We were stranded in scorching heat and couldn't continue the journey. To me, the blame lay with our production team in Vancouver. It was their van, and they assured us it was capable of making this arduous journey. I called to explain the situation and advised them I would charge the cost of repair to one of my credit cards; they, in turn, would be reimbursing me out of their commission money from the gig. They reluctantly agreed, and I set the wheels in motion to get the vehicle repaired.

We spent the night in a cheap motel. Late the next day, we got back on the road with a reconditioned transmission. We took it steady after that and made sure we had regular stops to keep the van from overheating and the transmission from exploding. Eventually, we pulled into Terrace and arrived at the venue. It was an older hotel but relatively clean, and the showroom itself was a reasonable size.

While unloading our equipment, we encountered the house band we were replacing for the next six weeks. They were not very friendly and rather full of themselves. They talked so much that I had to tune them out and randomly smile when making eye contact. Once we were set up, it was time for a sound check. I was appalled to see this other band standing at the soundboard with that "Impress me" look on their faces. After all, we were doing them a favor by filling in while one of their girls recovered from an illness. It was clear to me from day one these people were going to be a pain in the arse, and they were. Because of the intense scrutiny, I knew we would have some problems on our opening night.

Opening night arrived. We knew we didn't have enough songs to cover our contractual obligations. The songs we did have were different from the list we had sent to the club. I did the only thing I thought would help the situation and drank a lot of vodka before we hit the stage. In my drunken state, I staggered through the night, singing, laughing, and hoping for the best. When the night was done, everybody in the audience complimented us on our performance. I couldn't believe we got away with it. We rejoiced in our victory. The rejoicing was short-lived.

In the morning, I was summoned to the office for a meeting with the bar manager and arrived with a terrible hangover. He and the house band leader confronted me with the set list we sent them and asked for an explanation. Why were we playing mainly rock music and not the variety of dance songs on the list? Confronted with this question, I could only give one answer, so I lied through my teeth and told them they had received the wrong list. They presented me with the list we were assembling for our tour in Asia. It must have been sent in error.

It was almost true. They agreed to a compromise after a somewhat heated exchange where I threatened to quit, and they threatened to fire us. After all the saber-rattling was over, we were required to learn all the songs on the Asia list at a rate of two per day. This agreement equated to us playing at night and rehearsing in the club every afternoon to get the new material into the show. We had to substitute two old songs for two new ones every day until our nightly repertoire matched the Asia setlist. Failure to do so would result in instant dismissal. We couldn't afford to get fired or be stuck in Terrace without enough money to travel home. We had no choice in the matter, so we agreed to the terms and began working like hell to get the new songs rehearsed and in the show.

The duration of our stay in Terrace was rife with hostility between us and the house band. They were also in league with the sound man who was dating the owner's daughter. She didn't like us, and when the manager was away for one weekend, she set the wheels in motion for us to be fired. When I received the call from the soundman telling me the band was fired because we hadn't adjusted our set list, I went ballistic. After all our work to appease this backwoods club, they were going to fire us under false pretenses. I raised hell, and when the manager returned, he was most apologetic to me. The bitch who caused the problems, along with her sound man boyfriend, were reprimanded for making unjustified decisions above their pay grade.

As time passed, we came closer to the end of this ordeal and were ready to get the hell out of town. Before our final show in Terrace, we were told the Feldman agency would send an agent to evaluate us at the club, but nobody arrived. Instead, they requested a video recording to assess our progress and decide our suitability for an Asian contract. We were able to film a show and sent the footage directly to the Feldman agent, who saw us showcase at the rehearsal room in Vancouver. All we could do now was keep our fingers crossed and await his response.

I contacted our production team to see what other work might be available to us while we waited for a response from Feldman. Unfortunately, I was told there were no more gigs. It seemed we'd been hung out to dry. Our contract ended in Terrace, so we had to decide what to do next. One thing we had to take into consideration was that we had no transport. The production company had sent a driver to pick up the van after we arrived in Terrace and promised to sort out another mode of transportation for our return journey. Unfortunately, the other method of transport never came, so we were evicted from the hotel with our equipment, luggage, and no vehicle. This dilemma called for drastic action.

I suggested that rather than blowing our money to get back to Vancouver, we should go east and try our luck in Alberta. I still had a good relationship with Don, and although he was no longer active in the music scene, I knew he would help us. I wasn't happy with how the production company had left us in this hell hole with no way of returning to civilization, so I decided to use their commission money to get us home. I ran the idea by the band, and they enthusiastically concurred. I planned to ship the musical equipment, we would straddle the Greyhound with our luggage and make the long trip back to my house in Edmonton.

I contacted Paula, who agreed to let the band stay at our place. She was always supportive, so with this plan hatched, we put the wheels in motion and said goodbye to Terrace. It has to be noted that the time spent in Terrace is one of the worst experiences of my career to date! The mood on the Greyhound bus was one of quiet reflection and cautious optimism. I, for one, had reservations about what lay ahead but tried to remain positive in my demeanor. Paula picked us up at the Greyhound station when we arrived in Edmonton. We returned to our humble abode with our extended musical family. It felt so good to be back home. Of course, the house was crowded, but that was ok. That night when I climbed into bed, I breathed a sigh of relief and held Paula tight. I was home, I was happy, so life was good.

Getting the band working as soon as possible was essential, so I contacted Don and arranged a meeting. He was always excited when a new challenge was presented and met with us at his downtown office. As I have said before, he was no longer actively working in the music business but seemed to enjoy getting involved behind the scenes. He gave me some contact numbers for agencies in the USA and suggested we follow up with Feldman. We videotaped the show in Terrace and sent a copy to the agent in Vancouver, hoping he would enjoy it and get us booked into one of the Asian resorts. Unfortunately, this was not to be. He didn't like what he saw and suggested replacing our female singer with a girl who had a better stage presence and more charisma. I decided to give the band members a more general account of what he said rather than singling out our singer; since the guitarist was now dating her, there was no way she was being replaced, so I left it alone.

This revelation was a devastating blow. The whole point of putting this band together had been with a view to it being booked in the Asian market. Without the Feldman agency, there was no way we would be going anytime soon. Paula and I couldn't sustain having so many people living with us without some revenue being generated by the band. To add insult to injury, I got a response from Don's contact in Vancouver, who was supposed to negotiate a recording contract for me with the songs I'd recorded in the summer. He told me the songs weren't strong enough to warrant his endorsement, and I should look elsewhere for representation. I would later find out the reality of the situation: he had no relationship with any of the major labels and was full of shit.

Battered but not beaten, I sent packages to all the agents I could think of but only got a response from one agency in Edmonton. It wasn't very reassuring, but we had to work as Paula, and I were running out of money. We performed at a couple of local venues and made enough cash to stay afloat for a while. With the prospect of getting to Asia, or anywhere else for that matter, fading fast, the bass player decided to call it quits and returned to the States. I ended up playing bass for a while. I tried everything humanly possible to salvage the situation, but every avenue led to a dead end.

Finally, in desperation, I got the Blue Goose 2 back on the road. We used it for a short tour, culminating in us playing our final show in Lloydminster. Ironically, the last time I played there was my final gig with the Martin Andrew Band, and now this outfit would share the same fate. We went through the motions as best we could but knew it was over. Many fingers pointed at me when it was time to allocate blame, and perhaps they were right. The production company in Vancouver told me we were going to Asia, which turned out to be a false narrative. I had, in turn, fed this false narrative to them, and where had that got us? As we limped back to Edmonton with the bus engine backfiring, I felt utter despair about how the year had unfolded. It started badly and went from bad to worse. I worked as hard as possible and tried to do all I could to get things going, but every way I turned, I ran into difficulty. So, what next?

We arrived back in Edmonton, and the cloud of silence which had hung over us for the entire journey remained. No words were exchanged as the rest of the band collected their belongings while I remained stoic in the driver's seat. Then when their car was loaded, they simply drove away as I sat there in silence, waiting for Paula to come and take me home. I had no idea what I was going to do or how we were going to survive financially. My world was falling apart, and I was sinking deeper into the dark realms of alcoholism. The only thing I was sure of was Paula; I needed her now more than ever. She arrived in the minivan with a big smile on her face. I felt better just seeing her there. We drove home. It was a relief to be in the house again with no band members lounging around on our furniture. There was only one thing to do. Open a bottle of wine and celebrate.

Gallery 13

Rehearsing in Vancouver 1997.

Live show in Yellowknife 1997.

Contemplating a new lineup between sets!!

The new line up.

A break from recording with Paula at Scotty's.

Preparing for the feast.

The Bagel Pizza Indoor Picnic 1997.

All photographs from Martin Andrew private collection.

Chapter Fourteen

THE BAND HAD DISSOLVED. I WAS AGAIN WITHOUT ANY FORM OF employment, so it was time to take stock of the situation and make my next move. Paula was happily employed as a beer tub girl and waitress at Club Malibu in the West Edmonton Mall. Although it didn't pay much, it kept us afloat while I sought a way to generate income. As I searched for employment, I was still racking my brain for a way to move forward with my music career.

With the three songs I completed in Vancouver and the four I had previously recorded in Edmonton; I had enough material for a CD. I found a local company that dealt in short-run manufacturing and ordered five hundred copies of what came to be my first CD release. The project was completed swiftly, and "Like the Way that I Do" was soon released. One thing I did to promote the CD was get some airtime on a local radio station. Shannon Tyler was one of the girls who sang backing vocals on the recordings in Edmonton. She had since become a DJ at a local radio station. When I took the disc to her station manager, he was more than happy to put it on rotation.

I would like to believe his decision was based on the merits of the CD itself, but the reality is they played the song "Falling in Love" because she was singing on it. What did I care? My ego was beyond bruising. I was on the radio four times daily. I remember stopping at a red light when my song was played. I opened the windows in the car and turned up the radio. This minor achievement, for what it was worth, did manage to put a smile on my face that day.

I had no desire to try and put a band together to promote the disc and relied on word-of-mouth sales and a few local TV appearances. At one of these TV shows, I met an interesting character who introduced himself to me as a producer and told me he had his own show. I explained what I was doing, and he suggested we stay in touch as he could help me. I did voice-over work for him and interviewed the band Trooper at a show in Edmonton.

It was fun and a little different from what I was used to, so I continued to work with him and earned a meagre pittance for my trouble. We discussed how best to promote my CD. He suggested filming a video for the title track. I wrote a comedic storyline for the shoot and gathered as many friends as possible for a hysterical day filming in Don's backyard by the pool. Unfortunately, the video never saw the light of day because Mr. TV Producer didn't edit it, and I got tired of waiting for him. It was a shame because we encapsulated the fun element of the song; it could have been a valuable sales tool. I'd never filmed a scripted promotional video before and was very disappointed with this outcome. I put my heart and soul into every venture I pursued, only to come up empty-handed. At this point, I was getting tired of the futility of my efforts. Nothing was going my way, and I was unable to contribute financially on the home front, so I decided to get a "real" job.

Christmas was just around the corner. We desperately needed some extra money if we were going to have any kind of festive celebration. I don't get too excited about public holidays, but Paula and I had two small children awaiting Santa's arrival, and I wanted to please them. Rhonda, who was a dear friend of ours, arranged for me to have an interview at the hotel she worked at. I managed to charm my interviewer, the shipping and receiving manager, and became a full-time employee at the Mayfield Hotel.

I did a lot of warehouse work when I was younger, so it was a good fit for me. However, it was a hard slog. I had to get up around 6 am to be at work at 7:30 am. Most of the time was spent unloading trucks in freezing conditions, and to say the least, I was not having fun. My supervisor was a complete idiot; I didn't enjoy spending time with him at all. In addition, I had to stock up the freezers after unloading the trucks, so I spent most of the day being very cold and miserable.

No matter how hard I tried to fit in, I couldn't handle working in this so-called regular workplace. This mundane lifestyle was not for me; it only lasted about six weeks before I resigned. During my six weeks of employment at the hotel, I had access to the backstage area of the showroom. The Mayfield Hotel hosted dinner theatre shows. I often saw the actors and musicians arriving for work. I was so envious of them and often wished I were going to perform on the stage. Instead, I was stocking the bar for that night's performance, filled with envy and regret as the stage doors closed behind me and the artists gathered to revel in the wonderment of the entertainment world. It was a world that I seemed to have left behind me, but I knew I had to find my way back.

Despite our financial woes, we had a fun Christmas, but there was a lurking reality of starting another year without any real direction or idea of what I should do next. 1998 was now upon us; Don devised one of his finer schemes to make some money. He introduced me to a lady friend of his who was an entrepreneur and dabbled in some projects within the entertainment field. I use the word entertainment loosely as I participated in some ridiculous antics at her request to make a dollar.

One of the more memorable and embarrassing moments of performing in her fashion shows was when I had to dress up as "Adam." I and "Eve" put on our outfits, which for me, consisted of some skimpy underwear with leaves glued to them. Not only did it look ridiculous as we pranced around the bar, but it was also very uncomfortable as the glue and leaves scratched at my thighs like a rabid cat. Despite needing the money, I declined to work for her on any further projects.

Don was undeterred by the premature demise of my modelling career and offered to have me work as his assistant at the Investors Group. I could trade in my leafy loin cloth for a suit and tie. All I'd have to do is make phone calls and file documents. I had known Don for a long time, so working with him would be low stress. It was a new beginning in my short career in the world of high finance.

The office setting appealed to me; I enjoyed getting dressed up for work. The people working with Don were friendly enough, I was a bit of a novelty to them, not being from the same background, but we got along just fine. I worked with Don for several weeks. While doing his bidding by day, I was also recording with some local musicians at my studio by night. It was during this period that Kelly Douglas contacted me.

Kelly was a guitarist whom I met several times. He called me to see if I was still performing. I invited him to the house, and we chatted about possibly forming a rock duo. I hadn't intended to do this again following the previous disasters, but Kelly was a good mate. We would have a lot of fun if we did it all with a sense of humor, not taking things too seriously. I already had all the tracks from previous duos, so putting the show together was easy. I reconnected with the Banks agency, and we were back out on the circuit in no time.

Working with Kelly was a lot of fun. We got along well and enjoyed getting drunk before, during, and after the shows. At first, we used his van to get us and the equipment to the venues until disaster struck on one fateful trip to Didsbury, Alberta. His van (which doubled as his house) blew up, and we were stranded on the highway. The vehicle was a right off, so while he guarded the equipment, I was able to hitch a ride to the nearest town to look for an alternate mode of transport. I was lucky enough to happen upon a farmer who was selling a Ford F150. After cleaning some manure from the truck bed, I purchased the truck for a great price and returned to pick up Kelly. I have no recollection of what happened to Kelly's van. We may have left it at the side of the road, or the farmer may have picked it up and sold it for scrap. Whatever happened to it was no longer our concern. We managed to get to our gig in the new, albeit smelly, truck.

After our weekend in Didsbury, I drove us back to Edmonton, and Kelly moved in. Paula liked Kelly but often chastised him for encouraging me to drink so much. Of course, it was the other way around, but seeing Kelly getting yelled at once in a while was funny. Unlike the other band members who stayed with us, Kelly was different and became one of the family. The kids loved him. He would often take them to the store for Slurpee's and the occasional chocolate treat.

One of the funniest gigs he and I did was in Fort McMurray, Alberta. The night began with an array of young fillies flashing their ample bosoms at us as we thundered through our rock repertoire. We got so drunk that when we left the bar, I decided to take a shortcut through the park on our return journey to the hotel. How we didn't hit a tree, or anything else for that matter, is beyond me.

Kelly bedded down for the night, but I decided to roam the streets until I found a 24-hour cafe where I could satisfy my food cravings. I fell asleep face down on a plate of eggs benedict and was escorted off the property. I eventually returned to the hotel and woke Kelly up for a drunken chat. After many slurred words were exchanged, we finally fell asleep. It had been a fun night, but we would pay the price for our alcohol-induced euphoric experience the following day.

As we nursed our aching heads in the morning, we noticed the truck had a scrape down the side. Neither of us had any idea how it got there. We packed up our belongings and headed south towards Edmonton. When we got home, I explained to Paula why our new truck had a massive scrape down the driver's side door. I blamed the whole incident on Kelly, and subsequently, he got yelled at by Paula for leading me astray. There was never any real vitriol in Paula's words, and we always had a good laugh about whatever trouble Kelly and I got into. She was concerned about my excessive drinking, but trying to convince me to slow down was an exercise in futility, and she was aware of that.

Paula was looking for a new job, so I introduced her to a cantankerous older man who owned the infamous Kingsway Hotel in Edmonton. It was a rough joint, but I got her a job there, bartending and serving shooters to the hooligans who frequented the establishment. She settled into her new job. Kelly and I continued playing at any dive bar that would employ us. Life went on without incident for many months until one day Kelly and I were out of town when I received a call from Paula.

The neighborhood we were living in was not very pleasant, and some of the other occupants of the surrounding houses were less than friendly. Some teenagers had taken it upon themselves to Harass Paula by throwing not only insults at her but clumps of dirt as well. All she was trying to do was sunbathe in the privacy of our backyard when she was subject to both physical and verbal abuse.

Most of the women in the complex were morbidly obese; Paula had been the target for some young peeping Toms. When she told the teenagers to get lost, the trouble began. She was in tears when she called me; I was unhappy with the situation. I asked her to stay in the house until Kelly, and I returned. As soon as we arrived on the scene, the situation escalated. I told the teenagers in no uncertain terms what I thought they should do, and before I knew it, I had half the population of the projects on my doorstep.

It was like one of those old movies where the villagers march on a castle with torches and pitchforks. The only difference, this was no castle. Thankfully, they didn't have any pitchforks. Kelly and I were able to subdue the mob, but the damage was done. Paula didn't feel safe living in what had become such a hostile environment, and to be honest, neither did I. We decided to get out of the neighborhood as fast as possible before something more serious occurred, with one or both of us getting hurt. Kelly decided it was time for him to find his own place. We agreed to continue working together as a duo on the weekends.

I contacted a local realtor and met with an English lady who told me she had some listings that may suit our needs. I don't know quite what I was thinking at this point, but I got it into my head that I wanted to buy a house and buy it that day. I looked at her listings; most were so rundown they should have been demolished. I was ready to give up the search when she presented me with a property in fair condition.

The house was not in the most desirable part of the city, but it was a quaint little place, and the street seemed quiet and clean. I called Paula and told her I had found a house and was going to the realtor's office to figure out financing. It was not an expensive property, but we also didn't have much money saved, so how would I pull this deal off? We needed around $5000.00 for a down payment and were short about $4,500.00. I was convinced we could come up with the money, so I wrote a non-refundable check for $500 and signed the relevant documents agreeing to buy the house.

The next day I took Paula to see the house, and we were able to get a look inside. The family in residence had been renting the property for some time. We were disturbed by the unkempt nature of the people dwelling within and realized that, as renters, they had no vested interest in the upkeep of the property. The house itself was like a little English cottage. Paula and I fell in love with it and were happy to consider it our first home together. All we had to do now was figure out how to pay for it before we lost our deposit.

We devised a scheme to enter into a collaborative initiative between the Bureau of Indian Affairs and Paula concerning a business proposal. Paula is 50% Cree Indian and qualified for government funding for various entrepreneurial endeavors. Having committed to buying the house, we decided running a small business from the property would be a great idea. The idea was to build a recording studio in the basement and run an agency from an office constructed in one of the spare rooms. The house layout was conducive to accommodating the services we proposed, so work began on a business plan to illustrate our aspirations for the proposed music management recording company.

I'd never needed to create a business proposal, so I contacted Don to seek his counsel. He supplied me with the basic template for such a document, and I began working on it immediately. It was a long and arduous task, but I remained focused. With due diligence, the task at hand was soon completed. Paula had to attend many meetings with the Bureau of Indian Affairs. Finally, she convinced them the project was legitimate and viable as a potentially successful business. So, the fun began. Our original idea was to get a small grant with little oversight from the Bureau and would not require any financial records to be disclosed. However, Don suggested applying for a more significant grant. He reasoned that Paula could only apply for financial support once, so getting as much money as possible would be in her best interest.

We reluctantly took his advice as we preferred less scrutiny and wanted to be something other than micro-managed by the Bureau. If we secured a grant for a more significant sum, they would have a vested interest in our business for the next three years. Let's remember the main reason we wanted financial help was to secure a down payment on our future home. The business was never intended to be anything more than a means to an end. If the company failed, we would have to pay most of the money back for the more significant grant as opposed to not paying anything back for the smaller one.

Along with the large grant, we had to get a loan and put in significant capital ourselves. We were in over our heads and kept digging deeper every day. Time was running out for the rest of the deposit to be paid on the house, so we had to move forward with what was becoming a very tangled web of creative financing. Getting a loan was very difficult. Every bank in Alberta turned us down. We managed to secure a loan with a women's group called AWEIA, whose main goal was to help female entrepreneurs in their business ventures. As part of their loan criteria, we would need to make monthly statements available from our business so they could monitor our progress.

We jumped through all the hoops doing everything required of us. Finally, we had a loan secured and our capital in place. All we had to do now was show evidence of our financial agreements, and we could collect the grant money from the Bureau. However, there was just one slight problem. We had been led to believe we were getting a lump sum payment, but this was not the case. The Bureau informed us we would only be funded after we proved we had spent our loan money and capital investment. We had to buy things first and present our receipts to the Bureau, and only then would they release a percentage of the costs we had incurred from our grant money. This whole scheme backfired on us. The documents had been signed. We had no way out and couldn't use any of the money from the loans, capital investment or grant for the down payment on the house. We were in big trouble.

Don's eldest daughter Heather came to the rescue. I will be forever in her debt for what she did. We were hours away from losing the house when she called me and said she had talked to her grandmother about our situation. I'd met her grandmother numerous times over the years and found her to be very caring and wonderful. She was going to lend us the money. I couldn't believe it! This dear lady was lending money to Paula and I on a handshake and secured the sale of the property to us. When the dust settled, we had our house and grant but not quite how we'd expected.

I maxed out all the credit cards to get the capital required. We had a loan to pay back, along with a mortgage. We were more in debt than ever before and had to convince the folks at the Bureau of Indian Affairs we were running a successful business. A large amount of our proceeds was spent renovating the basement. When the contractors completed their work, a space had been created for a fully functional recording studio. Once that was done, we installed my musical equipment along with the new things we purchased to satisfy the terms of the agreement.

We achieved our goal of buying a house, but as I previously said, things had turned out differently than planned. We had so much debt it took a lot of work to keep pace with the bills. The studio made a little money but not enough to be considered a viable business. It seemed like I was on the phone with the Bureau most days, feeding them so much bullshit that even I started to believe it. It was critical to have them think we were doing well; otherwise, we would have to pay back the grant money. I convinced them we were making money by using rather creative accounting methods. Of course, the less said about that, the better, but this had to be one of the most stressful periods of my entire life.

Serendipity was about to enter my life again when I made an impromptu visit to a local strip club. The bar where Paula worked was part of a large complex that incorporated a nightclub and the strip club, I visited that day. I just popped in to see a friend of mine called Big Daddy Mike, one of the club's resident DJs. He mentioned that one of the other DJs had quit. He asked me if I would be interested in applying for the position. I applied, was hired, and started the very next day.

Once again, I worked as a strip club DJ during the week and played in a duo on weekends. It was like going back in time to when I worked at Rusty's, only now I was at a club called Pinky's. Working at Pinky's was a lot of fun, and since Paula worked in the lounge bar at the same facility, we could see each other occasionally during breaks. With both of us working at the hotel and me doing duo gigs with Kelly on the weekends, we were able to stay afloat. However, every day when the mail arrived at the house, I felt a sense of dread as there were so many bills. Our whole life was consumed with paying off our creditors, but we could only afford to pay the interest since the credit cards were maxed out. It created a vicious cycle where our money was used to pay off a debt that would never decrease.

Our situation was a less-than-desirable position to be in. The phone would ring most days with some official questioning me about the company's finances. I would have to lie through my teeth and try to convince them we were fiscally sound. We had no clients, and the business was floundering. The market was already swamped with agencies and recording studios, so even if we had tried to build the business, the chance of success was slim to none. All this grant had done was put us further in the hole than we had ever been. The one good thing was we were now considered homeowners, which felt good.

My gigging with Kelly ended as he decided to leave Edmonton and move on to the fairer pastures of Calgary. My next duo partner was a lady Don introduced me to. The original idea was for her to be a client of our nonexistent agency. Instead of flogging that dead horse, I saw an opportunity to make some cash playing live shows instead of trying to book her. She was a country singer. The idea was to have her sing country, and I sing rock. We rehearsed in the studio and employed the services of the Duke agency to furnish us with gigs. The appeal of a male and female duo made for an easy sale to the clubs, so they quickly got us bookings. I was not a big country music fan, but the mixture of country and rock songs worked with the crowd.

The constant stress in my life was taking its toll. I found it hard to sleep at night, and when I was awake, I constantly worried about how to survive financially. Paula always had a positive attitude and remained calm throughout all our wheeling and dealing, but I didn't share her strength and reverted to my old friend alcohol for some peace of mind. Duo shows with Kelly had been so much fun, and when we drank, we were usually in a celebratory mood. With my new duo partner, I was just going through the motions to get a paycheck. It wasn't that I disliked her; it was an incompatibility of personalities. We had nothing in common.

I drank more and more on the road and at home. Before getting close to the stage, I would consume half a bottle of vodka in my hotel room. Most of the gigs were done in a drunken haze. After the show, I would go to my hotel room and drink some more until I passed out. I had no idea how close to the flame I was flying. My history of liver problems should have had me drinking orange juice rather than the potions I poured down my esophagus.

It was a challenging period for both Paula and me. We struggled to keep the Bureau of Indian Affairs off our backs, and our debt load was unbearable. The stress level hit a new high; it seemed like things couldn't get any worse. Then in late March of 1999, I had just returned from a gig when my health started to fail. Despite the handfuls of painkillers, I was swallowing, I'd been drinking heavily and had a terrible hangover that wouldn't go away. My abdomen began to swell, and my temperature began to rise. I wanted to stay in bed, but I had to go to work at the strip club. I managed to get myself mobile but knew something was wrong. I had felt this way before, only this time, the symptoms were more severe than any previous occurrences.

Paula came to work with me in case my condition deteriorated. As it was, I only managed to work for about an hour before I had difficulty breathing and walking. After that, I simply had no energy. I knew then my liver was in bad shape, and I had to get to a hospital. We went to the emergency room, and I was seen by a doctor who seemed to have little interest in my condition. He said nothing was wrong with me in his professional opinion, and a good night's rest might put me right. He opined I would be better served by going home and resting in bed.

So, we went home, and things just went from bad to worse. My skin turned yellow as the jaundice set in, and the whites of my eyes became orange. The crashing headache and the pain in my swollen abdomen became unbearable. Paula took me back to the hospital. Once again, I lay on a bed waiting to be seen, hoping someone would take the time to do a blood test.

I remember lying on a gurney in the cold waiting area, wondering if this was it. Had I finally gone too far, and this time, I was not going to be able to recover from this senseless overindulgence? As I pondered my fate, I was approached by a specialist named Dr Bailey. He went out of his way to see me. He was not the doctor on call, but he observed how yellow I was and decided to look into my case. Dr. Bailey ordered a lot of blood work. Within a few hours, he had a prognosis for me. My liver was in terrible shape, and the toxins in my blood were at a very critical level. My pancreas, spleen, and kidneys were all affected, so I was sent to a ward for observation.

This was devastating news. When the doctor told me I had chronic liver disease, all I could think was I had gone too far this time and would die. Paula stayed with me for as long as was allowed, and then she was asked to leave. I struggled to hold back tears when Paula kissed me goodnight. How could I have been so stupid to throw away the chance of being the happiest man on the planet? Here was a woman who loved me and would stand by me right or wrong, and I'd been so stupidly selfish and drank myself into what seemed to be my deathbed. How was this going to affect the children, parents, brother, and friends? I was heartbroken and had no recourse other than to see what tomorrow would bring and hopefully beat this self-inflicted wound once again.

The following day I awoke in agony, my abdomen more swollen than ever and unbearable nausea. I had no strength and could barely get out of bed to go to the bathroom. I had an I-V in my arm because I couldn't eat or stomach drinking any water. Unfortunately, bad news travels fast. It was not long before I was told my mother was on the phone. Paula called the rest of the family, and my mum decided to phone the hospital to see what was happening. I talked to her briefly and tried to sound upbeat, but I am sure she saw through that facade. I was given a motherly dressing down with some words of compassion and encouragement.

Later that day, four doctors visited me and gave me their diagnosis and prognosis for my recovery. As I lay there in this pathetic and help-less state, I braced myself for the words they were about to utter. I was expecting the worst and hoping for the best, but what they told me was not what I wanted to hear. The professional consensus was I had severe liver damage caused by excessive drinking, and the toxins in my liver were so high they were unsure whether or not I would be able to recover. They said there was nothing they could do for me. It was possible I might be dead within two weeks if my liver continued to deteriorate and ended up completely failing. I was to be discharged that day and sent home with the hope I might recover in due course. This was the worst day of my life.

After they left my bedside, I sat in silence, wondering what the future had in store for me. It's funny how we often say things like " I don't care if I die" or " I want to go out in a blaze of glory." When you're faced with mortality, there is nothing poetic or romantic about it at all. I was scared of what might be ahead of me. I didn't want to die. I realized at that moment I had so much to live for. I had Paula, my family, and friends. These people loved me and wanted to share their lives with me. How could I have been so blind to what was important in life?

I had to recover from this and ensure it was the last time I would ever fall into the evil grip of alcoholism. The condition I found myself in was not new to me. I knew what to expect, but nothing could have prepared me for the agony I was about to endure. Jaundice sets in quickly with liver problems, and the bloodstream is subsequently poisoned. The condition makes your whole-body itch to the point where you want to tear your skin off.

When I was hospitalized in the '80s, the itching lasted about a week, causing terrible discomfort. Unfortunately, this time, it was going to be worse. Fourteen weeks of itching twenty-four hours a day is what I had to endure. I was prescribed a powder which, when dissolved in water and subsequently consumed, was supposed to suppress the intensity of the itching. Still, the side effect of ingesting this potion was extreme nausea and subsequent vomiting. So daily, I had a choice. I could scratch my skin bloody or spend the day vomiting with my head in the toilet bowl.

Nights were the worst. I couldn't lie in bed for long as the bed sheets intensified the itching by increasing the temperature of my skin. Most nights, I lay naked on the kitchen floor. Sometimes I would lie by the front door to catch the draft and cool my skin. It was a living hell. Paula was my nurse, taking me for a walk each day to exercise my leg muscles. I could only move at a snail's pace, but we made it around the block before I started wheezing and had to rest. I had to visit the doctor frequently to see if my liver was getting any better. The toxin levels were dropping, but I was by no means out of the woods.

Despite my condition, the creditors were relentless in their quest to recoup money from our accumulated maxed-out lines of credit. I was far from a full recovery but decided to return to work at Pinky's for extra income. All I had to do was talk on a microphone. I could sit most of the day, so it wasn't too physically or mentally challenging. I even managed to do a couple of duo gigs to get some extra cash. I would split my time between resting in the hotel room and playing on stage. The stage work was uncomfortable as it was hot, and I would start to itch. In between sets, I would take a cold shower and rest until it was time to hit the stage again.

Paula employed the services of a couple of ladies who were reiki healers. They offered to work on me for free. I had several sessions with them. It was a fantastic experience. They never touched my body, but the intense heat generated as they placed their hands over my liver was incredible. By each session's end, we were exhausted and sweating profusely. I'm not sure how reiki works, but it helped me, and I will forever be grateful to those ladies.

I was recovering slowly and able to work, but our debt load was out of control. Something had to give, as we couldn't sustain this financial burden any longer. One of the strippers I worked with had become a personal friend. One day while visiting, she suggested Paula might benefit from entering the world of exotic dancing. I did not initially favor it, knowing the kind of people involved in the industry, but it did make sense financially. She could generate a great deal more money stripping, but this was only a decision we would make after much discussion.

We weighed up the pros and the cons, the pros won. We decided to do a trial run and booked some work for Paula through the agency at Pinky's. Paula's debut was a total success. She was a natural enter-tainer and could jump into the industry without going through the usual "Rookie" stage of doing cheap shows and silly competitions. I knew a lot of the high-end girls. They assured me they would look out for her as she eased her way into the industry. Paula was soon up and running with a full work schedule. It was now her turn to hit the road and tour Canada while I stayed home and looked after the kids. This changed everything financially. She was able to make a lot of money fast, and in turn, we were able to pay down our debt load. The only downside was she had to travel a lot and would be away from the children for extended periods.

I spent the next six months recovering from my illness and working at Pinky's. I decided to stop playing with my duo partner as I had no interest in returning to the bar scene full-time. Since I could no longer drink, the prospect was less appealing than ever. I had a steady income from my DJ paychecks, and Paula was making great money out on the road. I managed to refinance the house for its new market value and, in doing so, cleared whatever outstanding debt remained. We were back in the black.

I'd been knocking on death's door only six months before this, and we were buried under a mountain of debt. However, Paula was now enjoying her new life as an exotic entertainer. I had recovered from a devastating self-induced setback. It seemed the light at the end of the tunnel was sunshine, not the usual floodlight of an express train about to hit us between the eyes. We were going to be alright. I had doubted my very being, but Paula was a tower of strength throughout, and I count my blessing for her each and every day.

On my 37th birthday, I gave myself a birthday present by surprising Paula. I was almost back to full strength and wanted to do something special. I blindfolded her and drove her to a flying school at a small airfield in the city. She was so excited to find I had rented a small aircraft, and we were going flying. We flew high above the clouds that day, and I cherished every moment. It was symbolic that we had risen above all our problems and were flying high again. At least, that's how I felt on that day. I was glad to be alive and with the one I loved. I could see a silver lining in the clouds. It felt good knowing we once again had a future together.

With my health steadily improving and our financial situation stabilizing, I could focus on the one thing that gave me genuine pleasure: my music. I had a high-quality facility in our home to record new song ideas without time constraints, so I used it and began working on a new CD. Again, I spent hours in the studio and enjoyed the creative process. There would be no arguments with annoying studio engineers or wannabe producers. If it sounded like crap, it was down to me, so I'd better ensure I got a good result. Towards the end of the year, I felt a great sense of calm in my personal life, and I'd grown to love Paula even more than I could have imagined. One night after a hard day's slog at Pinky's, we sat at the dinner table having some beans on toast. I'd been thinking about asking her to marry me all day and popped the question over a plate of baked beans. She didn't take me seriously at all. I had always told her I would never get married again, so why this change of heart?

I realized this woman meant everything to me, and I wanted to share the rest of my life with her. There was no doubt in my mind. I wanted her and only her to take my name in marriage. She shed a little tear when she realized I was serious and said yes. I was the happiest man on the planet, and my baked beans never tasted so good. We decided not to reveal our intentions to anybody, not even our closest friends or the children. We intended to shock everybody with the news of our union after the fact and not before. She and I agreed we didn't want a traditional wedding. Instead, we would aim for the tackiest wedding conceivable and have as much fun as possible. So where else other than Las Vegas would be a suitable destination for this debacle of romance?

The Road to the Manor

I booked a wedding chapel online. We were married on Christmas Day 1999. There would be no way of forgetting that wedding anniversary! We told the kids and our friends we were going on a quick getaway; nobody harbored thoughts of a suspicious nature. Vegas was a blast. We had such a good time. We stayed at the Imperial Palace and were married at the Little Chapel by the courthouse. It was as tacky as it gets with a preacher who walked with a limp and his hand out for a tip. The chapel was damp, with a Charlie Brown Christmas tree garnished with dilapidated tinsel. It was perfect!

The ceremony lasted five minutes. We were now Mr. and Mrs. Andrew; I loved the sound of it! We celebrated our honeymoon in Vegas at the Tournament of Kings show. Then it was back to the hotel to consummate the marriage. Vegas was fun, but I could never imagine living there. We checked out some of the entertainment; I had never seen such cheesy acts gracing a professional stage. The bands were so fake in their delivery. They played well, but the hideous costumes and the lack of sincerity in their dialogue with the crowd reminded me of a cabaret act in a Butlins holiday camp.

This place was not for me. Please remember I just said that. We arrived back in Edmonton on New Year's Eve, away from the hoards pouring into Vegas for a night of drinking and debauchery. It had been quite a year. As we moved into the new millennium, we had time to reflect on what could have been a tragic but self-induced ending to my life. Instead, we had beaten the odds together and rounded out the century by getting married. I felt good and very positive for the first time in a long time. I looked forward to getting some new material written, recorded, and hopefully sent to interested parties. The Internet was a whole new ball game for self-promoting, and I wanted to explore all those possibilities fully. The main thing was a sense of happiness, which had eluded me for a long time.

I managed to beat my drinking problem once and for all and had a great family life. We survived getting the house and the loan for the business and could stay afloat now that Paula was working as an exotic dancer. If there was any drawback, it was just that Paula was away from home a lot, which was hard for Randi, Mark, and I, who missed her so very much. That was something we would have to deal with, and we did.

Tanya and I developed a tremendous long-distance relationship; I arranged for her to come and visit me in Canada. I always had to cross the Atlantic to see her, but she was finally allowed to fly over to see me for the summer holidays since she was getting older. Seeing her without prying, judgmental eyes looking at me would be wonderful. I was ready for a change in my professional and private life. I wanted a new challenge in the entertainment world. There were several challenges in my personal life, starting with renovating our house and turning it into a cozy home. As the clock struck midnight, Paula and I welcomed the year 2000. It was a new year and a new millennium. We shared a loving embrace as the champagne corks popped and the fireworks etched images into the night sky.

Gallery 14

The first house we bought in Edmonton 1999.

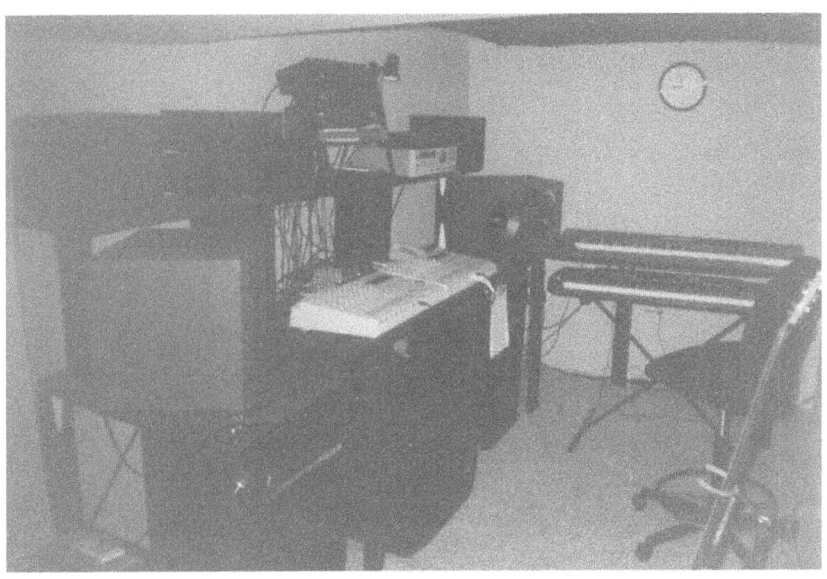

The recording studio control room.

Don and I hosting a BBQ at the new house.

Too much to drink.............again!

Paula in the back of the aircraft on my Birthday 1999.

Left: Big Daddy Mike at Pinky's. **Right:** Meeting Elvis in Las Vegas.

Getting ready for the big day by basking in the sun!

On December 25th, 1999, we tied the knot.

All photographs from Martin Andrew private collection.

Chapter Fifteen

I ENTERED AN ERA OF DOMESTICITY AND BEGAN TO ENJOY THE
challenges of owning a rundown house that needed a lot of tender
loving care. The property's basement was in good shape as it was
recently purpose-built for our recording studio project. However, the
upstairs and outside needed some work. I started painting the house's
exterior and got a little help from our new lodger. We decided to have
Marvin come and live with us as it served a dual purpose of giving him
a roof over his head and helping us out with the bills. He was a great
guy to have around the house and was affectionately referred to as
"Marvin the Bastard."

When the work on the outside of the property was completed, I
decided to employ the services of a contractor to renovate the inside.
We needed ceilings textured and walls painted, along with other minor
repairs I wanted to avoid tackling with my limited DIY skills. Having
scoured the yellow pages seeking help, Roger arrived on my doorstep
and offered his company's services. He was very personable, and we
chatted about everything besides the renovation.

It turned out he was a drummer, and we had a lot in common. Not
only did he paint my house, but he also stopped by for tea and coffee,
and we would chat about music. During this renovation period, Paula

was away a lot, stocking the war chest with funds so we could initiate and execute the necessary repairs to our home. I barely saw her. She was away for weeks. We would talk for hours on the phone at night. It was a challenging period for us, but one which was necessary.

I wasn't doing anything other than working on the house and recording songs in the studio. There would be the occasional project that would come my way but nothing of any real significance. Paula was making good money, but the trade-off was her travelling a lot. We were on a mission. We resigned ourselves to the fact that this was how things had to be, but we didn't have to enjoy. The house looked great. We only had one room remaining to decorate. I decided to do this room alone but ended up in a real mess when hanging the wallpaper. Roger was busy working elsewhere, so I contacted a friend of ours who was skilled in the art of wallpapering. Arianna worked with Paula at the Kingsway Hotel and was our close friend. She was the DIY queen, and I was glad to have her come to the rescue.

As we chatted during this decorating extravaganza, I mentioned to Arianna that I had an erroneous lump on my upper groin. It wasn't an unusual topic of conversation as we were close friends and broached all kinds of medical issues as part of our regular banter. I showed her the area of concern, and after a brief examination, she told me I had a hernia. I was shocked and amazed that I had not drawn this conclusion but ignored the symptoms, hoping they would just go away.

I tried to figure out how this happened. I narrowed it down to a couple of options. One could be the excessive lifting I did when working with the duo, or it might have been when I tried to move a large fridge into the basement by myself. I had taken a nasty fall as I slipped and fell down the stairs, rendering me prostrate under the refrigerator. Either way, this condition had to be handled before it worsened. The doctor scheduled me for surgery, and I was again under the knife. Once the surgery was completed, it would take many weeks to recover, so a period of convalescence would be the order of the day.

Following my release from the hospital, I took a leave of absence from the strip club, and Paula took some time off work for my initial recovery. When it was time for her to return to the road, it was just

Marvin, the kids and myself at the house. I can't say I was miserable but rather more frustrated at being incapacitated again. It took a while to get back on my feet, I wanted to return to work, so I eased back into my job as a DJ at Pinky's. Marvin and I decided to join some friends at the Sidetrack Cafe in Edmonton one night. The Sidetrack was known for having quality entertainment, and the food wasn't bad either. We discussed the local music scene during the evening's entertainment and how everybody's endeavors were progressing. During this conversation, a dear friend named Marcia presented me with a challenge that would take my entertainment career on a very different path for the next few years.

She talked to me about Jubilation's dinner theatre and indicated that, in her mind's eye, I would be a perfect fit for their production style. These shows incorporated song, dance, acting and were always comedic. I could sing and be funny sometimes, but could I perform as an actor? It was as if she had thrown down the gauntlet and challenged me to audition for one of these shows. I thought about it for a few days, then decided to give it a go. After all, what did I have to lose? I called the theatre box office at the West Edmonton Mall and asked if they were holding auditions. I was informed they were, and they booked me for an audition that week. I had to sing two songs and perform a three-minute comic monologue for the audition.

I had no problem singing two songs, but performing the monologue was a little unnerving. I decided to write my monologue instead of finding one online as I wasn't sure what would be suitable. At least if I wrote something, my delivery would be honest and could not be compared to the original comedian's performance. Marvin drove me to the audition, where I performed for the stage manager and a handful of cast members from the show. The audition went well. I felt good about my performance even though I was wrapped in bandages and still in pain from surgery. It must have gone quite well because I got a call back to perform for the director. Having done this, I was told there was a suitable role for me for their up-and-coming show.

The show was a spoof on the television series Magnum PI. They were looking for someone to play the part of the Englishman. Higgins was the character's name on the television show, but the name was changed to Huggins in the Jubilations production. It would be a perfect role for me to break into the world of musical theatre. I shared my enthusiasm with all present and told them I would love to participate in the production. They asked me a few questions about my experience in theatre. I rolled out a list of false and over-the-top accolades. I told them I worked at the BBC and had been involved in theatre shows for years. I'm sure they saw right through this, but at the time, I thought I managed to spew out all this rubbish reasonably convincingly.

The director was happy and told me to expect a call in the next few days. A couple of days went by, but the call never came. I was devastated. I thought I'd done so well, but nobody contacted me, so it was back to the drawing board and figuring out what to do next. Then, I received a call from the Kingsway Hotel informing me the facility had been sold and we would all be out of work in two weeks. Talk about getting blindsided. This was terrible timing. I was almost completely recovered from my surgery and ready to return to work full-time, only to be made redundant. Now what?

My acting career had finished before it started, and there were no band opportunities I cared to get involved with, so it was back to looking for a regular job. I went for an interview at the International Airport and became employed as one of the poor sods who stock the aircraft with meals and beverages. It was now very late in the year, and winter had set in. The prospect of doing this kind of work daily in the sub-zero temperatures of a Canadian winter was daunting.

The night before I was due to commence my newfound employment, I couldn't sleep. I was sick to my stomach with the whole prospect of what lay ahead. It was the same feeling I'd experienced time and time again since leaving school. I'd tried to walk the straight and narrow path of normality by working in a regular job, but it wasn't for me. I couldn't do it. The morning I was supposed to start work, I awoke Paula and told her I couldn't do this new job. She was so relieved. She didn't want me doing the job in the first place. My pride and the need to contribute financially toward our coexistence forced me to try and do this. Who was I kidding? Certainly not my beautiful wife.

She called the airport and told them I had an alternate offer of employment and would no longer need the position they made available to me. As it turned out, she was right. Within two days of turning down the job at the airport, I got a call from the director at the theatre offering me the part of "Huggins" in "Magnum PUI." I couldn't believe it! I would later find out they decided to offer me the role after my first audition but hadn't bothered to contact me because the show wasn't going into production for a few months. Either way, I was flattered and relieved to get the part.

The only problem now was I faked a resume and bluffed my way into this position without knowing the first thing about working in the theatre. Yes, I could sing, and it seemed I could be a tad comedic, but what about all the other elements in one of these productions? I was about to get a crash course in theatre etiquette and needed my wits about me to pull this off.

I had to wait a while before rehearsals began, but only briefly before being presented with my first script. As I opened the package, I had no idea what to expect or how big a part I would be playing in this production. The first page of the eighty-page script indicated that one of the characters would be making an introductory speech to the audience. I looked at this vast speech only to find out it was to be delivered by Huggins. As I looked at the subsequent pages, my heart began racing as I realized this would be quite the learning process.

I typed my lines onto separate sheets of paper and set about learning them. I wanted to be fully prepared when rehearsals began. I spent every waking minute reviewing the script. Gradually, I could retain the dialogue. I was determined to be ready for this challenge and aimed to dazzle the director with my newly honed thespian skills.

The show was to run in two cities, the first of which was Winnipeg in Manitoba. Winnipeg is where we would be rehearsing before the show opening. Then, after two weeks of intense rehearsal, the show would run for three months at the theatre in Winnipeg. When the run was finished in Winnipeg, we would open in Edmonton for three months with a possibility of doing a third venue in Calgary which the company was frantically trying to get open.

Before I left for Winnipeg, I had to go to the Edmonton theatre and join the ranks of the additional cast. Their job was to serve the customers and keep their energy level up while portraying a character related to the show. I could see how the show ran behind the scenes and got used to interacting with the audience. A big part of these shows was the interactive element with the audience. The cast members, along with the additional cast, were required to serve food and drinks as well as perform on stage. Having never been a waiter, this would undoubtedly require a new skill set to be learned by me. Many of the additional cast were young and immature. They went a little overboard with their characters, but I was to join their ranks for a night to get used to the theatre atmosphere. First, I had to pick a character, so I decided to be Rod Stewart for the night. Rod was not related in any way, shape, or form to the show, but it was a character I felt comfortable doing.

I spent the night waiting on tables and getting used to the lay of the land. It was quite a lot of fun, but I felt like an older man playing with a bunch of kids at a restaurant. I was keen to finish the training and be on my way to the big show. I worked that night alongside one of my future cast members. She was a veteran actor in Jubilations productions and was instructed to take me under her wing for the training process. She was a hard one to read, but we got along well. She told me I was fully trained and ready for action when the night was done.

I was instructed to make my transport arrangements for the journey to Winnipeg, so I had to decide whether to fly or take my car. At the time, I was the proud owner of an Oldsmobile, which seemed the most practical and economical mode of transport for my trip. So, with the car packed solid, I bade Paula farewell and started my journey to Winnipeg. It was now March of 2001, still freezing, and there was quite a lot of snow on the highway. However, the car was built like a tank, so the road conditions didn't bother me as I travelled east with a smile on my face and the radio blasting.

About two hours into my journey, as I was approaching the outskirts of Lloydminster, I heard a strange clunking sound coming from the engine. I was tempted to turn up the radio and ignore it, but the car was losing power, and the banging got louder. I knew I was in trouble. As I limped into a local gas station, the engine gave out a final bang and stopped. The motor had seized. All that could be seen was steam and smoke billowing from under the bonnet. This was a disaster. I was nowhere near my final destination and now had a wrecked car full of my things.

I called Paula to let her know what happened, then racked my brains for a solution to this predicament. I walked a few miles to Walmart and purchased two large suitcases. Having returned to the gas station, I transferred my belongings into the two suitcases and sold the car for scrap to the gas station's owner. I received $50 for the vehicle, which paid for a Greyhound ticket to Winnipeg and a subsequent taxi ride to the hotel.

When I got into my hotel bed, I was exhausted from the long trip and felt somewhat worse for wear. My throat was sore when I woke in the morning, and I felt ill. I could hear the other cast members in the hallway getting acquainted, but I chose not to join them. I was scared to death. I thought I'd bitten off more than I could chew. I remained in my room until there was a knock at my door I couldn't ignore.

I was invited to join the rest of the cast members for a quick meet and greet in one of the hotel rooms. They were all great people and made me feel very welcome. I felt more at ease with the situation after speaking to them. I looked forward to getting started with rehearsals. We had to be up at 6 am to get breakfast before driving to the rehearsal studio. The studio was set up with a mock stage taped on the floor. Before any acting took place, we had a read-through of the script. The days were long, hard, and split into three sections. We started with acting and blocking the show, followed by a vocal rehearsal, and rounded out the day with some choreography.

The choreography was the hard part for me. I had never done anything quite like it before. It took a while to pick up the steps. I spent hours in my hotel room working on the dance moves we'd been taught at rehearsal. The most frustrating thing of all was the cold I'd developed. I got a nasty throat infection, making it hard for me to sing during vocal rehearsals. I sensed the director was worried I might be unable to handle the workload. Of course, I assured him I could, but let's face it, I was the new kid on the block, so I couldn't blame him for having his doubts.

I struggled through the whole rehearsal process with the throat infection and finally had to go to a local clinic to get some antibiotics. By the end of rehearsals, I was somewhat ready. We'd crammed a lot into our two and a half weeks of rehearsing. We'd not only learned the show but had also been trained in skills pertaining to the service industry. We had to learn the computer system for ordering drinks and be able to carry trays of glasses to the customers. The computer I could handle, but taking a tray full of food and beverages to the audience terrified me. I hated that part of the job but agreed to do it, so that was that. When the opening night was finally upon us, I still had a script backstage and would run lines before going out to do certain scenes. I was terrified and exhilarated as I hit the stage for my debut performance as a theatre actor. This new avenue of artistic endeavor was indeed very satisfying. I was glad to have made this transition. Thank you, Marcia, for throwing down the gauntlet on that fateful night at the Sidetrack Cafe.

We spent three months in Winnipeg. The show ran for five consecutive nights each week. One element of each evening's performance I could have done without was childish and, in my mind, futile games we were forced to endure with the additional cast as a prelude to the show. It was supposed to create energy and enthuse everybody for the night ahead. The thought of having to run around playing "Simon Says" with a bunch of overgrown school kids just put me in a bad mood. Other than that, I looked forward to each night and became good friends with my cast mates.

We hung out at a piano bar at the hotel and would often have dinner together. It was a good time. As summer fast approached, it was time to return to Edmonton and open the show at the theatre in the West Edmonton Mall. The rest of the cast stayed in some condominiums provided by the company, but I stayed at home with Paula and the kids. This summer would be even more fun because Tanya was coming over for a visit. Life was good; I was thrilled to be home and able to perform by night and have my days to spend with the family.

Tanya and I spent a lot of time together during this period. I felt myself getting to know my daughter and finally having the relationship I'd wanted for so long. She was growing up, and we could discuss why I left England and pursued a career overseas. Tanya was very understanding and expressed an interest in coming to live with me. She had specific issues at that time and some problems at school. She'd been labelled a problem child concerning her attitude toward the teaching staff, although her academic capabilities were not questioned.

The mere idea of her coming to live with me was unbelievable. Of course, this would not happen immediately, but even having this to look forward to gave me hope. I loved my daughter from the day she was born. All I wanted to do was help her and create opportunities, so her life could be as fulfilling as humanly possible. It was a wonderful experience to have Tanya and the rest of my family come to see me perform at the theatre. I desperately wanted Tanya to see what I was doing. The night she was in the audience felt so gratifying to me. I introduced her, along with Mark, Randi, and Paula, to the cast. They had a great time, with the night being a tremendous success.

One of the girls in the cast lived on a farm. She told me her family farm had stables, and she enjoyed riding horses. Tanya had been riding horses in England for some time. She became quite an accomplished rider even at an early age. Paula and I had been paying for her lessons for many years as she had shown a keen interest in all things equestrian. I took Tanya to the farm, and she got to ride a beautiful horse. She had taken a few lessons while in Canada, so she was adept at riding Western style. I even got on the horse myself and bounced around the field, much to the amusement of all present. When the summer drew to a close, so did the show and the visit with my eldest daughter. Before she boarded the plane, she reaffirmed her desire to move to Canada. I could not have been happier. I looked forward to the day we would be reunited, and I could be a father to this beautiful child of mine.

The show never opened in Calgary as the theatre was not

completed in time to host us. However, I made it through my first theatre show, which was a success. The director and the rest of the production company were happy with me. It was agreed I would be in the next show, which would begin rehearsals in two months. I didn't bother looking for any other work in the interim but continued recording my new CD at the house and enjoyed spending time with Paula when she was home from her demanding touring schedule. My health was holding its own, and we kept pace with our financial obligations. I really couldn't have asked for more. Finally, I found my niche. I no longer had to work in sleazy bars playing old rock songs to a bunch of drunks. I had no desire to return to the bars and was perfectly content to work in the theatre. The crowds were large, and the money was steady. I looked forward to the next show. "WKLP Rock n Roll Radio."

For this next excursion to Winnipeg, I decided to fly. My last efforts at getting there by car had left a sour taste in my mouth, so I thought I would take to the sky for this trip. One of the other cast members and I boarded the plane and settled into our seats. It was a short flight ahead of us, and we enjoyed each other's company as the jet taxied out to the runway. The engines screamed, and we charged the runway like a rampant bull. We were soon off the ground and climbing into the sky.

I noticed we levelled out at a very low altitude during our ascent. This action made sense once the captain spoke over the intercom to inform us of a problem. At first, he was not specific, instead announced they would run some tests and assured us there was no cause for alarm. This was cause for alarm; I broke into an instant cold sweat. The sounds of revving engines and clunking resonated throughout the entire aircraft causing all aboard to question the safety and outcome of this flight.

Once again, the captain calmly spoke over the intercom and informed us the undercarriage was stuck and the jet stream would likely rip the wheels off if we climbed any higher. We had to land and get the wheels repaired. The only problem was that he was unsure whether the wheels were fully down and informed us of the possibility of them collapsing when we landed. If that were the case, the wing would likely hit the runway rendering this situation a somewhat unfavorable scenario as it was fully fueled and could explode upon impact.

As the plane slowly descended, I knew fate was out of my hands and asked the universal powers of nature for a favorable outcome. It was the most nerve-racking moment I have ever spent on an aircraft. Even when the wheels hit the runway, I had to hold my breath, wondering if the undercarriage would collapse. It didn't, and we taxied to a halt. When I was safely back in the terminal, I called Paula to inform her of the ordeal. We chatted for a while before it was time to get on an alternate jet. This time we took off, and all was well. After a short flight, I was in the fair city of Winnipeg, looking forward to getting started on the new production. After a short ride to the hotel, I unpacked my belongings in familiar surroundings. I enjoyed my experience the last time I was here and hoped to have a similar one on this trip.

The cast assembled for the meet and greet, most of whom were amiable. One of the female cast members was a bit above herself, but that wouldn't deter me from having a good time. The theatre in Calgary was finally open. We would be performing in three cities during this run. We signed on for nine months, and it would be a roller coaster ride for me. I had no idea at the beginning what was ahead of me; that's probably just as well. During rehearsals, we had a lot of fun in our downtime, and the cast became very close. We had parties at the hotel, and everyone bonded well, so we started as an excellent team.

Shortly into the run, some dissension in the ranks became apparent. One of the male members was an ad cast who had been given a chance to do a show due to his comedic physicality. It became evident he felt a closer kinship with his old ad-cast buddies and became ostracized from the rest of the group. One of the female cast members decided she was above the rest of us and became more annoying to work with daily. It would have been somewhat tolerable had she been as gifted as she thought, but this was not the case. These early rifts didn't heal and festered as the show progressed. The conflict disappointed me since I had relished every moment of the last show and enjoyed the time, I had shared with my old cast mates. Things were going to be different during this run.

I had written into my contract that I would not be required to serve drinks and could only be given light duties on the floor. I asked to include this legitimate clause in my contract to safeguard my well-being. Carrying trays full of drinks caused me to have pain in my groin. I did not want the hernia repair to fail, as this would mean I could no longer perform as part of this ensemble. They agreed when I presented my concerns to the company, and the clause was added. It antagonized the floor manager intensely. He tried everything to manipulate situations for me to recant the clause. However, I was adamant I would only do what had been agreed to, so he and I did not get along.

The atmosphere within the cast was getting decidedly frigid, and so was the Canadian winter. Then, on a snowy day in late November of 2001, I got a call from Paula which would cause me great anguish. She informed me of Tanya's expulsion from school in England. There had been allegations of drug use and alcohol consumption. She had also been accused of taking a weapon to school and associating with older girls who were indulging in ritualistic elements of the occult. It all turned out to be hugely exaggerated and primarily unfounded. Paula was also informed that Tanya no longer wanted to move to Canada. I was devastated. The dream of having my little girl with me was all but gone. I spiraled out of control into a deep depression and began to lose weight rapidly.

I couldn't eat or sleep. The more I thought about it, the worse I got. Finally, I went to a doctor to get some pills to calm my nerves and help me sleep at night. Unfortunately, this was the beginning of another addiction. I had finally freed myself from the grip of alcohol, but a new demon was waiting in the wings. I quickly became dependent on prescription drugs as they were the only way to ease my tension and relax at night. Having an addictive personality, to begin with, just made matters worse. Where I was supposed to be taking one pill, I would take a handful and enter into a state of complete oblivion.

Some nights I had to be held up on stage. I was more like Jim Morrison than the Johnny Rocket character I was supposed to portray.

It was becoming very apparent to all around me that something was wrong, even more so when I contracted viral bronchitis. Some nights between scenes, I would have my head down the dressing room toilet, hurling my guts up. A quick wipe down with a towel and a splash of cold water on my face, and I was back on stage.

As December approached, I was a complete mess. I now weighed 147 lbs., 33 lbs. shy of my weight when I started the show. I was gaunt and looked like I had prison pallor. I had to use an asthma pump to breathe and couldn't face eating much in the way of food. I was lucky if I managed to stomach a bread roll and some soup each day. Christmas was soon upon us, and I was addicted to prescription drugs. I couldn't function without them, so there was no easy way to kick the habit. I wasn't enjoying the show; the nights seemed endless. The best way to get through it was to stay stoned, which I did.

Eventually, the run ended in Winnipeg, and it was time to return to Edmonton. I was able to see my doctor and describe how I was feeling. He told me I should try Paxil to see if it helped my depression and anxiety. I agreed and now had a cocktail of drugs daily to keep me happy and help me sleep. Paula was travelling all over Alberta and ended up being away from home a lot of the time. She knew of my condition but had her contractual obligations to fulfil. I felt very lonely without her, but the situation was what it was.

I have always been my own worst enemy when all I have for company is myself. I tend to over-analyze things and create problems that don't exist other than in my twisted psyche. The run in Edmonton was tedious and unfulfilling for me; honestly, I only remember a little about it. There are, however, a couple of nights that stand out in my mind. When Paula returned to the city, she brought one of her colleagues to the theatre. I had fun dancing with them and involving them in the show. Randi celebrated her birthday at a show. I had a great time spoiling her and getting her on stage with me. Other than that, I spent most of my time in a medically induced haze, counting the days until the show ended.

When the run in Edmonton was over, Paula and I took a well-deserved break and jetted off to the Bahamas. Even that was fraught with annoyance, as at the beginning of our trip, we had to sit in the aircraft for an hour or so while they tried to clear the ice from the wheels frozen to the runway. We spent a few days in Fort Lauderdale before boarding a ship to the Bahamas. We were only there briefly but had so much fun. I was still taking pills but being with Paula calmed me a lot. I was able to remain coherent and enjoyed our time together. We rounded off our trip in Orlando before returning to the frozen wastes of Edmonton.

The vacation was terrific; I loved every moment of it. It was time to return to the show and a new theatre in Calgary. Nothing changed. I thought the new venue might inspire me, but I was wrong. It was not long before I took too many pills again and hated life. I was not taking Paxil anymore but had opted for alternate anti-psychotic drugs. Whatever I was swallowing, it was doing nothing for my well-being. That much was certain. The only good thing from the run in Calgary was a visit from the musical director who worked at the Mayfield Hotel. You may remember that the Mayfield was where I'd worked some years earlier when I was desperate for money. Back then, I was lugging boxes and stocking up the bar in the theatre while the actors prepared for their nightly performances. I had watched them with envy as I went about my menial tasks as a glorified errand boy. Could this be an opportunity for vindication? Would it be possible for me to return to Mayfield as an actor in one of its forthcoming productions?

The music director showed a keen interest in my talents, and we discussed the possibility of me being part of the next production. The Mayfield was regarded as the best venue in the city for musical theatre productions. It would be a significant upgrade into the major leagues if I could secure a position in one of their shows. I would have to be content with the fact that interest had been taken in me, and the possibility of being hired was indeed just that. On my days off in Calgary, I contacted some talent agencies, seeking employment as an extra. Calgary had several agencies. I'd approached a few of them with little success, but one gave me a contact number for the casting director who worked on the Mentors show; a Disney production. This number would come in handy later on, but for right now, I had to focus on making it to the end of the run I was currently involved in.

On Canada Day, we played a game of soccer which pitched ad cast and cast members against each other. Even Paula played in this contest and displayed tremendous skills on the pitch. Unfortunately, during the game, the outcome of a hard tackle resulted in the fracturing of my wrist. For the remaining two weeks in Calgary, I had my arm in a sling, and the director ended up writing the whole bizarre affair into the script. The nine months drew to a close, and I was relieved it was over. I had no desire to socialize at the end-of-show party, so as soon as my bags were packed, I loaded the car and drove back to Edmonton. Jubilations had run its course for me. I wanted to step up to the first division and secure a contract at the Mayfield dinner theatre.

For the duration of my nine months performing the WKLP show, I familiarized myself with the internet and learned how to use it as a marketing tool. I signed up for a site called MP3.com. This site allowed independent musicians to showcase their original music and have CDs manufactured for resale. I was able to advertise my music in the theatre brochures, which attracted many people to the MP3 site. I sold some discs and topped the MP3 charts with a couple of my songs. It was gratifying modestly but also made me realize it was time to change my thinking regarding my aspirations for a record deal.

The industry had changed and was a different ball game altogether from when I started. Anybody can market themselves to a worldwide audience these days with the simple click of a mouse. I could make money and achieve sales without a record label. I was self-sufficient and could record everything independently, so there was no overhead. This new approach would be my focus for the future. I would become an independent artist with his own record label, and to hell with the big companies. They would have little interest in me at my age, so why flog a dead horse? First, though, it was time to bask in the sun in Mexico with my beautiful wife and try to curb my prescription drug addiction.

Martin Andrew

Gallery 15

The new look for my acting career 2001.

TLA management head office.

Recording some new songs 2001.

Dance rehearsals for the Magnum show.

Tanya in the Theater lobby.

Vacation in the Bahamas.

Boating in Miami.

Left: Bahamas with Paula. **Right:** Mexico with Amanda.

Left: Florida. **Right:** Cruise ship party.

Celebrating Randi's Birthday at the Theater.

Hanging out with "Dickie Bongos".

Marvin the Bastard with Paula in the kitchen.

In the backyard with the kids.

All photographs from Martin Andrew private collection.

Chapter Sixteen

THE VACATION IN MEXICO WAS JUST WHAT I NEEDED TO RECHARGE MY batteries and boost my enthusiasm. We stayed at a beautiful location by the marina in Puerto Vallarta and enjoyed long, lazy days just basking in the sun. I was adhering to the prescribed amount of medication, so I could function and felt no need to overindulge. The only thing bothering me was the cast on my broken wrist. It hindered my ability to get a good suntan, and I was not too fond of it. I gave into my vanity and removed it by smashing it on a countertop and gouging it off with a bread knife.

During the vacation, my thoughts turned to what was next for me. An opportunity presented itself during the final run of the WKLP show when the music director from the Mayfield approached me at one of the shows in Calgary. The Mayfield was preparing for the sequel to the successful Christmas show "The British Are Coming" and may require my services. I was flattered and excited about the prospect of performing there. It was the best gig in town in that particular entertainment genre and would be a real feather in my cap should I get it.

Once we were back in Edmonton, I contacted the music director and scheduled an audition. They wanted to see me act out a comedic scene and sing some songs. I decided to do the famous parrot sketch from Monty Python's Flying Circus and would sing a couple of numbers from the show I had just completed. I asked Richie aka Dickie Bongos, a good friend from the WKLP cast if he would help me with the parrot sketch, and he agreed.

When it was time for me to audition, I had my lines rehearsed, but no parrot. We had a stuffed owl at the house, which had been used to scare off pigeons, so I took it to substitute for the infamous parrot. The audition went well, with me beating up on this stuffed bird, much to the surprise and amusement of the director. I sang my songs and was told they would let me know when they had made a decision. I knew that phrase all too well and hoped for the best but expected the worst.

My fears were unfounded. After being called back for a second and more grueling audition, I was offered the job. I was thrilled. I would be part of a cast of eight actors working alongside some of the best musicians in the city. It would be a triumphant return to the Mayfield, which was the place where I mopped floors and lugged boxes while listening in awe to the rehearsals in the theatre. This time I would be performing on the stage and not just admiring those, doing so from afar. Rehearsals were set to begin in October of 2002, and I was ready and raring to go. I wanted to be entirely focused on what I was doing. It was a big show and required a lot of diligence regarding the learning process. I got off most of the drugs I'd been taking and only used sleeping pills to ensure a good night's rest. It seemed as though I was finally getting myself back on track.

Since the onset of this mental health crisis, I'd been trying my best to help Tanya through her educational dilemma, having been expelled from school. She was fifteen years old and had all the problems of a teenager. She wasn't having the best time at home and had been out of school for quite a while. After numerous applications, she was accepted by a school in her designated district and could continue her studies. She had a lot of catching up to do, which created a great deal of pressure for a child her age.

During one of our long-distance phone calls, Tanya informed me she had a new boyfriend. The boy she was seeing was twenty years old. When I heard this revelation, I was not happy about it. However, it was decided she would come and visit for Christmas that year. She asked if she could bring her boyfriend. I agreed to this because I wanted to see what sort of character he was and, if possible, end what I considered an unhealthy relationship. I knew what he was after, and if I had anything to do with it, I would prevent it, or if it had already happened, I would stop it.

Before Tanya's Christmas vacation, I had a lot of work ahead of me getting prepared for the show. The script was long, and the show had about ninety songs. It was way more intense than any Jubilation show I had been involved with. To be honest, I kept thinking about the old phrase, "Be careful what you wish for." So, of course, I had wished for this, but could I do a good job and meet the required standards? Only time will tell.

The first day of rehearsals proved to be anything but intimidating as this was an equity union production, and everything had to be done by the book. The floor manager paid close attention to our rehearsal schedule and used a stopwatch to ensure we got our breaks at the appropriate time. The cast were all seasoned vets of the Mayfield shows and made me feel most welcome. The rehearsal process itself was different from what I expected. Vocally we rehearsed harmonies and were responsible and trusted to sort out our lead parts. The acting portion was also left for us to interpret to a certain extent. The director watched what you did and then fine-tuned it as he saw fit. The hardest part for me, as always, was the choreography.

The lady in charge of our dance routines (Christine) was stunning and very talented as a choreographer. The most intimidating and difficult routine was when I had to learn the steps for "Supercalifragilistic-expialidocious" and found out she was playing the part of Mary Poppins. However, Christine was very patient with me, and the routine became one of my favorites in the show. At the end of the day's rehearsal, I would go home and practice all the moves and lines I learned. It was hard to keep pace with all the edits and rewrites, but I wanted to ensure I was ready for opening night which was fast approaching.

We'd been in the rehearsal room for two weeks when the opening night was upon us. I recall we went to a local restaurant before the show when I expressed my concerns about not being fully prepared. Everybody else was of the same mindset, which I found very reassuring in a funny way. It was not long before we were standing behind the curtain, waiting for the show to begin. I was terrified and didn't feel confident that I was ready for this mammoth performance. When the curtain opened, and I saw this sea of anticipating faces, I was trembling with fear as I uttered my first words.

Through fear and trembling, I slowly settled into the show. It was great to be a part of this, not only for the content and the people I was working with but for the sheer fact I felt vindicated. Yes, I worked in this same building stocking shelves and unloading trucks in the bitter cold; I had even been invited on stage one night when a Tina Turner tribute artist named Hollie Vest had me roll up my trousers and gyrate to the overtures of "Proud Mary." I was back, and this time, I was an actor. Opening night was a huge success. I felt accomplished when it was over. The Mayfield was the big gig in town; I was so proud to be a part of it.

The show was scheduled for four months, which meant I would have a steady income for the duration, which was always good. As Christmas approached, I looked forward to spending it with my family and my eldest daughter, who was flying in from the UK. It was the first Christmas Tanya, and I would spend together since leaving the UK in 1989. It was an exceptional time, and I wanted to ensure everything was perfect for her stay.

The house was decked out with a ridiculous amount of lights; Paula made the place look amazing. She went to the airport to pick up Tanya and her boyfriend as I put the finishing touches of paint on the new porch I had been struggling to complete. I waited with bated breath until I heard the front door open and saw my beautiful Tanya standing before me. She looked fantastic, but the first impression I got from her so-called boyfriend was not so good.

He had a vacant expression, and when he opened his mouth to speak, it was the most inaudible dialect I'd ever heard. I didn't like him from day one, and he was affectionately known as the "Lab Rat" from that day on. I was determined to end this relationship, but it was Christmas, so I had to proceed cautiously. I most sincerely hoped Tanya would see him for the true idiot he was and dump him of her own volition. This kid wasn't even good-looking. I just couldn't figure out the attraction for the life of me, and I was not alone. Mark and Randi found him irritating and obnoxious, as did Paula and anybody else who came into contact with him. For now, though, Tanya was blind to all his faults, so we proceeded with the festive season culminating in a disastrous meal on Christmas day with all the frills of a dysfunctional family gathering.

I booked a table at a beautiful restaurant for the festive feast. I wanted the whole family together for a wonderful and memorable Christmas dinner. Unfortunately, the entire event was ruined by the lab rat, who decided he didn't like anything on the menu and wasted all his food which cost a small fortune. I had to excuse myself at one point before I exploded. Things didn't get any better as we approached the new year.

One particular night, things got heated between Paula and Tanya after Tanya, and I argued over something which, in retrospect, was quite ridiculous. Everything I hoped for was going to hell in a handbasket. As the time drew near for their departure, I had a fatherly discussion with Tanya about her relationship. She concluded it was not a healthy relationship and assured me once they got home, he would be history. I was very relieved to hear it. It had been wonderful to see her again, but Christmas had been a disaster for Paula and I, who had hoped for so much and ended up struggling just to put a smile on our faces.

As we entered the new year, my contract at the Mayfield was coming to an end. I was delighted that my dear friend Don McKenzie made it out to see me, as we hadn't seen much of each other lately. He had been busy with his investment work, and I had been out of town a lot with the theatre shows. We always connected via telephone but seeing him sitting in the audience that day was great. Don was always very supportive of my endeavors. This was a trait that never faltered over the years. He told me he enjoyed the show. We agreed to have a spot of tea at my house and discuss more in-depth what we were both doing.

We discussed many old and new things at our meeting, but Don had a few specific topics he wanted to talk about. He chatted about what his life meant to him and what kind of a legacy he would like to leave behind when he was gone. He was getting a few things off his chest. I felt such a discussion was a little premature since he appeared to be in good health. We parted ways, and unbeknownst to me, that would be the last time I would see Don alive.

A couple of weeks later, after a matinee show, I arrived home to find Paula in tears. She told me Heather called and gave her the bad news that Don had died. I broke down in tears and was devastated to hear that my good friend had passed away. That night I struggled to get through the show as I only kept thinking about Don and the great times we shared in this wild entertainment world. It was a tragic loss and the end of an era for me.

I was a pallbearer at his funeral. The turnout to pay tribute to this great man was huge. All those involved in the Canadian music scene were well acquainted with Don McKenzie and arrived in droves to pay their final respects. During the ceremony, the priest spoke very eloquently about Don, as did others who had known him. The priest handed me the keys to the Blue Goose 2. It was officially announced in the chapel that I was the proud new owner. It was a token gesture as the bus had no ignition keys, but it was one of immense meaning to me. Don was buried on a cold winter's day in February 2003. I will never forget him as long as I live. He was a great man.

The British invasion show was now at an end. I enjoyed it immensely but had never really settled into it. I don't know why; I knew what I was doing, but I was always a little uneasy before and during the performances. I hoped to be invited to perform in another show. This was highly unlikely as the theatre hosted many different productions, I knew I wouldn't be suitable for. I wasn't interested in returning to Jubilations, so I weighed my options and decided to make a call.

The call I made was to the man whose number I had acquired in

Calgary. He was a casting director, so I thought it would be worthwhile calling him to see if there were any openings for me in the Disney show "Mentors." As it turned out, he was the extras casting director, so the chance of auditioning for a significant part in the show would not be possible. Nevertheless, I arranged to meet with him. Our initial meeting went well, and he got me on set immediately.

Extra work is fun the first time, but after that, it can get a little boring. You sit in a holding tank for hours listening to everybody tell tall tales about how they are credible actors and just doing this for a few extra bucks. Any fool off the street can be an extra, which became apparent from my first experience on set. So why was I there? I was there because I needed the meagre income it could supply me, and I was hoping it might lead to better things. These were false hopes, although I got to appear in a movie called "White Coats" and was fortunate to be introduced to Dave Thomas, who directed the film starring Dan Akroyd.

I was never given a leading role or even considered for a minor one. I was just one of the crowd waiting patiently to be hustled on and off set with the rest of the wannabe actors. I deserved better than this, and not in an arrogant or egotistical way. I had done theatre roles and knew I could handle something more challenging than merely blending into the background.

One day I got a call to audition for a TV commercial. The commercial was for the Lutheran Church of Canada. I didn't care about the subject but was determined to get the part as this was a speaking role for national television. The audition went well, and I soon found myself on set. What a difference it was to be in a principal position. I was pampered beyond belief, and I must admit I enjoyed every minute.

We filmed the first part of the commercial at a local residence. I worked with a lady who played my TV wife and two children. Everybody worked well together, and we finished filming part one of the commercial by mid-afternoon. The second part of the commercial was filmed at a local cemetery. I couldn't believe it when we arrived at the place, I'd helped lay Don to rest only a month earlier. It was a very surreal experience as the scene we were filming was of a funeral, but in a way, it was strangely comforting. It was as if he was still watching me and taking pride in another achievement of mine. Soon my day of filming ended, but before leaving the location, I quickly visited Don's graveside.

Aside from a few other roles as an extra, limited opportunities were forthcoming for this aspiring thespian. However, I was struggling to find something to occupy my mind, so periodically I could be found hanging out at local bars chatting with old friends. On such an occasion, I ran into a man, who like others before him, would change my life. I decided to visit a local strip club and chat with my old friend Chris on this particular occasion. He and I worked at Rusty's, and I often dropped in to see him at the new club where he bartended. While sitting at the bar nursing a Diet Coke, Chris introduced me to an Elvis impersonator. I reluctantly entered into a conversation with him as I had a preconceived idea about how stupid impersonators were. My preconception was unjustified.

My first meeting with Robin was delightful and informative. First, we chatted about his show and briefly discussed what I'd been doing. Then, he asked me if I would like to do a show with him. At first, I thought he wanted me to hand him scarves and glasses of water, but he wanted me to join his show as a singer. Next, he asked me if I would like to impersonate Rod Stewart.

I had been plagued with people comparing my look to Rod's, but my hair was short and brown at this point in my career. Robin convinced me that by adding some highlights and spiking my hair, I could do a credible impersonation of the man in question. The last time I impersonated Rod was at Jubilations when I was learning the tricks of the trade for musical theatre. I enjoyed spoofing the spiky-haired rocker but wasn't that interested in this kind of work and never had been. I'd always thought tribute acts were so pretentious and, frankly, quite stupid. Robin was very persuasive and having spoken to him at length and hearing how much I would be paid, I agreed to try it.

Robin told me I could audition whenever I was ready, but sooner would be better. I sang a few Rod Stewart songs with the Martin Andrew Band, so I felt comfortable auditioning for this new role vocally. I bought a red jacket from a thrift store along with a couple of ties and added a lot of highlights to my hair. After some intense back-combing and excessive hairspray, I was ready to debut as a Rod Stewart impersonator. All I needed now was a sound stage to perform on for the audition, so I booked some time at the Edmonton Music Society facility. It had a small stage with a PA system, an ideal setting for a one-person show. Roger agreed to accompany me for the audition, run sound and film my performance. I acquired a couple of karaoke tracks for the audition and having run through the songs several times, I was ready.

When Robin arrived, he was not alone. All those associated with his show accompanied him, including his mother, who was his manager. I sang, danced, and did my best to look like the legendary rocker. When I was done, Robin and his entourage gave me their verdict. They loved everything about my performance, and I was hired immediately. He had shows already scheduled, so I had two months to get my act together then it would be time to start performing at the local casinos.

Around the same time as I was forging a new career as an impersonator, Paula had also been thinking about making a change. It was not so much a career change as an expansion of territories to work in. She'd been performing at the same venues for quite a while and wanted to explore the possibilities of working somewhere new. Paula is of native heritage and, as a Cree Indian with treaty status, can work anywhere in North America. She talked to several girls who worked in America and had been given favorable reviews.

Paula and I felt our respective careers had plateaued. Life in Canada was becoming stagnant. There was little work for me, and she was fed up with travelling and being away from home so much. A place that seemed able to solve all our problems was the very place where we had been married. Las Vegas. In Vegas, she could work at a club in the city without needing to travel. The problem with dancing in Alberta was she had to move around a lot as the club patrons were locals, and a fresh lineup of girls was required each week. In Vegas, the patrons were tourists, so the club's clientele changed every night, allowing girls to work in one club for as long as they liked. Since I decided to pursue a career as an impersonator, what better place to do it than sin city?

We discussed our options at length and decided in August of 2003 to head south and check things out by spending a week in Las Vegas. Robin's mother informed me her eldest son was also an Elvis impersonator who worked at the Stratosphere in Las Vegas. She was going to see him in early August, so we coordinated our trip with her. My first show with Robin was in late August, so I took my tracks and lyrics with me to continue learning the songs for the show. We boarded an aircraft to Las Vegas. After a short flight and shuttle ride, we checked into our hotel. We'd opted for staying at the Palace Station Casino as it was close to all the clubs we wanted to evaluate.

Our first day was spent checking out the local clubs. We chatted with several managers, who told us that Paula must complete a background check and file other documents with the city before being eligible for employment. Next, we hailed a taxi and visited all the relevant licensing facilities in Las Vegas. Having completed a background check, filled out the appropriate forms, and answered numerous questions, Paula was issued a Sheriff's card. She was now ready for her first day at work in Las Vegas.

I was so anxious for her as she caught a cab and headed off for her first day of employment in Sin City. I spent that afternoon trying to learn lyrics for my upcoming debut as a Rod Stewart impersonator. It wasn't easy; all I could think of was Paula and how she got on at the club. But I need not have worried. When she returned to the hotel, she gave me a full debriefing and told me how her day had been a success. She made some friends during her short day of employment at the club and felt comfortable with the new environment.

We met Robin's mother at the Stratosphere and attended the "American Superstars" show. Several celebrity impersonators were in the show, including Robin's brother Darren. I watched intently and visualized myself on the stage performing as Rod. If I was going to become a Rod Stewart impersonator, this seemed like the place to be. This trip to Las Vegas gave us a greater perspective of what life would be like in this vibrant city. We decided to take a serious look at the possibility of moving from Canada to the USA.

We finished the week celebrating Paula's birthday, basking in the sun, and discussing our next move. Upon our return to Edmonton, we contacted the American immigration authorities and explained our situation to them. They gave us the green light to apply for our green cards. We were told Paula didn't need a green card. Treaty Indians have no borders and can freely move around North America without visas or work permits. Since I was married to Paula, I would be approved for permanent residency, and so would Paula's children.

We were ecstatic to hear this news as it sounded like the application process would be straightforward and expedited with relative ease. I stress the word "sounded" as we found out later the information, we were given was erroneous at best. However, at this stage, it was full steam ahead. We acquired the relevant forms, filled out a mountain of paperwork, got pictures and various other notarized documents organized, and were ready to submit our application. When the package was signed and sealed, I breathed a sigh of relief and delivered it to the post office, where it could start its journey to the immigration office in Nebraska. Since we'd been told the process would be straightforward, we saw no merit in wasting time and began looking online for apartments in Las Vegas. We decided to put our home in Edmonton on the real estate market, assuming we would get a quick sale and be on our way post haste. Now it was the waiting game.

We found a suitable apartment at the Sahara Palms complex across the street from the Palace Station Casino. Having stayed at the Casino in August, we had a chance to survey the surrounding area, finding it safe and clean. It was an ideal location. The club Paula worked at during our reconnaissance trip was close by, so I booked our move-in date for October 5, 2003. At this stage, we were under the assumption that all three of us would be moving to America without any problems. I say only three of us as Mark decided to stay with his father in Canada, only Randi had shown a keen interest in moving to America.

In the meantime, it was business as usual with Paula out on the road, Randi in school, and myself preparing for my first show as "Rod

Stewart." I'd rehearsed enough material for two forty-five-minute sets. Before I knew it, I was sitting backstage at the Argyle Casino, waiting to be introduced. A bunch of friends had come to see my debut performance, but I couldn't relax for some reason. It was the first time I'd done a show like this. I was pretending to be someone else. Rod Stewart was a legend, so I had to make sure my interpretation of him and his music was authentic and believable.

I heard my introduction and walked out onto the stage. I was so tense that my throat wouldn't loosen up. I struggled to get through the first couple of songs, knowing everyone in the showroom was judging me. I was plagued with a sense of fear and dread during the first set, so relieved when it drew to its conclusion. It should have been so easy! I rehearsed for weeks preparing for this show, and here I was blowing it because I was so uptight. It was unacceptable; I was determined to do better in the second set.

I managed to loosen up and gained confidence as the night progressed. By night's end, I was screaming like a banshee as I belted out Rod's hits to an enthusiastic crowd. The night was a success, and I was officially on the roster as the new Rod Stewart impersonator in town. This portrayal of Rod came very naturally to me as there were a lot of parallels that could be drawn between the way he and I performed. I had never tried to emulate him, but the reality was I just looked like him and sounded like him when performing. People assumed I studied his every move before my debut. The truth is, I had not seen him perform since I watched Top of the Pops back in England all those years ago.

Many impersonators use a ton of makeup to look like the original artist. All I had to do was arrive at a venue with messy hair, wearing colorful clothing, and I was this apparent ringer for Rod. It was an easy fit for me, so I decided to exploit it for all it was worth. Fortunately, I liked his music; the more I sang it, the more I enjoyed it. I looked forward to the shows with Robin at the casinos in Edmonton, but my ultimate goal was to hone my skills at these venues and try my luck in Las Vegas. It was time to roll the dice.

Gallery 16

Promotional Show pictures from the Mayfield Theater.

Photographs courtesy of the Mayfield Dinner theater.

Martin Andrew

Happy faces! Christmas at West Edmonton Mall 2002.

Trying to enjoy the festive season at Casa Andrew.

Photographs from Martin Andrew private collection.

Gondola ride celebrating Paula's birthday August 2003.

First show performing as a Rod Stewart.

Photograph from Martin Andrew private collection.

Chapter Seventeen

OCTOBER WAS FAST APPROACHING, SO PAULA AND I MADE OUR FINAL preparations for the trip. First, we would drive to Las Vegas, and once Paula was settled into our new apartment, I would take the Greyhound home, leaving her with the car. In our absence, a friend stayed at our house in Edmonton. Marvin had been lodging with us for a while and was reliable, so we had no worries concerning Randi's well-being while we were away. Finally, the hour was at hand, and we set off on the long drive to Las Vegas. Crossing the border is always a bit nerve-racking, but we gained safe passage south. After driving for the whole day, we found a little motel and decided to get some rest. We were again on our way by early morning and finally pulled into Vegas at around 5 pm on Sunday, October 5th, 2003. We'd arrived early but decided to see if they would let us have the keys; otherwise, we would be back at the Palace Station for the night.

We were pleasantly surprised when we arrived at the complex. We talked to the lady at the office, and after signing a few papers, we were handed our keys. We drove to the rear of the complex and parked the car. It felt good as we unlocked the door to our new home and entered our new abode. We dropped off our luggage at the apartment and explored our new neighborhood. The surrounding area was relatively quiet, and our apartment was close to one of the swimming pools. We concluded this to be an ideal place to begin our American adventure.

We had no furniture, no television; we didn't even have a bed to sleep on, so we made a makeshift mattress on the floor out of our sleeping bags and got some well-earned sleep. The following day the sun was out; it was time to get organized. The first thing we did was make a trip to Walmart to get some furnishings for our new home. We got the bare necessities, including a small television and a futon to sleep on. Once that was in place, we decided to go to the immigration office to get our green cards.

As I've already stated, we were told this process would be straightforward, and we would get our cards immediately. Instead, having lined up for over an hour, we talked to an immigration official who dropped a bombshell of catastrophic proportions. The information we based so many decisions on was false. As a North American Indian, Paula could work and live in America without a visa or green card, but as far as I was concerned, it was a different story.

For me to live in America and get a permanent resident card, Paula would have to "upgrade" and then sponsor me, which could take years. It was disgusting and racially charged when they used "upgrade" to describe Paula's transition to becoming a permanent resident. We found out very quickly that when dealing with immigration officials, you just had to listen and keep quiet. They had no genuine interest in our situation and were dictatorial in dealing with us. We were told the same criteria applied to Randi, and as a British citizen, I had no rights in America. I was advised to return home immediately as I'd made my intentions clear about working and staying in America to an immigration official.

We walked out of that office with our dreams shattered. We had taken the plunge into what now seemed to be a bottomless pit of disappointment. What on earth were we going to do? Everything had been geared towards this move. The house in Edmonton was up for sale, and we had already leased the apartment in Vegas and signed a twelve-month contract. We were down but by no means out. There had to be a way to get this sorted out.

The Road to the Manor

We knew Paula had to apply for a green card, so we filled out the relevant forms and filed them. We had already sent forms to Nebraska for Randi and I and hoped those might be approved. Unfortunately, the chances were very slim, and even if they were approved, it could take years to get our permanent resident cards. My trip back to Edmonton wouldn't be so triumphant after all. I had to leave Paula alone and get on a Greyhound bus for the journey north. Knowing she would be alone and working extra hard to support two homes broke my heart. As the bus pulled out of the station, I felt ill and wondered if there was any way to salvage this situation. It seemed hopeless, but at the same time, I was determined to find a way out of this predicament.

When I arrived back in Edmonton, I had to break the news to Randi. She wasn't happy being separated from her mother. It had been different when Paula was away from home working in Alberta. Now, she was living in another country, and we had no idea how this situation would develop. I tried to assure her everything would be fine, but deep down inside, I had reservations. We weren't having much success with the immigration authorities. Whenever we thought we were getting somewhere, another disaster would befall us as we were given more wrong information. I went to see Paula before the year ended, but most of my time was spent in Edmonton trying to sell the house.

Randi and I spent Christmas with our good friends Roger and Cheryl and enjoyed a fabulous festive feast. They were staunch supporters of our move to America and keen to help in any way they could. During one of our many conversations, Cheryl pointed out that we might have some trouble getting Randi across the border as she was a minor and would need the consent of both her natural parents. This was going to be a substantial stumbling block.

When we asked for her natural father's permission, he refused to allow her to travel unless he was released from his obligation to pay child support for her. This prompted legal action and more expenses for lawyers as they sorted out an agreement. A judge would have the final say. We hoped no travel restrictions would be enforced. We were successful in our quest. It was made official that Randi was now in the sole custody of her mother, and her father was out of the picture.

Early in 2004, Paula sought legal advice about our situation and consulted with an immigration lawyer who painted a very different picture for us. There was a way to get us all to America. On my next trip south, Paula and I met with the lawyer and listened intently to what she had to say. She explained I could receive an O1 visa if I could gain sponsorship from an American talent agency and prove that nobody else in America could perform a Rod Stewart impersonation as well as I could. If I could get one of these O1 visas, Randi, as my stepdaughter, would be able to get an O3 visa allowing her to live in America and attend school. All of this would be coupled with a new application for permanent resident cards, as the other application I'd filed would likely be rejected. It was a long shot, but with our lawyer at the helm, it seemed we just might be able to turn our situation around.

I was sent back to Canada with two projects. First, I had to compile as much information about my musical career and how it pertained to being a Rod Stewart impersonator. Second, I had to find a Las Vegas agency to sponsor me. Over the years, I'd kept a lot of contracts and other memorabilia, which came in very handy when putting this dossier together. I dug up everything I could find. On my next trip to Vegas, I delivered a colossal parcel to our lawyer, whose job was to sort through it and compile a presentation to be reviewed by those who would decide my fate. The next thing I had to do was find an agent.

During this particular stay in Vegas, I found myself sitting in the lounge bar at the Venetian Hotel, watching a band. I asked them about the local scene and who they would recommend as a potential booking agent. They were most helpful and told me that Steve Beyer Productions was the town's biggest and best agency. I did a little research on the Internet and found this agency was indeed a vast enterprise. They had several impersonators on their roster. I felt confident if I could meet with Steve Beyer, he would be suitably impressed with my image, which may lead to a discussion of a possible sponsorship agreement.

I called his office and set up an appointment. It was a huge agency, but to my surprise, the man himself was relatively small in stature but very personable and not intimidating at all. I'd brought a video for Steve to look at, and although it was a reasonably basic recording, I felt comfortable having him review it. It was an accurate representation of the skill set I had to offer. I watched Steve's body language as the first track kicked in; I was elated to see he enjoyed the video immensely.

When asked if I'd be interested in performing "Rod" as part of a production show he was staging at the Venetian Casino on the strip, I couldn't believe my ears. He needed one more impersonator for the show and, having been suitably impressed with my promotional video, offered me a job. I broached the subject of having his company sponsor me. After a brief moment of pause, he agreed and offered to fill out any paperwork required by immigration. This was one of my better days.

The show was scheduled for April 30th, 2004. The showroom I was to perform in was C2K, with a capacity of around 1500. What a way to start my career in Las Vegas. Paula and I went to the law office and gave our lawyer the excellent news. I don't think she could quite believe it. I was delighted with the outcome of my meeting with the Steve Beyer agency. She continued her legal efforts on our behalf, and I returned to Edmonton, where preparations would begin for my Las Vegas debut.

For Randi's birthday in March of 2004, we decided to fly her down to Vegas to see what she thought of her future home. Randi spent some time with her mother and, by all accounts, thoroughly enjoyed the trip. We were so relieved she enjoyed herself on that mini vacation. We'd taken her ability to adjust to living in a different country for granted, but after this trip, those concerns were no longer an issue. Of course, this was a huge life change for her, but it seemed from her enthusiasm during the vacation she would be able to cope with uprooting from Canada and relocating to America.

Upon her return, I took her out for a birthday dinner at The Keg and listened with great intent as she thrilled me with tales of her exploits in sin city. I smiled at her as she spoke and admired this wonderful child before me. I was very proud to have her in my life and looked forward to a future with her and Paula. The idea of the three of us living together without having to travel all the time and being apart was so appealing to me. Things were looking good. As we finished our meal and drove home, I ran through different scenarios of what life would be like in the months and years to come.

By clinching the deal with Steve Beyer, I had met all the criteria required for the O1 to be submitted for approval. It was quite a lengthy process, but by paying an extra $1000.00 to the government, we could expedite things. Funny how money can always speed things up. The documents we'd compiled were first sent to the American Federation of Musicians in New York. They had to review the material and sign a document stating that I was indeed qualified to perform the task of impersonating Rod Stewart in such a fashion that nobody else in America would be suitable for the said position. They concurred this was indeed the case, and we were halfway to getting the O1 visa approval.

Next, the package and the letter had to be sent to the California immigration authorities for them to put their stamp of approval on it and for a visa request to be issued. The visa had to be issued in Canada, so we opted to have our final interview at the American consulate in Calgary. Along with the O1 I'd qualified for, an O3 would be issued to Randi, and we would both be allowed into America for one year to work and attend school, respectively.

With all the documentation being handled by our lawyer stateside, I was thrilled to be back in Canada to try and get the house sold and prepare myself for the forthcoming concert. There had been some interest in our humble home, and there was a strong possibility the interested parties would make an offer. Things were finally falling into place. It had been a long time coming, but ultimately, we were getting closer to our dream.

Paula decided to come back to Edmonton for a visit which coincided with my travelling back to Las Vegas for the show at the Venetian. We saw each other for a day or so before I had to catch a plane heading south. Arriving at the airport, I checked my bags and proceeded to the security checkpoint. The immigration agent questioned me about my frequent travel to America. I was lucky he was of a friendly disposition (a rare commodity in that profession), as he warned me, I'd been flagged and that subsequent trips across the border might not be without incident.

I boarded the aircraft. I was back on American soil three hours later. I took a cab to the apartment; staying there alone was weird. How Paula managed to be alone in that apartment for all those months was beyond me. She was a stronger person than I. Our car had remained in Vegas, so after a quick shower, I fired it up and headed toward the strip for the show.

When I entered the building, I was shocked at the size of it. The stage was enormous, sporting a massive projection screen high above it for those who needed a decent vantage point. I met the other impersonators. We sat and chatted for a while until I was called to the stage for my sound check. I was a little nervous, but with all eyes upon me, I blasted through my short set and was relieved that I didn't tense up and my voice was in good shape.

Following the sound check, it was the waiting game as we consumed cold cuts and bottled water in the green room. I was the opening act for the show, and there would be a grand finale with all the entertainers on stage. Steve Beyer was coming to the show to check me out, and the robotic television cameras in the establishment would be put to good use filming the night's performance.

Show time arrived. I launched onto the stage, giving the best impersonation of "Rod" I could deliver. The stage was so big I almost lost my breath from running around and interacting with the band. No sooner was I on, and it seemed I was off again. Time does fly when you're having fun. I received congratulations all around and marked the night up as a glorious success. Two scantily clad models escorted me around the audience as part of the night's proceedings. I'd been instructed to meet and greet those in attendance and pose for pictures. The whole night was excellent, and as it drew to a close, I felt so good that I couldn't stop smiling. Steve was happy with my performance and congratulated me on a successful night. It was official. We were now in business together.

I packed my things and headed out to find the car, which was easier said than done. In all the excitement, I failed to note where I parked the damn thing and spent about forty minutes searching for it. The slight frustration of misplacing the car could not cast a cloud over such a fantastic night. On my way back to our apartment, I drove the length of the Las Vegas strip. I had achieved something significant in performing at the Venetian that night and wanted to revel in the moment's glory.

The moment passed, and I was soon back at the apartment, lying in the darkness, still grinning from ear to ear and replaying the night's highlights. I drifted off to sleep that night with a feeling of great contentment. In the morning, it was back to the airport. After a short flight, I was back in Edmonton with Paula and Randi relaying the tale of my first show. The other good news when I arrived home was the house had been sold. That was it. All we had to do now was get the house packed down and figure out how to get everything across the border. As it turned out, that was the easy part.

We decided that moving a house full of our belongings into a small apartment in Las Vegas was not a realistic option, so we started looking for a larger property. Paula met a real estate broker at the club in Vegas, who offered to help us out. He told us he had a property that might be suited to our needs. It was a four-bedroom house his company owned, and we could lease it effective immediately. We broke the lease at the apartment complex enabling us to move into this larger home.

Another American friend of Paula's offered to drive the U-Haul truck for us. Marvin was on board for the trip south, and so was Amanda, a colleague of Paula's. Marvin would be travelling with Paula and our American driver in the U-Haul. Upon their arrival at our new house, Amanda would fly to Vegas and meet them there. Randi and I were to stay home in Edmonton as we still had to travel to Calgary to finalize our visa situation.

Once everything was in place, a U-Haul truck was rented, and the loading commenced. We bought a whole bunch of new furniture from Roger's store. Once that was loaded onboard, we gradually filled the truck with the rest of our belongings. Packing everything into the truck took a whole day. We gave what we couldn't take with us to some friends. What we couldn't give away, we threw away.

Finally, with everybody heading south and the cat on board the truck, Randi and I said farewell. It was a weird feeling as we watched the truck pull away. It was exciting but also a little worrying. Randi and I hoped their journey would be incident free and there would be no immigration issues at the border. With that in mind, we returned to an empty house. We had a few more days staying home before moving out and spending the rest of our time in Edmonton at Roger's.

Later that night, we visited Rodger and Cheryl and waited for a call from Paula. When the call finally came through, it was not the news I'd wanted to hear. They made it across the border without too many problems, and the bulk of the journey had been incident free. That being said, while travelling through the mountains, the guy who was driving the truck had increased the speed to a dangerous level. Fortunately for all aboard, they made it through the mountain pass, but when they reached the city's outskirts, a front tire blew out, and the truck careened off the road with Paula trying to stabilize it by steadying the wheel from the passenger's seat.

I was relieved to hear they were alright but far from pleased with the cavalier attitude and conduct of the driver. He had endangered everybody's lives and had no right to do that. I chatted with Paula as she waited for a tow truck to arrive and change the tire. We'd been lucky in so much as nothing was damaged other than the friendship with our American driver. Hearing they were finally in Vegas at our new home was a relief. We now had a beautiful four-bedroom house to fill with our new furniture and personal belongings. Randi and I readied ourselves for the next leg of our journey as the Vegas crew prepared to unload all our worldly goods into the new house. We would soon be on our way to Calgary for a final interview and to pick up our visas.

Paula had the newer car in Las Vegas, and I used our old Ford Tempo to get around. It was a bit rusty in places but mechanically sound. I gave it a quick tune-up and an oil change before starting our epic journey. Our first and only stop was to be in Calgary. Amanda had arranged for us to stay at her mother's apartment for a couple of days while we dealt with the business at hand. When we arrived at the American Embassy, we were interviewed together, and aside from a lot of waiting around, the visas were issued quite promptly. The Immigration official stamped my passport with an O1 visa and told me Randi would get her O3 visa stamp at the border. This didn't sit too well with me, but I wasn't about to argue with him, so we said our "thank you's" and moved along. Before the ink was dry in my passport, we packed our bags at Amanda's mother's and soon headed south toward the border. It wasn't long before we arrived and met with the immigration officials. I explained our situation and hoped we would be issued Randi's O3 without a problem. Instead, we were instructed to pull over and enter the building for questioning.

These so-called officials had to be the most sour-faced individuals I had ever encountered. It seemed they were determined to cause us grief and scoffed at the very fact I'd been issued an O1 visa. The O1 visas are given to people with an "extraordinary ability." The recipients are usually scholars, professors and other select academics. They couldn't understand how an impersonator had been issued such a visa. There were also mutterings from these idiots about Randi not having a visa and the possibility I was trying to kidnap her.

I was enraged by their foolish rhetoric but managed to hold my composure as I explained to them in great detail what we'd been instructed to do by the officials at the embassy. We stood before them for about half an hour, knowing our fate lay in their hands. What would be their decision? Would we be refused entry? As Randi and I engaged in small talk, they just stared at us like we were criminals. It was awful, but finally, they issued Randi with an O3 visa, and we were on our way.

We screamed with joy and relief as we pulled away from the border and cranked the tunes in the car. This was it. It was the start of a new beginning for us all. As we drove through the night, I had a lot of time to think about my life's journey so far. When I started in this crazy business at the ripe old age of eighteen, I felt that a few years into my career, I would be a media sensation and live the life of a rock star. My mother often used to say, "If you knew what was ahead of you, you'd never make it through." She was right in making that statement.

Life is a roller coaster ride of highs and lows. Yet, when we dream of success, we focus on the highs and never the lows. Life is about balance and the ability to continue life's journey while enduring all that comes your way. The choices I made, both good and bad, had forged the highway I was travelling on. That highway had taken me from my sheltered childhood in rural Suffolk to the bustling city beat of London's music scene. I'd travelled all over the UK, toured the European continent and crossed the Atlantic Ocean to pursue my dreams in Canada. However, my journey was far from over, and the road ahead beckoned me. If there's one thing I've learned over the years, it's that anything can happen, and however much you prepare for what lies ahead, you should always watch out for the curve ball.

Gallery 17

Randi on vacation with Paula at Hoover Dam.

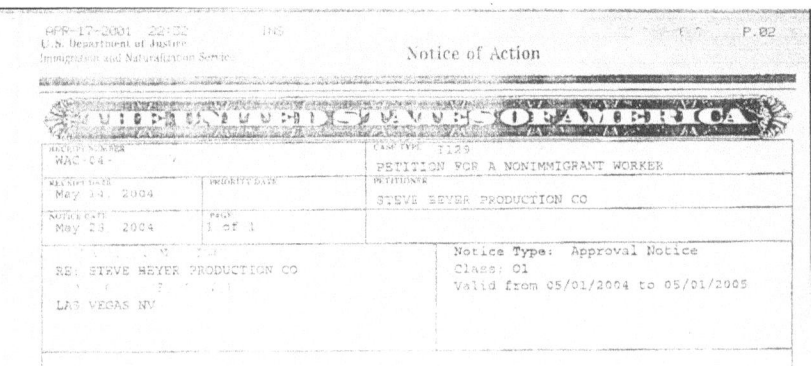

My first O-1 approval notice.

My first show in Las Vegas at C2K.

More from the show at C2K in May 2004.

All photographs from Martin Andrew private collection

Chapter Eighteen

In June of 2004, Randi and I arrived in Las Vegas. We had our respective visas, and it was time to embark on our new adventure. I was absolutely exhausted from the trip. The Ford Tempo had done well and completed our journey without roadside assistance. I recall the light raindrops accumulating on the windshield as we turned onto Craig Road. We were mere minutes away from arriving at the new house. As we approached the gates of our new community, I was about ready to collapse. Just a few more minutes and we would be at our destination. I called ahead to Paula and couldn't wait to see her smiling face. She greeted us as we pulled into the driveway and crawled out of the car. We were home.

After a quick cup of tea, I was ready for bed. Our new furniture was in place, and a California king-size bed was beckoning me. As my head hit the pillow, the reality of the situation hit me. We had made this big move, and there was great uncertainty about our future. So much to do. I needed to rest and think with a clear head. Both mind and body had to be in pristine condition for the challenges ahead. I stopped taking my prescriptions and needed to detox in order to think straight. Too much for this weary mind to think about, so it was time to close my eyes and sleep.

Martin Andrew

I awoke to the sounds of cheerful voices as Paula and Randi were engaged in the wonderfully tedious task of opening boxes and setting up the new décor. This was not my forte, but I helped out as instructed, and soon the house looked quite cozy. The rest period was over, and it was time for work. Paula was already working full-time at a club, and Randi was enjoying a summer vacation the like of which she had never experienced before. It was so hot! She spent a lot of time inside the house but, with a gentle nudge, made new friends in the neighborhood. Finally, it was time for me to meet with my agent and see what plans he had for me.

The whole idea of this move to Vegas was to become part of a show on the strip. I wasn't interested in touring anymore, and Vegas was a perfect situation for my aspirations. Here I could go to work on the strip, perform for people from all over the world and come home at night without the hassles of dealing with hotels and airports. The Steve Beyer Agency was the biggest and the best. Since he agreed to sponsor me, I had no doubt I would be placed in one of the tribute shows with relative ease.

Steve took me out on the strip to introduce me to the Las Vegas scene. I felt very important being walked into so many casinos and introduced as his new talent. Occasionally, I would get up and sing, receiving a very positive reception. The buzz of the strip was beguiling, and I couldn't get enough of it. I'd finally arrived and was in the right place at the right time with the best agent in town. Steve told me he would set up an audition with Legends in Concert, but in the meantime, he wanted to get me working and making some money.

My first official engagement was different from what I expected. I was to co-host a talent contest at Bally's, which would run for several weeks. It was suggested that this would be great exposure and kill some time while an audition was set up. I agreed to do the contest, so my first Las Vegas engagement began. The competition was a karaoke show with many singers performing who couldn't get hired in a professional setting. The majority of these characters were appallingly bad, but some talented folks were among them. I hated karaoke. I thought its only place was in a private setting, not a strip Casino. Track shows were becoming popular with venues simply because they were more cost-effective. All you needed was a person to run the equipment, and the audience entertained themselves. The standard of entertainment is usually quite pathetic, but all the karaoke singers boost each other's egos. It makes for an easy, if somewhat painful, night.

The contest ended after a couple of months of enduring some of the worst singing, I have ever heard. I had certainly gained some exposure, but not the kind I'd hoped for. I'd been lumped in with these lackluster performers and wanted to disassociate myself from them quickly. I didn't air my grievances to Steve or the other agents at the company. It would have been inappropriate to start rocking the boat and making demands at this early stage. I bit my lip and kept my fingers crossed for a chance to dazzle the producers at Legends in Concert.

I didn't have long to wait; soon, I was going to the production offices for my audition. I arrived at around 9 am with my full Rod apparel in place. I, along with Steve, entered the building with great confidence. This was my opportunity to be a part of what was considered by most the best impersonator franchise in the business. Naturally, my expectations were high. As I waited patiently in a somewhat spartan office, delusions of grandeur and a healthy paycheck were the main focus of my mind's eye. I expected to be escorted to a sound stage to perform for the company executives and show producers. Instead, I was greeted by a somewhat disheveled character and his colleagues.

There would be no sound stage to perform on. Instead, I was handed a portable CD player to play my audition tracks. Only one song was required, and I was to sing among the tables and chairs in the spartan office. One person had a camcorder, and the recording would be of me singing "Hot Legs" without a microphone. I could not believe how pathetic this audition was. How could I take this seriously? There was no way to project the strength of my live performance in this restrictive setting, so I hit play on the CD player and just belted out the song.

While I was singing, nobody seemed to be paying much attention. I could hear various conversations competing with my vocal performance. Four minutes later, it was all over. The cinematographer left the room, and a few pleasantries were exchanged before Steve, and I left the building. It had been a complete waste of time. The company already had two Rods, and I would be number three on the list. The Rod character was low on the food chain regarding impersonators, so the likelihood of me being hired was relatively remote.

It became apparent from this audition that the stacking order in Vegas for performers was not about talent, but more about first come, first served. The two other guys had worked with Legends for a while and were solid with the company. They didn't need a third for that particular character but put me on the list just in case. I could do the job well, and I had the same heritage as Rod, his look and voice, both spoken and in song. None of this mattered. I was third on the list, and it has remained that way.

Steve hoped Legends would hire me as his job would have been done, and he could make his percentage from me in perpetuity. I hoped they would hire me as it would have been a regular gig, and I wouldn't need to search for work in perpetuity, as mentioned above. I had no problem paying Steve a percentage, but as it turned out, we both lost out. After the failed audition, Steve felt obligated to keep me working in whatever capacity he could. There was always corporate work to pursue, but remember, two other established company options existed.

I did several corporate shows and had mixed feelings about them and the way I had to perform. I'd expected Las Vegas shows to be top-notch productions. This was the world's entertainment capital, but I soon realized that title did not reflect the work ethic of the productions themselves. I recall a show at the Mandalay Bay swimming pool. It was a luxurious affair with a Louis Vuitton cake worth more than my car. I was to perform with a live band, but to my dismay, the band did not know how to play the songs.

I always had copies of my tracks on hand, so I suggested I sing to those. I was informed that the band would not be paid if I did that, so I was given a solution. The band would play along to the CD, and the audience would be none the wiser. I couldn't believe my ears but had no choice other than to go along with the charade. It was a disaster. The band played the wrong chords in the wrong keys, and the drummer couldn't lock in the tempo. I felt like a complete idiot, but nobody else seemed to give a damn. They were right. The audience didn't care or even pay much attention to the main event. This was not an isolated incident, as it became apparent all that mattered was making as much money as possible for little effort.

My first year in Vegas was different from what I'd hoped for. I had experienced some of the worst cases of non-professionalism in my whole career and started to question whether or not I'd made the right move. I was contracted to the Beyer agency as they had sponsored my O1 visa, and I couldn't work outside that agreement. So, whatever they offered me, I had to take. It had been a fast decline from my first show at the Venetian when I thought I'd landed on my feet and hit the ground running toward my dreams of being a Las Vegas entertainer.

The gigs became progressively worse, with the occasional glimmer of hope every once in a while. The opening of the Neon Garage at NASCAR was a lot of fun to perform at. Still, the moment was short-lived. The misery of reality continued as I was offered a permanent position at the Tropicana, hosting a karaoke show. This was the lowest of the low, or at least I thought so until I was told to host bingo at the Western Hotel on Fremont Street. You read that right—bingo as Rod Stewart.

Paula and Amanda came with me to the venue. We arrived at around 2 pm for the afternoon session of bingo. As I walked into this seedy casino with my fancy clothes and spiked hair, I felt like a total Pratt. I was escorted to a podium and instructed in the fine art of bingo calling. Two hours of hell ensued as I called out numbers for the hopeless and homeless. Sitting in that chair, I concluded a change must be made, but how? I was grateful to Steve for his sponsorship, but he lost interest in my cause, and I had grown tired of his inability to get me where I needed to be.

My O1 visa was about to expire, and I wondered if Steve would renew it. The consequence of the visa expiring would have been devastating. The visa was the only way I could stay in the country while my petition for a green card was processed. It wasn't just about me. Randi was here on an O3 visa which was tied to my O1. If I had to leave the country, so would she, leaving Paula alone in Las Vegas. A lot was at stake, but a decision had to be made quickly.

I met many interesting people during my first year in the Las Vegas entertainment scene. Some were credible, and some were more dubious. Trying to figure out who's who was a real challenge and often led to disappointment. One such character of a more questionable nature I met was a self-proclaimed promoter and agent called JD. I didn't know much about him, but I heard he was a wealthy trust fund kid who liked to play the big shot. He had varying credentials depending on who you talked to, and I failed to find an endorsement from a person whose veracity was not in question.

JD approached me at a fundraiser I was performing at and said he wanted to work with me. He had nothing good to say about the Steve Beyer Agency and claimed access to a showroom on the strip. He wanted to sponsor me for my O1 visa and take over the reins. Nothing was happening to me with the Beyer agency. I was doubtful my visa would be renewed, so I decided to take a chance on JD. I had him email Steve to ensure there would be no animosity with the transition. Steve gave his blessing, and the change was made.

My early discussions with JD about his intention to have me perform in a strip casino sparked my enthusiasm. There would be no more singing to tracks or performing with bands who couldn't be bothered to learn the music. Instead, this was a chance for a full production show in a strip casino with a live band. I was told I could write the show and choose the band members myself. The venue was the Riviera Casino at the north end of the strip. It was an older venue but still had fantastic credibility and was a near-legendary property on Las Vegas Blvd.

There was a Neil Diamond tribute show performing in the showroom. The proposed idea was for that show to move to a different location and for mine to move in. JD, the tribute artist for Neil Diamond, and I met to discuss the proposed relocation. As we talked about the shows, everything seemed legitimate. If the main character from the Diamond show was on board and believed JD's proposal, then who was I to think otherwise? After the meeting, I was tasked with putting together a band. At the same time, JD worked out the contractual obligations for all parties concerned.

I wasted no time and advertised on the internet for musicians to join me in this venture. I didn't get a lot of replies, but one gentleman was very enthusiastic. He told me he was a bass player and wanted to meet ASAP. I arranged to meet him at the Cannery casino, which was local for me and easy for him to get to. The meeting went exceptionally well, better than I could have ever imagined. The bass player's name was Ray. He assured me he could assemble a whole band, including a name drummer from the eighties rock scene. He claimed to know Robert Sweet from Stryper and told me he would likely be interested in the project since Stryper was on an extended hiatus.

I was impressed with Ray; he came through with his promises. He assembled a whole band for me. I was still reluctant to believe that Robert Sweet would be even remotely interested in playing with an impersonator, but my doubts were laid to rest when I received his phone call. He was on board for the project, so the "Forever Rod" show band was formed. I explained the possibility of playing at the Riviera, which generated as much excitement with the band as it did with me. We rehearsed at Bill's house. He was one of the guitarists. The other guitarist was Ronee; he and I hit it off and became close friends.

We soon had a complete set of songs learned and a promotional video filmed but were still waiting for news on a start date at the Riviera. Every time I called JD, I was told he was sorting out the "language" of the contract. It was a reasonable explanation since he was dealing with a showroom on the strip, not only for me but for the transition of the Neil Diamond show to a new venue. Frustrating as it was, we just kept honing our talents to be ready for the show. During rehearsals, it became apparent that Ray was falling behind and unable to learn the material satisfactorily. Much as it pained me to do so, I had to let him go. He was the man who put the band together for me, so the decision on a personal level was tough. The other band members agreed he had to be replaced, so the search was on for a new bass player.

Ronee was a master guitar builder for Fender and an exemplary guitarist. He offered a solution to our problems. At the Fender factory in Corona, CA, he worked alongside another famous name who played in "Blue Murder" and alongside Jimmy Page in "The Firm." Enter Tony Franklin. Ronee set up a rehearsal at the Fender showroom, and we set off from Vegas for our first Jam session with the "Fretless Monster." Upon our arrival, I was introduced to Tony, and we were soon blasting through Rod's greatest hits. It was surreal to me when I looked back at the band I was playing with. My tribute show featured two prominent figures from the world of rock and roll: one on drums and the other on bass. It was truly unique, and I will never forget that day.

We discussed the show and the forthcoming residency at the Riviera during the rehearsal. There was some skepticism from Tony and the others, and it was in our best interests to confront JD. Something told me to call the Riviera and talk to the entertainment director to find out what was holding up the "Language " of the contract. Strictly speaking, it would not be common practice to do this when represented by an agent, but JD's constant excuses and kicking the can down the lane justified the inquiry. I got through to the entertainment director and asked him all my pertinent questions concerning the residency. He assured me he knew nothing about it and had never heard of JD. He also stated that the Neil Diamond show was to be a permanent attraction for the foreseeable future.

My heart sank. I had been duped. It was all a pack of lies, and I had unwittingly fed this same pack of lies to my band members. I told the guys what the entertainment director told me. There was a stunned silence in the room as the news sank in, followed by a mutual feeling of the situation being typical of the music industry. I was livid. I called JD and confronted him with the facts, only to hear him continue with his tissue of lies and deceit, claiming innocence in the matter and assuring me he would get to the bottom of it. He never did and disappeared from the Las Vegas entertainment scene shortly after this incident.

So now what? I had been made to look stupid, and there was no showroom on the horizon, let alone on the strip. I decided to showcase the Forever Rod show for all the Las Vegas agents, hoping they would see merit in my vision and secure some bookings for the future. It seemed this was the only way of keeping the band together. I booked a venue for the showcase but could not secure the interest of Robert and Tony. Robert was recording a new album with Stryper, and Tony didn't see a future in what I had to offer.

I managed to get a new drummer, bassist, and keyboard player for the showcase. The venue was the Railhead showroom at Boulder Station Casino. I sent invitations to every agent and promoter I could think of in the hope that some of them might appear. The show itself was a chronology of Rod's career. I was sick of the Legends-style shows and wanted to do something different. I put together videos that interacted with the performance and chronicled the rise to fame of Rod Stewart. I had multiple costumes and even recorded my voice telling his story during the video sections while I was backstage changing outfits. Finally, the curtain went up. The show began with a modest audience of friends, agents, and other curious onlookers.

We played our hearts out that night, and all in all, it was a successful venture. Many agents and promoters had come to see the show and were suitably impressed. The problem was they didn't know what to do with it. They all had such tunnel vision of what a tribute show should be and couldn't see past the ageing template of the Legends in Concert success. I was trying to offer a fresh approach, but they were looking for more of the same. I followed up the show with multiple calls to all present but was met with a wall of silence and no bookings for the act.

So much time and effort had been put into this venture, and nothing had come of it. With another year ending and no sponsor for my visa, I faced the same dilemma I'd encountered twelve months before. I needed a new sponsor and had no idea who that would be until one Sunday brunch at the Plaza Casino in downtown Las Vegas. I had been desperate for work and called Steve to see if he had any scraps, he could throw my way. He hired me to sing at the champagne brunch in Oscar's restaurant (named after the infamous Las Vegas Mayor) and said a piano player would accompany me. It sounded ridiculous, but I needed the work, so I agreed.

I crooned, "Do you think I'm Sexy" with my pianist doing his best to keep up and pranced among the assembled guests. One of the guests was a lady called Donna. She was an older lady and seemed to enjoy my performance. She asked me to join her at her table and informed me she was an agent during our conversation. She had been around since the days of the mob. I enjoyed hearing her regale tales of the old days. I explained my situation to her, and she immediately offered to help. Over a glass of champagne and a few ripe strawberries, my problems were solved. I had sponsor number three ready to take me under her wing.

I got a three-year O1 visa for myself and an O3 of the same duration for Randi. This would cover us until we were eligible for our green cards, meaning no further sponsors would be necessary. Donna was a lovely lady. I looked forward to working with her and finally getting some credible venues to perform in. Donna often told me about how things worked in the old days. For example, she had been able to present a performer in the afternoon and have them perform that night, back when the mob was in control. However, those days were long gone, and she struggled to find me anything at all.

I had experienced situations like this in the past when I would meet credible people who were past their prime. Denny, Don, and now Donna had all been heavy hitters in their day, but the sun had gone down on that horizon long ago. I have always considered myself a very loyal person and was prepared to persevere with what was rapidly becoming a no-win situation. Donna was extremely kind, and although she could have pulled the exclusivity clause, she told me to seek work anywhere I could instead. She was still my sponsor, but this broadened the scope of my search and gave me a far greater chance of success. Unfortunately, the gigs were very sporadic, and there was not much money to be made. The band was falling apart, and the dream of a "Forever Rod" show on the strip was all but gone.

One day, I got a call from Donna about a rather intriguing offer of employment. She informed me that an agent in LA was looking for a drummer and asked if I would be interested in auditioning. This was totally off the wall and made no sense to me at all. I was a singer, not a drummer, so I gracefully declined the offer. However, she was adamant that I hear her out as this was an acting gig, and she thought I would be the perfect fit for the role. I decided to hear what she had to say. From what I could gather, it was a documentary about impersonators. They needed somebody who looked like Rod Stewart to play the drums, or at least fake doing so. I was still unconvinced, so she arranged for the director to call me.

I was shocked to hear about the project when the director contacted me. He told me they needed my character to tie the storyline together for a documentary featuring the likes of Mick Jagger, Elton John, Ringo Star, Paris Hilton, and Bob Geldof. The list continued; they were all very famous characters. I commented that it was quite an ensemble of impersonators he procured, at which point he informed me all the people involved were actual celebrities. The project was called Platinum Weird, the brainchild of Dave Stewart from The Eurythmics.

They were filming a "Mockumentary" about a fictional band called Platinum Weird, which had been around in the '70s, and Dave Stewart was re-launching the act with Kara DioGuardi. The whole thing was fake but endorsed by some of the biggest names in the business. My job was to portray the original drummer "Brian Parfitt." They wanted me as I had a perfect look and an authentic cockney accent at my disposal. As soon as I knew what this was all about, I drove to Hollywood and auditioned for the part. I was hired on the spot and secured my position in the documentary as the original drummer from Platinum Weird. It aired worldwide, and I was sharing the screen with the best of the best in the industry.

Having enjoyed this experience, I signed up with a few acting agencies in the Las Vegas Valley. There was not a lot of credible work on offer, but plenty of background positions, which, although tedious, allow you to be around some exciting productions. I recall working on a movie called Domino, where I could sit and chat with Micky Rourke. He was fun to chat with. I was a great admirer of his acting ability. Oceans thirteen was an entertaining film to be a part of. If you look closely at the final scene filmed at the airport, I managed to get myself in frame with Brad Pitt.

If I were to act, I would need to do more than hang around on set as an extra. I didn't want to be that annoying guy pointing out to all my friends that I was on the screen for a couple of seconds while the lead actors were pulling focus. You know, rather like I did in the previous paragraph. I wanted a leading role but would have to wait several years before that opportunity presented itself. So instead, I had to focus on making money as best I could. This took the form of playing in a cover band, a Bon Jovi tribute band and continuing the struggle as a Rod Stewart impersonator. I was still writing songs and releasing CDs periodically, but there was no steady income or firm direction to follow.

I got a call one day from John Stewart. His claim to fame was that he created Legends in Concert and ran it successfully before parting company with the franchise. His was a name I had heard and been told various things about him, some good and some bad. I wanted to make my mind up, so I listened to what he said when he called me. His latest show was on a London double-decker bus. The "Show Bus of the Stars." There would be more than one of these vehicles, in various cities, with tribute artists performing at least four times a day. I was told I could make at least $2500 a week and was asked to show up at Steve Beyer's office for a green screen photo shoot.

It sounded like fun. A little strange but fun, nonetheless. I was in if I could make that kind of money, and it was a steady gig. I went down to Steve's place for the photo shoot and met with Mr. Stewart. He seemed a little self-centered and self-serving, but if the gig was legit, I wasn't complaining. After the photo shoot, things moved fast and before you could say, "Tickets, please," we were on board the bus doing a promo video on the Las Vegas Strip. There were full-size pictures of us impersonators on display all over the bus. Being on this open-top bus with the whole strip cheering and waving at us felt good.

The Road to the Manor

Just before the schedule was finalized and the bus tours were about to begin, I was called into Steve's office for a chat. He had an offer for me. He was co-producing a show which would be performed at a casino in Oregon. It was a 10-week run, and he wanted to know if I was interested. The show would feature me as Rod Stewart and Doug Starks as Sammy Davis Jr. The production was called "The Great American Songbook", and I would need to sing some of the old standards from the songbook in question. The other producer had seen a video of me singing Rod's songs but wanted to hear me performing some standards. I hurriedly called a piano player friend, banged out a couple of songs, and sent them in for approval. I was hired. The only problem was I had signed up for the show bus.

I was unsure what to do and turned to Steve for advice. He had his reservations about the show bus and the wages I'd been promised. Working for Steve, I knew I would be paid what I was offered, and the gig would be a sure thing. I passed on the show bus with the proviso that I could perform alongside the other artists upon my return. All parties agreed, and after a couple of weeks of rehearsing the new show, we were off to Oregon.

The Four Feathers casino was our destination. We drove to Canyonville, Oregon, in convoy. I'd just bought a Mazda Miata, which had very low mileage and was extremely good on gas, so that would be my mode of transport for the journey. We stopped off in Reno to catch a show and, the following day, arrived at our destination. Canyonville was very small, but the casino was quite large and clean. We were given rooms at the hotel for the night and told in the morning we would be moving into an alternate residence for our ten-week stay.

The night in the hotel was great, but the new accommodations could have been more desirable. Bugs and ants ruled the roost; it was rustic living at best. There were four of us in the cast. Karen, Tina, Doug, and I got along and worked well together on stage. The show was a relatively low-key event, as we performed in a small lounge at the casino. The show comprised acting, singing, and dancing. It reminded me of the productions in Canada.

Shows can become tedious as you get into the run, and some unauthorized antics are often necessary to keep one's enthusiasm. One day, Doug and I spent hours sewing a whoopee cushion into one of the stools the girls sat on during a particularly romantic part of the show. Then, when Karen sat down for her heartfelt solo, the cushion let rip! Doug and I were backstage, rolling on the floor, laughing. During a lecture from the sound engineer at the end of the show, it was pointed out that shadows of our legs kicking in the air and peals of laughter could be heard at the back of the room.

Another night, I was singing out in the audience when I noticed a bride celebrating her big day. I approached the table and straddled her while singing suggestive lyrics. She began to lean back as I leaned forward, and suddenly, there was an audible "Whoosh" sound as her hair ignited. There were candles on the tables, and her hair went up like a Molotov cocktail. What a sight it must have been as I climbed onto her, beating her on the head to try and put the flames out. I thought I would be sued, but she and her new husband told me it was the best part of the night, and they would never forget it. For that matter, neither would I.

Days turned into weeks. The show chugged along for the duration. We spent many days visiting wineries and taking in the scenery. Oregon is a beautiful state. I really enjoyed its serenity, but by the end of ten weeks, it was time to return home. We finished our final performance and hit the road that night. The drive home gave me plenty of time to think. The same challenges I faced arriving in Las Vegas were staring me in the face three years later. It was now 2007, and I'd still been unable to secure a steady gig.

The Road to the Manor

Gallery 18

Living the dream! Vegas 2004.

Faux famous people in the land of the impersonators.

The showbus of the stars.

By Donna Wauhob

Watch for the name of Martin Andrew, a Rod Stewart look-a-like. He looks so much like Rod that you would swear it is him. Martin's show is called, "Forever Rod - The Show." Martin's band recreates the Rod Stewart experience from his early days with The Faces—throughout the glamour of the 1980's to the more sophisticated Rod of the 1990's. The world class musicians perform all of the hits that made Rod Stewart a living legend. The show is a chronological exploration of Rod's career with live music cleverly integrated into documented visual displays. The show captures the man and his music. You will learn about his humble beginnings basking in a London tube station, to a string of hits from MAGGIE MAY to DO YA THINK I'M SEXY. The timeless and legendary hit songs of Rod Stewart brought to life both visually and audibly by a world class professional band. Up to 90 minutes of Rod Stewarts greatest hits can be performed in a single show or split into smaller sets as required. Rod's brightly colored jackets, loud shirts, tartan ties and blonde spiky hair, all replicated along with his trade mark sleek moves. The 5-piece Rock n Roll band relentlessly pumps out hit after hit as Forever Rod pays tribute and gives the ultimate salute to a living legend.

The new kid on the block!

The Road to the Manor

Tony, Ronee, Robert, Me, Bill.

Admiring the scenery in Canyonville with Doug Starks.

Backstage & Backwoods.

Karen, Me, Doug & Tina.

The Road to the Manor

BRIAN PARFITT
DRUMMER ORIGINAL PLATINUM WEIRD

Several Sources Foundation

~ 2nd Annual ~
Night of 1000 Stars

~

"V" Theater at the Desert Passage
Aladdin Hotel & Casino
Las Vegas, Nevada
Friday, November 5, 2004

We extend our Heartfelt Gratitude and Appreciation to
"The Night of 1000 Stars" Headliners and Talent
~
Clint Holmes
~
Mark Pfister, ABC TV, Master of Ceremonies
~
"Mr. Bojangles, The Ultimate Entertainer"
Starring
Ted Levy and Eric Jordan Young
~
Kevin Lyons Band featuring Mabel Brown
Scott Goodkin, Motivational Speaker
Brian Jaffe, Auctioneer
~
Bill Fayne
Gayle Steele
Kelly Clinton
Downtown Gordie Brown
Elisa Fur
Gayle Ritt
The Checkmates
The Christopher Puppets
Grant Griffin
Bill Acosta
Freddy Bell
George Bugatti
MRS – Mary, Rose and Shelly
The Shirelles
The Drifters
·Martin Andrew as Rod Stewart·
Christopher as Nat King Cole
Geena Maddux
The "X" Girls

Platinum Weird Mockumentary.

All photographs from Martin Andrew private collection.

Chapter Nineteen

IN 2003, WHEN PAULA AND I FIRST ARRIVED IN LAS VEGAS, WE LIVED in relatively modest accommodations at an apartment complex by the Palace Station casino. It was a convenient location close to the clubs where Paula worked, but we aspired to find something more conducive to our joint needs. I was not too fond of the proximity of neighbors and the inevitable parking space dilemma of dealing with those who thought allocated covered areas were an invitation to abandon vehicles at their leisure. We needed a house, so we got a house. This was the property Randi and I arrived at in June 2004.

We lived in a gated community and entered into a lease-to-own agreement. It was short-lived when the landlord tried to steal the $20,000.00, we paid him for leasehold improvements to the property in the shape of a swimming pool. After a brief court battle, we got our money back and moved out of that property and into the one next door. It was a genuine case of "Out of the frying pan and into the fire."

We were persuaded to buy the house by the lady who owned it and just happened to be a Realtor. We put down our $20,000.00 as a deposit and got a mortgage with IndyMac Bank. The deal seemed too good to be true, and we soon discovered it was. When we bought our house in Canada, we had a lawyer handle all the legalities, but here in America, it was all taken care of by a "Lender." We were so naive and trusting of our newfound realtor friend that we signed the papers and thought our 1% mortgage was outstanding.

It would have been a great deal if it had been a 1% mortgage, but that was not the case. We soon discovered that 1% was merely an optional payment against the ever-increasing percentage rate, which started at 7.5%. Within the first few months of making our optional payment, I noticed the amount we owed increased rapidly. When I made inquiries to our lender, the full scope of the tryst became apparent. If our goal were to pay this mortgage down, it would cost us an ever-increasing amount of money. That financial situation, along with all our other immigration costs, would put a heavy burden on Paula and I to make money and make it fast. Paula was more than pulling her weight, but I struggled to hold my own. This was just the beginning of our financial woes and the economic turmoil facing the nation and the world.

Thanks to the amount of money Paula could generate and the sporadic earnings of my endeavors, we stayed afloat as time ticked on. All of this was playing heavily on my mind as I returned from my exile in Oregon. I had been earning good money for the last ten weeks, but now it was time to see what opportunities awaited me in Las Vegas. Unfortunately, Vegas was slowing down, and by late 2007, there were slim pickings. Nevertheless, the opportunity was still there to perform on the show bus, so I knuckled down and made myself available.

When this lucrative engagement was brought to my attention, I was told the remuneration would be very satisfying to my balance sheet: as there was the possibility of performing four times a day and seven days a week. Unfortunately, the actuality of the situation was far from that. I was offered two to three shows per week at a rate of $100 per show. What choice did I have? I took whatever I could get and began performing on the bus. It was so ridiculous I could barely believe I was a part of this debacle. The bus itself was constantly breaking down, and the exhaust fumes when it was running were unbearable. Most attendees did not exceed four people, and their interest level was limited at best. Occasionally, we would get the upper deck full, but the somewhat useless sound system was barely audible in those instants. It was a joke, and I was a part of it.

I kept thinking that all I wanted to do was perform on the strip, so technically, that is what I was doing. One of the performers used to refer to the bus as a rolling stage to make his life less miserable and retain some semblance of dignity among his peers. There was no way of sugarcoating this. We were singing to a handful of people on a smelly old bus, becoming the laughingstock of the Las Vegas entertainment scene.

I couldn't make enough money from doing this alone, so Paula had an idea of how to make some extra cash. She was good friends with the guy who ran the valet car service at the club where she was employed. Some girls who perhaps had too much to drink after a long shift often needed a ride home and didn't trust the cab drivers. I became the trusted driver who would tend to all their impaired needs.

Around the same time this opportunity came along, so too did another. An agent from the Steve Beyer agency called me and asked if I would be interested in running a karaoke show at the Tropicana. I had worked there before running a karaoke show and hated every minute of it, but I couldn't turn this offer down. Our financial situation dictated my career choices at this time, so I accepted the offer and started work immediately. I now had three forms of employment and could create a schedule to capitalize on each position's income. I would strictly do day shows or early evenings on the show bus and work as a KJ at the Tropicana Wednesday through Saturday. My hours were 8 pm until midnight and sometimes a little later on the weekend. When I finished at the Tropicana, I would head to the strip club and drive the girls home until the sun came up.

With these three jobs, I could contribute significantly to our war chest, and the financial burden would soon be under control. It couldn't have come at a better time, as the great recession and economic collapse were quickly upon us. The housing market took a nosedive, and we were so far upside down on our mortgage that we might have to walk away from this tragic situation. We bought our home for $300,000.00 in 2005; by late 2008, it was valued at a paltry

$97,000.00. The interest rate on our mortgage had climbed to a staggering 10.5%, and the monthly payments, along with our other financial obligations, were excessive. Despite all this, we chose to keep our home and make ends meet as best we could.

We had desperate monetary problems, but I felt strangely content with my situation. It wasn't what I'd envisioned, but I was working, making money, and that had to be enough for the meantime. This period allowed me to determine the best approach to achieve my ultimate goals. I was determined to make the best of this situation, and to be honest, some fun things happened during this time. The show bus was like a dial tone to me. It never changed and didn't require much thought, so I approached it in a very automated fashion. However, I always tried to ensure the people I performed for witnessed a good performance. At least the best performance I could give on that ridiculous piece of junk.

The taxi service I offered at the strip club was mostly fun, but some girls could be a bit of a trial. Due to their intoxication, some could not remember where they lived, so apparent short journeys became challenging. One night to my complete dismay, a girl decided to relieve herself in the compartment on the passenger side door. I'm unsure how she managed it, but she filled the molded plastic receptacle with fresh urine without spilling a drop. The money was good, and the job, although not that rewarding, had its moments.

The karaoke show at the Tropicana was not where I wanted to be, so I consciously developed a new show style. As a result, I attracted quite a healthy following and garnered a rather eclectic bunch of amateur performers who made for some fun nights. Preston, Heavy Metal Howard, Stiffler, Dave who can't behave, Crazy Larry and Igor, to name a few. I was often joined by colleagues who enjoyed the spectacle and would add a little professionalism to an otherwise talentless display of epic proportions. On one such night, I was introduced to a lady who would play a significant role in my career in the years to come. Her name was Samira.

It was a regular night of karaoke hell when I noticed a couple of people at the back of the room whom I'd worked with. During the night, they, in turn, introduced me to their friend who was visiting from Canada. I was told she was a Tina Turner tribute artist and asked if I would invite her to sing with me on stage. Of course, I was happy to oblige and called upon her at the appropriate moment to sing "Hot Legs." Usually, when a singer joined me on stage, they were either inept or, if actually a singer, relatively reserved in their performance. Samira broke with tradition and exploded like a fireball when she hit the stage. She was a fantastic singer. I hadn't encountered such energy from a performer in a long time, certainly not at a karaoke show.

When the performance ended, she left the stage with me standing there, wondering what had just happened and wanting to learn more about her. After the show, I had a brief encounter with her and was able to talk for a short while. I told her how impressed I was with her performance and suggested we stay in touch to perhaps work together in the future. I handed her my business card, and she was gone into the night as quickly as she arrived. I had high hopes she would contact me, but I wouldn't hear from her for a long while. I later learned she discarded my business card, but fate or destiny was at play, and our paths would cross again in the coming years.

Things continued with my three modes of employment for quite a while. Life was good but becoming increasingly dull. The show bus was becoming less fun, and the audience, or lack thereof, didn't help much in ingratiating my enthusiasm. Driving inebriated strippers around had lost its appeal, and the karaoke show drove me mad. An opportunity was about to present itself, and things about to change.

One night at the end of a bus show, the poor sods who had bought a ticket were disembarking the "double-decker" showroom when I noticed a couple of interesting characters on the sidewalk. Our drop-off location was close to the Harmon Theater. Two of the performers from one of the shows were taking in the night air. I saw them looking at the bus with an element of disbelief and wonderment, and as I hit the side-walk, they approached me. I was inundated with questions about the show bus and asked if I would be available for any other work.

There was an open position for a character in the show they were performing in, and they wondered if I would be interested. The show was called "Rock Star the Tribute," featuring a cast of rock star tribute artists and a live band comprising actual rock stars. I was indeed interested. The Harmon Theater was a credible venue; I'd seen a lot of advertising on various media outlets. I told them I was curious, and we exchanged numbers.

I was soon contacted by the show management and asked to make myself available for an audition. The audition was quick; I was hired after a couple of verses of Maggie May. The show's producer assured me I wouldn't regret my decision. Although the remuneration wasn't fantastic, it was enough for me to walk away from the other three ventures I had been manacled to for so long. All I had to do was sing four songs for my set and make myself available for the finale. I was welcomed to the show with open arms and joined the "Rock Star" cast.

The other ensemble members portrayed characters such as Steven Tyler, Ozzy Osbourne, and Joan Jet. The band had a rotating cast of some credible players and others less plausible. What I mean by this is they were advertised as rock stars from famous bands, but some were very far removed from the original members of the acts they claimed to be part of. Some guys stood out and became friends, while others I found to have more ego than legitimate claims of being a rock star.

The cast of impersonators was no different. It ranged from complete idiots to some charming people. It was a typical Vegas show full of smoke and mirrors with a hint of real credibility. I was a part of it, so who am I to claim to be superior to the rest? I'd wanted to be part of a legitimate Las Vegas show since arriving, and here I was in 2010, performing two shows nightly at the Harmon Theater. There were no complaints from me, at least not yet.

The attendance at the show was modest at best. The Harmon was a small theatre. It wouldn't have taken much to fill it, but a sold-out night was never achieved. It became apparent fairly early on that the producer was dangling a carrot that wasn't there. He insisted he had a deal with the timeshare companies, and we would have a massive influx of audience members within a few weeks. These weeks turned into months. Soon we were told the show would be moving to the

Riviera casino as the deal with the timeshare companies was imminent, and we needed a more extensive showroom.

It all sounded great, but we didn't know that the producer had not been paying the rent at the Harmon, and we were doing a runner without paying the bill. We packed up our gear and moved the show to the north end of the strip. The Riviera was a legendary casino, and I was so happy to be performing there. After the debacle years ago of being promised a showroom only to find out it had all been a pack of lies, this seemed like vindication. The theatre was beautiful. We shared the facility with Andrew Dice Clay. This was it. This had to be it! I would be performing nightly at a casino that had hosted the likes of Liberace and Elvis. What could possibly go wrong?

It was a good crowd for opening night, as many complimentary tickets had been issued to ensure a capacity crowd. I waited patiently backstage until it was my time slot, then bolted onto the stage with the enthusiasm of a teenager. It was a fantastic feeling performing at the Riviera right up until it wasn't. I put every ounce of energy into my performance and was nearing the end of the set when disaster struck. I was running to the back of the stage toward the drummer when I decided to do a quick 180 and heard a loud pop. At the same time as the audible pop reached my ears, my left leg seemed to double in size, and I was in excruciating pain.

I hung on to the mic stand and kept singing as best I could, but something was seriously wrong. The pain got worse, and my mobility was literally at a standstill. I looked at the guitarist on my left flank and mouthed, "I'm in trouble!" I had to mouth the words and not yell them because we all used in-ear monitors and could only hear what was going through the mixing console. I could hardly shout down the microphone about my condition, so mouthing the words was my best option. After several attempts to get my point across, he finally acknowledged me and gestured to the monitor technician.

I wasn't sure why he was telling the monitor tech about my situation, but soon after that, my monitor mix changed drastically, and I was subjected to intense high frequencies. The guitarist misinterpreted what I said when I mouthed, "I'm in trouble," and instructed the monitor tech that I needed "more treble." It added insult to injury as I struggled to make it through the song. Finally, the lights went down, and while the crowd cheered, I fell to the stage and crawled off in agony.

After the showroom cleared, I was taken to the hospital, where they discovered a hole in my left calf muscle. The pop I heard was the muscle exploding. The consequent swelling was because the outer sleeve of the muscle hadn't torn, so the blood had nowhere to go. I was loaded up with painkillers and sent home. This was a disaster. Opening night, I sustained an injury that could very well keep me out of the show for the foreseeable future.

Nevertheless, I was determined to return to the stage the following night and reclaim my glory. I told the producer I could ham up the performance with a walking stick. He thought it was a fun idea and gave me the go-ahead. What I should have taken into consideration was the effect of the painkillers. The pills numbed the pain but also caused me to be very dehydrated. Minutes before I went on stage, I realized I couldn't get my throat lubricated enough to sing. I tried everything, but nothing worked. My intro began, and there was no escape. I had to go on stage. I limped on with my cane to a bewildered audience who couldn't quite comprehend what they were witnessing. I couldn't hit a note to save my life and ended up talking through the set while the other singers in the wings attempted to cover my vocal parts.

It was pathetic; I had never felt so stupid on stage. The set ended with the subdued overture of a pitiful golf clap and me limping off the stage. Despite the words of encouragement from some of my colleagues, I knew the game was up. As I left the theatre that night, I knew my days of performing at the Riviera on the Las Vegas Strip had ended. It had only taken two disastrous nights, and it was all over.

Since I had no medical insurance, I couldn't afford the surgery I needed to relieve the pressure in my leg, so I spent the next six months either lying in bed or hobbling around the house, aided by a walking stick. I fell into a depression and tried to drown my sorrows with a cocktail of alcohol and painkillers. I was still in touch with some of the cast from the show and could keep abreast of all the gossip and goings on at the theatre. Unfortunately, the show was losing ground rapidly, and the number of people attending was dwindling. There was also some drama taking place, and the cast split into two groups. By the end of the run, the split was official, and the original show returned to the Harmon Theater with the other faction remaining at the Riviera.

What we still didn't know about at this time was the behind-the-scenes financial debacle taking place. The "Rock Star the Tribute" producer was a grifter. He was taking money from vulnerable investors and making them promises about financial gain while using their funds for self-enrichment and running the show into the ground. By this time, he had used several different venues and been thrown out of them for not paying the rent. I will never understand how he managed to get the show back into the Harmon Theater. Due to his defaulting on payments, we suffered an embarrassing eviction, but somehow, he managed to work a deal to get us back on the Harmon stage.

My leg healed, and I was keen to return to the show. There were now two versions, but only one was available to me. The faction who chose to stay at the Riviera deemed the Rod Stewart character unsuitable for their new adaptation, so I returned to the fold at the Harmon. A couple of other members were added to our latest incarnation, and we began performing again with the promise of large crowds and the reality of small ones.

It was only a short time before getting paid became a problem, and we were always told the bank was the cause of our financial hardship. By this time, I was starting to question the integrity of our fearless leader and decided to take a stand. I called the producer and instructed him I would only perform that night if paid in full for the two weeks' money owed. This declaration must have struck a nerve as, within hours, the entire cast was informed the show was closing and we should pick up our equipment and belongings immediately.

Shortly after this, as we dug deeper, we discovered more about the producer and his lies. We were owed a considerable amount of money and decided to sue the producer. A court battle ensued, with us being victorious but unable to get any compensation. The judge told me she was happy I won and wished me lots of luck collecting the funds owed. Unfortunately, luck was not enough, as I and the others who won the case never got a dime. A couple of the cast members and I tried to salvage our careers by forming a cover band, hoping to make a few bucks in the local clubs. It was an exercise in futility and the band we called "All In" achieved nothing more than filming a promotional video at my expense. I had to think of something else to do, but what? The never-ending question of how to pick up the pieces and start again. It was becoming all too familiar territory. I was getting truly sick of it.

I contacted a colleague who worked with me on a variety of projects. Gina was adept at impersonating several characters. We devised the idea of developing a Rod Stewart and Shania Twain show. Incorporating country and rock and roll was a solid concept as it would appeal to a broader audience than a solo character. Flashbacks to my duo days in Canada taught me this. However, we would still need to find a suitable venue for live performances. As chance would have it, our mutual friend Tony Sacca had a club on the Fremont Street Experience. It was more like a complex than a stand-alone theatre with a bar and restaurant attached. He offered us the showroom, PA system, and lights for free. It was an incredible offer, so I rehearsed a new show with my old friend Gina.

Gina had a full-time position at the Flamingo Casino as a beverage manager and earned a decent salary. I, however, had no income other than the money I could make from performing, so it was in my best interest to get this show up and running as quickly as possible. Gina and I performed as our respective characters many times, so putting a set of songs together was easy. We wouldn't be performing with a band but decided to employ the services of a couple of sexy dancers. Jessica Wood was a beautiful young lady whom I worked with at the Harmon Theater. She was a very talented dancer and extremely good-looking. I asked her if she would like to participate in the new show, and she accepted the offer. I left it up to her to find another girl and asked if she would choreograph some routines.

Rehearsals went well, and we were soon ready for opening night. It was quite a thrill to be running a show and having no producers other than Gina and myself to deal with. However, we learned fast there were still people other than producers who could influence a show's success.

We employed the services of one such entity. A company offered the service of sending people to your venue to be audience members, ensuring the venue was packed and, in turn, creating the illusion of a successful show. We used this service and asked the company to supply audience members for opening night. As a result, we were packed to capacity, and the performance was solid. We looked forward to a long run at the Las Vegas Rocks venue.

Despite our best advertising efforts and canvasing people wandering around the Fremont Street Experience, we could not increase our paid ticket sales. The room looked great with all the free audience members in attendance, but we needed more than that to pay us a living wage. This situation didn't affect Gina as much as it did me. The show was my sole income, which was not enough to live on. Paula joined our ranks and was employed as a bartender in the restaurant for a short while. She, too, was experiencing a lack of sustained income at the club she was working at and decided to try and supplement her earnings by joining us on a part-time basis. We were barely making ends meet when a strange Russian man approached me. This Russian had seen me perform at the Tropicana and the Harmon Theater. He advised me that he had an offer for my consideration. He wanted to take me to Vladivostok for a series of Christmas shows and asked if I would be interested. Nothing much was happening with our show, so I asked Gina what she thought about taking a couple of weeks off at Christmas and starting again in the new year with some fresh enthusiasm. She was in agreement, so I told the Russian I was willing and able to take him up on his proposal, and so began the preparations for my venture to the Far East.

In Vladivostok, I would be performing with a live band and required to make concert appearances at two rock clubs. With all preparations in place and my Russian travel visa ink barely dry, I was on a plane heading for the far east before you could say "borscht." It was a long flight with a lengthy stopover at Seoul airport before finally arriving in Vladivostok's frozen wasteland. My first impression of this Russian city was that it reminded me of Canada, bloody freezing! Having cleared customs with relative ease, I waited for the Russian to arrive as I warmed my hands on a sadly inadequate cup of airport coffee.

Upon his arrival, I was transported to my hotel and told to rest as we would meet with the club owners the next day. The hotel was satisfactory if not a little rustic in nature. My room had a great view overlooking the water of a nearby estuary. The only problem was the water in the estuary was frozen, and all other aspects of the scenic surroundings were blanketed in snow. It was -23 and blowing a blizzard. There were no English channels on television and nothing I could understand in the magazines in the lobby. This was indeed a different world I had entered into, but for now, it was time for some well-earned sleep.

My driver and the Russian picked me up the next day. We met with the club owners to discuss my upcoming shows. Unfortunately, the people I was introduced to were some of the most unsavory characters I have ever encountered. Big, fat, and bolshy! The Russian had to interpret the content of the discussion, but I could understand the mood by the volatility of the dialogue. They seemed to enjoy yelling, and most of the meeting was peppered with sporadic outbursts of foreign profanity.

The meeting was finally at an end, with the most significant negotiation being the discussion about me singing Jingle Bells. After a fiery exchange, it was decided I would not be required to sing the song. I met the band that day, and through the interpretation skills of the Russian, I could communicate with them quite easily. They were well rehearsed, and the show came together very quickly. I was treated to a nice meal as we discussed the final touches for the performance, which would be making its debut the following night.

Showtime! The place was packed, and I couldn't wait to hit the stage. This crowd was amazing. There were beautiful women as far as the eye could see, which was in complete contrast to the somewhat disheveled-looking male members of the audience. My enthusiasm was not letting up as I blasted out Rod's greatest hits. It was a relief and a contrast to the lackluster audience I'd been performing to in Las Vegas. I loved every minute of it. By the end of the set, I was in a cloud of euphoric bliss. Who knew Vladivostok could be so therapeutic for my rock n roll soul?

After performing a few shows, I had some days off before we ventured to the next club, so it was time for sightseeing. The Russian proudly displayed me to the local community as I was given a guided tour of the city and its landmarks. I was wined and dined for the duration, enjoying every moment of my faux fame. It was a smooth ride until I decided to have a midnight snack one night. The hotel was furnished with a beautiful dining area with plenty of food in a buffet-style setting. My understanding of buffets was the food being checked regularly, with fresh items replacing those past their prime. Unfortunately, I was unaware of a public holiday and the resulting lack of protocol at the hotel's buffet. I decided to have some fish, pate, cheese selection and other sweet treats. It was delicious, and I indulged my hunger cravings to the full. The only problem was this food had been left from the previous day, as the catering staff had failed to clear it away: due to their probable enthusiasm for the upcoming public holiday. The disaster was about to strike.

I had an important show coming up, performing for many friends of the club owners. These friends were very dubious characters with ties to organized crime. Other dignitaries would attend, and I was told to stay in character and present myself to the assembled masses as Rod Stewart at all times. I discovered the reason for this was that many people were coming to see who they thought was the real Rod Stewart. This did not sit well with me, and I would generally have refused to do it. However, considering who I was dealing with in this situation, I agreed to comply.

I began to feel ill shortly after eating at the buffet. The feeling intensified. It became apparent I had food poisoning. I have never felt the intensity of nausea I did during that period. I was constantly experiencing an evacuation of all fluids and all solids from all orifices. I thought I was going to die. I was burning up, so I opened my window to try and cool the room and get some fresh air. The temperature was frigid, and snow blew on my bed sheets due to a crosswind. This was a

Hell that had frozen over. I knew I had an important show coming up, and there was no way I could cancel it. I had to get better.

When show day arrived, I was fragile but determined to perform. After a long hot shower, I got dressed and made my way to the hotel lobby. A driver picked me up, and soon I was in the dressing room at the club. I still had cold sweats and intense cramping in my stomach, but the show had to go on. I dressed and sat on a couch, sipping water, hoping to get through this ordeal and keep the local mafia happy. The club hired some dancers for the show. They proceeded to get ready in my dressing room. I remember sitting, watching these beautiful women getting naked right in front of me and hoping I wouldn't throw up all over them.

It was 30 minutes until showtime when the Russian arrived and inquired about my well-being. I told him I was desperately ill and not sure how I would be able to perform. The Russian had a solution. He handed me a tablet and instructed me to take it with a glass of water, assuring me I would feel better in minutes. I had nothing to lose, so I took the pill and waited for the miracle cure. Within a few minutes, my head was spinning, and my stomach was cramping, causing severe pain. I thought I'd been given cyanide or something harmful instead of a miracle cure. I rushed to the bathroom and, for the first time in my life, was throwing up what looked like black tar. The vomiting lasted for several minutes and stopped as quickly as it started.

When I gathered my senses and cleaned myself up, I felt better. The Russian remedy, indeed, was a miracle cure. To this day, I have no idea what he gave me, but it worked. As I exited the bathroom, he greeted me with a smile and a glass of water. It was showtime. I performed to a sell-out crowd of duped dignitaries who paid a lot of money to see the actual Rod. After the show, I sat with the club owners at the main table and was offered caviar and champagne. I gracefully declined their offer, citing a tender stomach lining and a pallet lacking the sophistication to enjoy such fine dining.

I was in a fragile state for the remainder of my stay in Vladivostok, but able to perform at all the venues without any cancellations becoming necessary. It had been quite an experience: beautiful women, toothless men, various criminals, and outstanding musicians. Despite my health issues, it was a worthwhile trip. I was handed an envelope full of US dollars at the airport, and the Russian said farewell. It was a long flight home, and I looked forward to returning to work with Gina to continue developing our fledgling show.

As I touched down in Las Vegas, I was relieved and happy to be home. Travelling is fun. I still enjoyed visiting foreign places, but I missed home and looked forward to a nice cup of tea and a few days off to recover. Not so fast, Martin Andrew! As I regained my cellular signal, I noticed multiple messages from Tony Sacca. I hoped to hear good news from him, but soon a "coup de grace" was delivered.

I was under the impression that his club was indeed his and he was the boss. However, this was not the case. Tony was merely a tenant, and he was being evicted. His eviction meant that Gina and I no longer had a showroom and had to get our things out of the building before the doors were locked. No feet up and a cup of tea for me. No sooner had I got home and dropped my cases off than it was time to make my way to the club to collect my belongings. It was not the triumphant return I'd envisioned.

I met Tony and Gina at the club, and a somber atmosphere set in. We had not been successful with the show, and it became apparent Tony had failed with his business venture. We hugged each other before going our separate ways. I had no clue what I was going to do. I had no agent and no prospect of any work. Paula's part-time job was gone, and the big money she used to make in the strip clubs was not there anymore. In addition, we had a mortgage crippling us and were still trying to pay off legal fees. All these money woes were not going away. If we didn't devise a game plan soon, we would sink even faster into a sea of debt and despair. It was time for radical change.

The Road to the Manor

Gallery 19

Martin Andrew has Rod Stewart's look, sound and suggestive microphone moves down cold in "Rockstar."

Rockstar the tribute Live at the Harmon theater 2010.

My theater debut in America.

Birthday picnic for Paula's 36th.

A day out at Venice beach.

The Road to the Manor

Show promo.

Live show in Vladivostok.

Touchdown in Russia.

Billboard in downtown Vladivostok.

The Road to the Manor

Hanging with the girls at the club in Vladivostok.

A Russian sauna experience that haunts me to this day.

All photographs from Martin Andrew private collection.

Chapter Twenty

2010 WAS ENDING, AND I WAS SEARCHING FOR A NEW WAY TO MAKE A living. My efforts to be part of or to create a show in Las Vegas had yet to amount to any credible claims of success. I was not part of the "in-crowd" and had consequently ostracized myself from the local musicians, entertainers, and agents. Having put so much time and effort into forging a career here in the United States, I expected to be more successful. Instead, there were no more big paydays from Paula working at the strip clubs, and I had no income at all. Vegas had changed, and it was time for us to do the same.

A friend I worked with when I was driving girls home from the Strip clubs had a suggestion. He was working as an armed security guard and making reasonable money. He suggested I take the PILB armed guard exam and obtain a license to become a security guard. I could now carry a handgun since I had achieved permanent residence status in America. I completed a course to obtain my CCW license and gained all the required qualifications for my new line of work. Is this what it had come to? My dream of being a Las Vegas entertainer became the nightmare of becoming an armed security guard. So be it.

I have never been one for sniveling in a corner, feeling sorry for myself. I instead opted for doing a job I hated and sniveling privately in my head while earning a crust. I took my friend's advice and got hired by a private security company. All I had to do was wear a cheap black suit, carry my 9mm handgun and stay awake. It was a boring existence, but I could make a few bucks and contribute to paying down our debt load. I opted for working the night shift as I hated dealing with the people who attended busy conventions during the day. The night shift was quiet, and I spent a lot of time with my thoughts and a couple of other guards whose company I enjoyed.

I stayed in touch with Gina throughout this new endeavor. She was still working at the Flamingo as a beverage manager. I told her I was struggling with this new way of life, and she suggested a venue change. The Flamingo was hiring security officers for the pool season. She thought, if I were to be working as a security guard, why not do it by a pool full of scantily clad young ladies? Of course, her offer was strictly for working at the pool, and my mind strayed to the allure of working with scantily clad young ladies. The head of security was a good friend, so she made the necessary introductions, and I was hired on the spot.

My first port of call was attending the mandatory two-week security academy course. I had been used to working for the other company and having no training or challenging duties other than staying awake. However, this was a different beast. I was instructed to attend the academy for academic and practical hands-on training. Many new hires were a little suspect in the academic department, but we all paid close attention to our instructors. There was quite a lot to learn as a security officer in a casino with many responsibilities.

I completed the course with my colleagues, and we were shipped out to the Flamingo for six weeks of hands-on training with a Field Training Officer. The shifts were ten hours in duration and four days a week. I was put on the night shift from 8 pm until 6 am. Everything from transporting millions of dollars in cash to scraping drunks off the bathroom floors had to be experienced within six weeks. We had access to everywhere in the casino and the ability to arrest those causing trouble. Reports had to be written, and at any given time, anything could happen and often did. At the end of my training, I was cut loose and sent out to the pool area for the summer season. This was going to be fun, or so I thought.

There were plenty of scantily clad young ladies poolside, but as the temperature soared, so did the drinking habits of the clientele. We spent most of our time treading carefully around fresh vomit, trying to control the unruly men and women who were there to party hard. Trying to handcuff a rambunctious young lady fighting with you and barely covered in a skimpy bikini is no easy task. Trying to curb lewd acts below the water line also presents quite a challenge as you try to stay hydrated in the blistering heat.

It was not what I'd expected; the days were long and hard. All these people on vacation having a wonderful time while I was there trying to police the situation had no compatibility with my heart's desires. Most of the men and women present just viewed the security officers as "killjoys," and that's basically what we were. We only said no, and they didn't like it. It was a very negative setting. It didn't do me any favors looking the way I did. I would be approached daily by well-meaning guests, who pointed out that I looked like Rod Stewart and should consider being an impersonator. Apparently, there was good money in it.

We were sent inside to work when the weather finally cooled down, and the pool closed for the season. The day was split into five periods, each consisting of two hours spent in a different part of the casino. Anything could happen at any given time, and it soon became apparent to me that the casino played host to two very different worlds. There was the world the tourist lived in, where they enjoyed fine dining and a flutter at the sportsbook. On the other hand, there was a decidedly darker side to life in the casino, which we experienced daily. Assaults, heart attacks, drug dealers, pimps, prostitutes and even the occasional dead body to deal with. We were privy to it all as the radio traffic in our earpieces flooded our heads with the day's trauma and criminal activity.

I could spend the next few chapters recounting all the crazy situations I had to deal with, but one, in particular, stands out in my mind. I was working the day shift and had been sent to Bills Gambling Hall for a couple of hours as they were short-staffed. No sooner had I arrived when a call came through about a disturbance in one of the hotel rooms. I requested backup but was denied as we were short-staffed and advised to proceed with caution. I was not too bothered about this as it was around 9:30 am, probably a couple arguing about some indiscretions from the night before.

As the elevator doors opened on the second floor, I witnessed a truly bizarre sight for so early in the morning. A young woman was naked and running along the hallway, screaming, "He's got a gun...He's going to kill me!" She ran passed me and ducked into a room the maids were cleaning. The door slammed, and there was an awkward silence. I was slightly perplexed at the sight I just witnessed. I was about to call dispatch to update them on the situation when I noticed a man standing in the hallway staring at me. He was located in the direction from which the naked lady had been running. Did he have a gun? Was murder on his mind?

I decided to introduce myself and find out what was happening while being mindful of what could potentially be a dangerous situation. The man acknowledged me. I asked him to keep his hands where I could see them. Although I wore a Kevlar vest, I had no firearm and was unprepared for an armed assault. We were issued a retractable baton which helped deter the occasional drunk, but no match for a handgun. Nevertheless, we entered a cordial dialogue, and I called dispatch to relay to them the situation I was dealing with.

The man remained calm, and the more we spoke, the better I felt about his demeanor. It was part of the job to deal with various people in different situations. This daily routine led to an understanding of people and an ability to judge the credibility of what they told you. Every story has two sides, and this one was no exception. When my backup arrived, I interviewed the naked lady along the hallway.

When I reached the room, she had sought refuge in, she was sitting on the bed, swaddled in a hotel bath towel courtesy of the domestic workers on site. I asked her what had caused her to streak through the hallway screaming blue murder. She was keen to tell her side of the story. She said that a one-night stand had turned violent. Her apparent intention was to go to the gentleman's room for a late-night drink, and in turn, he raped her at gunpoint. It was a serious allegation and could not be dealt with by our in-house security alone. Instead, Las Vegas Metro police were called and took over the investigation.

This story may seem like a clear-cut case of rape at gunpoint, but it was far from that. This particular routine was quite commonplace in the casino, and you, the reader, deserve an explanation. What would happen on any given night to an unsuspecting, if somewhat gullible, gambler was what played out here. A man is gambling and flashing around a lot of money. A pretty girl catches his eye, and he becomes elated with his good fortune at the poker table. His ego kicks in as he allows her to join his fun. The girl suggests sexual fulfilment, and they, along with his substantial winnings, retreat to his hotel room. She asks him to shower before they hit the sheets. While he is soaping his under-carriage, she gets dressed, steals his money, and leaves the room. This routine should occur before he has time to rinse the conditioner out of his hair.

On this occasion, the man suspected the girl had an ulterior motive and merely ran the water while observing her through the crack in the door. He witnessed her stealing his Rolex and confronted her before she had time to strap on her thong. The game was up, so she needed to create a diversion. I witnessed the diversion of her running and screaming along the hall, causing me to separate the two parties for questioning. The claim that she had been raped and a gun was involved guaranteed the involvement of local law enforcement. When a girl claims to be raped, they are offered transport to a local hospital by ambulance. This offer ensured the naked lady could exit the casino and seek sanctuary at a local medical facility. Once there, she could refuse treatment and leave the premises relatively quickly. Her pimp could then pick her up and drop her at a new location to seek out another gullible gambler.

It was just one of many scams we had to deal with both day and night at the Flamingo, but it made for an interesting shift at work. I would continue working as a security officer at the Flamingo for two years as I desperately tried to claw my way back into the entertainment business. It was exciting some of the time and demoralizing most of the time, but at least I was employed and bringing in some money. Toward the end of my tenure at the Flamingo, Paula decided to retire from exotic dancing and move into the mainstream labor force. There were a couple of reasons for this. First, the clubs were attracting more and more hookers keen to do a little extra for the clientele, and Paula had grown tired of the lifestyle that accompanied the job.

Paula had initially entered the business in Canada when I fell ill, and we were experiencing a heavy dose of financial trouble. She made good money in both countries, but things were changing. Paula was getting older, and hanging around young hookers had no appeal. It was time to move on and integrate into the workforce she had not been a part of for so many years. This was a significant change for her. There were lots of rules and regulations and a paycheck that didn't come close to the money she had been used to.

She landed a job at Harrah's, and on occasion, while I was working at the Flamingo, we could see each other. Paula worked at the spa's front desk and would sometimes be sent to the Flamingo to help. She and I met on more than one occasion and discussed our situation. Here I was in a security uniform, and there she was in her spa attire, with both of us proudly sporting our name tags. We had gone from enjoying the high life and big bucks of the early 2000s to this, and it only took a little over a decade to do it. It felt like defeat anyway we looked at it, but with bills to pay and no other opportunities readily presenting themselves, we were firmly entrenched in this new lifestyle.

After my time at the Flamingo came to an end, I was still able to work in the security field. I had my armed guard card and CCW permit, which allowed me to carry a concealed weapon. There were always plenty of security jobs in Las Vegas, and if you had the credentials, you could find employment relatively easily. I worked for many different companies. On one occasion, I was employed by a gold mining company in northern Nevada. This was, without a doubt, the most dangerous employment situation I have ever been in. I was part of a team of six armed guards whose job was to protect the assets of a gold mine and ensure that no trespassers encroached on what turned out to be disputed territory. Unfortunately, a bunch of hillbillies who lived in the hills claimed some of the land and were determined to undermine our efforts to secure it. It was an extremely volatile situation.

There were frequent attacks on us, with gunshots ringing out in the night. In addition, they would shoot up the equipment and vandalize buildings regularly. Unfortunately, the local law enforcement was on their side and offered no assistance to us. What made matters worse was the crew I had to work with was somewhat dysfunctional. Most of them were ex-military with all kinds of mental issues. They enjoyed firing rounds at anything that moved and would even shoot near your feet when trying to get a few minutes of relaxation.

The job didn't last long as the mining company went bust, and my fellow guards shot rounds into some protected buildings owned by the Bureau of Land Management. These two factors caused me to beat a hasty retreat back to Las Vegas to avoid being arrested and charged with malicious damage to government property. I knew how hard it would be to get monies owed to me by the company, so I declined to get involved in any legal litigation. I had been down that road before with the show at the Harmon Theater and experienced the bitter taste of financial defeat. It was time for a new job.

I found new employment with relative ease. Same shit, different uniform. I was past caring; I did as I was told. The days passed without incident as I mulled over a multitude of ideas and scenarios where I would be back on stage and enjoying life again. I did, however, have a more pressing concern that had to be dealt with. I had some health issues, so Paula and I decided to combine a visit to see family and friends in Canada with a medical check-up.

Paula had accumulated some paid leave, and I was given time off without any problem, so we booked our flights and headed back to the Great White North. We stayed with our good friend Roger and, before my impending colonoscopy, visited with Mark and some other friends. I contacted the casting agent who helped me break into the Canadian movie industry as an extra. After my procedure, we agreed to see each other and catch up with all the local gossip.

The Road to the Manor

I was soon out of the hospital and able to meet with my friend. During our discussion, he told me about a production he was involved in and how he thought I would be ideal for one of the characters being cast. This tickled my fancy, and he subsequently suggested a screen test. He had access to a small film crew and was prepared to come to Roger's house to capture the magic I was ready to deliver. A date was set, and we filmed a couple of scenes from the movie script provided. It felt good to be doing something creative again. It seemed so ironic that I had to return to the city I'd left to achieve this. The screen test was completed and sent to the director for review. Now it was the proverbial waiting game. Our time in Canada ended, so Paula and I boarded a plane to head south.

It was not long before I got a call from my friend up north telling me I had landed the part of the male lead in the forthcoming production of a movie called "Forbidden Playground." I was to portray a club owner married to a cheating wife. This was a dream come true, and all from a visit to Canada to have an exploration of my colon conducted. I was soon furnished with a script, and in the latter part of 2013, I was on a plane heading back to Edmonton for my debut as a lead actor in a feature film.

I arrived a couple of days before we started filming and settled in at Roger's house. I spent every waking moment reviewing the script and committing my lines to memory. There was no way I would be the weak link on set; I took the whole process very seriously. I received my call time for the first day of filming and tried in vain to get some rest. I slept with the script on my pillow and, during the night, often glanced at it as I tried desperately to fall asleep.

It was an early call to set; I didn't want to be late, so I set off as the sun rose. I can remember how wonderful it felt driving to that first shoot location. I was on the highway as the sun crept into the sky. It was a beautiful morning. I was ready to give my best performance, but first, I had to stop daydreaming and concentrate on the directions I'd been given. I arrived at the location and was surprised to find nobody there. I was early but expected to see some trucks or crew members readying the set for our first day of filming. Instead, there was not a soul in sight, so I sat in the front seat of the hummer I'd borrowed from Roger and rehearsed my sides.

As call time approached, a few people drifted into view. It became clear to me this wasn't a high-budget movie Hollywood style, but rather a low-budget film Edmonton style. It didn't matter to me. So long as everyone involved brought the same enthusiasm as I had to set, we would be in good shape to make this movie. In this hope, I would be satisfied as all involved were doing this for the passion of making the movie, rather than the little money we would be paid for our trouble.

I introduced myself to all present and was made to feel very welcome. There was a very informal atmosphere as most people involved in making this movie knew each other from the local enter-tainment scene. I was the outsider but was welcomed by all. We soon got to work on the first scene, and I enjoyed every minute. Aside from one exception, my fellow cast members were fun to work with; it was a great team. I struck up a great relationship with the leading lady, Samantha Grant and also enjoyed the company of the director, Kevin Matlo.

I could spend the next part of this chapter re-living all the scenes I was a part of, but that would be far too self-indulgent. So instead, I would like to recount a few memorable moments I shared with Saman-tha. The first was the day we did the bedroom scenes. I had seen many movies with torrid sex scenes, and now it was my turn to spend the best part of a day in the bedroom with Samantha. She is a beautiful lady; we hit it off on the first day of filming. I felt somewhat relaxed about our bedroom scene but was unsure how it would all play out. The scene could be filmed in many different ways, so it was down to the director to decide. Kevin opted for a tender love scene, which began with us undressing slowly before gracing the sheets with our semi-naked bodies.

We kept our underwear on and simulated a passionate love scene. It was surprisingly easy to ignore the cameras and focus on what we were doing. I would be making a false statement if I said it was awkward or, in any way, uncomfortable. I was in bed with a beautiful woman, and it was fun. We were both professional about our approach to the scene but also had a few laughs during filming. Good times. The scene in the movie lasts about a minute, but we spent much longer than that getting it done. In one particular shot, where our hands clasp together as the music reaches the peak of a crescendo, I wasn't even in bed. To get the right angle, I had to kneel next to the bed and reach up to grab Samantha's hand. The suffering we endure for our craft!

Another scene with an entirely different feeling was when I discovered my wife had slept with my son's schoolteacher. In this scene, I explode angrily and cause my wife (Samantha) to tear up. The scene's intensity caused some of the crew to become visibly upset. After about six takes, Kevin stopped us from doing it again. Samantha was a little distraught after we finished filming, and to be honest, so was I. It's strange how something which is fiction and contrived can tug at your heartstrings. But we were in the moment so much that it felt like an honest confrontation with tears. In moments like that, you've honed your craft and fashioned a scene that will hopefully move an audience in the same way it has impacted you.

Three weeks passed in the blink of an eye, and we were celebrating our potential achievements at the wrap party. There was talk of the Paramount film company in Hollywood showing interest in this production. To have Paramount pick up this project would be incredible and could lead to all kinds of opportunities. I had reservations about this rumor, but it lent an air of intrigue. As an artist, you can't help but get sucked into the vortex of wishful thinking and the possibility of your career taking off. Rationale dictates caution in one's thinking, but the idea of climbing the ladder to fame and fortune often throws the caution of that rationale to the wind.

I said my farewells and looked forward to returning to see my newfound friends when a premiere date for the film had been set. But, for now, it was back to Las Vegas and the age-old quest to make money before the red carpet beckoned. I was able to pick up where I left off with relative ease, and begrudgingly settled back into the mundane routine of being a security guard. I hated it. I was the leading male actor filming a feature film a few weeks earlier. Now I was in a stupid uniform dealing with idiots.

Soon after my return to this less-than-satisfying form of employment, I was contacted by an acting agency in Edmonton. A critically acclaimed show called "Blackstone" was looking for an actor to play the part of a crown prosecutor in an upcoming episode. It had been suggested that I would be suitable for the role, so I was offered an audition. I was familiar with the show as my friend who filmed my audition for Forbidden Playground was the casting director for Blackstone.

It was agreed I would film a short scene at my house in Las Vegas and submit the footage for review. I diligently set about filming and presenting the scene in short order. I was pleased to be offered the part. I was going to play an attorney on television. I was thrilled to participate in such a brilliant production and headed north in early 2014. I remember arriving at the film set and being amazed at the size of the production. My first day on set while filming Forbidden Playground had been a very modest experience with a humble crew and just personal vehicles in a small parking lot. However, this was a different ball game. They called this particular location "The Circus," which was an apt description. Numerous trucks, trailers and a large contingent of cast and crew were displayed. I was welcomed on set and ushered to my trailer. My trailer?

I had my own trailer with a complimentary fruit basket and other goodies. I was treated so well and couldn't help but reflect on my polar opposite life in Las Vegas. One minute I was a security guard working at a low rental facility dealing with drug dealers and hookers. Next, I was lounging in my trailer, awaiting an escort to set. No pun intended! It was a roller coaster life I was leading, but I had no idea how soon it would be before I came off the rails and had a near-fatal crash.

Having consumed some delicious fruit, I was advised it was time for hair and makeup to be tended to and was led to the appropriate trailer to ready myself for the set. During the application of my makeup, a wonderful lady called Prudence drew attention to a lump in my neck. This was not something I was unaware of. Throughout my career, when experiencing a throat infection, my glands swelled up and caused me a great deal of discomfort.

Before I arrived in Edmonton, I had experienced such an infection some weeks previous, but the swelling in my neck had not gone down this time. It didn't bother me much, as the lump in my neck was not painful. It looked unsightly, but I had chosen to ignore it since no discomfort was associated with this growth. I explained all this to Prudence, but she was very concerned for me and suggested I see a doctor upon my return to the USA. Something about her demeanor and tone of voice made me take notice of her concern. I resided myself to the fact that a prognosis from a qualified physician may indeed be required.

I put aside all my concerns as I was escorted to the set to film my scene. Once again, I was the center of attention and loved every minute of it. I worked with skillful actors, which made for a good scene. It is much easier to deliver a strong performance when you have competent people to work with, and this experience did not disappoint. I wish I could have stayed longer and had a more prominent part to play in the episode, but for now, it was over and time to get to the airport.

Upon returning to Las Vegas, I continued working in security but also decided to put an advertisement on Craig's list for any musicians or singers looking to collaborate in the search for working opportunities. I was desperate. Craig's list was a last resort; it usually generated a lot of responses from total idiots. However, on this occasion, I got lucky. A female singer responded and advised me of some cruise ship opportunities. I had never worked on a cruise ship, so I was interested in hearing what she had to offer. As it turned out, it was very little, but she managed to get us involved with a local top-40 dance band.

This went against the grain for me as I enjoyed playing rock music and had little to no interest in this genre of bubble gum crap. I bit my lip and showed up to rehearsal with my bass guitar and a somewhat open mind. The songs were challenging as most of the repertoire was dance hits from the 1970s. The driving rhythm for the songs was created by drums and bass, with little going on in the guitar department: which suited the guitarist rather well. He was the band leader, whom I hoped would be more competent with business as his guitar skills were sadly inadequate. I put him in touch with my old friend Steve Beyer. Soon we were filming a promo video on Steve's sound stage. That very same day, Steve booked us at a venue in Laughlin, and my career as the bass player in a dance band began. Oh, Joy.

Before we set off for our debut gig in Laughlin, I made an appointment to see my doctor to evaluate the lump in my neck. This appointment led to a subsequent referral to a specialist who would take a biopsy and submit the tissue for testing at a laboratory. I repeated this testing process three times, with all results returning inconclusive. However, the ENT specialist still had concerns and suggested I see his colleague if he were available. His colleague was a top surgeon in the country specializing in throat surgery for cancer patients. The mention of the word cancer sent shivers down my spine, but I doubted there was room for concern. I was lucky enough to get an appointment with Dr Wang and was able to see him quickly. It could have taken up to six months to see this sought-after surgeon, but the wait time was a mere two weeks on this occasion. The appointment coincided nicely with completing our less-than-memorable contractual obligations as a dance band in Laughlin. Upon my return, Paula and I attended the appointment with Dr. Wang.

I was convinced I was fine, and the lump in my neck was no more than a blockage. However, now I was in the hands of Dr Wang, who would determine the root cause of this erroneous lump. A camera was inserted in my left nostril and then fed through my nasal passage and into my throat to explore and evaluate. Within minutes, Dr Wang found a growth and advised me that he deemed it necessary to proceed with a surgical biopsy. The biopsy was performed within a few days of this discovery. After the procedure was completed, I awoke from the anesthetic and was presented with the diagnosis.

As Paula stood over me, holding my hand, Dr Wang told me the back of my throat had disintegrated while the procedure was being performed, and the lab results confirmed his worst fears. I had throat cancer. I couldn't believe what he was telling me. Aside from a touch of fatigue, I had been in no discomfort and felt pretty good. There was no mistake. I had stage three cancer, and without further treatment, I would be lucky to make it to the end of the year. It was devastating news. I hadn't smoked for over twenty years, so what had caused this? I was told the cause of my cancer was a direct result of having contracted the HPV virus. Paula was her usual upbeat self and assured me we would beat this. As I lay there, I was unconvinced. A tidal wave of self-pity engulfed me as I drifted helplessly into an ocean of despair. Everything came to a sudden stop. It had to. There was no guarantee I would survive beyond the end of the year, so my complete focus had to be on fighting this dreadful disease. There would be no more band and no more singing. Other than cancer, the premier of the film I'd been a part of had crept up on me. Forbidden Playground was finally ready. I had even written the title song for the movie during the post-production months, and now it was time to see the finished product.

Before Paula and I booked our airline tickets to Edmonton, we secured a date for my surgery upon our return. October would be challenging, but I just wanted to enjoy the film premiere for now. We arranged to stay with our son Mark. I was able to invite friends and family to this red-carpet event. It wouldn't have all the glamour of a Hollywood premier, but I was determined to enjoy every moment of this wonderful occasion.

All our glad rags were on full display as we entered the auditorium. It was a wonderful reunion with the cast and crew as we settled into our seats to enjoy the movie. It was quite surreal to be in a theatre watching a film in which I had a lead role. Although I tried to immerse myself in the film's fantasy, I kept thinking about what lay ahead of me with my health challenges. When the credits rolled, the cast received a standing ovation. It is a moment I will remember and cherish for the rest of my life. I may not have been part of a blockbuster sensation, but I was part of a labor of love that had been so rewarding.

After the photographer's shutters fell silent and the handshaking was over, the task of telling some of my colleagues about my condition was upon me. They were as shocked as I had been and lent me enormous emotional support. I didn't want to tell any of them before viewing the film as I felt that would have been inappropriate and self-serving. I did, however, feel they would like to know. If I concealed things from them, they might have been hurt by my action or inaction, as the case may be.

With the celebration and revelation over, it was time to return home and prepare for my forthcoming surgical procedure. I publicly announced this on Facebook and privately contacted close family and friends. I was overwhelmed by the outpouring of kind words, which gave me an essential boost to my somewhat subdued mood. Paula was always very optimistic about the outcome of my surgery, but I had my doubts. I thought this could be the end of the road for me. There was no more time for discussion or doubt as the day finally arrived for me to go under the knife.

It had been explained the procedure would be performed using a robotic device called the Da Vinci system. Using this mechanical system dramatically increased my chances of survival, and the trauma to my neck and face would be significantly reduced. I was checked in at the hospital, and preparations were made for my surgery. The waiting was the worst part. Once I had the gown and cap on, I just wanted to get it over with and hopefully wake up with all cancer removed. A smile from the surgeon and an injection into my vein caused my speech to slur and my vision to fade. My life was now in their hands as consciousness gradually drifted into the darkness of induced sleep.

Agony! I awoke in so much pain I couldn't believe it. It felt like someone tried to cut my head off with a bread knife. I had tubes and wires all over me, and my vision was blurred. The one thing the pain told me was I had survived the five hours of surgery. The question was, had the surgery been a success? I was told they removed fourteen lymph nodes and a tonsil and managed to remove all the cancerous tissue from my throat. It was great news and well worth all the pain and discomfort I was experiencing.

I was hospitalized for about a week until I regained enough strength to return home. I looked awful. Frankenstein came to mind as I squinted at my reflection in the bathroom mirror. I was terribly swollen, and it was tough to swallow. The pain medication was not strong enough, so I eventually asked for the most potent narcotic available and was given a prescription. I knew I would probably get hooked on these things, but one battle at a time. For now, I just wanted to get out of pain, and I would deal with any addiction issues later.

I was told to relax and rest as much as possible, but within two weeks of my release from the hospital, I foolishly returned to Laughlin with a new band and performed for a few weeks in a somewhat diminished physical state. I had to be helped onto the stage and have somebody put my bass guitar strap around my bruised and swollen neck, but I was able to perform. The gig itself was alright; it was the problem I brought home with me that caused all kinds of issues. The accommodations in Laughlin were less than desirable, and I picked up some bed bugs during my stay there. Upon my return home, these bugs ended up in our primary bedroom, and we had to fumigate the house.

Paula and I spent the best part of two months sleeping downstairs on adjacent couches. She would go to work during the day, and I would watch television until she got home. Aside from the hospital visits and the never-ending pain, we enjoyed camping out together. Paula was working at the Spa in Harrah's. I would, on occasion, go to the gym to try and strengthen my right shoulder. During the surgery, some nerves had been cut, and my shoulder slumped forward, resulting in little to no strength in my arm.

My physiotherapist gave me a regimented exercise course and told me to work through the pain. It wasn't easy, but it was a case of using or losing it. I struggled at first, but as each week passed, I could push myself harder and regained a near-full range of motion in my shoulder and arm. However, I had difficulty smiling and often looked like a stroke victim. This was not because of my mood. The skin on my neck and face had been peeled back during surgery. This led to a lot of numbing in my face and neck, causing all kinds of problems when trying to create facial expressions. To this day, I still have no feeling in parts of my neck and face. I am also prone to muscular spasms occasionally.

It was a long road to recovery, but I was walking along it, determined to regain my former strength and perform on stage again. The whole family came together, and for once, we had all our children under one roof with their respective partners. After my neck healed sufficiently, I had to undergo six weeks of radiation therapy to make sure the cancer was entirely eradicated. Every weekday, I travelled to the radiation clinic and received treatment. I didn't notice much happening for the first couple of sessions, but by the end of six weeks, I had dropped a lot of weight, and my neck was burnt and blistering. No matter, I had my family and friends around me and a sense I would recover from this ordeal and be able to pick up where I left off.

The end of the year was fast approaching, and we found ourselves still buried under a mountain of debt. Although Paula had insurance covering many of my medical bills, expenses undermined our financial recovery. I couldn't work and was unable to earn money to contribute to our fiscal dilemma. We had never fully recovered from the financial crash of 2008, and our two mortgages had out-of-control interest rates. A decision had to be made and made fast, or we would lose everything we had worked so hard for. Despite my physically weakened state, the old grey matter in my head was still functioning quite well. I procured the services of a lawyer and gained some legal insight into our financial situation. We always diligently paid our bills despite any hardship we may have endured. However, this matter of principle and pride had to come to an end. To get a better deal on our first mortgage, I was instructed to contact the bank and make an offer.

Our situation required some basic mathematics to be applied to make us a viable commodity for a mortgage adjustment. The lawyer told me by continuing to pay our mortgage, the bank would consider us ineligible for any percentage reduction on the loan. Their interpretation of our situation is that if we could keep our mortgage payments current, we must have sufficient income to honor the loan conditions. If we refused to pay and told them we had no money, they would foreclose on us, and we would be homeless. The idea was to stop paying the mortgage for a few months and send the bank our financial records for them to calculate how much we could afford.

I stopped the mortgage payments and cooked the books using the guidelines laid out to me by the lawyer. The bank finally agreed to negotiate, and we went from a 10.5% mortgage rate to 3.0%. This in itself was significant, but there was more work to be done. We had enormous credit card debt and a second mortgage we couldn't afford. All of this was garnished with a double helping of medical bills, which meant we were on a one-way trip to financial ruin. It was time to do something I had avoided my whole life. I had to file for bankruptcy.

I felt ashamed and beaten, but I could find no sensible alternative. I approached a local law firm and started the filing proceedings for Chapter 13 bankruptcy. Doing this would eliminate the second mortgage and several other debts. A structured monthly payment would enable us to clear our remaining debt after three years. We would have no credit or credit cards, and the stigma of doing this would stick to my soul for the duration.

I had been in Vegas for over ten years, and this was my landmark achievement after a decade of hard work. Bankruptcy! When all the documents had been collated and submitted to the court, my presence was requested at the law office for a final signature. I signed those papers on December 31st, 2014. I remember returning to the house in a haze of sadness and regret. I thought I'd done everything right. Clearly, this was not the case, or what I had done was not enough. Life is so unpredictable. My mother's words kept resonating in my head. "If you knew what was ahead, you'd never make it through."

Yes, I was down, but I refused to be out. I had made some significant gains and achieved accolades I would not have thought possible many years ago. This may have been a time of regret, but it was certainly not one to wallow in self-pity. I was getting stronger and had beaten cancer. If I could overcome that, I would have a fighting chance to conquer any other obstacle. As I pulled into the driveway of my Las Vegas home, I knew what lay ahead would not be easy, but there again, it never had been.

Martin Andrew

Gallery 20

On the set of Blackstone as Mr. Cogburn.

Left: Hanging out with Eric Schweig. **Right:** What a duo!!!

Paula and I at the premier of Forbidden Playground.

On set with the police.

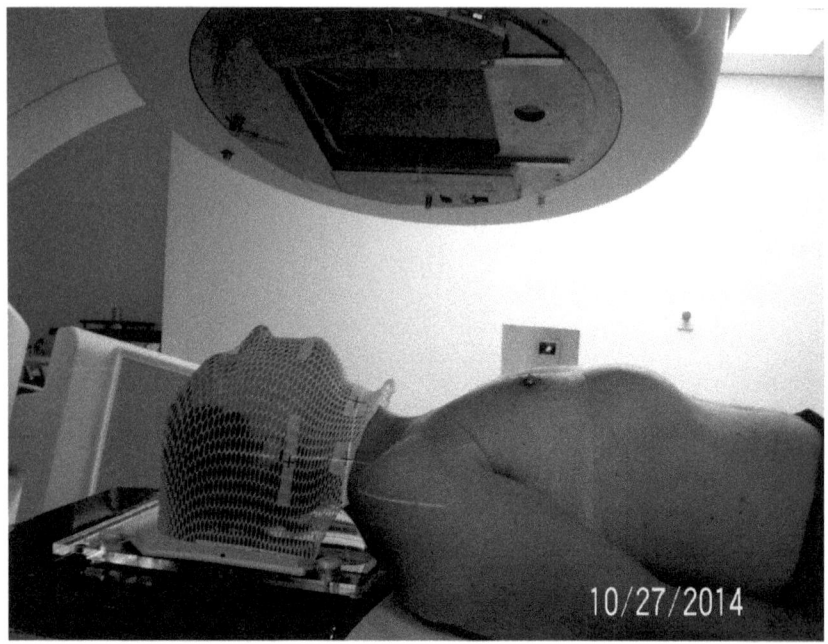

Radiation treatment.

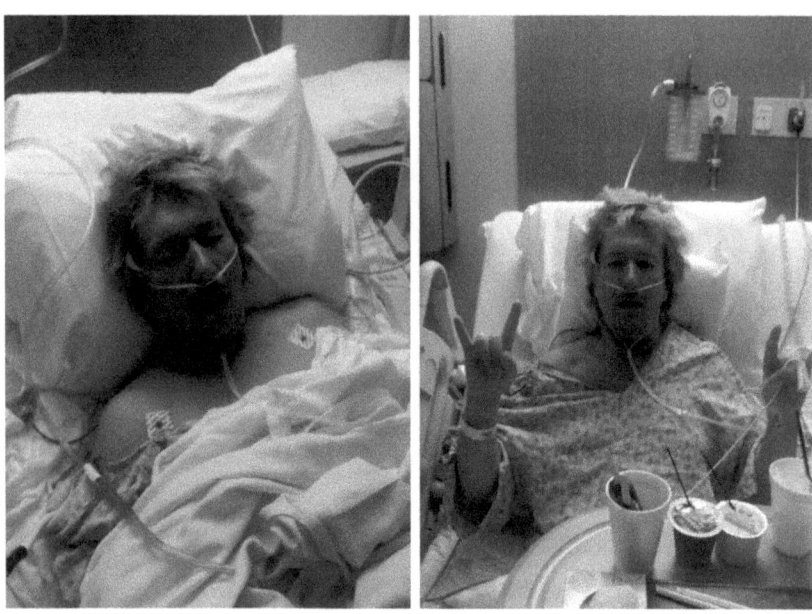

Radical neck surgery for throat cancer 2014.

Recovering with my family.

All photographs from Martin Andrew private collection.

Chapter Twenty-One

A NEW YEAR WITH NEW OPPORTUNITIES AND CHALLENGES WAS NOW upon me. I had survived throat cancer but was far from being fully fit. The surgery and radiation had taken their toll on my mind, heart, body, and soul. Despite this setback, there was no time to waste. The previous year and its challenges also had some high points. My family and friends surrounded me, and my eldest daughter Tanya showed keen interest in moving to America. For her, this would be easy. Her mother was American, so as a birthright, she could automatically become a citizen and not face all the challenges I endured to work and stay in the country.

The opportunities afforded me were limited at best, as Las Vegas had changed a lot since my arrival over a decade ago. There was no residency beckoning to me, and the corporate gigs I had been blessed with some years ago shifted their focus to other forms of entertainment. In addition, Paula and I still had financial obligations despite my being in Chapter 13 bankruptcy. Her income from working at the spa would not be enough for us to break even, let alone get ahead.

As chance would have it, I talked with an old friend, Martin Groves. He was living in America, but we had forged a friendship as teenagers in Bury St. Edmunds many years ago. He was now the vice president of an insurance company and keen to help me recover financially. He suggested I become a life insurance salesperson. I had never considered such a career but decided to try it since my phone wasn't ringing off the hook for entertainment work.

Martin arranged for me to work at a local office in Las Vegas. At the time, he was based in Texas but frequently visited Las Vegas during business travels. Before starting to work and selling policies, I had to take the state exam. It was the first time I'd done something like this since I was back in school in the late 1970s. The thought of learning all the legalities of the Insurance business concerned me somewhat, but it also presented me with a challenge I desperately needed.

I'd been coasting along for such a long time in my music career that there was not much in the way of challenges presenting themselves in any way, shape, or form. With the Rod tribute show, all I had to do was learn about thirty songs for my live performance shows. Once that was done, there was not much else that needed doing. Rod fans wanted to hear all the classic hits, so there was little need to expand the repertoire once those were learned. I played bass guitar in some cover bands and a couple of tribute shows, but once again, once the classic songs had been learned, you could coast through the shows and enjoy the spectacle on the dance floor.

This new learning bout would be a real challenge, so I decided to work diligently, acquiring knowledge for the state exam. I studied the curriculum and soon realized this undertaking would not be a cakewalk. I knew very little about this field of endeavor, and the language was difficult to understand. So many legal terms to comprehend and State laws to retain.

I studied for two months until the course material was completed. I took numerous mock exams and got an average percentile of 95%. Finally, I was ready for the state exam and submitted my application. I secured an appointment in reasonably short order and went to the examination facility. It was like being back at school. We were ushered into a room and seated at a computer booth. Strict testing rules and regulations had to be adhered to at all times. If you looked around the room or even uttered a word without raising your hand, it was grounds for immediate disqualification.

I sat facing the computer screen and awaited instructions to begin the exam. We were told we had four hours to complete it, and I was keen to get started. I had consistently done well on my mock exams and was sure I could complete the testing without too much trouble. The word was given, and the testing began. I remember the sheer horror as I skimmed through the questions looking for something I understood. None of this made sense. Where were the questions from the mock exam? I understood they might be worded slightly differently, but what was in front of me may as well have been in a foreign language.

The curriculum I studied so diligently for the best part of two months and the mock exams aced would have no bearing on what was now in front of me. Why? I'd been given the wrong study program. It was the wrong bloody course! I wasn't made aware of this until after the exam, but can you imagine how mad I was when this was revealed? Nevertheless, I answered enough questions to gain an 80% average over the entire examination, split into three parts. I passed! I was now licensed to sell life and health insurance in Nevada.

Martin Andrew Insurance Salesman. It didn't quite have the ring to entice people to converse with you at a party, but that was my new title. Following this fantastic result at the testing center, I joined the other salespeople at the local office. I was inducted into the masses of hungry sales staff who were bombarded with promises of wealth and grandeur during brainwashing sessions led by the company's top salespeople. Those who had not achieved specific sales goals were ridiculed, and others that had conned some poor unsuspecting pensioner out of their limited social security funds were celebrated.

The biggest challenge ahead of me now would be fitting in with this new crowd. I was assigned to a team along with a team leader who would show me the ropes. A couple of days during the week would be spent on the phone making cold calls to people who had little interest in listening to my scripted introduction. If an appointment was made, then a follow-up visit would ensue. I attended several meetings with the team leader and watched his technique with great interest.

First was a video presentation followed by a lecture on how foolish it was not to be interested in getting a policy. I wasn't too fond of this song and dance. It was not about getting people covered with a good life insurance policy, but rather a way to line your pockets with their hard-earned cash. The more policies you sell, the more chance of becoming a team leader and taking a percentage from your fellow team members. It was no more than a bloody pyramid scheme.

I was grateful to Martin Groves for this opportunity, but I quickly discovered this line of work was not for me. However, I didn't feel this had all been for nothing. On the contrary, I was rather pleased that despite studying the wrong course, I'd managed to pass the state exam. All my years as a rugged little rocker had not impaired my ability to learn and retain. This time of study proved that to me. Although I ended my career as an Insurance salesman after only a few weeks, I had no real regrets. I hadn't given up any entertainment contracts to do this work and regained faith in my academic abilities. With my insurance days behind me, it was time to take another look at my career.

I was approached by a duo known as the "Edwards Twins." They wanted me to be part of a show they were producing at a theatre in Boston. I met Anthony and Eddie Edwards at the Tropicana casino some years ago. Anthony Cools introduced us; the twins were interested in working with me. They were identical twins who performed multiple characters but often had other artists make guest appearances in their specialty shows. One such show focused on the music of the 1970s, and they wanted me to perform as Rod Stewart.

I flew to Boston and was introduced to other cast members who paid tribute to 1970s icons. The show was great fun, but a conversation with one of the other entertainers would lead to my involvement in yet another production. During lunch, my fellow entertainers and I often discussed other interests and productions we were involved in. At one such meeting, I talked about an Idea I had for an all-star tribute show with theatrical attributes.

Most of the tribute shows I'd seen were just a collection of characters with no real purpose being presented to the audience for why they were together on the same stage. The "Spirit of Rock n Roll" had been my pet project for some time. I explained my vision of a scripted production with a storyline. I wasn't the only one present with such a vision. I listened intently to one of the other performers with similar interests. We agreed to collaborate, and I was asked to write a script for the show idea presented to me.

Upon my return to Las Vegas, I began work on the script. The show idea grew into reality with a tour being booked in Canada. Once again, I would be returning to the north for work. The irony was not lost on me that I'd generated great opportunities in Canada by moving to America. I wasn't complaining, and in the fall of 2015, I was on my way to rehearsals for the forthcoming production.

We rehearsed for a couple of weeks and headed out for the first show in Winnipeg. The show's management and producers booked various venues across western Canada. Some of these were appropriate, others were purely farcical. They could sell enough tickets to fill smaller venues, but there was a problem regarding the 2500-seat theatres. On two occasions, I had to call my casting director friend to get hundreds of paid audience members to fill the stalls, although the balconies remained ominously empty. We appeared in television interviews and filmed multiple promo videos but to no avail. Although the tour was fun, it lost thousands of dollars at the box office.

Egos had been stroked, but the only thing wagging was the dog. It was a financial disaster, but the makings of a good show had been apparent during these limited engagements. After three weeks of travelling and performing, it was time to get back to the drawing board if this production were to have any future value. However, before returning to Las Vegas, I had to make a pit stop in Edmonton. Before the tour, I noticed a lump in my abdomen. It wasn't cancer this time, just a rather painful hernia needing repair. I had an appointment with a surgeon in St Albert and would spend a few days of recovery with my son Mark before returning home.

The journey was challenging as I was only a week out of surgery, but I made it home in one piece. I was racking my brain, trying to figure out the best way to move forward with this show. Touring was expensive, and without some serious corporate sponsorship, the financial outcome of any other tours would likely be the same: thousands of dollars in the red. It wasn't my money being wasted; my fee was paid, so why the big concern? Longevity is the simple answer to that question.

The end of 2015 was looming fast. Before I had time to figure out the best way to move forward with this new show, I received a telephone call. I couldn't believe my ears when I heard the unmistakable accent of the Russian. He had an offer for me. He wanted me to return to Vladivostok for three weeks during the festive season. This time I would be joined by my old friend Ronee, whom I worked with on several projects over the years. We had both been to Vladivostok on separate engagements but would be joining forces this time.

The Russian wanted us to perform a ZZ Top tribute and the Rod Stewart show. For ZZ Top, I would play bass and stick on a beard. For the Rod show, Ronee would be the guitarist. Other musicians were provided for us, and all expenses would be handled. Ronee and I always had fun together, so we agreed to the terms and prepared for a Christmas extravaganza in East Asia. The flight to Vladivostok was long, and we arrived feeling somewhat jet lagged. However, there was no time to be wasted. We were whisked away from the airport to an awaiting studio for rehearsals. We had both worked with local musicians. Rehearsals were brief as the players had done their homework. The following day would be our first show, but first, we were introduced to our accommodations which were home for the duration of our stay.

We had both experienced Russian hospitality and stayed at a good hotel on our last respective visits. Unfortunately, such a precedent would not be the case on this trip. Where we were taken was reminiscent of a Gulag. Dirty concrete and brick walls surrounded our compound, garnished with a heavy amount of razor wire to keep people out or keep us in. We climbed a rickety metal staircase thick with ice and opened the door to our awaiting abode. It was terrible with two tiny rooms, no pictures on the walls and a bed in each with wafer-thin mattresses.

Ronee and I had made many road trips over the years. Complaining was not in our nature, so we just smiled and unpacked our things. There was no television, a shower with no water pressure, and a fridge that barely worked. The refrigerator was the least of our worries as it was so cold in the apartment, we didn't need it. This would be our home for three weeks, so we had to make the most of it. We were going to perform at a different venue from our previous engagements, so we hoped the experience would be somewhat decent.

The club did not disappoint. It was small, and the stage was tiny but adequate for us to enjoy our performances. The dressing room was a different matter entirely. We had to get changed in an area where the kitchen staff got dressed for their shifts. They were none too impressed with us encroaching on their space, but we managed to work around them, and an air of conviviality was achieved.

Opening night was a huge success; we played our hearts out to a very enthusiastic crowd. The familiar social interactions took place after the show, with the local females enjoying our company and the males tolerating our presence. We noticed early on that the Russian used us as a conduit for him to get to know women in the club. He considered himself the local hero who contracted musicians from Las Vegas to perform at the club. He would parade us around and act like a big shot, hoping to land a lady or two each night. It was a side of him we were unaware of on our previous engagements in Vladivostok.

Things were going well at the club, but life at the Gulag was not much fun. We spent most of our time at a local tearoom managed by a fellow Brit. We passed our time sipping tea and eating copious amounts of fruitcake. It's safe to say we had reservations about the enjoyment and musical fulfilment we were experiencing. Nevertheless, we were there and going to make the most of it, whatever challenges may come our way. Little did I know I was about to face one of the most significant challenges of my life as I sipped my tea and ordered a second slice of cake.

Before departing on this trip, Paula and I visited our doctor for what was supposed to be a regular check-up. Paula noticed a small bump on her neck and asked me to check it out. It was about the size of a small pea. I thought it was nothing to worry about, nor did she, but we decided to consult our doctor for safety's sake. The doctor thought there was nothing to worry about but wanted to get a biopsy to be sure. At the time, we nervously joked about how similar this was to me finding a lump in my neck that turned out to be cancer. However, the lump in my neck was huge; this bump on Paula's was just the size of a pea, so surely there was no need for genuine concern.

Out of extreme caution, Paula had a surgical biopsy performed by the same surgeon who saved my life. Before the results were available, I'd left on my trip to Vladivostok. Now, I know what you are thinking. How could he leave his wife when there was a chance, she may have a severe illness? The simple truth is that neither of us thought it would amount to anything. We thought it was just a bit of gristle: a little lump barely visible and benign. How wrong we were.

One day as I sat in my cell at the Gulag, I decided to call Paula for a chat and see how things were back home. She told me the biopsy results had been revealed to her, and she was diagnosed with Non-Hodgkin's Lymphoma. I couldn't believe my ears. How could this be happening? I had barely recovered from my battle with cancer, and now my wife would face this life-threatening disease. I broke down and wept. It was the saddest day of my life by far.

Paula was very calm and resolute. She was the one comforting me! I had to pull it together, but it would not be easy. Words I had spoken during my ordeal with this disease came back to haunt me. I said, "Nothing could ever be worse than receiving a cancer diagnosis." I was wrong. Finding out that someone you love has cancer is far worse. I felt helpless. I was so far away from home with another couple of weeks to go. When the telephone call ended, I crumbled to the floor.

Ronee was so kind to me when I relayed the news to him. He listened to me and shared words of comfort like only a true friend would or could. I was at my lowest ebb but knew we had a job to do, and there would be no early release. We performed as usual at the club that night, but my heart was not in it. My thoughts were with my dearest Paula. I just wanted to be home to care for her, but I was here at the club.

After the show, I sat at the bar alone with my thoughts when a beautiful young lady approached me. She couldn't speak English, so I asked the Russian to translate for me. He took it upon himself to make some lewd remarks to the young lady, who, in turn, unleashed a verbal onslaught directed toward me. I was confused and asked what had just happened. He explained by telling me what he said and laughed at me. It was not the time or the place; I tore into him with a verbal onslaught of my own. When I was done, I left the bar and went upstairs to the dressing room.

The Russian followed me. He was enraged that I dared to chastise him in front of his friends in the club. He swung a fist at me. I moved just in time for him to punch a hole in the wall and injure his hand. I was not backing down and told him our relationship would be strictly business. The friendship was over. I probably overreacted to the situation, and antagonizing him was not a good idea, but I didn't care at that time. I told Ronee what happened, and he stood firmly beside me. He didn't need to do that. He could have easily sided with the Russian and continued our show dates without having to look over his shoulder, but he chose not to.

From that point on, he and I became very isolated and were made to feel extremely unwelcome. We continued to perform as professionals do, but there was a definite atmosphere at the club. At one point, things got so ugly Ronee contacted the American Embassy. They came to the club, making their presence known. We were working for some less-than-desirable people, and who knows what they had in store for us at the end of the contract. Another more sinister contract?

The ordeal ended on January 1st, 2016. We gathered our belongings and were driven to the airport. The journey was fraught with concern as we didn't know what our escort had in store. The driver and his accomplice talked to each other and frequently scowled at us in the rearview mirror. Although we had no fundamental understanding of what they were saying, it was apparent from their voices the dialogue was derogatory. The journey was very disconcerting, with neither of us convinced our final destination would be the airport.

Our bags and guitars were unceremoniously thrown onto the sidewalk when we arrived. The doors slammed, the wheels spun, and we were left standing at the side of the road. With great haste, we passed through security and boarded the plane. The flight home was a somber affair for both of us. It hadn't been the fun trip we expected; the Russian was no longer a friend. Ronee and I sat in different areas of the aircraft. It was a time of silence and solitude. I just wanted to get home and wrap my arms around Paula. She was now facing the fight of her life, and I needed to be in her corner.

Once back in Las Vegas, Paula and I spent our time at doctors' appointments, scheduling her treatment. She underwent several weeks of chemotherapy to aggressively attack the cancer, which was rapidly reproducing in her blood. She was fitted with a port in her chest, and the potentially lifesaving treatment began. It was heart-wrenching to see her hooked up to this elaborate machinery pumping a cocktail of chemicals through her veins. She never complained, despite being constantly nauseous and gradually losing her hair.

I remember the night at home when Tanya shaved Paula's head. Tanya shaved half her head in an act of support for Paula's ordeal. Our daughters were of great comfort to Paula at this time as they stood vigil by her side. Mark had to endure from afar but showed great strength of character and unwavering concern for his mother's well-being. The image of my dear Paula's vulnerable appearance will stay with me forever. It's an image symbolizing a time when I was helpless to ease the physical pain of someone who was everything to me. All I could do was what Paula wanted me to do, which was to carry on as usual. She was as convinced about beating her cancer as she had been about me winning my battle. Although my concern never diminished, I had confidence in her and was able to respect her wishes, getting on with the job at hand.

Since my arrival in Vegas, I looked for an opportunity to be part of a show with a proven ability to survive the fragility of a long-term engagement. So many shows in Las Vegas, such as "Legends in

Concert," had been running for years. Much as I despised the tired format of that particular show, the performers in it were getting a regular paycheck. I'd tried to produce a show in Las Vegas when I did the "Rod & Shania" tribute. However, I knew how expensive that little venture had been on the Fremont Street Experience and leasing a space on the strip was unrealistic.

I was convinced that a residency was the way to go, but where to find a venue was the million-dollar question. However, a chance meeting with an old friend was about to change all that. In my early days of performing in Las Vegas, I met a man called Steve Bach. Steve was, and is, a very accomplished musician who worked with many credible artists and a tribute band in Los Angeles. He and I toyed with the idea of working together, but very early in our collaborative scheming, he was offered a position with Cirque de Soleil. This position took him away from Los Angeles, and he became a music director for a Cirque show in Macau.

A project I'd been involved with some years before the Canadian tour introduced me to some members of the Cirque clan. As a result, I was hired to perform in a play by the British National Theater of America. The play was written by Matt Charman and entitled "A Night at the Dogs." My co-stars in the play were British and from various Cirque shows on the Las Vegas strip. The play was a great success, and friendships were forged.

So back to the venue dilemma. I'm figuring out how to find a suitable venue for a residency when I get invited by one of my Cirque friends to see a show, he appears in. I gladly accept; Paula and I enjoy a wonderful evening of acrobatics and other stunning theatrics. After the show, we are invited to see the backstage area and get a guided tour of the inner workings of this spectacular production. When the tour concluded, we got into an elevator and pressed the ground floor button. Within seconds we were at our destination, and the doors opened.

As Paula and I exited the elevator, I brushed by a man with a face familiar to me. I kept walking for a few steps before I abruptly stopped in my tracks. After a brief pause, I turned to see who appeared so familiar. It was Steve Bach. We hadn't seen each other in years. It was one of those movie moments where both parties looked confused and called out each other's names tentatively yet excitedly. Steve was the music director for the show we just witnessed. We negated our plans without further ado and made haste to a nearby lounge. There was so much to talk about. We stumbled over each other's words and laughed until our sides hurt. We agreed to have lunch and continue our conversation over a toasted bagel and a fine, medium roast.

Steve and I got together at the Bagel Cafe in Summerlin, with me not knowing how many things were about to change. After our preliminary small talk, I told him about the show I was involved in and my dilemma in finding a theatre for the production. We agreed that a Las Vegas venue was unrealistic, but Steve offered an alternative. He had been Andy Williams and Jim Stafford's music director at theatres in Branson, Missouri. Steve knew a lot of people in Branson and suggested there may be an opening for a residency at one of the theatres.

I relayed this information to the show producers and management team. A recon mission was planned to evaluate the possibilities of leasing a theatre in Branson. Steve had a particular local producer in mind who he contacted at my request. We were in luck. There was an empty theatre complex opposite this producer's theatre; he even had the keys if we wanted to take a look. I contacted the producers in Canada, and they agreed to look at the Branson property.

The property had three business areas, all housed in the main building. A bar, coffee shop, and box office were on the ground floor. The theatre itself was on the second floor. The building was reasonably sound, but it would take a lot of work to prepare the theatre for the show. The Canadian producer decided to lease all the businesses and take over the complex. A tentative deal was reached with all present, and great enthusiasm filled the air.

So that was it. The show was moving to Branson for a residency. I volunteered to start the renovations and arrived in Branson in early May 2016. I was able to stay with the now "Co-producer" of the show. Steve and I were offered production deals at the initial meeting. Still, those evaporated in short order, along with the comical spreadsheets and other dangling carrots we bore witness to. I worked long hours at the facility, gradually developed a theatre floor plan and submitted other ideas for the bar and coffee shop. I even managed to get Paula employed as the bar manager.

After a few months of long, laborious days, the facility was taking shape, and it was almost time for the cast to arrive. The show was to comprise the main cast and musicians from the Canadian tour, with one significant addition, Samira. She was the extraordinary lady I met all those years ago at the Tropicana casino, and now we'd get a chance to work together in Branson. Unfortunately, despite being (what I considered) the best tribute to Tina Turner on the planet, she was only employed initially as a backing singer.

I returned to Las Vegas and was happy Paula responded well to her therapy. After her last treatment, we consulted with her oncologist and decided to travel to Branson. I can't tell you the relief I felt finding Paula in better health than when I left for Branson in May. She had a long road to full recovery, but by the time we left Las Vegas, she was in remission and ready to begin our new adventure.

It took the best part of two days to get to Branson. All cast members were assembled and almost ready to go when we arrived. While I was gone, the producers deemed it necessary for the musicians to help with various tasks, including building a stage in the bar. Unfortunately, one of the guitarists fell through the stage and injured his leg. His name was Jimmy Craig, and he became one of my very few close friends during our time in Branson. Despite his injury and various things lacking in the production department, the show opened in August 2016.

It was decided early on that we needed alternate shows to fill our calendar, so I developed "Legs" and a show called "Rockers Rollin'." These two shows would bring me, and the others involved, the most pleasure. "Legs" featured a tribute to ZZ Top and Tina Turner, and "Rockers Rollin' " featured tributes to Rod Stewart, Mick Jagger, and Tina Turner. It was my way of getting Samira's talents to the forefront instead of burying her in the background as a backing singer. Samira, Jimmy, and I became the three Amigos. We were joined by

Steve's son Sebastian, who was affectionately referred to as the "Buzzard."

Performing in three shows six nights a week requires a great deal of stamina. There was a gym at the apartment complex where we were housed. This facility became a second home for the duration of my stay in Branson due to Samira, an enthusiastic fitness trainer. Jimmy and I would join her at the gym, and "coach concrete", as she was affectionately known, would put us through our paces. It was a hard slog at times, but the benefits outweighed the pain we endured. I managed to lose a few pounds and gain some extra muscle which would be of great benefit during our long work weeks.

The main show lost its allure very early due to a mixture of annoying egos and a lack of vision from the so-called producers. The cast soon split into two camps, and a cloud of angst hung over every performance of the main show. The ticket sales were pathetic. We often performed for six people in a two-hundred-seat theatre. Many nights were cancelled, which didn't do much for morale as we sank deeper and deeper into a quagmire of discontent. We'd relocated to Branson, hoping to have a theatre we could return to for multiple seasons, but the dream was becoming a nightmare.

There were often moments of comic relief, most inadvertently supplied by Samira. She was a very talented lady with a penchant for destroying any inanimate object encountered. I remember she came to visit Paula and I one day at our humble Branson dwelling. Within minutes, she had torn down the curtains, and the curtain rail was in pieces at our feet. She decided to let in more sunlight, but devastation and destruction always seemed to follow her intended good deed.

Samira was not immune to accidents during her performances as "Tina", and I recall several nights when I could hardly contain my laughter. One time she arrived on stage wearing her "Thunderdome" coat and realized she had removed her dress. It became an issue when I went to remove her coat for the next song. She hysterically scurried off the stage as I proceeded to lead an impromptu blues jam with lyrical content describing her near-naked experience.

On more than one occasion during her performances, she had a wardrobe malfunction resulting in all present trying desperately to contain our laughter. A bra insert was seen one night flying through the air before being kicked repeatedly by a high-heeled shoe until it was obscured from view by the drum riser. Another night, when her dress came undone, she was able to do a quick twirl and re-attach the garment without missing a beat. Samira was no backing singer. Instead, she was a fantastic entertainer who kept us all smiling when it would have been so easy to wear a frown.

Things didn't improve. By the end of the season in December, the shows had all but collapsed with a deep-rooted animosity between the two camps and little festive cheer. Paula had done her best to get the bar up and running, but after a short visit to Canada in December to get some blood work done, she returned to Branson only to find out she had been fired. I was relieved as I didn't want her to be around such toxic people housed in such a hostile environment. A few weeks before we returned to Las Vegas, Randi and her husband Ed came to celebrate Christmas. We made the most of it, but I'm sure it was a big disappointment for them. Not too many smiling faces were to be seen, and the theatre I'd hoped to give them a tour of was now closed for the season. It had all come crashing down, and before we knew it, we were back on the road heading for Las Vegas.

We endured a treacherous journey back to Las Vegas as we encountered heavy snow and freezing temperatures. It was a two-day journey, and the one night we tried to sleep at the side of the road was an exercise in futility. We huddled in the car to try and stay warm, but it was all in vain. We had our little convoy, with me leading the way in the truck and Paula bringing up the rear in the car. The heater in the truck stopped working, which made for a miserable trip, but with the bright lights of Las Vegas in sight, we were just glad to be home.

It would be easy to conclude the season in Branson was just another failure to add to my growing list of disappointments. I, however, did not see it that way. I'd forged relationships with some wonderful people and enjoyed the "Legs" and "Rockers Rollin'" shows. I also enjoyed working with Jimmy, Samira, and The Buzzard. The creation of our new shows was in its infancy and needed more development time to branch out independently. The key was to have a central location for us to be together to finish what we started.

More challenges presented themselves when Paula and I arrived home. First, on inspection of our property, we found the hot water tank had sprung a leak and flooded part of the ground floor. As a result, there was extensive damage to the downstairs bathroom. Fortunately, we had an insurance policy to take care of the repairs. The other challenge was created by a call I received from one of the producers in Branson. The good news was despite the poor attendance, loss of money and cast infighting; a decision was made to go ahead with a second season. It was music to my ears. Not because I particularly wanted to return to the toxic situation I had just left, but more because it was the perfect place to get our new shows ready.

I was fully prepared to accept the new offer when one of the conditions of my return stopped me in my tracks. The producers, with a decision based on pure malice and insecurity, refused to renew Samira's contract. They said she was a troublemaker and caused too much drama, which was utter bullshit! Samira was, and is, a great performer who caused no problems. However, she had to endure a great deal of animosity and jealousy because she was likeable and talented. This condition for my return would have split up our newfound team and was a non-starter for me.

I refused to return to Branson without Samira being part of the team, and a stalemate ensued. The producers now had a real problem. I was integral to all three productions and scripted the main show. The script was registered to me, so subsequently, I would not allow them to continue performing the main show as portrayed in my script. I received numerous emails attacking me and my new friends but refused to respond or enter negotiations. My decision was final. No Samira, no show!

Gallery 21

Samira and I in Branson.

Photograph by Stormy Schumacher.

Jimmy and I doing a ZZ top tribute.

The three amigos!!

Photographs by Stormy Schumacher.

Samira doing time in Branson.

Photograph from Martin Andrew private collection.

Photographs by Stormy Schumacher.

Thank you and goodnight!

The harsh reality of how fragile life can be. Paula in the fight of her life 2016.

Photograph from Martin Andrew private collection.

Chapter Twenty-Two

AFTER DRAWING A DEEP LINE IN THE SAND, COMMUNICATION BETWEEN the producers and myself went dead. I was in close contact with Samira and kept her abreast of the situation, as none of the producers had the guts to call her directly. Samira and I were determined to work together and develop our "Rod & Tina" show. The enjoyment we experienced was mutual, and there was definite chemistry between us when we performed on stage. At this point, we were unsure if returning to Branson was a realistic option. Despite my leverage over the producers, they were adamant at the time that Samira could not return. We would have to find other ways of getting back together to get our show on the road.

Samira had been asked to perform at a friend's party in Vancouver and was keen to have me in the show. After a brief negotiation with her friend, I was included in her performance as a special guest. I was very excited about this show despite the fact it was a one-off performance. It would be the first time we could work together outside the toxicity of the Branson experience. I boarded a plane in early January 2017 and flew to Vancouver.

Samira allowed me to stay at her house. I was given the guest suite, which was more than ample for my needs. She had a beautiful home, and I was made to feel very welcome. I met some of her friends and family. We spent a few days before the show enjoying some local attractions. We talked at length about the situation in Branson and agreed if we could return there, it would be the path of least resistance for developing our show.

The day before our performance in Vancouver, I woke up with a nauseous feeling that wouldn't subside. It progressively worsened during the day, and I was throwing up every twenty minutes by the evening. I had the worst fever and couldn't stop throwing up throughout the night. Samira spent the night mopping my brow with a cold cloth and holding a bowl for me to empty my stomach into. By the morning of the show, I was empty, and aside from a few dry heaves, I felt the tide had turned. Although a little fragile, I was determined not to let the side down and prepared myself for the evening's performance.

It was a fun night; our performance was a great hit with everyone in attendance. This singular performance confirmed we needed to work as a team. We hoped performing solo shows would now be a thing of the past. A wave of excitement washed over us like a baptism of sorts. Our focus was now on getting Samira back in the cast for season two in Branson. I would have to open negotiations with the producers and see if they were prepared to bend.

After numerous emails and text messages, I got my way. Samira was reinstated, and we would return to Branson in February to prepare for the new season. I was under no illusion that any of the problems of season one would not be a part of season two. All I needed Branson for was to get us together under one roof to prepare the "Rod and Tina" show. We needed promotional video material, and Branson would be the ideal place to complete this task.

Jimmy stayed in Branson over the winter and informed me about the production team's mood. From what he told me, it became clear we'd be in for a relatively cold reception. I didn't care. I was focused on one thing and one thing alone. I could smile and wave; while bestowing the anger inside me upon these contemptuous individuals, the recipients being none the wiser. I looked forward to it.

The Road to the Manor

As predicted, our reception committee was less than sincere in their welcoming, so we just ignored the frigidity of the situation and set about getting the shows up and running. The familiar sight of Paula working behind the bar was a distant memory as some locals had taken her place in a management capacity. It seemed like the bar, which once had aspirations of being a classy musicians' retreat, turned into a spit and sawdust joint. Our wages were significantly reduced, and the production value of the theatre was lackluster at best. Nevertheless, it was good to be back.

I could write a book about my unpleasant experience in Branson, but that wouldn't be productive. What happened there can stay there, but some things are worth mentioning for the record. Something unrelated to the shows affected me deeply. Things I was unprepared for but had to face up to during my time there. Before proceeding with these revelations, a word of thanks. I would have struggled to cope with what unfolded without my newfound friends. So, to Samira, Jimmy, and the Buzzard, I say thank you for your enduring friendship.

The shows at the theatre were lumbering along under a cloud of disdain and animosity. Nothing had changed since the first season. We went through the motions with forced smiles on our respective faces. Then, I received some shocking news on March 10th, 2017. My father died. I knew he was ill, and the prognosis received from his doctor was not good, but I was not prepared for this tragic news. I collapsed on the floor and was consoled by Samira and Jimmy. I'd never had a close relationship with my father and hadn't seen him in three years, but I was devastated to hear of his passing: no more phone calls or visits. The finality of the situation became very apparent, and this caused me great anguish. I spoke to my mother, who was in shock and heartbroken. They had been a couple for over fifty years and, in their way, forged a loving relationship that endured.

Samira and Jimmy stayed with me throughout the day. After I regained my composure, we visited a lake. The serenity and peaceful nature of this location were what I needed in my fragile state of mind. My father loved the water, and it seemed appropriate to spend some time at the water's edge to reflect on his life and subsequent passing. I have no religious beliefs, but I was with two friends who were people of faith. A Muslim and a Christian. I asked them if they would say a few words to honor my father. Samira spoke in Arabic, and Jimmy in English. Both articulated some beautiful words. I will be forever grateful to them for the consolation they offered me.

I performed at the theatre that night and was flanked by my dear friends. Fortunately for me, the performance was the Tina and ZZ Top Show. We enjoyed it with a genuine air of happiness in our group's demeanor. I'd been allowed to cancel the show but refused to do so. The show must go on, and it was the best thing for me to do at that time. We paid tribute to my father with music and song. The one connection he and I had was our genuine love of music. It seemed a fitting tribute to the man I wish I'd known better.

Arrangements were made for me to attend his funeral, and I soon parked my rental car in the driveway of my childhood home. When I entered the house, I was greeted by my brother and his wife. After exchanging a few pleasantries, it was time to see my mother. She was in a terrible state, both physically and mentally. She put a brave face on, but it was clear she had suffered a loss that would devastate her well-being and her entire future. It was a somber affair as my mind occasionally drifted to thoughts of an unrealistic expectation that my father might suddenly appear.

Before the funeral, I went to see my father's body as he lay in the chapel of rest. Looking at this motionless figure, I could not equate the body before me with the man who lived. He looked so different. So small. I had to see him with my own eyes to turn the page and move on. He was at peace. I knew he would want me to get on with my life and not waste time mourning him. He was a very pragmatic man in life, and I was prepared to respect what I believed to be his wishes in death.

The funeral was tough for me. I volunteered to write and read the eulogy, thinking I could get through it without being overrun with emotion. I had stood in front of thousands of people over the years, but this was different. Familiar faces, their eyes locked on me as I stood stoically at the church lectern. From my first utterance, my voice began to tremble as I relayed the words written to the compassionate onlookers. I was unable to regain my composure and struggled to finish the eulogy. As I returned to my seat, my brother's strong arms engulfed me, consoling me as I wept uncontrollably. I was supposed to be a tower of strength for my mother but had displayed diminished capacity in that role as I sat with my head hung low.

A small gathering surrounded the grave as my father was lowered into his final resting place. We all sprinkled a handful of dirt onto his coffin. The image of my mother hesitantly casting a single rose into the grave is etched into my memory. We returned to the house for light refreshments after the burial ceremony. Then, it was time to regale tales of the man who had been and would now be the subject of fond memories. My dear friend Graham and his wonderful family attended, and their calming presence comforted me.

Graham had been a friend of mine since my early teens and was almost a surrogate son to my mum and dad. He often visited my parents and would help them with a variety of chores. Sometimes Graham would sit and have a cup of tea, listening intently to my mother as she told tales of old. The sheer fact he took time out of his day to check in on them was a testament to his strength of character. He had proved himself to be a true friend. It was so good to see him and his family on that day.

My mother tried to stay busy and, as usual, was a fun host despite the circumstances of the gathering. She was a real character who could always raise a smile and a glass of sherry or two. I found a quiet moment to talk to her and assess her state of mind. She let her guard down and confided in me that she had no desire to continue living without her beloved partner. Physically, she was in a real mess. She underwent dialysis treatment three times a week and spent the rest of her waking hours sitting in a chair. She'd been a heavy drinker and smoker her whole life, a habit that continued despite her health problems. She was fading fast, and my father's death would speed up her demise. I could do nothing but assure her she was loved, and I hoped she could find new meaning for waking up each day. My words were spoken in vain, but they had to be said. I just hoped for the best but had to prepare myself for the worst.

I said farewell to all in attendance and boarded a plane returning to America. The loss of my father was hard to come to terms with, but the best course of action for me was to get busy and keep busy. I wrote a new set of songs and asked Jimmy if he would play guitar. He agreed, and we started to work on recording the new material for my forthcoming CD. We worked on the songs by day and performed at the theatre at night. I hadn't collaborated with a guitarist in a long time. Jimmy was an excellent player, so his contribution brought new life and a unique sound to the compositions.

I was asked to perform with some old friends in California in May. "Jumping Jack Flash" paid tribute to the music of The Rolling Stones. I worked with them several times as part of their "Stones & Stewart" show. During our negotiations for the upcoming show, I suggested involving Samira. They agreed, so Samira and I got time off and flew to California for a show in San Juan Capistrano.

This would typically be just another show and wouldn't be on my list of things to write about in this memoir but for a minor glitch. Everything was as it should be, and the show began in its regular, smooth fashion. I was dressed for my performance while Samira was still getting ready to join me. The dressing room was about a hundred feet from the outdoor stage, and the pathway was a little rugged. I was wearing runners, so my journey to the stage was without incident. However, this would not be the case when Samira had to make her way to the stage in high heels.

I completed my set, and it was time to introduce Samira. Somebody was supposed to tell her it was showtime but forgot. Due to the distance from the stage to the dressing room, it was hard to hear what the person on stage was saying. That person on stage was me, and as the band played the intro for the arrival of Samira, I called for her to join me. I tried to call her at least three times before she heard me. In a panicked, semi-dressed state, she ran along the cobbled path toward the stage.

It was indeed a sight to behold. This tiny person in a spiky wig yelled, "I'm coming!" as she trotted bow-legged toward the stage. I think the crowd enjoyed her entrance more than the show, but the fun was not over yet. Due to our delayed flight, we missed the soundcheck. For the encore, it was decided Samira, and I would join the lead singer from the Stones tribute band, singing a verse of Honky Tonk Woman, which we both knew. To our sheer horror, the song was in the wrong key for both our vocal registers. I could sing my verse an octave higher, but Samira sounded like a Barry White soundtrack from a '70s porn film. The moment was immortalized when captured during a split second of still photography, in which our expressions said it all. It had been a challenging day, but we enjoyed every minute of it, and it was a wonderful distraction from the mundane routine of Branson. After the show, we returned to Branson, and the ordeal continued until another devastating sucker punch was bestowed upon me.

On July 21st, 2017, my brother called; I was told my mother was dead. Within four months, I had lost both parents. I cannot begin to describe the anguish and pain this caused me. I won't pretend we were a close family, as that had never been the case. I'd left home when I was nineteen years old and rarely visited my parents in the early years of relocating to London. Instead, I flew across the Atlantic often and nurtured a more mature approach to our relationship in later years. They were my parents, but now they were gone.

It was a carbon copy trip to England for my mother's funeral. I was meeting old friends, giving a heart-wrenching eulogy with tea and light refreshments to follow. It seemed robotic as I tried to understand what it all meant. Our childhood home would now have to be sold along with all the furnishings that couldn't be transported to my brother's home or my house in Las Vegas. It was the end of an era. There would be no more family home in Bury St. Edmunds.

My brother and his wife vacated the premises before I did, leaving me nothing to do but think. I felt as empty as the house looked. The outline of pictures on nicotine-stained walls was now a sad reminder that all things must come to an end. It was a final, sad farewell as I reversed my rental car out of the driveway onto such a familiar street. I took one final look at what was now to become just a memory. I drove away from what had been my family home for the last fifty years, knowing I would never set foot inside it again. It was time to move on. When I returned to Branson, my entire focus was on finishing my album of new songs and getting the "Rod & Tina" show ready for presentation to all agents. The album was taking shape, but I needed one more song. I decided to write a song in memory of my parents. The song is called "The Hands of Time" and became the title track for the new album.

My old friend Martin Groves showed up in Branson and began to take a keen interest in the new show I was developing. He had worked in the music industry, offered to help us with the business end of things, and constructed a website for us. The only thing we needed now was a name for the show. So, we discussed possible show titles one night when Samira, Martin and I were out for dinner. After evaluating several suggestions, we called the show "Reunited."

The reason we settled on this title was because it reflected the concept of the show. The storyline dealt with the re-launching of Tina's career. Rod Stewart and many others in the industry played an integral part in bringing the new Tina to the forefront of the live music scene by singing duets with her. My script was based around a fictitious reunion of the two singers looking back over their colorful careers. Samira and I spent long hours fine-tuning the script while Martin Groves developed a logo for us and began work on the new website.

We needed some video footage and photographs for our new show to use as promotional material. To this end, we asked a wonderfully talented local photographer for a favor. Stormy Schumacher created a fantastic portfolio of live performance images, and I set about putting together a biography for the new act. By the end of the season, we were ready to contact the list of agents I collected from various sources. When the producers announced the date for our final show at the theatre, we were more than ready to move on.

The second year in Branson served its purpose, and as the theatre closed its doors for the last time, we all breathed a sigh of relief. It had been a harrowing experience in some respects, but we'd come out of this debacle on top. It was now time to go our separate ways. We would not be a part for too long, as I suggested we reconvene at my house in the new year. I had two extra bedrooms, so it would be easy to house both Jimmy and Samira. In addition, the Buzzard was just a short car ride from Las Vegas, so getting everyone together for rehearsals and shows would be easy.

We embraced each other before dawn on a cold December morning and said our goodbyes. It was not a goodbye but more of an "au revoir" situation. After two days of travelling, I pulled into my driveway. It felt so good to be home. I could now enjoy Christmas and see the new year arrive, knowing I'd be working with my friends on our new project. My album was near completion, and I looked forward to spending time in the studio applying the finishing touches. I was delighted with how the album turned out. Jimmy added so much texture and color with his guitar-playing skills, and I looked forward to recording Samira's voice when she and I reunited in the new year. For now, it was time to relax and enjoy the festive season.

2018 had begun, and there was a lot to get on with. I had been contacted by a lady in Reno named Stephanya, who had a job offer for me. She produced a show called "Simply the Best," which was a tribute to the music of Tina Turner. She asked if I would be interested in appearing in her show when it opened later in the year. There was no conflict of interest here. Samira and I agreed it would be a good idea for me to do this as it might lead to new contacts for our show. So, with that contract waiting in the wings, I decided it was time to get every-body back together.

We readied ourselves for our first show early in the year. The Steve Beyer agency had taken an interest in our new product and decided to showcase us at the upcoming NASCAR race. I performed at this loca-tion several times. My tribute to Rod Stewart was one of the main attractions when the Neon Garage opened all those years ago. I had a good repertoire with the agency and felt confident they would like us.

Days before we were due to perform, Samira developed a sore throat and lost her voice. This was not good for our first performance, or any performance for that matter. We loaded her up with lozenges and hoped for the best. Unfortunately, it was a windy day at the racetrack, which played havoc with our costumes. The show we were contracted to perform that day was to showcase the tributes to ZZ Top and Tina Turner. The agency had seen me perform as Rod many times, so it was essential to introduce these new acts to them.

We hit the stage and played our hearts out. Stick-on beards blew like flags in the wind as Samira strutted around the stage, ducking high notes when necessary. The crowd loved it! I was convinced we would receive a rave review from the agents in attendance. When we exited the stage, we were flooded with compliments from the audience and agents alike. It was a hit! After our triumphant debut performance, we returned to my house for a well-deserved cup of tea.

Before I could make an appointment at Steve's office, I was contacted by phone with some news I wasn't expecting. The agents had not been impressed with our performance despite the adulation we received from the crowd. The criticism was directed toward Jimmy's vocal capability in recreating the Billy Gibbons experience. They felt his vocals were weak and not representative of the character. Jimmy's portrayal was integral to the show, so they deemed us nonviable. On the other hand, they agreed he was a fantastic guitarist, and Samira's interpretation of Tina Turner was excellent. Still, it was not enough to sway a viability decision in our favor.

There were already a few "Tina" impersonators in town, and I was all too aware of the other "Rods" available for bookings. Plenty of great guitar players, and only a limited number of positions were available. We had nothing new to offer. The most prominent agency in Las Vegas turned us down, and I had to relay this information to the others. I have never been one to sugarcoat things, so I let them have it right between the eyes. Jimmy felt he had let us down and wanted to leave. I told him we were a team and should stick together despite the negative comments from the agency. I was able to dissuade him from going, and so began a long conversation about what we should do next.

We knew we had a great act (despite the review given by the Steve Beyer agency) and decided to continue developing our show. We continued for the best part of the next two years with limited success, but some memorable and fun experiences are worthy of note. We played to sold-out crowds in venues around the country, from Waco, Texas, to Los Angeles, California. There are, however, a couple of places that stand out in my mind for differing reasons.

We were invited to play at the Hard Rock casino in the Dominican Republic. There were two Hard Rock venues. We experienced sell-out crowds at both. The Dominican was an exciting place. Our host/promoter was a wonderful character. Juan Carlos wined and dined us in a fashion becoming of real rock stars. The advertising campaign was excellent. I witnessed my image on billboards standing over forty feet tall. It was an authentic rock-star experience, and we enjoyed our time in the Dominican. I was housed in a villa with a private pool and a fully stocked bar in my suite. I would have enjoyed it, but I was only there for a few hours due to an early flight.

Samira was fortunate to be offered a contract to perform at the Glen Arbor golf course in New York for a private function. The special occasion was the celebration of golf legend Gary Players' birthday. It was glamour and glitz at its finest. I remember playing bass onstage and watching Samira tease and tantalize the audience. Suddenly I noticed a face in the audience from many movies I'd seen. It was Michael Douglas watching Samira as she provocatively delivered each song in a way only, she could. What a night that was!

Another wonderful moment for me, unrelated to our performing schedule: receiving my American Citizenship. It had been a long, complicated, expensive road, but now the journey was at an end. I was sworn in and received a warm welcome to the United States of America. It was a time for celebration with both friends and family. I now held dual citizenship, and my days of immigration woes were at an end.

We continued pursuing the dream of getting a residency or at least a viable touring schedule. Still, we could never quite get enough work to sustain us financially. I ended up introducing Jimmy to some old friends of mine from the security industry, and before long, he was working as a full-time security officer. Unfortunately, this was not why he came to Las Vegas, and it became apparent he was unhappy with how things turned out.

I was fortunate to work in Reno for several weeks as part of Stephanya's production. It was a fun experience and a regular paycheck, but as with many shows, there was no follow-up of any significance to capitalize on the initial success. I had occasional offers to make guest appearances in other shows, but by the end of 2019, our once-close relationship was beginning to fracture. Samira and I began to focus on working together using tracks instead of a full band, leaving Jimmy increasingly isolated. There was no blame to be laid; we were just casualties of an industry that didn't take prisoners. The Buzzard was firmly entrenched in the LA music scene. My contact and conversations with him diminished as time passed. The year ended with Samira leaving for a well-earned break and me being invited to perform, as part of a New Year's celebration, with yet another show.

Before Samira and I parted company, she was offered a short tour in Mexico and arranged for me to participate. This was, perhaps, the start of something good. Track shows were easy. All you have to do is plug in a phone and sing along to pre-recorded music. It's like karaoke in costumes. I had been so against doing this style of show and desperately wanted to perform with a band. However, I was prepared to do what was necessary to keep our partnership together.

I rang in the New Year at the Feather Falls Casino in Orville, California and flew back to Las Vegas the next day. I spent most of January preparing for February. February was the month when Samira would be returning to Las Vegas, and rehearsals would begin for our forthcoming tour in Mexico. I was excited to be reunited with her as we endeavored to keep our fledgling partnership alive. However, just before we left for Mexico, there were a couple of other contractual obligations to fulfil.

My dear friend Melonie contacted me and asked if Samira and I would sing at the nursing home where her grandmother was a resident. I met Melonie when I performed at Grandma Rita's 80th birthday party. We hit it off and became close friends. Samira and I were thrilled to be part of this celebration. The reaction of Grandma Rita was worth its weight in gold when we burst into song, to her total dismay. Samira lined up another private party for us where I was to be a surprise guest singer. I wore a wig and moustache to stay incognito, facilitating my undetected mingling among the partygoers. The location was a beautiful property in Las Vegas; we had a most convivial night. We were just so happy to be singing together again. We had no band, but as singers, we were doing what we always did. Samira was so much fun to work with, and I looked forward to our time in Mexico.

Before we left for Mexico, there were disturbing news reports about a virus causing some alarm worldwide. In addition, there was talk of a pandemic. I had never heard of a pandemic and had to look up the word's meaning. I didn't pay too much attention to this, and most people were not overly worried about it at the time. We thought it was probably another news story designed to scare us all into buying more Lysol products. I gave the reporting little credence and looked forward to heading south for some fun in the sun.

Our accommodations were a bit rustic when we arrived in Mexico, even by Mexican standards. However, we made the most of it, and the tour was soon underway. We had so much fun. The gigs were often underproduced, but we were determined to enjoy ourselves in whatever situation presented itself. It was a glorious time by all accounts. We had little to do during the day. After working out, we lounged by the pool and basked in the hot sun. At night we sang from our hearts to an adoring audience who made us feel very welcome.

It was what we'd been working towards for so long. Of course, it wasn't what we'd envisioned during our time in Branson, but this would be a great way to make a living, and I had no complaints. During our stay in Mexico, we discussed plans for the future and were happy to work together again. We had a deep respect for each other's integrity and talent. This was a winning team, and we could envision a bright future ahead of us. The only thing casting a shadow of doubt on this bright future was the increasing concern over the growing pandemic.

We saw news reports as things worsened. I began to take the situation very seriously. There were reports of respiratory failure and multiple deaths all over the world. Could this be happening? It seemed almost apocalyptic. As our time in Mexico ended, I remarked to Samira half in jest that these might be our final shows for quite a while.

On our journey to America, we noticed many people wearing face masks. There was even an incident on the plane where a passenger became embroiled in a heated argument with one of the crew members who inadvertently touched her with a dirty towel. Things were getting serious; we had no idea how serious they were about to become.

After a brief stopover in Las Vegas, I took Samira to the airport for her final journey home. We spent a few hours together sipping coffee and contemplating what lay ahead. Our concerns lay with our future and the world's future as a whole. If this pandemic were as bad as predicted, we would be in for a rough ride. I said my final farewell to Samira and hoped I would see her soon. When I returned home from the airport, my conversation of concern continued with Paula.

Jimmy was still living at my house and working as a security guard. He and I discussed the situation and concluded it would be best for him to leave Las Vegas and return to his father's home. There were news reports of highways being shut down as the pandemic spread, and states desperately tried to contain this medical emergency. Jimmy embarked on his journey, leaving Paula and I alone in our home. All we could do was watch the news reports as the crisis unfolded.

It had been a roller coaster ride for the last two years. Our home had been used as a base camp for the band and, at times, created a somewhat chaotic living situation. The pandemic was upon us, and the world was about to change. Once again, I would have to find a new path of endeavor to travel on, but for now, it was time to hunker down for the long haul. People were dying in droves, and neither Paula nor I wanted to become a casualty of this pandemic. The whole world came to a standstill, and us along with it. All we could do now was wait and see how bad things would get.

Gallery 22

The Coach house in Los Angeles.

Waiting for our flight at the Las Vegas airport.

Hello Texas.

The Road to the Manor

The day I became an American Citizen.

Photograph from Martin Andrew private collection.

Hands up!

I think the song is in a different key... Help!!!!!!

Photograph by Scott Schmitt.

Photograph from Martin Andrew private collection.

The Buzzard, Jimmy, Samira, Me & Mike at work.

… and at play.

Photographs from Martin Andrew private collection.

Performing in Reno with Amanda aka Maggie.

Getting ready for a show in Palm Springs.

Photographs from Martin Andrew private collection.

In the UK with my dear friend Graham.

Photograph from Martin Andrew private collection.

RIP Mum & Dad.

Photograph from Martin Andrew private collection.

Chapter Twenty-Three

THE WORLD HAD NOT WITNESSED SUCH A DEVASTATING EVENT IN OVER a hundred years. Despite politicians' attempts to call for calm, it became very apparent what was taking place would change the world forever. Businesses worldwide closed their doors as the new normal began to sink into the minds of the global population. Las Vegas was about to join many other cities worldwide as it slowly, but with increased urgency, closed its doors and fell silent.

The Las Vegas Strip was now like a ghost town awaiting the outcome of this global disaster. Nobody knew how this would play out, but it became evident we would be in this for the long haul. Food and water became scarce, and mandates were put in place by state governors to encourage people to stay home and wear facial coverings around others. It seemed we were part of some dystopian movie as time progressed and the grip of Covid-19 took a firm hold on us.

With venues closed, I was unable to work as an entertainer. All future shows which had been tentative were now a distant memory as cancelled contracts became commonplace within the entertainment industry. I was very concerned about our financial well-being. Paula was still able to work but for how long? Nothing was certain. I even resorted to becoming an Uber driver briefly, but I didn't consider it a safe environment to work in. Not only was there the possibility of getting robbed at gunpoint but now there was a chance of catching a killer virus.

I still had my credentials for being an armed security guard and decided to see if I could strap on my 9mm and find employment. So many businesses were forced to close their doors, and it left them in a vulnerable position. However, security companies were happy to post guards at these vacant premises, so I was immediately hired when I applied.

My first posting was at a warehouse complex in southern Las Vegas. I was once again in uniform, driving a patrol car around a lot of empty buildings eight hours a day. It was so quiet, with only the occasional homeless person passing through to break up the monotony. No aircraft flying overhead in what used to be a busy Las Vegas sky. No traffic on the highways and no bustling crowds to be seen anywhere.

Just weeks before this, I had been in Mexico with Samira performing to enthusiastic crowds in various exotic locations. Lazing on a lounger by the pool seemed such a distant memory as I struggled to get comfortable in my ageing patrol car. I couldn't succumb to this and knew I had to find something to occupy my mind. With so much free time, I decided to write a new album. I had eight hours a day to develop new song ideas, so the process of writing the "Lookalike" album began.

During my time at the warehouse complex, I got most of the song ideas for the new album into demo form. While recording the new album, the security company assigned me to a new location on the Las Vegas Strip. The Benihana restaurant at the Fashion Show Mall would be my new place of employment. This was a far cry from the laid-back situation I became accustomed to at the warehouse complex.

One of the female managers at the restaurant had been threatened. It was my job to ensure she was kept safe. This duty was to be undertaken while tending to all other security concerns at the establishment. Nevada's Governor decreed some restaurants could open and offer a takeaway service. My job was to ensure that people observed the six feet social distancing rule and behaved themselves while on the premises. This I duly did, and aside from a couple of minor incidents, everything ran smoothly. The threat to the manager seemed to be no more than just that as she went about her business without being troubled by the would-be assailant.

During the summer of that year, an incident shook up the world in a very different way. A policeman slowly killed George Floyd on live television, and the world erupted in protest. Las Vegas was about to see the people's wrath as they marched along the strip to protest this brutal crime. It was a powder keg just waiting to be ignited as the masses gathered close to where I was working. The nature of the crime was deemed racial because a white policeman slowly suffocated George Floyd to death. America was no stranger to a racial divide, but the intensity and the fury from that night will never leave me as long as I live. Shots rang out, and a policeman received a bullet wound to the head as he stood guard outside the Trump International Hotel. Within a few moments, helicopters were overhead. I witnessed more police activity than I'd ever seen on Las Vegas Boulevard. It was chaos as the Police and National Guard stood firm while the massive crowd approached.

I monitored the situation outside the restaurant when the crowd started advancing toward me. The advance turned into a charge as the protesters tried to evade the massive police presence. I noticed two small children running ahead of the crowd and attempted to corral them behind a large concrete planter pot. I was terrified they might fall and be trampled to death. However, I was able to keep them safe as the crowd pushed past me. I gestured to the on-looking staff in the restaurant to lock the doors, which they duly did until the anger-fueled protesters passed by.

I was happy to have helped these vulnerable children and wondered why they had been subjected to such dangerous circumstances. My inquiring mind was answered when a female protester began yelling profanities at me. These were her children. I was told in no uncertain terms it was my fault they had been put in danger. I was perplexed and bewildered by her attack on me. All I wanted to do was keep her children safe. Her take on the situation was very different from mine. I was a white man, in uniform, with a gun. Someone who looked just like me had perpetrated this heinous crime the world had seen play out on live television. In her eyes, I was the enemy. I had never experienced such hatred directed toward me for my skin color and job. So, was this racism I was experiencing? The lady in question who spewed this hateful rhetoric towards me was white.

The unrest continued over the next few days, and my position at Benihana became increasingly untenable. I was involved in several altercations, some of which became physical. I was amazed at how many people wanted to become aggressive toward me. After all, I was in uniform and armed with a loaded gun. Unfortunately, my armed presence wasn't much of a deterrent. There was no respect for me or my uniform, so I asked the supervisor for a reassignment to a quieter location.

As Christmas was fast approaching, there seemed to be no end to the global pandemic strangling the planet. However, as I did my rounds through the new neighborhood I'd been assigned to, a subtle attempt was made to put a brave face on things as people decorated their houses with modest displays of tinsel and colored lights. At this point, it felt like I might never be an entertainer again. Now that may sound a little over dramatic, but at the time, nobody knew what would happen next.

It seemed like the world was spinning out of control. We had social and economic unrest, a presidential election that divided the country and a pandemic with no end in sight. To top it all, I learned about the passing of my dear friend Scotty. He'd been such a great friend to me. I grieved his death with a heavy heart. Yet with all this turmoil, I had to focus on finishing my new album. It was the only thing I had any control over. So as the year drew to a close, I worked hard to get the songs completed against the backdrop of world despair and the certainty of uncertainty.

2021 began much as 2020 had ended. Paula worked at the daycare, and I was a full-time security guard. Everyone close to me, family, and friends, had been dealing with the daily challenges of making ends meet. Some had been more fortunate than others. There were government grants and funding for those who lost their jobs. Some of my colleagues got weekly money from the government, far surpassing what they had earned as entertainers. Unfortunately, I missed that boat and was firmly entrenched in the "essential worker" workforce along with Paula.

The new year brought a new location for me to work at. A nursing home was under construction. It was my job to see that no tools or building materials went missing. We were a three-person crew, each of us spending eight hours at the building site. I settled into the swing shift working from 3 pm until 11 pm. I liked this shift as the site workers usually completed theirs by 4 pm. After locking the gates, I had the run of the place to myself.

Most of my time was spent roaming around the building site, checking windows and doors, ensuring no vagrants broke in trying to use the facility as a safe haven to sleep for the night. It wasn't exciting, but I was safe and glad to be away from people. I'm by no means an antisocial person by nature, but these were difficult times. People were agitated and prone to violent outbursts. If you got too close, somebody might sucker punch you or, worse, infect you with the deadly virus. I was more than content to be on my own.

I had a lot of time on my hands during shifts and decided to put them to good use. There was little to no activity at the nursing home, so I buried my head in my phone and decided to start looking for some entertainment work. There were no live shows, so many entertainers did podcasts or voice-over work. I had no aspirations for hosting a podcast but decided to look for some voice-over opportunities.

I downloaded an app called "Backstage" and signed up to see if I could find some credible situations. So many apps you can download are utter rubbish, but this one seemed to have some credibility. I landed a paid gig within a few weeks of answering adverts. I was to play a Southern sheriff in a slasher series. I did voice-overs for several episodes before the series faltered and disappeared into obscurity. Aside from the $200 I got paid for my trouble, what was more important to me was that I'd been paid for doing something I enjoyed within the realms of the entertainment industry. It ignited a fire of hope, and I began scouring the app for other opportunities. There were no in-person auditions, so everything was done by phone. Taped auditions were the name of the game. I must have done about ten every week until one day, I saw an advert that caught my attention.

It was just another day at the nursing home when an opportunity presented itself which would change my life forever. I remember it was a hot day; I'd parked my car next to a portable toilet to take advantage of the shade. Unfortunately, the toilets were frequently overflowing, and the stench from this particular one was overwhelming. The pong was staggering! However, getting out of the sun seemed a fair trade, so I put up with the stench and scoured my app for auditions. There was one advert in particular that caught my eye. It said a major network was looking for a person to play a butler as co-host in a forthcoming reality show. It also stated that a British accent was preferred but not necessary. It sounded too good to be true; I felt well suited for the role. I decided to fill out the application and see if I could garnish a response. I thought it was probably a fake ad, but I decided to follow through with the application process despite my reservations. A few days passed without a response to my application arriving in my email inbox. I thought my first instinct of it being fake was correct, so I continued searching for other opportunities. Then one fine day, an email arrived while I sat in my car in a more aromatically pleasing setting. It was a response to my application for "The Butler" role on a forthcoming reality show. Could this be for real? I truly hoped so.

A producer called JP asked me to be available for a Zoom inter-view. A time was set, and I was instructed to dress in "butler attire." My hair was blond and a little long, so I decided to slick it back to create a more formal look. I wore a dress shirt, tie, and a suitable waist-coat to complete the required appearance. I sat patiently in front of my computer, waiting for the invitation link to open the Zoom meeting. Soon I was face to face with JP, and the interview began. We hit it off immediately; he made me feel very at ease. He asked a lot about my background in entertainment and listened intently as I tried to impress him with my list of self-perceived achievements.

An hour passed as we challenged each other's intellect. I tried to forge a bond with my new friend. Finally, he informed me if offered the position; I would work on a show aired on the Fox network. However, he did not reveal the show's name at this time. Nevertheless, he seemed credible, and I took him at his word. It was a magnificent opportunity. I hoped his on-camera enthusiasm was as genuine as mine.

The interview was almost at an end when JP threw down an artistic gauntlet. He said, "ok, be a butler for the next two minutes." I was not prepared, but without missing a beat, I spun a yarn of epic proportions in what I considered a butler's style. As I became more enthusiastic and comfortable with the role, I saw JP laughing. Was he laughing with me or at me? There was no turning back; I completed my butler interpretation awaiting his critique.

He was genuinely pleased with my performance and assured me he would edit the footage and pass it up the chain of command. Our meeting came to an end. I was told I'd be contacted if the review of my interview was positive. My computer screen went blank along with my mind. I sat in stunned silence for a few moments trying to register in my head the gravity of the situation I was now in. If I got this role, it would change everything. National television recognition was at stake, and I was desperate for this break.

For those of you who have had no dealings with the entertainment world, particularly the world of television and film, I feel it incumbent upon me to make things clear. All the excitement and anticipation was on my side. To the network, this was just business as usual as they made up their minds during the casting process. For me, it was time to hurry up and wait. They would call me when they were good and ready. This made for a very stressful situation. So much was at stake. If I got the role, I would be firmly entrenched in this production and elevated to a new level of credibility within the entertainment world. It would be true of my colleagues' perception and the viewing public. If I failed to get the role, I would be doomed to walk the grounds of the nursing home amid the constant stench of overflowing toilets. I had to get the part, but that decision was not one for me to make.

A few weeks passed before JP contacted me with some good news. I had impressed the executive producer, and another Zoom call had been organized for me to meet her. I was also told that having made the shortlist for the role; this meeting was important. I had to shine as I would only get one chance at this. No pressure. The day soon arrived, and I was in a virtual meeting with SallyAnn Salsano. She was a giant in the industry. Her reputation and resume preceded her. To say I was a little nervous would be an understatement; however, after a short while, she relaxed me, and the interview commenced. We covered much of the same ground with similar lines of inquiry from the initial consultation with JP. It felt like she wanted a first-hand look at me to ensure I was qualified for the job. I did everything possible to assure her I would fit the role perfectly. Once again, I received the same set of instructions when the interview was at an end. Please don't call us; we'll call you. She would make her final decision and recommendation to the network in due course. Now it was time to hurry up and wait.... again!

It seemed like an eternity as weeks passed without a decision. I just needed to know so I could lick my wounds or prepare for the new challenge ahead. Finally, the waiting was over. I received a call from the network advising me a contract had been drawn up for me to evaluate. It was the news I'd been waiting for. I was elated and scared to death in the same heartbeat. For a brief moment, I started to second-guess myself. Was I up to the challenge? Had I finally bitten off more than I could chew? Be careful what you wish for! Enough of this nonsensical thinking! I was ready for this.

As a new team member representing himself, I had little chance of challenging the contract's language. I signed on the dotted line without hesitation. The last time I signed a contract like this was for a record deal, back when I was with Heretic. That contract was far less consequential than the one I just signed, but it made me remember the feeling I experienced all those years ago. It was the feeling of moving up the ladder of success.

With the contract signed and an agreement reached, things moved quickly. First, I had to be measured for my costumes, so the wardrobe designer was dispatched from Hollywood and arrived on my doorstep. I spent a whole day trying on outfits as we developed the desired look for the butler. The ground floor of our home was converted into a giant dressing room with costumes strewn all around. I was having my very own "Pretty Woman" moment!

By day's end, the outfits were ready to be sent away for final alterations. We were one step closer to the beginning of production. Fox completed several background checks on me to see if there were any skeletons in my closet. To my surprise, they found none. I can't tell you what a relief that was. I had a lot of paperwork to fill out for payroll and various other bureaucratic annoyances to take care of, but soon the tedium of the moment ended. My flight was booked, and I would take the red eye to Atlanta, Georgia, to begin this new adventure.

I was exhausted when I arrived at my destination but made haste to retrieve my bags and await the ground transportation the network provided. A somewhat surly driver arrived and ushered me into a car. It was a reasonably short trip to the hotel. I was happy to reach my destination, as the conversation during the journey had been less than stimulating. I noticed JP waiting for me at the main entrance and looked forward to finally making his acquaintance in person. JP announced a revelation of epic proportions. I was told the network decided I would be the leading man instead of being a co-host on the show. I had not anticipated a change and was shocked yet happy with the news. I was going to host a reality show on prime-time television. It was fantastic news! Despite my best attempt at a calm and collective disposition, I must have appeared as giddy as a schoolboy.

JP informed me no less than ten days were imposed for a mandatory quarantine. Due to the strict Covid protocols, this was non-negotiable, and I was escorted to my room. I was concerned about being cooped up in a hotel room for such a long time. My concerns were soon laid to rest as I approached the double doors to my room. I was housed in the Presidential suite for my stay. This room was more extensive than some apartments I lived in. I had a couple of bathrooms and a formal dining/lounge area for entertaining. Alas, there would be no entertainment due to Covid-19 restrictions, but claustrophobia would certainly not be an issue in this humble dwelling.

The Road to the Manor

I was instructed to call JP if I needed anything. After a firm hand-shake, he left, and I was able to relax. Having settled into my room, it was time for some well-earned rest. It was a lot to take in. I was treated like royalty, still trying to accept the idea that little old me would host the show. Just a few weeks before this, I was sweating in the hot sun of Las Vegas in the midst of the constant stench of overflowing toilets. Now here I was, luxuriating in the Presidential suite. I lay down and fell asleep with a massive smile on my face.

Despite my being in quarantine, there was a lot of preparation to do before filming commenced. I was given a brief description of various activities I would have to be familiar with to teach specific protocols to the contestants on the show. I use the term contestants as dating shows usually have many ladies competing for a single man's affection. I hadn't been told anything else about the show and wasn't even aware of its title. It was not an issue, as my curious mind was at rest. I focused on learning everything from line dancing to dining etiquette.

A few days into my stay at the hotel, I was invited to join a Zoom call with some producers from the show and the writer. It was time for them to meet me and vice versa. I think it's fair to say I was more enthusiastic about the meeting than they were. All they'd been told about me was that I was a Rod Stewart impersonator who answered an advertisement on the Backstage app. It was hardly a glowing resume for someone about to host a reality show of this caliber, so I had to break the ice and win them over. When the call connected, I saw four faces staring blankly at me as a noble attempt to be cordial took effect. I could understand their concerns and decided to address them head-on by engaging fully and trying to dispel any misgivings they may have about my capabilities. We talked at great length. The longer the conver-sation, the better the atmosphere. Josh, Chris, Clay, and Zach's minds had been put at ease. It was time to work as a team to get this show rolling.

I was taken to the location where we were filming to familiarize myself with the layout of the building. Lake Shore Manor was an impressive structure situated on Lake Lanier. We spent an entire day walking through the house and exploring the vast grounds. It was a massive production with more cameras and crew than I'd ever seen on a movie set. I was to take note of the locations where "Robocams" had been installed and get acquainted with the property's layout. To be convincing in this role, I should at least know my way around the kitchen.

I must admit to being a little overwhelmed with the sheer scope of this project, and my inquisitive mind began asking questions. What was this production? Might it be something I had seen? I was not a big fan of reality television, so I was somewhat clueless about the genre. As our first day of filming was fast approaching, I still had a lot of preparation to do. I wanted to be ready for this and make no mistakes. I spent hours rehearsing in my suite, trying to learn a variety of etiquette challenges and create a persona for my character.

I talked to the producers about my role and asked what I considered a fundamental question. What was the butler's name? They hadn't finalized anything, so I asked if I could use mine. They agreed and deemed I would be known as "Martin the Butler." It was essential to me as I wanted the character to be credible, not just comic relief. In addition, I didn't want to be called something tired and predictable, so by using my name; I felt I would have a better chance of establishing "Martin Andrew" as the host of the show. With my wardrobe in place and my etiquette skills highly polished, Martin the Butler was driven to Lake Shore Manor for the first day of filming. I had my very own driver and a fancy vehicle. It wasn't because I was a big star, but merely to satisfy covid protocols and ensure I didn't get sick during production. Nevertheless, being driven to the set felt good. I was welcomed by the producers and escorted to my dressing room.

I was given the "Theater Room" at the Manor, which was entirely satisfactory. It had comfortable chairs, couches, and a massive projection screen, fully equipped with all the streaming networks you could imagine. I was also assigned an assistant; Mr. J. Wiggins would look after me on and off set. It was truly incredible, and we were just getting started. Call time was fast approaching, and I was whisked away to hair and makeup to prepare for my first scene. It was time to bring "Martin the Butler" to life. When my session in the makeup chair was complete, and my tie sported a neat Windsor knot, I looked in the mirror. I was impressed. Even I could believe I was a butler, but would the producers be equally impressed? I made my way to the front of the house, where cameras and crew were waiting. I was issued an earpiece, a concealed microphone from the sound department and made first contact with the control room.

Everyone was happy with the visual aspect of the butler, but would my skills as a performer be a suitable attribute for this new line of work? We would soon find out. The first scene was about to be filmed. There was no more time for doubt or indecision. I was told to greet the ladies as they arrived at the Manor house. Two vintage Rolls Royce's were their chariots for the night, but first, it was time to introduce the gentlemen. Gentlemen? Plural? There are two of them? The night's first surprise was two young men instead of the traditional singular male. I was told one was very wealthy and the other not so much. It was an exciting twist, but I was more concerned with not getting wet as it started to rain. The men arrived in brand new Rolls Royce SUVs. It was quite a sight watching them glide slowly toward the front steps of the Manor with beads of rain clinging to the pristine wax finish of the vehicles. I greeted the men, and in doing so, my career as a reality television host began. It was almost dawn when all parties arrived, and I'd ceremoniously ushered them into the house.

We had been on set for hours; I couldn't believe how long this took. Twenty ladies and two gentlemen joined me at the Manor that night. All we seemed to have achieved was a short drive to the house and an equally short walk to the rear of the property. How naive I was in my thinking. Just because this was reality didn't mean everything happened in real-time. It was a production, just like any other. My time spent on scripted television and film productions should have prepared me for this.

By the time all was said and done, we wrapped the first day's shoot at around 9:30 am. I was so fatigued and jittery. I had consumed a large number of energy drinks along with copious amounts of coffee and was beginning to crash. Before I was allowed to get changed and driven back to the hotel, I was told a big announcement would be made. Was I to be fired after my first night? Hopefully not! SallyAnn gathered us together and said the show we were filming did indeed have a name. Joe Millionaire!

Joe Millionaire was a groundbreaking concept of reality television in 2003, and we were relaunching it with a new twist. During the show's first incarnation, many unsuspecting ladies were deceived into thinking the eligible male had inherited over $50,000,000. The lady who reached the final was informed he was no more than a humble construction worker with limited financial success. The show garnished critical acclaim at the time. It boasted millions of viewers who tuned in each week to witness the spectacle.

The show's latest incarnation would feature "two Joes," one worth over ten million dollars, with the other being broke. The ladies would be made aware of this but wouldn't find out who was who until the climactic conclusion of the show. "Joe Millionaire for Richer or Poorer" was born that night, and I hosted this latest adaptation. It was fantastic news. I couldn't believe I was a part of this. I was told by the producers I'd done a great job on our first night of filming. They were happy with me, and I was with them.

The drive home to the hotel gave me time to digest the information I was privy to. I was so tired but couldn't stop thinking about how much fun I had in front of the cameras. I was allowed to be me and introduce a lot of my personality into the show. I was being Martin Andrew. Nobody was calling me Rod anymore; I can't tell you how good that felt. Yes, the butler was an exaggerated version of me, but I was ok with that. I would be known as Martin Andrew for this production and not just "the guy who does Rod Stewart."

We filmed in Georgia for the best part of a month, working long and grueling days. Due to the Covid protocols, there was little time for socializing other than our interactions on set. I think I had two days off during filming, which was spent resting or preparing for the following day's shoot. So, there are no tales to tell about wild parties or debauched experiences, as there were none. I signed a nondisclosure agreement with the network, so I am limited in what I can say about the inner workings of the production. So, what can I say?

The Road to the Manor

It was my most outstanding career achievement, and I was so proud to have been a part of it. As I have previously disclosed, this was not my area of expertise and being a part of the reality genre was not a priority in my quest for success. I cannot attest to the veracity of other shows in this genre, but from my perspective, Joe Millionaire was extremely genuine. It was as authentic as possible. I learned so much about this type of show.

When I first arrived on set, I approached filming as I did on any other project I worked on. You take direction, make your marks, and do your best to portray a character accurately according to the director's vision. In some respects, it was the wrong approach, as I hadn't factored in the interaction with real personalities and their emotions. The ladies and gentlemen were just being themselves. They were in a fantasy bubble where emotions ran wild, and there was no retreat or escape. All their strengths and flaws were captured on camera twenty-four hours a day.

Summoning the Ladies at the Manor.

Come rain or shine the show must go on.

The Road to the Manor

That's a wrap folks!!

Promoting the show on Fox 5 Las Vegas.

Paula and I with Annie, Jennie & Amanda. Fan
appreciation party at Mandalay Bay Las Vegas.

All photographs from Martin Andrew private collection.

The Road to the Manor

This bubble we were in was a world unto itself, and you become immersed in an alternate reality. After a while, it becomes easier to ignore the cameras. Before long, you can expose your true self and all the vulnerability accompanying that persona. I found myself becoming more emotionally involved with the cast and crew. I made new friends behind the cameras and became a surrogate father figure to the ladies and gentlemen of the show. We were a dysfunctional unit. This experience would bond us together for life.

When filming wrapped, we said our farewells and hoped we had captured something special during our time together. After the usual monotony of the travel day, I was whisked away to the airport and arrived back in Las Vegas. I was driven to my house, and as the limo pulled away, I stood briefly to collect my thoughts. It felt like a dream. Time had gone by so quickly. Now I was home, and it was time to relax. I wanted to shout from the rooftops that I was the new host of Joe Millionaire, but I couldn't say a word. The network advised me that a press release was in the works, but I should remain silent until given the green light. I'm sure many of my friends thought I was a tad aloof and slightly pretentious when deflecting their questions, but I had no choice. It was a multi-million-dollar production, and a leak from me could negatively impact the press release.Finally, the news broke, and every major outlet covered the press release. I couldn't believe my eyes when I saw an article in Variety magazine featuring me. I had been in the press before but nothing like this. It was worldwide! Joe Millionaire was back, and Martin Andrew was the new host. I couldn't help but feel a sense of pride as I foraged through countless articles. So many hardships over the years, and now this. Had it all been worth it? Absolutely! Once the world knew about the show, the countdown was on for the first episode to air on prime time. Episode one was set to be televised on January 6th, 2022. What a way to finish out 2021, knowing that 2022 would begin with my national and international television debut. Some things still had to be done, and I was asked to be part of the Christmas advertising campaign at Fox.

A car was sent to my house, and I was flown first class to Los Angeles. A waiting limousine delivered me to a swanky boutique hotel in Hollywood. I was given a healthy expense account to make the stay more pleasurable. My dear friend Chris Kenny paid a visit to the hotel. Chris was the primary writer for the show. He and I had become close friends during filming. He often visited me in the theatre room, chatting between takes.

Chris had been responsible for getting hot food delivered to my dressing room. I had an air of timidity when complaining about the cold meals left outside my door, and Chris stepped in to make things right. It was time for me to return the favor. I had this healthy expense account, but it was in the form of credit for use at the hotel. Chris and I proceeded to the bar. He drank the expense account while I nursed a Perrier water. Now we were even. During my brief stay in Hollywood, I filmed a commercial with a distinct Christmas flavor alongside the other show hosts and Fox celebrities. I felt I was on top of the world and very important until a rather angry young lady approached me.

I finished filming my part of the Christmas commercial and was told to help myself to lunch in the catering area. After changing out of my butler clothing into civilian attire, I did just that. I was confronted by a young lady in the catering area and asked what I was doing. I told the rather irate young lady I was having lunch. She advised me the food was for production staff and I had no right to be in the catering lounge. I was to leave immediately. I was dismayed by this attack but kept calm and decided to explain to her what I was doing at the studio. I must confess I was tempted to say, " Do you know who I am?" but clearly, she didn't. When I explained I was filming a commercial for Joe Millionaire and gave my name, she rustled through some papers as her face turned red. The next few minutes were filled with the overtures of apologies and gestures of an obsequious nature. I just laughed and encouraged her to do the same thing. I was the new kid on the block, and she was just doing her job. I enjoyed my lunch, and we both had an amusing story to tell.

After my short stay in Hollywood, it was all about the waiting game. The world was still buried deep in a global pandemic, so Christmas was a quiet affair spent with family. Paula and I celebrated the dawning of a new year as 2022 was now officially in play. It was a mere matter of days before Joe Millionaire premiered on prime time; the excitement was killing me. January 6th was here, and a few hours before the show airing, I received a knock at my door.

A gourmet cake arrived with a beautiful congratulatory message from SallyAnn and her team at 495 Productions. It really was the icing on the cake. A cup of tea was freshly brewed, and a generous slice of cake lay on my plate as I watched the clock countdown. It was time for the two-hour special of Joe Millionaire to begin. I could hardly believe this was happening, but I was on television, hosting the show. What a journey it had been to get to this pinnacle of my career. It's a feeling I will cherish forever.

So, there you have it. Over forty years of struggle had finally paid off. The young teenager who listened intently to his aunt and uncle's tales of show business all those years ago finally achieved his goal. Things had not turned out the way I'd anticipated, but then again, things rarely do. I could offer up so many cliches in my final comments, but that would be somewhat self-serving and pretentious, don't you think? What I will say is this. I second-guessed myself all the time. I became desperately disheartened and deeply depressed on occasion. I was sidetracked and often ruined opportunities by having a bad attitude. I struggled with alcoholism and prescription drug addiction. I didn't rehearse enough when I should have, and I sometimes mistreated people. One thing I didn't do was give up. If you give up, the probability of success doesn't diminish; it disappears. So, what is the secret of success?

I get tired of hearing successful people say, "Just believe in yourself, and you'll make it to the top, just like me." There is no guarantee of success just because you believe in yourself, but what I do think is this. You stand a fighting chance if you refuse to give in and stay the course, firmly believing in your talents. Writing my memoirs has given me a greater insight into myself by reliving the journey I call my career. I genuinely hope all who read this might learn from my mistakes and, perhaps, gain a degree of wisdom and encouragement from the words shared on these pages. My journey continues, and I wish everyone safe travels in their life's endeavors.

Toodle Pips!